CAMBRIDGE SOUTH ASIAN STUDIES

INDIA'S EXPORTS AND EXPORT POLICIES
IN THE 1960s

CAMBRIDGE SOUTH ASIAN STUDIES

These monographs are published by the Syndics of Cambridge University Press in association with the Cambridge University Centre for South Asian Studies. The following books have been published in this series:

India's Exports and Export Policies in the 1960s

DEEPAK NAYYAR

CAMBRIDGE UNIVERSITY PRESS

CAMBRIDGE

LONDON · NEW YORK · MELBOURNE

Published by the Syndics of the Cambridge University Press
The Pitt Building, Trumpington Street, Cambridge CB2 1RP
Bentley House, 200 Euston Road, London NW1 2DB
32 East 57th Street, New York, NY 10022, USA
296 Beaconsfield Parade, Middle Park, Melbourne 3206, Australia

First published 1976

Printed in Malta by
Interprint (Malta) Ltd

Library of Congress Cataloguing in Publication Data

Nayyar, Deepak.

India's exports and export policies in the 1960s.

(Cambridge South Asian studies; 19)

1. India – Commerce. 2. Export marketing.
3. India – Commercial policy.
I. Title. II. Series.

HF3784.N39   382'.6'0954   75-46206
ISBN   0 521 21135 2

TO MY MOTHER AND FATHER

with affection

CONTENTS

Contents

Contents

LIST OF TABLES

Tables

Tables

Tables

PREFACE

This study is a modified version of my doctoral dissertation at the University of Oxford. It is a product of the research carried out at Queen Elizabeth House, Oxford, during 1972 and 1973. I would like to thank my colleagues for an intellectually stimulating environment, and the staff for providing me with all the research facilities. My greatest debt is to Paul Streeten, without whose constant help and encouragement this book would never have been possible.

Conversations with Manmohan Singh, whose previous work on the subject provided the starting point for the study, clarified many of my early ideas. For subsequent discussion on different aspects of the work, I am grateful to Max Corden, Prabhakar Narvekar, Utsa Patnaik and Frances Stewart. Special thanks are due to Angus Hone who read through an earlier draft and made many valuable suggestions. Ian Little, Peter Oppenheimer and Maurice Scott provided several criticisms, most of which I have stubbornly resisted; these did, however, lead to a strengthening of the argument at some places. The errors that remain are, of course, mine.

This book seeks to analyse India's export performance and export policies during the 1960s. When the research was carried out, 1970/71 was also the latest year for which systematic information was available. In the years since then, the Indian economy has witnessed certain new developments, many of which may have a bearing on export trends. The principal conclusions emerging from the book, however, are not affected by these occurrences in any significant manner. Given the time lags inevitable in publication, it is almost impossible for any book to incorporate the latest developments in a constantly changing economic scene. Nevertheless, in a short postscript, I have attempted to bring the analysis of export trends up-to-date and to discuss the broader implications of the current economic crisis in India for the export sector.

It needs to be said that many of my ideas have changed since the manuscript was completed. Had I been writing now, I might have asked a somewhat different set of questions and, perhaps, written an altogether different book. However, as no comprehensive analysis of India's export performance in the 1960s is available so far, this book should at least fill a gap in the literature.

I should like to thank Bob Townsend, the Librarian at the Institute of Commonwealth Studies, Oxford, for his assistance in obtaining some documents and publications which were not readily available. Elizabeth Sweetnam, Mary Whipp and Phil Duynhouwer deserve special mention for having painstakingly typed parts of the manuscript.

My wife, Rohini, helped in innumerable ways; most of all by putting up so cheerfully with my preoccupations. Without her constant moral support, the book would have taken far longer to complete.

March 1976   DEEPAK NAYYAR

ABBREVIATIONS

DGCIS	Director General of Commercial Intelligence and Statistics
ECAFE	Economic Council for Asia and the Far East
FAO	Food and Agriculture Organization
GATT	General Agreement on Tariffs and Trade
IJMA	Indian Jute Mills Association
LDCs	Less Developed Countries
NCAER	National Council of Applied Economic Research, New Delhi
RBI	Reserve Bank of India
UNCTAD	United Nations Conference on Trade and Development

c.i.f.	Cost, insurance and freight
f.o.b.	Free on board
kg	Kilograms
ton	Metric ton
n.a.	not available
Rs	Rupees
$	US dollar

A NOTE ON STATISTICAL TABLES

1. In India, the primary source for export statistics is the *Monthly Statistics of the Foreign Trade of India*, published by the Director General of Commercial Intelligence and Statistics, Calcutta. The annual fiscal year figures are published in the March issue each year. The phrase 'statistics published by DGCIS, Calcutta' at the foot of tables in the text refers to data obtained from this primary source.

2. Indian export and other statistics relate to fiscal years beginning 1 April, whereas figures on world trade and exports from other countries usually relate to calendar years. In making inter-country comparisons, as far as possible, we have tried to obtain comparable calendar year figures for India. Where this has not been possible, it is noted in the text.

3. The devaluation of the rupee in June 1966 gave rise to an artificial jump in the rupee value of exports. In order to overcome this problem and make export statistics comparable over the decade, the data on export value have been converted into US dollars at the rate of Rs4.76 to the dollar before devaluation, and Rs7.50 after it.

4. The convention with regard to time periods is as follows. Each is explained by an illustration:

   (a) 1965 refers to the calendar year;
   (b) 1965–1968 refers to a period of calendar years;
   (c) 1965/66 is used to denote the fiscal year beginning 1 April 1965 and ending 31 March 1966.
   (d) 1965/66–1968/69 refers to a period of fiscal years beginning 1965/66 and ending 1968/69.

Introduction

The purpose of this study is to analyse India's export performance
and policies in the 1960s. Several reasons prompted the choice of the
period 1960 to 1970. The pioneering work undertaken by Manmohan
Singh on India's export trends in the 1950s is the last comprehensive
analysis of the subject.[1] That was a decade in which export earnings
were virtually stagnant, and the export sector of the economy was
largely neglected. However, a great deal has happened since then.
The year 1960 provided a turning point and there was a reversal of
policy characterised by concerted efforts to promote exports.
Although this led only to a moderate growth in exports, and India
continued to experience difficulties in her attempts to mobilise the
external resources required to finance the development process, there
was a marked change in the composition of exports. A systematic
empirical analysis of the causal factors underlying India's export
performance in the 1960s would not only help in the evaluation of past
policies, but would also suggest guidelines for the future.

The study is divided into three parts. Part One provides the background. Chapter 1 outlines the approach for analytical purposes and
identifies the possible factors that could have affected export growth.
Chapter 2 highlights the main features of India's export performance
during the period under review.

The second part (Chapters 3 to 9) attempts an empirical analysis
by adopting a micro economic approach to the problem, and considers
the performance of individual export industries. Given the diverse
commodity composition of exports, an exhaustive study of all the
commodities would have been beyond the scope of this work. Thus,
in order to confine the empirical aspect of the study to manageable
proportions, I have selected eleven export industries which, on the
average, accounted for more than 60 per cent of the country's total
export earnings. Apart from being the major foreign exchange
earners, these industries also constitute a fairly representative sample
of the export sector in India and should, therefore, give a reasonable
idea of the factors affecting export performance. While jute goods

[1] M. Singh, *India's Export Trends* (Oxford, 1964).

and cotton textiles account for most of the traditional exports of manufactures, tea, cashew kernels and tobacco are the principal exports in the category of processed products. Among the exports of unprocessed raw materials, minerals such as iron ore, manganese ore and mica form a substantial proportion. As for non-traditional exports, the discussion is confined to manufactured leather, chemical products and engineering goods. The factors and policies that influenced the trends in exports of each of the selected commodities and commodity groups are investigated in detail.

While the policies affecting individual exports are discussed in the various chapters of Part Two, an attempt is made, in Part Three, to take a macro economic view of export policy. Some of the important policy issues emerging from the empirical analysis are taken up for detailed discussion. Chapter 10 considers the effect of domestic policies towards exportables and evaluates the efficacy of the export promotion measures adopted by the Government. Chapter 11 analyses the impact of the June 1966 devaluation of the rupee on export performance in the following years. Chapter 12 attempts to assess the benefits of bilateralism as an instrument of trade policy. This is done by looking into the consequences of bilateral rupee trade with the socialist countries of Eastern Europe on India's export growth.

The concluding observations in Chapter 13 attempt to identify the salient features of the Indian export experience and to draw together the lessons emerging from the study.

It must be stressed that this book is concerned with India's export performance and policies in the period 1960/61–1970/71; when the research was carried out, 1970/71 was also the latest year for which information was available. The years since then have witnessed certain new developments such as the recent boom in primary commodities, the sharp rise in prices of crude oil and the current economic crisis in India, all of which may have some bearing on India's export performance now, and in the near future. The broader implications of these recent developments are taken up for discussion in Chapter 14. This postscript also brings the analysis of export trends up to date.

Part One
General

I

An outline of the approach

It is well known that during the first decade of economic planning, trade policies in India tended to emphasise import substitution and to neglect export promotion. However, in the 1960s, there was a definite realisation that export growth was an extremely crucial factor in the development process. As a result, exports were given a high priority and export promotion became an important aspect of economic policy.[1] In this study, we shall attempt to analyse India's export trends and export policies in the period 1960 to 1970. Since the foreign trade sector is subject to both domestic and international economic forces, a country's export performance is influenced by a variety of factors. Therefore, as a starting point, it is necessary to outline a general method of analysis which would bring out the main determinants of India's export growth.

We know that the quantum and value of exports from any particular country are largely determined by: (a) the foreign demand for its exports; (b) the commercial policies abroad which affect the trade in products exported by it; (c) the domestic supply of exports, which in turn depends on the domestic production and consumption of exportables; and (d) the domestic policies towards exportables. This kind of rudimentary theoretical analysis is quite useful if one wants to highlight the basic factors which affect exports. In practice, however, such an approach is not sufficient because it remains at the aggregative level. For the purpose of empirical analysis, we need a method that explores in greater detail the causal factors to which changes in export earnings over a period of time can be attributed.

An immensely simplified model that has been frequently used in studies on the export performance of individual countries is the constant-market-share analysis of export growth.[2] Its basic assump-

---

[1] See *Third Five Year Plan*, Government of India, Planning Commission (New Delhi, 1961), pp. 137–41.

[2] This type of methodology was first used by H. Tyzynski in his article 'World Trade in Manufactured Commodities: 1899–1950', *Manchester School for Economic and Social Studies* (September 1951), pp. 272–304. Subsequently, the model was developed further and applied by, among others, P. R. Narvekar, 'The Role of Competitiveness in Japan's Export Performance: 1954–58', *IMF Staff Papers* (November 1960), pp. 85–100; and R. M. Stern, *Foreign Trade and Economic Growth in Italy* (New York, 1967).

tion is that other things being equal, a country's share in the world market for exports should remain constant over time.[3] In this method, any increase in a country's exports can be divided into four parts which are attributable to the general growth in world trade, changes in the commodity composition of its exports, changes in the market distribution of its exports, and changes in competitiveness. Although such statistical analysis has the virtue of being easily applicable, it is far too aggregative and does not go into the factors that actually determine each of the four components.[4] For instance, a country's competitiveness in exports is influenced by several factors such as changes in technology, changes in domestic demand and supply conditions, and changes in government policies, none of which find place in this oversimplified model.

Thus, in the following sections of the chapter, we shall briefly examine the factors underlying the changes in world demand, commodity composition, market distribution and competitiveness of a country's exports. This approach would not only bring to light the policies and variables which could have affected India's export performance during the period under study, but would also provide us with a framework for an empirical analysis of the trends in India's principal exports.

Growth in world demand

It is obvious that any change in a particular country's exports is at least partially attributable to changes in world demand for those products. Over a period of time, the trends in world demand are, in

[3] The crux of the hypothesis follows from this assumption. According to it, for any given period of time, the actual increase in a country's exports can be statistically divided into four components. First, there is the export growth which would have taken place if this country's exports had grown at the same rate as total world exports. Second, there is the export growth which would have occurred if the country's exports of each commodity had increased at the same rate as world exports of that commodity. Third, there is the export growth which would have ensued if the country's exports to each market had expanded at the same rate as world exports to that market. And finally, there is the export growth which would be attributable to improved competitiveness. For a detailed theoretical exposition of the constant-market-shares method of analysis, see E. E. Leamer and R. M. Stern, *Quantitative International Economics* (Boston, 1970), pp. 171–9.

[4] Hence, we shall not make any attempt to divide India's actual export growth into the four statistical components. Instead, we shall analyse the factors underlying each of these components, and then go on to a detailed study of the performance of India's principal export industries.

turn, determined by the growth in foreign incomes, foreign income elasticities of demand for this country's exports, changes in tastes, and changing supply conditions in competing countries. Clearly, all these factors have an important bearing on a country's export performance in so far as they affect the demand for its exports. However, they are external to the exporting country, and as such, it can do very little to exercise any influence over them.[5] Therefore, in our analysis of India's export performance we shall consider the extent to which the trends in world demand constituted an inhibiting or a stimulating factor; it is possible that in some commodities a stagnant world demand held back export growth, whereas in others, a rapidly growing world market benefited Indian exports.

Changing commodity composition

Given a commodity composition, a country may fail to maintain its share in the world market, i.e. its exports may not keep pace with the expansion in world trade, if the demand for most of its exports is growing relatively slowly. This would be true for any country whose exports are concentrated in primary products, raw materials or other commodities, the demand for which is income inelastic and hence growing slowly. In these circumstances, an unchanging commodity composition might well become a major constraint on export growth. If a country in such a position wants to increase its exports, there are three alternatives open to it. First, it can attempt to increase the total world demand for its exports, but this possibility is somewhat remote because as pointed out above, an individual country cannot normally influence the growth in world demand. Second, it can try to increase its share of the given world market, but this alternative is available to the country only if it is a small or marginal supplier of the particular export commodity. On the other hand, if it is a large and important supplier in the world market for that commodity, any attempt to increase its relative share of world trade is likely to be met with retaliatory action from the competing countries, and therefore may not succeed. Third, it can endeavour to alter the commodity composition by gradually shifting its exports away from primary products and raw materials, in favour of manufactured goods.[6] In view of the fact

[5] In some products, advertising and R and D methods which promote the commodity in new uses might be able to bring about a slight shift in the demand curve, but in general, such techniques can make only a marginal impact.

[6] One obvious method of doing this would be to increase the domestic processing of raw materials and primary products before export.

that the world trade in manufactures is growing very rapidly, such changes in the commodity composition of exports would probably aid export growth. It has been shown that during the 1950s a large proportion of India's exports were concentrated in commodities which faced stagnant or slowly growing world demand.[7] Hence, our analysis of India's export trends since 1960 must examine the changes, if any, in the commodity composition and their impact on export growth.

Changing market distribution

The market distribution also affects a country's exports. A country may fail to maintain its share in world trade if most of its exports go to markets which are relatively stagnant. Conversely, exports may increase faster than the world average if they are sold in rapidly growing markets.

Consider a situation where a country's export markets are unchanged over a long period of time, and are concentrated in one or a few countries.[8] If these markets are relatively stagnant or are growing very slowly, a static market distribution of exports might constrain export growth. Also, in the short run, it may not be possible for the exporting country to change its markets because of rigidities in the export structure. Such rigidities arise if the country is committed to a particular export market through its investment in distribution channels and market contracts. Let us now turn to the situation where it is possible for the exporting country to change its markets. If the new markets are dynamic and expanding faster than the old ones, a shift in their favour would accelerate export growth. For example, as we shall show later, in the case of some Indian exports, Japan and the USSR provided rapidly growing markets during the 1960s, whereas the older UK market was relatively stagnant. Thus, it is possible that in such products a shift in the market distribution helped the export effort. However, this should not be taken to mean that unchanged export markets always hamper export growth, and a

---

[7] See Singh, *India's Export Trends*, pp. 140–50. He found that in the period 1950–1960, the world demand for some of India's most important exports such as tea, cotton textiles, tobacco, jute manufactures, mica and lac did not register any significant increase.

[8] Such market concentration is quite common in the case of developing countries, and is often the direct consequence of colonialism. It is for this reason that the UK was a very important export market for India during the 1950s.

changing market distribution always fosters exports. What actually happens is a matter for empirical investigation and would depend on the type of products, the state of existing markets, and the growth potential of the new markets.

Competitiveness

In the long run, a country's ability to compete effectively with other sources of supply in the world market is perhaps the most crucial determinant of exports and export growth. The export competitiveness of any country is influenced by a number of factors. Among them, price is frequently regarded as the most important, because changes in export prices directly affect export performance. This factor has also been most emphasised in recent literature on the subject.[9] However, price is by no means the sole determinant of export competitiveness. The following analysis attempts to set out a simple framework which outlines all the factors and policies that might have affected the competitiveness of Indian exports. Broadly speaking, changes in competitiveness can be explained in terms of: (*a*) changes in export prices relative to those of the competitors' in the world market, (*b*) changes in trade policies adopted by the government, and (*c*) the effect of non-price factors. We shall now examine each of these elements of competitiveness, in turn.

Relative export prices

In any given market, one would expect the demand for exports from two competing sources of supply to be a function of relative prices, so that variations in export shares would be attributable to changes in relative export prices. But, in fact, the mechanism through which price affects competitiveness varies according to the product. As such, it is necessary to distinguish between homogeneous and heterogeneous products. In the limiting case of a homogeneous product there is a single world price, and a particular country's export competitiveness is reflected in its ability to export at that price, which in turn is directly dependent on its cost of production.[10] In the case of heterogeneous products, however, we find that relative export prices of competing

---

[9] For a comprehensive survey, see J. M. McGeehan, 'Competitiveness: A Survey of Recent Literature', *Economic Journal* (June 1968).

[10] We are assuming that this country is a small supplier in the world market and hence a price taker. But if it is a major exporter, it may be able to influence the world price by regulating the quantity supplied.

suppliers assume much greater importance.[11] It is worth noting that most products, and in particular manufactured goods, fall into this category. In all such differentiated products, relative prices are determined by the export prices of the individual country and the prices of competing commodities in the world market. Over the latter, the exporting country cannot exercise any influence. Therefore, export prices quoted by an individual country have a direct impact on its competitiveness.

There have been several empirical studies on the competitiveness of exports, and most of them show a clear association between prices and export performance.[12] However, price is only the apparent influence, and it would be difficult to analyse the competitiveness of Indian exports merely in terms of prices, which themselves are the outcome of an interaction of many factors. Therefore, it is necessary to examine the determinants of export prices, which are, the costs of production, the pressure of domestic demand and the bottlenecks in supply, if any. Although the effect of each of these on price competitiveness cannot be singled out, they are taken up separately for analytical convenience.

Before going into this, it is necessary to point out that some factors influence competitiveness in general, while some others influence competitiveness in particular products. For instance, a general inflation in the economy would raise the costs in all industries, including export industries. Assuming that there is no inflation in the economies of competing countries, this means that the competitiveness of all exports would be affected adversely. In other words, general changes in the price level of any economy would affect the competitiveness of all its exports, although not necessarily in the same proportion and to the same extent. On the other hand, changes in the prices of particular factor inputs or raw materials would affect the export competitiveness of some particular products alone. It would be useful to keep in mind the distinction between the general and the specific competitiveness effects.

Cost of production: Like all prices, export prices are closely related to costs. It follows that India's competitiveness in the world market would have been partially influenced by changes in the cost structure

---

[11] Of course, once we allow for product differentiation, factors like quality, brand-names and other non-price influences must also be taken into account. The impact of such non-price factors on export competitiveness is discussed later in this chapter.

[12] For the results of these studies, see McGeehan, pp. 244–8.

of her export industries. The main determinants of costs are factor productivity and factor prices. Therefore, at any given point of time, the difference in costs of production (hence export prices) as between competing countries can be explained almost entirely in terms of differences in factor productivity and differences in factor prices. For the same reason, over a period of time, a country's cost competitiveness depends upon improvements in factor productivity and the trend in prices of factors of production, in its export industries as compared to that of its competitors.

Pressure of domestic demand: In any economy, changes in the level of domestic demand exercise an important influence on domestic prices and costs. Given the fact that export commodities frequently enter into domestic consumption and almost inevitably employ domestic inputs in production, the pressure of domestic demand is likely to affect the price competitiveness of exports. Thus it would be useful to examine how the level of domestic demand might affect a country's export performance.

Consider first, an inflationary situation in which domestic demand is at a high level and rising steadily. Other things being equal, the direct effect of the pressure would be an increase in the domestic absorption of exportables and a reduction in the quantity available for export.[13] In the case of India, this factor may have been particularly important because a large number of exports, e.g. cotton textiles, tea, coffee, tobacco, sugar, spices, vegetable oils and footwear are consumer goods, the demand for which is bound to increase with the growth in population and rising income levels. However, such increases in domestic consumption are possible at given prices. But in an inflationary situation, the pressure of domestic demand also leads to a rise in prices. Unless there is a matching inflation abroad, the price rise would affect export performance adversely in three ways. In the first place, it would improve the relative profitability of domestic sales as compared to exports, and thereby divert exportable supplies to the home market. Second, it would raise the cost of inputs, which would in turn inflate production costs in the export industries and worsen price competitiveness. Third, it would lead to a resource allocation away from the export sector because production for the domestic market would be relatively more attractive.

---

[13] In the manufacturing sector, rising domestic consumption could also lead to lengthening delivery dates on export orders, thereby inducing foreign buyers to look elsewhere for supplies. Hence, in a situation of growing domestic demand, manufactured exports might suffer even if there is no change in prices.

Take now a situation of recession in which domestic demand falls to a low level. *Ceteris paribus*, at given prices, the direct effect of this recession would be an increase in the quantity available for export. Lower prices during the recession would also improve the competitiveness of this country's exports. If prices continue to fall, input costs would be reduced even more so as to improve competitiveness further. What is more, in a recession when no domestic sales are possible at the margin, producers may be willing to export at a price lower than the average costs, as long as they recieve something in excess of their marginal costs in order to recover a part of the fixed overhead costs. This reasoning suggests that a domestic recession is likely to improve the general competitiveness of exports and have a favourable effect on export performance.[14] It might be interesting to test this hypothesis by investigating the performance of some export industries during the recession in the Indian economy from 1965 to 1967.

So far we have analysed the general competitiveness effect of a fall in the level of domestic demand. In individual firms and industries, the impact of a recession on competitiveness would depend largely on prevalent cost conditions. Export industries which are subject to decreasing costs and derive distinct economies of scale, would incur an increase in average costs as a result of the reduction in output thereby worsening their price competitiveness, whereas in an increasing costs situation the competitiveness would improve.

Supply bottlenecks: Apart from the costs of production and the pressure of domestic demand, supply constraints in export industries also influence the price competitiveness and physical availability of exports. For example, export supplies may be restricted by an inadequate infrastructure, difficult production conditions, or shortages of domestic materials and imported inputs. While some factor scarcities directly affect cost competitiveness through higher input prices, other bottlenecks constitute a physical constraint on the output available for export. Such supply bottlenecks are quite common in India, and we shall examine the extent to which they limited the volume of exports.

Trade policies

Let us now turn to consider the effect of trade policies on the competitiveness of exports. Exchange rate variations are an important

[14] The obvious exception would be a situation where the recession is foreign in origin and the relative competitiveness in the world market remains unchanged.

instrument of trade policy available to governments for the purpose of attaining external balance. Such changes in the exchange rate directly affect the returns to exporters and consequently influence competitiveness. For instance, devaluation of the currency in any country reduces the foreign exchange price of its exports and/or increases the domestic currency returns of exporters, thereby improving competitiveness. Clearly, depreciations in the exchange rate are aimed at improving the general competitiveness of a country's exports. This was one of the objectives underlying the devaluation of the Indian rupee in June 1966. Hence, it would be interesting to investigate the impact of the devaluation on export performance.

In practice, however, a country might adopt trade policies which are discriminatory rather than uniform, and as such have a differential effect on the competitiveness of particular products. Just like exchange rate alterations, these policies are adopted for the purpose of attaining balance of payments equilibrium. Generally, they take the form of measures aimed at increasing exports and reducing imports. The effect of export promotion policies is quite straightforward. Direct export subsidies and all other forms of export incentives raise the domestic currency returns per unit of foreign exchange earned by exporters, thereby raising the relative profitability of exports and improving competitiveness. As against this, the levy of export duties and the imposition of export controls reduces the incentive to export, and has an adverse effect on competitiveness. Although the impact of import substitution policies on export competitiveness is not so straightforward, it is certainly significant. Let us take the example of import restrictions. They might affect the competitiveness of exports adversely by (*a*) raising the cost of importable inputs used in the export sector, and (*b*) lowering the relative profitability of producing exportables as compared to importables. During the period under study, the Indian Government employed a variety of export promotion measures, imposed export duties on some commodities, and continued its policy of import restrictions. Therefore, in the following chapters which are devoted to empirical analysis, we shall evaluate the role of these trade policies.

Non-price factors

In addition to relative prices and trade policies, export competitiveness is also dependent upon factors which are not reflected in prices. In fact, non-price factors such as designing, quality, marketing efficiency, credit, delivery dates and commercial policies abroad have an important bearing on a country's ability to export and its potential for expanding exports. This is particularly true for non-traditional exports of manufactures wherein competitive ability is to a large extent determined by the above non-price factors.[15] Let us therefore consider possible effects of some of these factors on the competitiveness of exports.

(a) *Designing*: The standard of designs depends largely on the state of technology and innovating skills in the exporting country. Given the fact of rapidly changing consumer tastes in the world market, it is likely that modern and up-to-date designing would improve competitiveness, whereas old and unchanging designs may affect it adversely.

(b) *Quality*: There are two aspects to this factor: the improvement of quality over time and the maintenance of quality control at any given point of time. In the long run, quality improvement always fosters competitiveness and is particularly significant in the case of manufactured goods. At times, however, exporters may harm their long term interests by slipping up on the quality of goods actually delivered, to meet the export contract. Thus, any laxity in the production or packaging process which might lead to sub-standard or erratic quality would certainly worsen the country's export competitiveness. This is quite a serious problem in India, and it is likely that a few careless exporters may have harmed the country's reputation as a reliable exporter.

(c) *Marketing*: Aggressive marketing methods can help a country break into new markets, specially in the case of non-traditional exports of manufactures. In real terms, marketing efficiency is constituted by the following: (1) the ability to extend export credit, (2) maintaining good public relations as the basis for an effective advertising technique, (3) providing an after-sales service, and (4) ensuring a prompt fulfilment of export orders in accordance with the promised delivery dates.[16] It is obvious that efficient marketing would improve a country's export competitiveness.

(d) *Commercial policies abroad*: Tariff and non-tariff barriers in the importing countries also exercise an influence on the export com-

---

[15] On the other hand, in the case of primary products and semi-processed materials, price competitiveness is relatively more important although factors like packaging and quality control can play a significant role.

[16] It is necessary to point out that whereas the keeping of delivery dates only requires efficiency in the production process, advertising and after-sales service impose selling costs on the exporter, and the extension of export credit involves a temporary export of capital.

petitiveness of a country.[17] It has been argued that escalated tariff structures and other protectionist commercial policies adopted by the advanced countries have discriminated against exports from developing countries.[18] Whether or not such policies had a restrictive effect on India's exports is a matter for empirical investigation, but in general, one can say that trade barriers abroad worsen a country's export competitiveness, whereas trade preferences lead to an improvement in it.

In the above paragraphs, we have discussed some of the main non-price factors that affect export competitiveness, but in actual fact, there may be many others. Although such factors are not easily quantifiable, their importance cannot be underestimated, and we shall take them into account in our analysis of India's export trends.

Summing up, we have outlined the various factors and policies that may have influenced India's export growth in the 1960s. However, this chapter has explored just the theoretical possibilities. In practice, the significance of each of these factors can be assessed only on the basis of a detailed empirical analysis. Therefore, the following chapters will attempt to study India's export performance within this general framework.

---

[17] Strictly speaking, tariff barriers abroad are price factors that affect the foreign demand for a country's exports. However, for the sake of analytical convenience, we have bracketed them with non-tariff barriers which are non-price factors.

[18] See for example, H. G. Johnson, *Economic Policies Towards Less Developed Countries* (New York, 1967).

2

Export performance in the 1960s:
an overview

As a preface to a detailed empirical analysis, this chapter reviews India's export performance during the period 1960 to 1970. It is useful to begin such a survey by examining the overall trend in exports. Table 2.1 outlines the main changes in the value and volume of exports over the decade.

It shows that export earnings increased rapidly from 1960/61 to 1964/65.[1] However, in the next two years, the value of exports registered a definite decline. This reversal of the trend is not visible if one looks at the export figures in terms of rupees. In fact, the decline is concealed because of the devaluation of the rupee in June 1966.[2] From 1967/68, the dollar value of exports once again showed a rising trend. By 1968/69, the foreign exchange earnings had recovered and were significantly higher than their previous peak in 1964/65. After that, there was a moderate but continuous increase in exports.[3] The

[1] It has been suggested that the spurt in export earnings in the early 1960s was partially a result of the inclusion of Goa in the Indian Union. Jagdish Bhagwati and Padma Desai argue that the addition of Goa's foreign trade boosted India's export figures; cf. *India: Planning for Industrialisation*, OECD (Oxford, 1970), p. 396. To some extent, this is certainly true, but it must be pointed out that the Goa trade figures were not included in India's export statistics until 1963/64, (see footnote to Statement 80 in RBI Bombay, *Report on Currency and Finance, 1966/67*). Even if we were to exclude Goa's exports thereafter, which were approximately $38 million per annum at that time, the rising trend would be deflated a little, but the overall picture of rapid export growth would not really be altered.

[2] Therefore, in order to make export statistics comparable over the decade, and to deflate the artificial jump in rupee export earnings after June 1966, the data on value of exports have been converted into US dollars at the rate of Rs4.76 = $1 before June 1966, and Rs7.50 = $1 after that date. This practice of converting export figures into their dollar equivalents will be adopted throughout the study, wherever comparisons over the entire period 1960 to 1970 are necessary. The dollar has been used for no reason other than convenience. Its parity remained unchanged throughout the period under study, whereas both the rupee and the pound sterling were devalued during the 1960s.

[3] At the risk of a slight digression, in this connection it is necessary to draw attention to the recent controversy about the 1970/71 export statistics. The matter came to light when it was discovered that the DGCIS export figure for 1970/71 was much

TABLE 2.1 *India's exports in the 1960s*

Year	Export earnings in $ million	Export value index 1960/61 = 100	Export volume index 1960/61 = 100
1960/61	1349.4	100.0	100
1961/62	1387.2	102.8	105
1962/63	1440.1	106.7	112
1963/64	1666.5	123.5	126
1964/65	1714.9	127.1	135
1965/66	1692.5	125.4	124
1966/67	1556.5	115.3	119
1967/68	1598.3	118.4	122
1968/69	1810.5	134.2	142
1969/70	1884.4	139.6	143
1970/71	2046.9	151.7	153

Source: Statistics published by the Director General of Commercial Intelligence and Statistics (DGCIS), Calcutta.

Note:
(a) Statistics relate to Indian fiscal years beginning 1 April.
(b) The figures for export earnings have been converted into US dollars.
(c) The value index has been calculated from the data on value of exports.
(d) The quantity index computed by the DGCIS has 1958 as base year, but the 1960/61 index happens to be 100 as well. Hence, we have used it for base year.

greater than the one compiled by the RBI on the basis of exchange control records. There has always been some divergence between the two sets of statistics because: (a) the DGCIS data include exports to Nepal, and re-exports, which the RBI data do not; and (b) there is a time lag between the actual export shipment and the receipt of the exchange control documents by RBI. In 1970/71, however, the discrepancy of $163 million was far too large to be explained away in terms of these factors. The basic explanation is to be found in the fact that halfway through the financial year, in November 1970, the DGCIS changed its procedure for recording exports. Whereas, until then, exports had been recorded on the basis of actual shipments, under the new method, exports came to be recorded when the bills of consignment were approved for shipment. This switchover in procedure naturally led to double counting in the following months, so that a significant proportion of the increase in 1970/71 exports was statistical rather than real. For a detailed discussion on the controversy, see Sarwar Lateef, 'Export Performance: What happened in 1970–71?', *The Statesman* (New Delhi, 11 March 1972); and 'Fourteenth Report of the Fifth Lok Sabha's Estimates Committee', *Ministry of Foreign Trade: Export Promotion Measures*, Lok Sabha Secretariat, (New Delhi, April 1972), pp. 26–9. Therefore, it is clear that the actual value of exports in 1970/71 was less than the $2046.9 million reported by DGCIS. However, in our study, we have had to rely on the DGCIS data, because a detailed breakdown of export statistics is available only in this series. But it will be useful to keep in mind the slight overestimation implicit in the 1970/71 figures.

trend is much the same if we look at the quantity index of exports. Between 1960/61 and 1970/71, while the value of exports grew by 51.7 per cent, the volume increased by 53 per cent. Over this period, export earnings grew at an average rate of 4.46 per cent per annum.[4] The average annual value of exports increased from $1512 million in the quinquennium 1960/61–1964/65, to $1765 million during the period 1965/66–1970/71. This modest growth does stand out in sharp contrast with the stagnation in export earnings during the 1950s. As a matter of fact, the average annual value of exports barely changed from $1268.7 million in the five-year period 1951–1955 to $1266.2 million during 1956–1960.[5]

The expressed objective of economic planning in India has been that the external resources required to finance development must be constituted increasingly by export earnings. Therefore, at the aggregate level, it would be interesting to consider the extent to which the modest increase in exports during the 1960s contributed to this objective of self-sustained growth. Table 2.2 compares the trend in exports and imports, and brings out the corresponding position of foreign exchange reserves. We find that the ratio of exports to imports fluctuated around 60 per cent from 1960/61 to 1967/68.[6] In this period, the foreign exchange reserves were also more or less constant at a level of about $600 million. However, in the last three years of the decade, there was a marked change. The proportion of imports financed by export earnings increased rapidly, and exchange reserves began to accumulate for the first time. To some extent, this reduction in the gap between exports and imports was attributable to export growth in the late 1960s, but a mere glance at the import trends is sufficient to confirm that it was equally, if not more, due to the sharp decline in imports.

So much for an aggregate view. Let us now turn to consider how far these overall trends were reflected in the export performance of individual commodities. Once again, the picture was quite different from what it was in the 1950s. Between 1951 and 1960, the foreign exchange value of most of India's major exports remained stagnant; cashew kernels, coffee, and iron ore were the only commodities whose

---

[4] This has been calculated as a simple average of the growth in exports each year over the preceding year. The compound rate of growth works out at 4.2 per cent per annum but we cannot attach much weight to it because of the tentative nature of the 1970/71 figure.

[5] Cf. M. Singh, *India's Export Trends* (Oxford, 1964) p. 9.

[6] The export-import ratio had dropped from a high level of 83.4 per cent in the First Plan period to an average of 56.2 per cent in the second half of the 1950s (see Singh, p. 11); and it was this trend that continued.

TABLE 2.2   *India's foreign trade and exchange reserves*

Year	Exports in Rs million	Imports in Rs million	Export–import ratio in percentages	Foreign exchange reserves in Rs million ($ million)
1960/61	6 424	11 216	57.3	3 036 (637.8)
1961/62	6 606	10 916	60.5	2 973 (624.6)
1962/63	6 853	11 315	60.6	2 951 (620.0)
1963/64	7 932	12 228	64.9	3 058 (642.4)
1964/65	8 163	13 490	60.5	2 497 (524.6)
1965/66	8 056	14 085	57.2	2 980 (626.1)
1966/67	10 949	19 017	57.6	4 784 (637.8)
1967/68	11 987	20 076	59.7	5 386 (718.1)
1968/69	13 579	19 086	71.1	5 767 (768.9)
1969/70	14 133	15 821	89.3	8 210 (1094.7)
1970/71	15 352	16 252	94.5	7 323 (976.4)

Source: RBI Bombay, *Report on Currency and Finance*, *1966/67*: pp. S6–7 for the years 1961/62 to 1964/65; and *1970/71*: pp. S6–7 for the years 1960/61 and 1965/66 to 1970/71.

Note:

(a) All figures relate to Indian fiscal years starting 1 April.

(b) The export–import ratio has been calculated by expressing exports as a percentage of imports.

(c) All figures on trade are in million rupees, so that for the period after June 1966, the data are in post-devaluation rupees.

(d) In the case of foreign exchange reserves, gold has been valued at Rs53.58 per 10 grams up to May 1966 and at Rs84.39 per 10 grams thereafter.

(e) The figures in brackets in the last column are the exchange reserves in terms of million US dollars.

exports increased rapidly in that period.[7] Table 2.3 which brings out the changes in foreign exchange earnings derived from India's principal exports, during the period 1960 to 1970, reveals that the trends were a little more complex and export performance varied substantially from commodity to commodity. Exports of cashew kernels, iron ore, engineering goods and iron and steel increased rapidly throughout the decade. In the early 1960s, export earnings from jute manufactures, tobacco and oilcakes also grew rapidly, but this trend was reversed in the latter half of the decade. The exports of tobacco and oilcakes, which reached a peak in 1964/65, declined and stabilised at a slightly lower level, thereafter. However, the exports of jute manufactures fell steadily after 1965/66. On the other

[7] For a description of the stagnation in India's exports during the 1950s, see Singh, *India's Export Trends*, pp. 14–15 and Bhagwati and Desai, *India: Planning for Industrialisation*, pp. 373–5. To avoid repetition, the details have not been introduced here.

TABLE 2.3   Trends in the value of India's principal exports: 1960–1970 (in $ million)

	1960/61	1961/62	1962/63	1963/64	1964/65	1965/66	1966/67	1967/68	1968/69	1969/70	1970/71
Jute manufactures	283.9	304.2	327.0	330.7	353.9	384.1	334.7	312.1	290.7	275.5	253.9
Tea	257.5	255.0	269.4	256.7	259.4	215.7	212.7	238.8	206.6	162.8	193.5
Cotton textiles	120.9	101.3	97.0	114.1	134.7	132.9	102.8	105.9	117.3	115.5	130.0
Cashew kernels	39.7	38.1	40.7	45.0	61.0	57.6	61.3	57.4	81.2	76.6	69.4
Tobacco	30.7	29.5	37.8	44.3	51.2	41.1	28.9	46.5	44.2	43.6	41.9
Iron ore	35.8	36.6	41.7	76.5	78.6	82.7	93.0	99.7	117.9	126.2	156.4
Engineering goods	14.1	16.4	19.8	28.2	35.3	39.7	41.5	55.3	113.3	141.8	155.5
Leather and leather manufactures	52.5	51.4	47.5	55.4	57.5	59.3	82.7	71.3	96.9	108.7	96.2
Manganese ore	29.5	21.9	16.6	17.4	27.6	23.2	19.2	14.8	18.0	14.8	18.6
Mica	21.3	20.3	21.8	19.3	20.5	23.7	19.1	20.1	18.0	20.3	20.8
Oilcakes	30.0	36.4	66.8	74.3	83.5	72.8	67.4	60.6	65.9	55.3	73.9
Coffee	15.2	18.9	16.0	17.5	28.2	27.2	21.3	24.2	24.0	26.2	33.5
Fats and vegetable oils	17.9	12.2	27.5	41.9	14.8	8.6	4.1	5.3	15.6	6.6	9.4
Chemicals	15.1	16.4	16.5	14.5	21.6	23.3	20.0	21.0	31.8	40.5	48.5
Sugar	6.9	32.2	37.7	56.9	45.0	23.5	24.2	21.9	14.0	11.8	39.1
Spices	34.9	36.8	29.0	33.7	35.1	48.5	39.4	36.3	33.5	46.0	51.8
Coir manufactures	18.3	23.5	25.3	25.0	24.2	22.5	19.8	17.0	18.4	17.9	n.a.
Iron and steel	20.5	20.3	4.8	7.6	21.7	26.0	34.1	73.1	105.3	115.7	120.9
Footwear	6.5	5.1	5.8	7.6	9.0	11.0	11.7	12.2	12.2	12.0	15.3
Raw cotton and waste	24.3	42.8	35.8	35.4	30.0	27.5	23.4	25.9	21.0	23.7	21.9
Total including others	1349.4	1387.2	1440.1	1666.5	1714.9	1692.5	1556.5	1598.3	1810.5	1884.4	2046.9

Source: Statistics published by DGCIS, Calcutta. Figures for engineering goods are, however, taken from data published by the Engineering Export Promotion Council, Calcutta in Home Bulletin 12 September 1968, 30 July 1970 and 12 August 1971.

Note: Statistics relate to Indian fiscal years beginning 1 April and have been converted into US dollars.

TABLE 2.4   *World trade and India's exports*

Year	World exports in $ million	India's exports in $ million	India's exports as a percentage of world exports
1960	128 100	1331	1.04
1961	134 100	1386	1.03
1962	141 500	1403	0.99
1963	154 100	1626	1.06
1964	172 500	1705	0.99
1965	186 400	1688	0.91
1966	203 800	1577	0.77
1967	214 500	1613	0.75
1968	239 000	1754	0.73
1969	272 400	1835	0.67
1970	311 500	2026	0.65

Source: UN *Statistical Yearbook, 1967*, pp. 385 and 391, for the years 1960–62, and *1971*, pp. 383 and 389, for the years 1963–1970.

hand, the earnings from exports of leather and leather manufactures, coffee, chemicals and footwear, which were more or less stagnant in the first half of the decade, expanded rapidly after 1965/66. None of the remaining principal exports registered any growth. The value of tea exports, which was quite stable until 1964/65, showed a decline in the later years. The exports of cotton textiles, mica, coir manufactures and raw cotton were stagnant throughout the period under study, as indeed they had been in the 1950s. It is not possible to discern any definite trend in the exports of sugar and spices owing to the wide fluctuations in value. Exports of manganese ore and vegetable oils also fluctuated sharply in the early years of the decade, but on the whole, revealed a downward trend.

In the foregoing paragraphs, we have attempted to highlight the principal features of India's export performance in the 1960s. In accordance with the approach outlined in the preceding chapter, we shall now examine the trends described above in the context of: (*a*) the general growth in world trade; (*b*) the changes in commodity composition of exports; and (*c*) the changes in export markets.

India's share in world exports

World trade grew at a phenomenal pace during the 1960s, and the value of world exports in 1970 was nearly two and a half times its value in 1960. Table 2.4 shows that India's export growth did not keep

TABLE 2.5   *Export growth by country groups* (in $ million)

Country group	Exports in 1960	Exports in 1970	Percentage increase
Developed market economies	85 700	223 900	161.3
Centrally planned economies	15 000	32 900	119.3
Less developed economies	27 400	54 700	99.6

Source: UN *Statistical Yearbook*, *1967*, p. 385, and *1971*, p. 383.

pace with this increase in world exports. Consequently, India's share in world exports declined continuously, and fell from 1.04 per cent in 1960 to 0.65 per cent in 1970. This trend is nothing new. India's share in world exports declined from about 2 per cent in 1950 to approximately 1 per cent in 1960.[8] It is worth noting that in the period under study, the decline was accelerated only after 1964. Over the decade, world exports rose by about 143 per cent, whereas India's exports increased by merely 52 per cent. If India had managed to maintain her 1960 share in world exports, her exports in 1970 would have been $3226 million, i.e. roughly 60 per cent more than they actually were.

Undoubtedly, a large proportion of the expansion in world exports was attributable to increased exports from the developed countries. Thus it might be argued that a developing country like India could not have maintained its share in world trade. However, the data in Table 2.5 show that India's exports did not even keep pace with the general growth in exports from less developed countries.

This relatively slow growth is often explained in terms of the fact that the bulk of India's traditional exports were concentrated in commodities such as jute manufactures, tea and cotton textiles, the world demand for which was growing very slowly.[9] But, as we shall see in the next section, even a shift in the commodity composition of exports away from these commodities, during the 1960s, did not arrest the fall in India's share of world exports.

Changes in commodity composition

A preliminary idea of the changes in the commodity composition of exports can be obtained by examining the changing shares of individual commodities in total exports. Table 2.6 traces the percentage

[8] See Singh, *India's Export Trends*, p. 11.
[9] The trends in world demand for these particular commodities, and their impact on India's export performance, are analysed in detail in the following chapters.

TABLE 2.6 *The percentage share of principal exports in total export earnings*

	1960/61	1961/62	1962/63	1963/64	1964/65	1965/66	1966/67	1967/68	1968/69	1969/70	1970/71
Jute manufactures	21.0	21.9	22.7	19.8	20.6	22.7	21.5	19.5	16.1	14.6	12.4
Tea	19.1	18.4	18.7	15.4	15.1	12.7	13.7	14.9	11.4	8.6	9.5
Cotton textiles	9.0	7.3	6.7	6.9	7.9	7.9	6.6	6.6	6.5	6.1	6.4
Cashew kernels	2.9	2.8	2.8	2.7	3.6	3.4	3.9	3.6	4.5	4.1	3.4
Tobacco	2.3	2.1	2.7	2.7	3.0	2.4	1.9	2.9	2.4	2.3	2.1
Iron ore	2.7	2.6	2.9	4.6	4.6	4.9	6.0	6.2	6.5	6.7	7.6
Engineering goods	1.0	1.2	1.4	1.7	2.1	2.4	2.7	3.5	6.3	7.5	7.6
Leather and leather manufactures	3.9	3.7	3.3	3.3	3.4	3.5	5.3	4.5	5.4	5.8	4.7
Manganese ore	2.2	1.6	1.2	1.0	1.6	1.4	1.2	0.9	1.0	0.8	0.9
Mica	1.6	1.5	1.5	1.2	1.2	1.4	1.2	1.3	1.0	1.1	1.0
Oilcakes	2.2	2.6	4.6	4.5	4.9	4.3	4.3	3.8	3.6	2.9	3.6
Coffee	1.1	1.4	1.1	1.1	1.6	1.6	1.4	1.5	1.3	1.4	1.6
Fats and vegetable oils	1.3	0.9	1.9	2.5	0.9	0.5	0.3	0.3	0.9	0.4	0.5
Chemicals	1.1	1.2	1.2	0.9	1.2	1.4	1.6	1.3	1.8	2.2	2.4
Sugar	0.5	2.3	2.6	3.4	2.6	1.4	1.6	1.4	0.8	0.6	1.9
Spices	2.6	2.7	2.6	2.0	2.1	2.9	2.5	2.3	1.9	2.4	2.5
Coir manufactures	1.4	1.7	1.8	1.5	1.4	1.3	1.3	1.1	1.0	1.0	n.a.
Iron and steel	1.5	1.5	0.3	0.5	1.3	1.5	2.2	4.6	5.8	6.1	5.9
Footwear	0.5	0.4	0.4	0.5	0.5	0.7	0.8	0.8	0.7	0.6	0.8
Raw cotton and waste	1.8	3.1	2.5	2.1	1.8	1.6	1.5	1.6	1.2	1.3	1.1
Total including others	100.0	100.0	100.0	100.0	100.0	100.0	100.0	100.0	100.0	100.0	100.0

Source: Table 2.3

contribution of India's principal exports to total export earnings. The striking fact to emerge from these figures is the rapidly declining importance of traditional exports. There was a dramatic fall in the share of tea and jute manufactures in the second half of the 1960s. The share of cotton textiles, manganese ore, vegetable oils, mica, raw cotton and coir manufactures in total export earnings also declined steadily over the decade. In contrast, the share of the relatively new exports such as engineering goods, iron ore, leather and leather manufactures, oilcakes, chemicals and iron and steel registered a significant increase; the expansion was particularly substantial in the case of engineering goods and iron ore. Among the older exports, there was a slight increase in the percentage share of cashew kernels. On the other hand, the contribution of some commodities, viz. coffee, tobacco, spices and footwear to total export earnings, remained virtually unchanged throughout the 1960s.

In considering the relative share of individual commodities we grouped exports according to their growth, i.e. whether they increased slower, faster, or at the same rate as total export earnings. These changes are of interest in themselves. However, in view of the fact that world trade in manufactures grew far more than that in primary products, it would be more meaningful to group commodities according to the extent of processing involved in the output finally exported. For the purpose of analysing export growth, such groups would provide a better index of the shifts in commodity composition of exports.

Table 2.7 highlights the changes in the composition of India's exports as between: (*a*) food and beverages, (*b*) raw materials, and (*c*) manufactured goods. It shows that the average annual share of food, beverages and tobacco (a commodity classification constituted mostly by semi-processed products) fell from 34.4 per cent in the three-year period 1960/61–1962/63 to 28.4 per cent during 1968/69–1970/71. At the same time, the average annual share of raw materials and other unprocessed products fell slightly from 20.6 to 17.6 per cent, whereas that of manufactured goods rose from 42.4 per cent to 53.3 per cent of total export earnings.

A further detailed breakdown of the above commodity classification is provided in Table 2.8, which suggests that:

(*a*) The declining exports of tea were primarily responsible for the reduced share of food, beverages and tobacco in total exports. Increases in the exports of coffee, oilcakes and cashew kernels did not make up for the loss in tea exports.

TABLE 2.7   *The overall composition of Indian exports* (in percentages)

Year	Food, beverages and tobacco	Raw and crude unprocessed materials	Manufactured goods	Other items
1960/61	33.3	20.2	43.3	3.2
1961/62	34.0	20.1	42.7	3.2
1962/63	35.9	21.5	41.1	1.5
1963/64	34.5	20.9	44.0	0.6
1964/65	35.4	19.7	44.5	0.4
1965/66	32.7	18.7	47.9	0.7
1966/67	32.6	19.8	47.3	0.3
1967/68	33.4	17.7	48.4	0.5
1968/69	29.3	17.7	52.5	0.5
1969/70	26.8	17.4	55.1	0.7
1970/71	29.0	17.7	52.3	1.0

Source: Calculated from statistics published by DGCIS, Calcutta.

(*b*) There was a decline in the percentage share of nearly all the traditional raw material exports, e.g. mica, manganese ore, hides and skins, raw cotton, etc. However, this decline was almost totally compensated for by the extremely rapid increase in iron ore exports.

(*c*) Although the share of manufactured goods in total exports increased only moderately, the changes in composition within this commodity classification are very interesting. The traditionally exported manufactured goods were jute products and cotton textiles. All other exports of manufactures can be defined as non-traditional, in the sense that during the 1950s, most of them were relatively insignificant; and even in the year 1960/61, they constituted a very small proportion of total exports. Table 2.9 summarises the results of section III in Table 2.8.

We find that the share of traditional manufactures in total export earnings fell from 30 per cent in 1960/61 to 18.8 per cent in 1970/71, whereas, over the same period, the share of non-traditional manufactures rose from 11.4 per cent to 31.7 per cent. It should be noted that most of these changes occurred after 1965/66.

Changes in export markets

Consider now, the markets for India's exports. Table 2.10 outlines the directional changes in exports, and brings out the changes in relative shares of the different export markets. The UK, the US, the USSR

TABLE 2.8   Commodity composition of India's exports: a detailed breakdown: 1960–1970 (in percentages)

	1960/61	1961/62	1962/63	1963/64	1964/65	1965/66	1966/67	1967/68	1968/69	1969/70	1970/71
I. FOOD, BEVERAGES AND TOBACCO	33.3	34.0	35.9	34.5	35.4	32.7	32.6	33.4	29.3	26.8	29.0
Tea	19.1	18.4	18.7	15.4	15.1	12.7	13.7	14.9	11.4	8.6	9.5
Coffee	1.1	1.4	1.1	1.1	1.6	1.6	1.4	1.5	1.3	1.4	1.6
Cashew kernels	2.9	2.8	2.8	2.7	3.6	3.4	3.9	3.6	4.5	4.1	3.4
Tobacco	2.3	2.1	2.7	2.7	3.0	2.4	1.9	2.9	2.4	2.3	2.1
Sugar and spices	3.1	5.0	4.6	5.4	4.7	4.3	4.1	3.7	2.7	3.0	4.4
Oilcakes	2.2	2.6	4.6	4.5	4.9	4.3	4.3	3.8	3.6	2.9	3.6
Others	2.6	1.7	1.4	2.7	2.5	4.0	3.3	3.0	3.4	4.5	4.4
II. RAW MATERIALS AND OTHER UNPROCESSED PRODUCTS	20.2	20.1	21.5	20.9	19.7	18.7	19.8	17.7	17.7	17.4	17.7
Iron ore	2.7	2.6	2.9	4.6	4.6	4.9	6.0	6.2	6.5	6.7	7.6
Mica and manganese ore	3.8	3.1	2.7	2.2	2.8	2.8	2.4	2.2	2.0	1.9	1.9
Fats and vegetable oils	1.3	0.9	1.9	2.5	0.9	0.5	0.3	0.3	0.9	0.4	0.5
Raw cotton and waste	1.8	3.1	2.5	2.1	1.8	1.6	1.5	1.6	1.2	1.3	1.1
Hides and skins	1.4	1.3	1.5	1.1	1.2	1.4	1.4	0.6	0.4	0.6	0.2
Other crude and raw Materials	9.2	9.1	10.0	8.4	8.4	7.5	8.2	6.8	6.7	6.5	6.4
III. MANUFACTURED GOODS	43.3	42.7	41.1	44.0	44.5	47.9	47.3	48.4	52.5	55.1	52.3
A. Traditional											
Jute manufactures	21.0	21.9	22.7	19.8	20.6	22.7	21.5	19.5	16.1	14.6	12.4
Cotton textiles	9.0	7.3	6.7	6.9	7.9	7.9	6.6	6.6	6.5	6.1	6.4

B. Non-traditional

Iron and steel	1.5	1.5	0.5	1.3	1.5	2.2	4.6	5.8	6.1	5.9
Machinery and transport equipment	1.1	0.7	0.9	1.1	1.4	1.4	1.8	3.3	4.0	4.9
Metal manufactures	0.3	0.3	0.5	0.5	0.5	0.5	0.9	1.3	1.7	1.8
Non-metallic mineral manufactures	0.4	0.6	2.3	2.1	2.2	2.3	2.7	3.8	3.5	3.2
Non-ferrous metals	—	—	0.3	0.1	0.1	0.1	0.1	—	1.2	0.8
Leather and leather manufactures	3.9	3.7	3.3	3.4	3.5	5.3	4.5	5.4	5.8	4.7
Chemicals	1.1	1.2	0.9	1.3	1.4	1.3	1.3	1.8	2.2	2.4
Silk and woollen manufactures	1.1	1.2	1.5	2.0	1.6	1.3	1.3	1.5	2.1	2.1
Paper, rubber and wool manufactures	0.2	0.2	0.2	0.4	0.4	0.5	0.5	0.9	0.7	0.9
Miscellaneous manufactured articles	1.8	1.5	2.2	2.2	2.7	2.4	3.0	3.4	4.5	5.0
Total including others	100.0	100.0	100.0	100.0	100.0	100.0	100.0	100.0	100.0	100.0

Source: For sections I, II, and IIIA: Tables 2.6 and 2.8; for section IIIB on the non-traditional exports of manufactures: statistics published by DGCIS, Calcutta—the percentages have been calculated.

Note: Non-metallic mineral manufactures include items such as asbestos, cement products, building materials, glass, glassware, pottery, precious stones, etc. The group of miscellaneous manufacture articles includes products like sanitary and plumbing fittings, furniture, travel goods, clothing, footwear, sports goods, printed matter, office supplies, precision instruments, photographic goods, etc.

TABLE 2.9 *Composition of the exports of manufactures*
(as a percentage of total exports)

Year	Traditional manufactures	Non-traditional manufactures	Other manufactured goods	All manufactures
1960/61	30.0	11.4	1.9	43.3
1961/62	29.2	10.9	2.6	42.7
1962/63	29.4	9.4	2.3	41.1
1963/64	26.7	12.6	4.7	44.0
1964/65	28.5	14.4	1.6	44.5
1965/66	30.6	15.3	2.0	47.9
1966/67	28.1	17.3	1.9	47.3
1967/68	26.1	20.7	1.6	48.4
1968/69	22.6	27.2	2.7	52.5
1969/70	20.7	31.8	2.6	55.1
1970/71	18.8	31.7	1.8	52.3

Source: Table 2.8.

and Japan have been treated separately from their regional groupings owing to their individual importance as markets for Indian goods.[10]

A study of the table reveals that exports to the UK declined steadily, while exports to Japan, Eastern Europe and the USSR increased very rapidly throughout the 1960s. This was a marked change from the historically determined pattern of export markets which had remained unaltered in the 1950s. There was a moderate but steady rise in exports to the USA and West Asia, although exports to the ECAFE region and the EEC countries did not register any significant increase. Exports to the EFTA countries other than UK, and the African continent were virtually stagnant, except for the sudden spurt in exports to Africa in 1970/71.

In absolute terms, India's exports to UK fell from $363.1 million in 1960/61 to $227.2 million in 1970/71. Over the same period, exports to Japan increased from $74.3 million to $271.3 million, to USSR from $60.7 million to $279.8 million; and to the East European countries from $43.7 million to $202.5 million.[11] Although there

[10] Of the regional groupings, some need explanation. Eastern Europe includes Bulgaria, Czechoslovakia, East Germany, Hungary, Poland, Rumania and Yugoslavia. The ECAFE countries include Afghanistan, Australia, Burma, Ceylon, Hong Kong, Indonesia, Iran, Pakistan, Malaysia, New Zealand and Singapore. The grouping West Asia includes Aden, Bahrain, Iraq, Jordan, Kuwait and Saudi Arabia.

[11] The rapid expansion in India's exports to the USSR and East European countries was largely because of the bilateral trade agreements, which are discussed in detail in Chapter 12.

TABLE 2.10 *India's export markets, by countries and regions: 1960–1970 (in $ million)*

	1960/61	1961/62	1962/63	1963/64	1964/65	1965/66	1966/67	1967/68	1968/69	1969/70	1970/71
UK	363.1	338.8	346.2	344.6	352.2	306.1	269.8	305.3	268.6	220.0	227.2
USA	215.8	243.6	242.9	273.5	309.2	310.4	293.3	276.6	312.4	317.2	276.5
USSR	60.7	67.8	80.5	109.6	164.0	195.4	164.5	162.4	197.7	235.1	279.8
Japan	74.3	85.3	92.8	123.8	128.2	120.0	143.3	181.2	211.1	239.1	271.3
Eastern Europe	43.7	67.8	114.6	119.6	138.9	133.6	136.5	138.8	157.5	175.0	202.5
ECAFE countries excluding Japan	224.1	202.2	212.1	265.5	244.2	214.0	179.1	179.9	245.0	264.9	275.7
EEC countries	108.9	118.3	116.7	130.9	120.0	116.1	118.9	119.0	148.6	133.9	131.5
Africa	103.1	118.4	105.2	97.8	97.3	129.9	95.9	93.6	97.0	117.5	185.7
West Asia	48.6	50.4	48.7	63.1	56.7	60.7	52.3	59.4	89.6	97.3	68.9
EFTA countries excluding UK	12.6	14.8	19.9	24.9	21.1	21.0	17.8	18.7	20.6	24.4	25.3
Total including others	1349.4	1387.2	1440.1	1666.5	1714.9	1692.5	1556.5	1598.3	1810.5	1884.4	2046.9
Relative shares: in percentages											
UK	26.9	24.4	24.0	20.7	20.5	18.1	17.3	19.1	14.8	11.7	11.1
USA	16.0	17.6	16.9	16.4	18.0	18.3	18.8	17.3	17.3	16.8	13.5
USSR	4.5	4.9	5.6	6.6	9.6	11.6	10.6	10.2	10.9	12.5	13.7
Japan	5.5	6.2	6.4	7.4	7.5	7.1	9.2	11.3	11.7	12.7	13.3
Eastern Europe	3.2	4.9	8.0	7.2	8.1	7.9	8.8	8.7	8.7	9.3	9.9
ECAFE countries excluding Japan	16.6	14.6	14.7	15.9	14.2	12.6	11.5	11.3	13.5	14.1	13.5
EEC countries	8.1	8.5	8.1	7.9	7.0	6.9	7.6	7.5	8.2	7.1	6.4
Africa	7.6	8.5	7.3	5.9	5.7	7.7	6.2	5.9	5.4	6.2	9.1
West Asia	3.6	3.6	3.4	3.8	3.3	3.6	3.4	3.7	5.0	5.2	3.4
EFTA countries excluding UK	0.9	1.1	1.4	1.5	1.2	1.2	1.1	1.2	1.1	1.3	1.2
Total including others	100.0	100.0	100.0	100.0	100.0	100.0	100.0	100.0	100.0	100.0	100.0

Source: Statistics published by DGCIS, Calcutta. The data on the absolute value of exports have been converted into US dollars, and the percentages have been computed.

Note: All figures relate to Indian fiscal years beginning 1 April.

was no similar expansion in exports to the USA, in absolute terms, it was a very important market, and foreign exchange earnings derived from it averaged $301.7 million per annum in the three-year period 1968/69–1970/1. Exports to the ECAFE countries excluding Japan were subject to considerable fluctuations, but over the decade as a whole, they registered a slight increase and averaged $268.5 million per annum during the period 1968/69–1970/71.

These trends in the absolute value of exports are reflected quite closely in the changing relative shares of different markets. Table 2.10 shows that UK's share in India's exports fell by more than half, from 26.9 per cent in 1960/61 to 11.1 per cent in 1970/71. At the same time, the share of the USSR market increased from 4.5 per cent to 13.7 per cent. Similarly, the East European countries also trebled their share in India's exports, which rose from 3.2 per cent to 9.9 per cent. The relative share of the Japanese market increased from 5.5 to 13.3 per cent. The proportion of India's exports absorbed by the US market in 1970/71 was slightly lower than that in 1960/61. However, the terminal year figures conceal the fact that exports to the US reached a peak in 1965/66, and in that year, the share of the American market was a little more than 18 per cent. Of the remaining regions, the share of exports going to ECAFE countries other than Japan declined marginally, while the share of the African continent registered a slight increase. The shares of the West Asian, EEC and EFTA countries remained virtually unchanged.

In this chapter we have outlined some of the main features of India's export performance during the 1960s. The trends emerging from our preliminary analysis can be summed up as follows.

(*a*) Over the decade as a whole, exports grew at an average rate of about 4 per cent annum. Although, in the context of the phenomenal expansion in world trade, this growth was relatively slow, and India's share in world exports fell continuously throughout the period under study, it was a distinct break from the past stagnation in export earnings.

(*b*) In the second half of the 1960s, there was a dramatic decline in the exports of tea and jute goods, which had been India's major foreign exchange earners until then, but non-traditional exports of manufactures, which were relatively insignificant until 1960, registered a marked increase.

(*c*) The UK, which had been a crucial trading partner in the early post-independence years, lost its traditional position as the most important market for India's exports, an increasing proportion of which went to Japan, USSR and the East European countries.

Apart from these findings, our discussion brought to light the wide disparities in export performance as between different commodities and commodity groups. Given the diverse commodity composition, it is clear that no single aggregative analysis would suffice to explain India's export performance. Therefore, in the chapters that follow, we shall adopt a micro economic approach, and analyse the performance of each of India's major exports.

Part Two
Empirical analysis: a micro approach

3

Jute manufactures

In 1960, India was the largest producer and exporter of jute manufactures in the world. It accounted for 45 per cent of the estimated
world production of jute manufactures, and for almost three-fourths
of world exports. Jute goods were also the single most important
export, which constituted 21 per cent of the country's total foreign
exchange earnings. By 1970, India had lost this position of dominance
in the world market. Although the Indian jute industry still accounted
for 38 per cent of the world production,[1] its share in world exports
fell to less than 50 per cent of the total, and only 12 per cent of the
value of Indian exports was attributable to jute manufactures.

The main changes in India's exports of jute manufactures over this
period are summed up in Table 3.1. It shows that in the first half of
the 1960s, exports grew steadily in terms of both value and volume,
and that the foreign exchange earnings derived from jute goods
reached a peak level of $384 million in 1965/66. After that, however,
there was a marked and continuous decline in exports. The fall in
export earnings was not as pronounced as that in volume, because of
an increase in the unit value of exports. The improvement in unit
value was partially a result of rising prices, and partially, as we shall
show later, an index of a change in the type of jute manufactures
exported.[2]

We shall now investigate the extent to which these trends were a
consequence of changes in world demand, on the one hand, and
domestic factors that affected competitiveness, on the other.

[1] India's production of jute manufactures fell from 1065 thousand tons in 1960
to 978 thousand tons in 1970, whereas the estimated world output rose from
2386 thousand tons to 2598 thousand tons. See Commonwealth Secretariat,
London, *Industrial Fibres: A Review*, vol. 16 (1966), p. 183; and vol. 20 (1973),
p. 199.

[2] New items like carpet backing fetched higher prices per unit of weight as compared to the traditional sackings and hessian.

TABLE 3.1 *Exports of jute manufactures from India*

Year	Volume in thousand tons	Volume index	Value in $ million	Value index	Unit value in $ per ton
1960/61	799	100	283.9	100	355
1961/62	803	101	304.2	107	379
1962/63	849	106	327.0	115	385
1963/64	930	116	330.7	116	356
1964/65	960	120	353.9	125	369
1965/66	900	113	384.1	135	427
1966/67	736	92	334.7	118	455
1967/68	753	94	312.1	110	414
1968/69	653	82	290.7	102	445
1969/70	571	71	275.5	97	482
1970/71	550	69	253.9	89	462

Source: Statistics published by DGCIS, Calcutta.

Note: All data relate to Indian fiscal years beginning 1 April. The indexes and the average unit value have been calculated from the absolute figures on value and volume.

World exports and the demand for jute goods

While analysing India's jute exports in the context of developments in world trade, it is necessary to compare the growth in Indian exports with the expansion in world exports, and to examine the factors underlying the changes in world demand for jute goods.

Consider first, India's share in world exports. Table 3.2 outlines the trend in world exports of jute manufactures and brings out the changes in relative shares of the main exporting countries. We find that although the average annual volume of world exports increased slightly from 1145 thousand tons in the three-year period 1960–1962 to 1197 thousand tons during 1968–1970, the average annual volume of Indian exports fell by 27 per cent, from 822 thousand tons to 600 thousand tons. As a result, India's share in world exports dropped from 71.7 per cent in 1960–1962 to 50 per cent in 1968–1970. The striking thing is that all the changes occurred in the second half of the 1960s, and it was in this short span of six years that India rapidly lost ground to Pakistan in the world market for jute goods. Between 1964 and 1970, India's exports of jute manufactures fell by almost half, whereas Pakistan more than doubled its exports. Consequently, India's share in world exports crashed from 74.8 per cent in 1964

TABLE 3.2 *Exports of jute manufactures from the major exporting countries (in thousand tons)*

	1960	1961	1962	1963	1964	1965	1966	1967	1968	1969	1970
India	862	731	872	904	1064	970	739	767	679	571	550
Pakistan	191	205	233	235	235	287	363	371	454	495	487
Belgium	49	44	52	58	56	58	61	58	67	61	55
UK	16	16	17	18	15	14	11	8	8	9	9
Others	59	43	45	45	52	58	55	50	48	48	50
World Total	1177	1039	1219	1260	1422	1387	1229	1254	1256	1184	1151

Relative shares (in percentages)

	1960	1961	1962	1963	1964	1965	1966	1967	1968	1969	1970
India	73.2	70.4	71.5	71.7	74.8	69.9	60.1	61.2	54.1	48.2	47.8
Pakistan	16.2	19.7	19.1	18.6	16.5	20.7	29.5	29.6	36.1	41.8	42.3
Others	10.6	9.9	9.4	9.7	8.7	9.4	10.4	9.2	9.8	10.0	9.9
Total	100.0	100.0	100.0	100.0	100.0	100.0	100.0	100.0	100.0	100.0	100.0

Source: Commonwealth Secretariat, London, *Industrial Fibres: A Review*, for 1960–1963: vol 16, (1966), p. 186; and for 1964–1970: vol 20 (1973), p. 202.

Note: Figures for the period 1960–1963 have been converted into metric weights, and rounded off to the nearest thousand.

TABLE 3.3   *World imports and consumption of jute goods*
(annual average: in thousand tons)

Country groups	1961–1963	1964–1966	1967–1969
Developed market economies:			
Imports	758	848	915
Consumption	1258	1361	1426
Centrally planned economies:			
Imports	56	162	146
Consumption	516	775	771
Less developed economies:			
Imports	412	443	342
Consumption	1137	1298	1317
World total:			
Imports	1226	1453	1403
Consumption	2931	3434	3514

Source: FAO Rome, *Monthly Bulletin of Agricultural Economics and Statistics* (February 1971), pp. 10 and 13.

to 47.8 per cent in 1970, whereas, at the same time, Pakistan increased its share from 16.5 per cent to 42.3 per cent.[3]

It is quite surprising that although India managed to retain her share in an expanding world market during the period 1960 to 1964, by actually increasing her exports, she was not able to maintain even the absolute level of her exports after that. On the other hand, in the latter half of the decade, Pakistan succeeded in increasing its share of a contracting world market. India's relatively poor export performance clearly needs an explanation, and we shall go into that, a little later in the chapter.

To some extent, the growth in India's exports from 1960 to 1964 can be explained in terms of the expansion in world demand. Table 3.3, which highlights the trends in world imports and consumption of jute goods, reveals that there was a moderate but significant increase in the world import demand for jute goods until the mid-1960s. However, in the following years, the growth in the consumption of jute goods tapered off, and there was a fall in world import demand. A disaggregation of these trends shows that:

(*a*) in the developed market economy countries, imports as well as consumption of jute goods increased very gradually throughout, although the pace slowed down towards the end of the decade,

[3] The share of other exporting countries remained almost unchanged at a level of 9–10 per cent.

(*b*) in the centrally planned economies, both imports and consumption rose rapidly in the first half of the 1960s, but the trend was reversed thereafter. The level of consumption stagnated, and the imports actually fell by 10 per cent between 1964–1966 and 1967–1969;

(*c*) in the less developed countries, consumption increased steadily throughout, but imports which rose slightly between 1961–1963 and 1964–1966, fell by 23 per cent in 1967–1969.[4]

Thus we see that the fall in the absolute level of imports after 1964–1966 was largely due to a substantial reduction in imports by the developing countries. The primary reason for this decline in import demand on part of the LDCs was the policy of import substitution, which led to the establishment of jute mills in many of these countries, dependent on domestically grown or imported raw fibre. Our hypothesis is confirmed by the fact that although jute consumption in LDCs increased a little between 1964–1966 and 1967–1969, imports decreased by 23 per cent. The impact of import substitution is indeed quite obvious, but the developing countries accounted for only one-third the total world imports of jute manufactures. It is therefore necessary to examine the possible reasons for the virtual stagnation of consumption and import demand in the developed countries, particularly after 1964–1966. In fact, the reasons are fairly well known, and, in general, fall into two broad categories: (*a*) the emergence of substitute materials such as paper and plastics; and (*b*) the development of alternative methods of transporting goods e.g. bulk handling, consumer packaging and containerisation. The next section attempts to analyse the effect of these factors on the exports of jute manufactures during the period 1960 to 1970.

Competition from substitutes

From time to time, there were scarcities of jute which resulted in high prices of jute goods.[5] Temporary stoppages in the supply of raw jute,

---

[4] According to a FAO commodity note, the fall in the imports of jute goods by the centrally planned economies and the developing countries was attributable to heavy reductions in purchases by seven major importing countries, which were, Burma, Argentina, Nigeria, USSR, UAR, Cambodia and Thailand. It is pointed out that these reductions were greater than the significant increase in imports by Kenya, Tanzania, Indonesia, Iran and Rumania, which occurred in the same period. See FAO Rome, *Monthly Bulletin of Agricultural Economics and Statistics* (February 1971), p. 10.

[5] During the period under study, prices of jute goods rose sharply in 1961, 1965, 1966 and 1967; see *Impact of Synthetics on Jute and Allied Fibres*, FAO Commodity Bulletin Series, no. 46 (Rome, 1969), p. 108.

and imbalances between the supply and demand of jute manufactures also led to considerable price fluctuations. To an extent, such fluctuations were only normal in an industry which draws its basic raw material from agriculture. But at times, partial crop failures were aggravated by strikes and political problems in the main jute growing and manufacturing areas.[6] The users of jute in the world market thus had to guard against these uncertainties by stockpiling, and, more important, by searching for alternatives.

The principal jute manufactures are yarn and cloth. As a woven fabric, jute has traditionally been the cheapest material for making bags, wrappings or bales for the transport of goods.[7] For many years, jute yarn has also been used in the manufacture of woven carpets, although of late, pre-woven jute carpet backing has come into increasing use. Jute products faced varying degrees of competition in their different markets. We shall look at each of these markets in turn.

The bag market

It is now generally accepted that the demand for jute as bag-making material has been declining for two reasons. First, fewer bags are being used in transportation and distribution.[8] Second, bags are being made from other cheaper materials.[9] Alternative techniques of transportation and distribution that have been developed include bulk handling, consumer packaging and containerisation. Substitute materials that have emerged are multiwall paper and plastics.

Over the last two or three decades, the development of bulk handling has been a part of the general process of mechanisation. The trend towards bulk handling has been particularly marked in developed countries, where commodity production and its processing are geographically concentrated, and where labour costs are relatively high. In such cases, deliveries made in bulk save on labour time. According to one study,[10] the trend towards bulk handling has been significant both in shipment from producing area to factory, and from factory to

[6] For example, the India–Pakistan war in 1965.

[7] Woven jute goods can be classified into: (a) 'sacking' which is a loosely woven fabric made from inferior quality jute; (b) 'hessian' or 'burlap' which is a more expensive and finer fabric made from superior quality jute; and (c) 'carpet backing' which is like hessian, but is woven on a much broader loom. There are other jute products, e.g. canvas and cotton bagging, but these constitute a small proportion of the total output.

[8] The development of bulk handling and new retail techniques which started replacing jute in the 1950s, is described extensively by M. Singh, *India's Export Trends* (Oxford, 1964), pp. 43–7.

[9] For a detailed discussion on the emergence of synthetic materials as competitors of jute, see *Impact of Synthetics on Jute and Allied Fibres*, Chapter V, pp. 33–98.

[10] Ibid. p. 33.

wholesale point. It is quite obvious that this change in transportation methods has little to do with the relative price of jute bags.[11]

The growth of consumer packaging has been reinforced by the effects of bulk handling. Once bulk has been broken at the factory stage, commodities can be packed into small containers for direct sale to customers. However, consumer packaging has developed quite independently as part of the whole new world of supermarkets and rapidly changing retail techniques. The recent changes in marketing methods which led to the establishment of supermarkets, have also resulted in a growing proportion of food products being moved in ready-to-cook or instant form. In other products also, manufacturers are increasingly supplying retailers directly with pre-packed ready-to-take-home consumer packages. All these changes in marketing techniques, which are also quite independent of the relative price of jute goods, have eliminated the use of the traditional jute bag or container.

In the sphere of export shipments, an alternative technique that has been developed is containerisation. In principle, this method is akin to bulk handling. It does away with the need for the hardy jute bag by packing commodities into huge containers for shipment. Of course, bags are not completely eliminated, for within the container the product is packed in bags; only these bags need not be strong because it is the container which takes the rough handling.

So far, we have considered reasons for the declining use of bags in transportation, which are quite independent of the price of jute goods. Let us now analyse the reasons for the growing use of materials other than jute, in bag-making.

Jute bags have faced intense competition from alternative materials, for many decades.[12] Multiwall paper bags, which were developed in the early 1950s, have captured many of the jute markets owing to lower and relatively stable prices. However, despite the lower prices, paper bags could not entirely replace jute bags because of their negligible re-use value, low tear strength and sensitivity to moisture and wetting. On the other hand, apart from re-use value (which accrues to the buyer and not the seller), jute bags have the advantage

---

[11] This is proved quite well by Singh, *India's Export Trends*, p. 45.

[12] Before and during the Second World War, the shortage of jute led to the emergence of cotton bags/sacks as substitutes. However, after the war, when jute supplies were again fully available, the jute sack captured its lost markets largely owing to the cost advantage. But, jute prices rose sharply once again in 1951. At this time, paper was readily available in Europe and North America. Multiwall paper bags were developed, and these offered intense and effective competition to jute sacks in the 1950s. Jute bags have not been able to recapture the markets lost to paper during this period.

that they can be handled roughly without snapping, and can keep agricultural products which need moisture and air to survive.

The more recent competitors of jute bags have been plastic film bags made out of low density polyfelin or polyvinyl chloride (PVC). These plastic bags began to compete with jute only in the early 1960s. Apart from their cheapness, the basic advantage of these bags over jute and paper sacks is that they are moisture resistant. This attribute makes them ideal for the transport of chemicals, fertilisers and hygroscopic materials. Hence, the main area in which these plastic bags compete with jute is in the fertiliser sack market.[13] Plastic sacks do have the disadvantages of low strength and low friction quality, which make them difficult to handle. Therefore, jute bags still need to be used for products which need to breathe and for export shipments, which inevitably come in for rough handling.

The carpet backing market

Apart from packaging, the most important outlet for jute products is the carpet backing market. This market began to develop in the mid-1950s, and became a booming one in the 1960s. High incomes in the developed countries have led to higher living standards giving rise to increased expenditure on home furnishings. As a result, the demand for carpets has been rising rapidly, particularly in the US.

All carpets need some kind of backing to strengthen them. In woven carpets, backing yarns are woven into the carpet fabric for this purpose. In tufted carpets, which are capturing an increasing proportion of the carpet market owing to their relative cheapness, the tufts are stitched into a pre-woven backing by multi-needle machines. These days, in addition to such primary backing, carpets are given a secondary backing in order to increase their stability and grip. In fact, secondary backings are quite common in tufted carpets. Therefore, in some countries the demand for carpet backing has increased faster than the output of carpets. The fact that the production of tufted carpets in the US alone increased by roughly 350 per cent between 1960 and 1969, rising from 99 million square yards to 455 million square yards, is a sufficient index of the boom in demand for carpet backing in the 1960s.[14] It also accounts for the rapid

[13] Plastic bags are bound to fare better, partially because of their anti-rot property, and partially because, as pointed out by the FAO study (p. 35), fertiliser manufacturers themselves are often large petrochemical companies, which also produce plastic bags and prefer to ship their fertilisers in their own products.

[14] This means that the output of tufted carpets grew at a compound rate of 21 per cent per annum; see *Jute Chronicle*, a bi-monthly publication of the Indian Jute Mills Association (IJMA) (Calcutta, July/August 1970), p. 83.

growth in American imports of hessian cloth over this period.[15]

It would appear that although jute products were facing intense competition from paper and plastic film bags, they had a virtual monopoly in the carpet backing market, where they were the cheapest and most suitable fabric. Even in the bag market, some inherent qualities of jute ensured that it could not be completely replaced. This was certainly true until the mid-1960s.

Prospects changed distinctly thereafter. In 1964, the synthetics industry developed polypropylene (PP) and high density polyethylene (PE), which have become the main competitors of jute products both in the bag, and in the carpet backing markets. PE competes only with jute bags, and PP competes with both bags and carpet backing. It has been observed that owing to lower costs of production and characteristics like lightness, high tensile strength, low water absorbency and anti-rot properties, these materials could completely replace jute products in the world market.[16] However, a recent FAO study pointed out that there are certain incalculables, because of which the process of substitution may not continue indefinitely until jute is eliminated.[17] These incalculables include the re-use value of jute bags, and the consumer acceptance of jute-backed carpets; lighter synthetic backings may not be easily accepted by buyers of carpets.

The American market for jute

Until now, we have analysed the development of substitutes in general terms. It is also important to consider the impact of these developments on the exports of jute manufactures from India. In doing so, we shall take the example of the US market, which, as is evident from

[15] See Table 3.5.

[16] PP and PE are woven polyfelin fabrics and are a petrochemical product which can be produced in most developed countries. According to the FAO report relating to the impact of synthetics on jute (p. 12), costs of production of these materials are likely to be lower than woven fabrics like jute, for the following reasons: (a) low raw material costs, which would decline over time with improvements in technology and economies of scale; (b) polymer sheets are slit into tapes so that the need for, and cost of, spinning into yarn is eliminated; (c) being a tape, its area of coverage is greater than that of a fibre, so that raw material costs are lower per unit of coverage; (d) the tapes have considerably higher tensile strength than jute and can therefore be woven in high speed looms, which have a relatively high productivity. In fact, during the last three or four years, the advent of high-density and high-speed tufting machines has pushed jute out of a considerable proportion of the carpet backing market. This is because jute threads cannot stand the strain of high-density needling at high speed. (See a report in *Jute Chronicle* March/April 1970, p. 32).

[17] *Impact of Synthetics on Jute and Allied Fibres*, p. 3.

TABLE 3.4   *Market distribution of India's jute exports.*
Relative shares of import markets (annual average: in percentages)

	(1) 1960/61–1962/63	(2) 1964/65–1966/67	(3) 1968/69–1970/71
USA	32.9	37.7	45.7
USSR	3.1	13.6	16.3
Canada	5.1	5.2	6.4
Australia	7.3	5.9	4.6
UK	5.2	4.0	1.9
UAR	2.5	5.4	3.7
Argentina	3.8	2.4	0.4
Total including others	100.0	100.0	100.0

Source: Commonwealth Secretariat, London, *Industrial Fibres: A Review*, for column (1): vol 14 (1964), p. 177; for column (2): vol 17 (1968), p. 188; and for column (3): vol 20 (1973), p. 203.

Note:

(a) Figures relate to Indian fiscal years beginning 1 April.

(b) The percentages have been calculated by expressing the volume of exports to a particular country as a proportion of the total volume of exports for each year. These have been averaged for the three-year periods.

Table 3.4, was by far the most important consumer of Indian jute products in the 1960s. What is more, the US purchased the bulk of its burlap import requirements from India. Table 3.5, which shows the trend in American jute imports and brings out the change in India's relative share of the US market, confirms this fact. Except in 1969 and 1970, more than four-fifths of the US imports originated from India.[18] Therefore, if we consider the American market for jute bags and carpet backing in the period 1960–1970, we should get a fair idea of the impact of the developments outlined above on Indian exports.

In the US, the commodities which have traditionally been the largest consumer of jute bags are animal feed and potatoes. During the 1960s, however, animal feed was shipped increasingly by bulk handling, and potatoes were moved more and more in 5 to 15 lb consumer-packs rather than 100 lb burlap bags.[19] In addition, when-

[18] It is noticeable that India gradually lost her share of the US jute market after 1965. The ground lost by India was promptly captured by Pakistan; see *Industrial Fibres: A Review*, vol. 20 (1973), p. 204. The factors underlying this relatively poor export performance are discussed in the next section, which is devoted to an analysis of the competitiveness of Indian jute manufactures.

[19] *Impact of Synthetics on Jute and Allied Fibres*, pp. 38–9.

TABLE 3.5   *Imports of hessian cloth (burlap) by the US*
(in thousand tons)

Year	Total imports	Imports from India	India's percentage share
1960	243.2	203.5	84
1961	234.0	196.4	84
1962	290.5	246.6	86
1963	344.6	294.8	86
1964	329.4	278.2	84
1965	336.4	287.8	86
1966	353.3	284.0	80
1967	338.2	276.5	82
1968	375.6	298.9	80
1969	358.7	270.8	75
1970	318.0	205.3	65

Source: Commonwealth Secretariat, London, *Industral Fibres: A Review*, for 1960–1964:
vol 16 (1966), p. 189; for 1965: vol 19 (1970), p. 204; and for 1966–1970: vol 20
(1973), p. 204.

Note: Figures for the period 1960–1965 have been converted into metric tons.

ever burlap prices rose above their long term average, as they did
in 1961 and 1966/67, paper bags captured many of their markets.[20]
For instance, in 1966/67, a 10-oz, 100-lb burlap bag sold for 22
cents while an equivalent 3–4 ply paper bag was priced at only 15
cents. During the same period, the price of a 100-lb jute bag for
potatoes was 15 cents, whereas an equivalent paper bag cost only
10 cents.[21] Therefore, although paper bags also lost their markets
to bulk handling techniques, they gained a little at the expense of
jute bags.[22]

The phenomenal expansion of the US carpet industry led to a
rapid growth in the demand for jute carpet backing, which in turn,
was primarily responsible for the substantial expansion in American
jute imports in the early 1960s. Table 3.5 shows that the volume of
US burlap imports increased from 243.2 thousand tons in 1960 to an
annual average of 336.8 thousand tons in the three-year period
1963–1965. However, this trend did not last long, and the growth

[20] Ibid.

[21] Ibid.

[22] The declining demand for jute bags in the animal feed and potato trade did not
show up in the total consumption of burlap bags in the US, because of increased
government purchases of sandbags, for use in Vietnam; see ibid. p. 40. However, this war-created demand provided only a temporary reprieve for jute
bags.

TABLE 3.6 *Carpet backing materials used in the US* (in percentages)

Year	Primary backing			Secondary backing			Jute used as a proportion of all carpet backing
	Jute	Synthetics	Others	Jute	Synthetics	Others	
1968	80.6	16.0	3.4	71.1	18.9	10.0	76.1
1969	66.6	29.7	3.5	75.9	17.4	6.7	70.9
1970	62.7	31.0	6.3	64.0	29.0	7.0	63.3

Source: IJMA, *Jute Chronicle* (January/February 1971), p. 8.
Note: The 1970 figures are based on the average for the first three quarters.

of American import demand for jute levelled off in the latter half of the decade. The basic reason was that the development of poly-propylene in 1964 provided the carpet industry with a synthetic alternative to jute for the purpose of backing. A few years later, the jute carpet backing market suffered a further setback when new developments in the carpet industry led to the adoption of high-density and high-speed tufting machines. As pointed out earlier, jute threads cannot stand the strain of needling at high speeds. Thus, synthetic materials steadily increased their share of the American carpet backing market. This substitution is brought out quite clearly by Table 3.6. Between 1968 and 1970, the share of jute in primary carpet backing fell from 80.6 per cent to 62.7 per cent, while the proportion of synthetic backing increased from 16 to 31 per cent. Similarly, the share of jute in secondary carpet backing also declined sharply. The emergence of synthetics in the American market led to an absolute reduction in jute imports during 1969 and 1970, which naturally had its impact on India's exports of jute manufactures to the US. Exports of carpet backing were the worst hit, and dropped steeply from 219 thousand tons in 1969 to 138 thousand tons in 1970.[23] Thus we see that although the growing demand for carpet backing helped India's jute exports through most of the 1960s, even in this market, jute products were threatened by increasing competition from synthetics towards the end of the decade.

Competitiveness of India's jute industry

We have already observed that in the years after 1964, India rapidly lost her relative share of the world market for jute manufactures to Pakistan. Table 3.7, which compares the exports of different types

[23] See Chairman's Report, IJMA Annual Meeting 1970, *Jute Chronicle* (March/April 1971), p. 27. As we shall show later, this dramatic fall was partially due to non-price factors such as strikes.

TABLE 3.7 *Exports of jute goods from India and Pakistan* (in thousand tons)

Year	Sackings		Hessian		Carpet backing		All jute goods	
	India	Pakistan	India	Pakistan	India	Pakistan	India	Pakistan
1964/65	259	153	480	66	109	7	950	233
1965/66	248	192	456	86	100	13	896	302
1966/67	181	244	360	96	134	20	734	371
1967/68	157	239	385	113	150	26	751	392
1968/69	83	229	310	107	200	27	650	449
1969/70	56	242	262	203	205	33	569	506

Source: IJMA *Jute Chronicle* (January/February 1971), p. 17.

Note: Figures relate to Indian fiscal years beginning 1 April, and have been rounded off to the nearest thousand. As these have been compiled by the IJMA, the data for India do not tally exactly with the official trade statistics on the aggregate volume of jute exports in Table 3.1, but the difference is very small indeed.

of jute goods from India and Pakistan, in the latter half of the 1960s, confirms this observation. A study of this table makes the following facts quite clear: (*a*) Between 1964/65 and 1969/70, India's exports of sacking fell drastically from 259 000 to 56 000 tons. Apparently, this loss was a direct gain of the Pakistan jute industry. (*b*) Exports of hessian from India declined by nearly half in these five years, whereas Pakistan more than trebled her exports. (*c*) The only redeeming feature in the export performance of the Indian jute industry was the rapid expansion of carpet backing exports. Pakistan's share of this market was nominal.

Clearly, the above trends cannot be explained in terms of falling import demand or stagnant world consumption. Between them, India and Pakistan provided a little more than 90 per cent of the world exports of jute manufactures, throughout the decade. Therefore, the answer must lie in the relative competitiveness of their jute industries. Let us now consider the factors that could have influenced competitiveness.

Relative prices

Price competitiveness over a period of time is determined by changes in the cost of production, and the pressure of domestic demand. We shall look at each of these factors in turn.

Costs of production: In the jute manufactures industry, the raw fibre is by far the most important constituent of the cost of production. According to several estimates,[24] the cost of raw jute accounts for about 60 per cent of total costs in an average jute mill. Hence, one can get a fair idea of the cost competitiveness of the jute industry in the two countries by comparing the trends in raw material costs over the decade.

Before making such a comparison, it is necessary to provide the

[24] Cf. (*a*) 'The Competitive Position of Jute Manufactures in West Europe and the Far East', *Monthly Bulletin of Agricultural Economics and Statistics* (March 1962), p. 3, according to which, raw material costs constituted 56 per cent of the total costs in India, and 49 per cent in Pakistan. (*b*) The Report of the *Pakistan Jute Enquiry Commission*, Karachi, 1961, estimated that raw jute constituted about 55 per cent of total costs in Pakistan; the figure was estimated to be slightly higher for a typical Indian mill; see p. 145. (*c*) In 1970, it was reported that raw jute accounted for 60 per cent of the total costs in the Indian jute industry; see Chairman's Report, IJMA Annual Meeting 1970, *Jute Chronicle* (March/April 1971), p. 28.

TABLE 3.8   *Production and imports of raw jute in India*
(in thousand tons)

Year	Production	Imports	Year	Production	Imports
1960/61	947	75	1965/66	1040	218
1961/62	1482	84	1966/67	1184	298
1962/63	1286	53	1967/68	1367	—
1963/64	1451	21	1968/69	691	110
1964/65	1369	106	1969/70	1221	—
			1970/71	1104	—

Source: RBI Bombay, *Report on Currency and Finance*, *1966/67*, p. 42; and *1970/71*, p. 85.
Note: All figures relate to agricultural years beginning 1 July and ending 30 June. The data
have been converted into thousand tons from the number of bales. Production figures include the output of both jute and mesta. Mesta accounted for 20 to 30 per cent of total
output in these years.

historical background to the position of raw jute supplies in the
two countries. At the time of the division of the country in 1947, the
main jute growing areas were in Pakistan. These were also the best
jute lands, in terms of the relatively high yield and the superior
quality of the fibre grown. Thus, while the Indian jute industry was
deprived of its main raw material source, Pakistan was left with the
raw fibre, but without a processing industry. As a result, India concentrated its efforts on increasing the production of raw jute, and
Pakistan set about establishing manufacturing capacity. To begin
with, India imported large quantities of raw jute from Pakistan, but
the increasing hostilities between the two countries soon put an
end to this trade.

In the 1960s, therefore, the imports of raw jute were minimal,
and the Indian jute industry was primarily dependent on the domestic
production of fibre. This fact emerges clearly from Table 3.8, which
outlines the changes in raw jute supplies. We find that the position
regarding the availability of raw jute improved substantially in the
first half of the 1960s. There is no doubt that this was one of the main
factors underlying the rapid growth in India's export of jute manufactures in that period. After 1965/66, however, there was a marked
deterioration in the position of raw jute supplies, and it was in these
years that India steadily lost her share in the world market for jute
products.

A noticeable feature of the above table is the considerable variation in the level of output. Such fluctuations occur because jute is
grown as a cash crop by farmers whose main alternative is rice. Hence,

TABLE 3.9   *Wholesale price index of raw jute in India and Pakistan*

Year (1961/62 = 100)	India	Pakistan
1961/62	100.0	100.0
1962/63	72.5	86.0
1963/64	73.5	86.3
1964/65	91.0	117.8
1965/66	131.6	124.4
1966/67	156.4	132.8
1967/68	111.4	108.0
1968/69	166.5	127.0
1969/70	144.1	108.6
1970/71	145.4	120.1

Source: For India: RBI Bombay, *Report on Currency and Finance, 1969/70* and *1970/71*, p. S30.
For Pakistan: CSO Karachi, *Monthly Statistical Bulletin* (January 1966), p. 3200; (July 1971), p. 787; (January 1972), p. 86.
Note: The figures relate to Indian and Pakistani fiscal years beginning 1 April and 1 July respectively. The wholesale price index published by the CSO, Pakistan, has 1959/60 as base year. The above figures have been calculated by taking the 1961/62 index, which was 119.88, as 100.

the acreage planted with jute in any particular year, is determined largely by the relative prices of jute and rice in the previous year, and the extent of available food supplies.[25] Owing to variable supply conditions, raw jute prices are also subject to sharp fluctuations.[26] This is borne out by Table 3.9, which compares the trend in raw

[25] In India, the output is particularly sensitive to changes in the area under cultivation, because all increases in raw jute production have been obtained by extending the cropping area. The average yield per hectare which was 1043 kg in 1950/51, 1049 kg in 1960/61 and 1025 kg in 1970/71, scarcely changed in two decades (see *Report on Currency and Finance, 1970/71*, p. 85). Efforts at improving the productivity were half-hearted, and far from successful. For example, till as late as 1965/66, only 8 per cent of the total jute acreage benefited from fertiliser, and barely 12 per cent of it employed improved varieties of seed. The impact of other agronomic practices, such as line sowing and plant protection, was also marginal; for details, see *Jute Development: Retrospect and Prospects*, Ministry of Food and Agriculture, Government of India (New Delhi, April 1967). It is clear that a significant improvement in productivity would not only have increased the availability of raw jute, but would also have made the fibre relatively cheaper for the manufacturing industry.

[26] The Government of India has recently announced price support measures for jute farmers in order to overcome this problem, and to ensure a steady supply of raw jute. However, in an area where subsistence farming is the rule, and food shortages are fairly common, it is not clear whether such price incentives would actually increase jute production. It may not even be desirable, if it leads to a lower rice output. Clearly, more efforts must be made to raise the yield per acre. For that, it is necessary to provide jute farmers with inputs, credit and knowhow.

TABLE 3.10   *Wholesale price index of jute manufactures in India and Pakistan*

Year (1961/62 = 100)	India	Pakistan
1961/62	100.0	100.0
1962/63	90.9	92.4
1963/64	81.9	86.0
1964/65	93.0	104.7
1965/66	118.6	126.1
1966/67	123.4	109.1
1967/68	106.4	94.7
1968/69	133.3	100.3
1969/70	154.5	102.4
1970/71	170.7	113.1

Source: For India: RBI Bombay, *Report on Currency and Finance*, *1969/70* and *1970/71*, p. S30. For Pakistan: CSO Karachi, *Monthly Statistical Bulletin* (January 1966), p. 3200; (July 1971), p. 787; and (January 1972), p. 86.

Note: The figures relate to Indian and Pakistani fiscal years beginning 1 April and 1 July respectively. The wholesale price index published by CSO Pakistan has 1959/60 as base year, but in order to facilitate comparison, we have computed the above figures by taking the 1961/62 index, which was 113.49, as 100.

jute prices in India and Pakistan. It is difficult to discern a general trend because of the fluctuations. All the same, it is quite clear that after 1964/65, prices of raw jute in India rose much faster than in Pakistan, which must have adversely affected the competitiveness of the Indian jute industry. In addition, the Pakistan jute industry had the advantage of access to relatively better quality raw jute.[27]

It is sometimes suggested that the Indian jute industry was relatively more efficient than its counterpart in Pakistan, so that the disadvantage implicit in high raw material costs may well have been neutralised. This was certainly true in the 1950s.[28] However, in the last decade, the Pakistan jute manufacturing industry went through considerable transformation and modernisation, and the situation may have changed completely. Unfortunately, no comparative estimates of the manufacturing costs in the two countries are available. But, to the extent that raw material costs and efficiency in the manufacturing process are both reflected in the final product price, India must have lost the competitive edge attributable to greater efficiency, during the 1960s. Table 3.10, which brings out the changes

[27] It is generally accepted that the quality of the Indian jute fibre is not as good. What is more, approximately one-fourth of India's raw jute supply was constituted by mesta (see note to Table 3.8), which is an inferior quality substitute for jute.

[28] For details, see Singh, *India's Export Trends*, p. 53.

TABLE 3.11 *Production, exports and consumption of jute goods in India* (in thousand tons)

Year	Production	Exports	Export–output ratio in percentages	Consumption	Consumption–output ratio in percentages
1961	997	760	76.2	278	27.8
1962	1231	874	71.0	303	24.6
1963	1324	890	67.2	333	25.2
1964	1271	1000	78.6	378	29.7
1965	1336	929	69.5	378	28.3
1966	1120	746	66.6	405	36.2
1967	1157	769	66.5	388	33.5
1968	1085	673	62.0	435	40.1
1969	893	579	64.8	380	42.6
1970	955	539	56.4	441	46.2

Source: RBI Bombay, *Report on Currency and Finance, 1966/67*, p. 56; and *1970/71*, p. 108.
Note:
(a) The above figures relate to IJMA mills only.
(b) Exports and consumption do not add up to production because of changes in stocks.
(c) The export–output and consumption–output ratios have been calculated by expressing exports and consumption as a percentage of total production.

in wholesale prices of jute manufactures in the two countries, shows that prices were relatively stable in Pakistan, whereas they rose steadily in India. The difference was particularly marked towards the end of the decade. Between 1966/67 and 1970/71, the wholesale prices of jute manufactures in Pakistan were virtually unchanged, but over the same period, the wholesale price index in India moved up from 123.4 to 170.7. Clearly, this trend must have helped the export drive of the jute industry in Pakistan.

Pressure of Domestic Demand: During the period under study, the market for jute goods in India expanded very rapidly. Table 3.11, which outlines the changes in the production and consumption of jute goods in India, reveals that the average annual domestic consumption increased from 305 thousand tons in the three-year period 1960–1963 to 419 thousand tons during 1968–1970. At the same time, the proportion of total output absorbed by the domestic market increased from 26 per cent to 43 per cent. The effect of this pressure of domestic demand on the exportable surplus was made worse by the fact that there was a continuous decline in India's production of jute manufactures after 1965. Thus, it is not surprising that exports, which accounted for over three-quarters of total production in 1961, constituted only 56.4 per cent of the output in 1970.[29]

To some extent, this increase in domestic demand for jute goods was only to be expected. In India, packaging is by far the most important end-use for jute goods. Foodgrains and agricultural products have always been packed in jute bags. However, industries such as textiles, cement, sugar and fertilisers also provide an important source of demand. Given the fact that during the 1960s, agricultural production in India rose by 20 per cent, and industrial production increased by 80 per cent,[30] the growth in domestic consumption of jute goods was certainly not very much.

It should be pointed out that the bulk of the domestic demand was for sacking,[31] and as such, could only have curtailed a part of the exportable surplus of jute manufactures. A look at Table 3.7 suggests that the pressure of domestic demand may indeed have reduced the exportable surplus of sacking, exports of which fell markedly, but no definite or conclusive evidence is available in this context. It is possible that the tax on exports of jute manufactures after June 1966 made the domestic market relatively more attractive. In a recent study, Laumas has shown that during the period 1960/61–1964/65, domestic prices of jute goods rose much faster than export prices, and that the latter were consistently lower than the former.[32] On this basis, he concludes that the domestic market was relatively more profitable in the early 1960s. Unfortunately, it is not possible to extend this data beyond 1964/65, or to comment upon it, because Laumas obtained it from a private unpublished source.

Trade policies

Trade policy affects the competitiveness of an industry if it raises or lowers the domestic currency returns per unit of foreign exchange

[29] This problem was not as acute in the case of Pakistan, because, in relation to the total output of its jute industry, the domestic market was not very large. In fact, during the period 1964/65–1967/68, on the average, 82 per cent of Pakistan's total output of jute goods was exported; (calculated from production figures in the CSO Karachi, *Pakistan Statistical Yearbook, 1968*, p. 164, and export figures in Table 3.7).

[30] The index of agricultural production rose from 142 in 1960/61 to 170 in 1969/70, and the index of industrial production moved from 100 in 1960 to 180 in 1970; see *Report on Currency and Finance, 1970/71*, p. S16–18.

[31] See *Jute Chronicle* (March/April 1971), p. 28.

[32] P. S. Laumas, 'Exports of Jute Manufactures from India: An Alternative Hypothesis', *Economia Internazionale* (February 1971), p. 132–3.

earned by exporters. Such changes can be brought about either by officially altering the exchange rate, or by subsidies and taxes on exports which change the effective exchange rate. In the case of jute manufactures, government policy in India was a mixture of both methods, while in Pakistan, only subsidies and taxes were used.

In the 1960s, the jute industry in both countries was subjected to several changes in export policy. A comparison of the two, in the following pages, makes one fact patently clear. Whereas, in India, the Government did not attempt to subsidise the jute industry in any way, in Pakistan, export policy was operated in a manner such that the jute manufactures industry was subsidised heavily throughout the decade.

In 1959, Pakistan introduced the bonus voucher scheme as an integral part of its export policy. Stated briefly, the scheme operated as follows. Exporters who surrendered their foreign exchange earnings to the central bank at the official exchange rate, were given a certain proportion of the f.o.b. value of their exports as an import entitlement, which was termed 'bonus vouchers'. During the period under study, the bonus rate for the jute manufactures industry varied between 20 and 40 per cent of the export value.[33] These foreign exchange vouchers were transferable, and could be sold freely in the open market. Given the tight regime of import controls, the vouchers naturally fetched high premiums, thereby providing an effective cash subsidy to exporters who sold them. But this was not all. The apparent subsidy offered by the scheme was compounded by cheaper availability of raw jute, exports of which were subject to a tax. In addition, the foreign exchange earned by exporters of raw jute had to be surrendered at the official exchange rate. This combination of policies led to the expected result where the effective exchange rate for exports of jute manufactures was much higher than the official rate, and that for exports of raw jute was lower than the official rate.[34] The estimates reproduced in Table 3.12 provide confirmation. The

[33] For a description of this method of export promotion, see Q. K. Ahmad, 'The Operation of the Export Bonus Scheme in Pakistan's Jute and Cotton Industries', *Pakistan Development Review* (Spring 1966).

[34] It would be interesting to analyse why such policies were followed. The conventional reason is that a developing country should export manufactures rather than raw materials, specially when a simple process is involved. This was probably one of the factors which prompted the Pakistan Government in its export promotion efforts. Aziz Khan suggests another possible reason which may have been responsible for these policies; see *The Economy of Bangladesh* (London, 1972), p. 93. He argues that this taxation of raw jute and subsidisation of jute manufactures was a classic example of fiscal policy being employed to effect a transfer from the poorer farmers to the richer capitalists.

TABLE 3.12 *Effective exchange rates for jute and jute goods in
Pakistan*

Year	Raw jute (Rupees per dollar)	Jute manufactures (Rupees per dollar)	Effective subsidy on jute manufactures in percentages
1959/60	4.14	6.86	44
1962/63	4.24	7.20	51
1965/66	4.52	6.64	39
1968/69	4.75	9.84	107

Source: A. R. Khan, *The Economy of Bangladesh* (London, 1972), p. 90.
Note: The effective subsidy on jute manufactures in the last column has been calculated as the
difference between the effective and official exchange rate of Rs4.76 = $1.

figures also show that the exports of jute manufactures were subsidised heavily since 1959/60, and in 1968/69, the effective subsidy
amounted to as much as 107 per cent. In view of the fact that exports
of the major input raw jute were taxed, it is clear that the effective
protection afforded to the jute manufactures industry in Pakistan
was even higher than that implied by the subsidy. Estimates of effective protection in the mid-1960s range from 183 to 406 per cent.[35]

In sharp contrast to this heavy subsidisation, the Indian jute
industry was relatively ignored. Until February 1964, exports of raw
jute were subject to a very small tax, which was a hangover from the
1950s, and was prompted by the scarcity of raw jute supplies in
India. Perhaps this may have been of marginal help, but otherwise,
during the 1960s, the Indian jute industry was one of the few export
earners which did not receive any subsidy whatsoever, and had to surrender its foreign exchange earnings at the overvalued official exchange rate. The 57.5 per cent devaluation of the rupee in June 1966
would normally have done a great deal to improve the competitiveness
of India's jute manufacturing industry vis-à-vis Pakistan. In fact,
however, its effect was greatly reduced by the simultaneous imposition
of duties on the exports of jute manufactures.

Table 3.13 sets out the rates of these export duties, which varied
as between different jute products, and were revised from time to
time in the post-devaluation period. The *ad valorem* incidence of
the export duties is not apparent because they were fixed in terms of

[35] S. R. Lewis, *Pakistan: Industrialization and Trade Policies*, OECD (Oxford, 1970),
p. 80. The sharp divergence in rates of effective protection arises from the different methods of treating non-trade inputs.

TABLE 3.13 *Export duties on jute manufactures in India* (in rupees per ton)

Year	Imposed/changed with effect from	On hessian	On sacking	On carpet backing	On jute specialities	On other jute goods
1966/67	6 June 1966	900	600	900	900	600
1967/68	25 May 1967	750	450	600	600	600
	February 1968	500	250	No change	Exempted	No change
1968/69	19 June 1968	No change	No change	No change		250
	1 March 1969	200	150	No change		150
1969/70	10 December 1969	No change	No change	300		No change

Source: RBI, Bombay, *Report on Currency and Finance, 1966/67 to 1970/71.*
Note:
(a) There was no change in export duties during 1970/71.
(b) Hessian excludes carpet backing and other specialities. Sacking includes cloth, bags, twist, yarn, rope and twine.

rupees per unit weight. All the same, it is possible to estimate their *ad valorem* equivalent by expressing the duty per unit weight as a proportion of the average unit value at the time of devaluation. Using this method, the rate of export duty in June 1966 worked out at 18.7 per cent for carpet backing, 26.7 per cent for hessian, 23.8 per cent for sacking, 29.8 per cent for other jute goods, and 24.5 per cent for jute manufactures as a group.[36] In the following years, these duties were gradually lowered, but the duty on carpet backing and hessian remained quite significant until the end of the decade.

It is clear from the above that the jute industry could not have derived much benefit from the 1966 devaluation. According to our estimates, the *net* devaluation (after discounting for the tax on exports) was only 16.5 per cent in the case of jute manufactures.[37] This policy is difficult to understand in a period when raw jute prices, within India, were abnormally high, and Indian jute manufactures were being subjected to increasing pressure in the world market, both from Pakistan and from synthetic substitutes. It is important to note that in the period 1966–1970, while the Government levied duties on the export of jute goods, India rapidly lost her share of the world market to Pakistan.

In all likelihood, these export taxes were prompted by the objective of maintaining the foreign exchange price of jute manufactures, in the belief that a substantial net devaluation would invite retaliatory action from Pakistan, which would inevitably lead to a terms of trade loss for both countries. But, according to the Reserve Bank of India, some of the export duties were at least partially intended to mobilise the windfall profits that would accrue to exporters following the devaluation.[38] On balance, it is difficult to say which was the dominant motive underlying the export duty on jute products. Clearly, any fiscal revenue-raising objective was totally misplaced, although the terms of trade argument had some element of logic in it. In a duopolistic market situation, it is obvious that India would have found it difficult to increase its relative share of the market by improving its price competitiveness. To that extent, the export duties were justified. However, in all the preoccupation about pre-empting retaliatory action by Pakistan, it was forgotten that a larger net devaluation would have been a good *defensive* measure against the latter's *aggressive* export policy based on the bonus voucher scheme. Such a policy might well have helped India to maintain her relative

---

[36] For details of the calculation, see Table 11.2.
[37] See Table 11.3.
[38] See *Report on Currency and Finance*, 1966/67, p. 124.

share in the world market for jute manufactures. In fact, it is quite surprising that, being the larger duopolist, India did not react to the increasing encroachment of her market share by Pakistan.

At this stage, it is necessary to point out that the increased share of Pakistan in the world market did not necessarily mean a genuine long term improvement in the competitivenes of her jute industry. The export policies adopted by the Pakistan Government were biased heavily in favour of jute manufactures, and against raw jute. The resulting multiple exchange rate system raised the domestic currency returns on manufactured jute exports so much that the domestic entrepreneurs were bound to respond to the high profits incentive. Some doubts have been expressed as to whether this heavy subsidisation of the jute manufactures industry actually constituted a net foreign exchange gain to the Pakistan economy.[39]

Quite apart from the economic merit of such measures, our analysis in the foregoing paragraphs has shown how export policies in India and Pakistan reinforced each other, resulting in India's declining share of the world market for jute goods.

Non-price factors

The trends in India's exports of jute manufactures during the past decade can be explained largely in terms of relative prices and trade policies. All the same, there were a few non-price factors which may have exercised some influence on export performance.

For example, the sharp decline in India's exports of jute manufactures during 1970 may be partially attributable to:

(a) the loss of eighty-nine working days at Calcutta port during the year 1970, owing to the bargemen's and stevedores' strikes;[40] in fact, this stoppage of work at the port hit export shipments of jute fairly hard; and

(b) the long shoremen's strike in America and the simultaneous recession in the US economy during 1970, both of which factors, led to a dramatic decline in the US consumption of jute goods in 1970/71.[41]

The aforesaid short term factors may not have been significant over the decade as a whole, but their importance should not be underestimated, because it is such temporary stoppages in supply that lead to an increasing use of substitutes.

[39] For a detailed discussion on the economic wisdom of these subsidisation policies, see Lewis, *Industrialization and Trade Policies*, pp. 129–31.
[40] See Chairman's Report, IJMA Annual Meeting 1970, *Jute Chronicle* (March/April 1971), p. 27.
[41] *Report on Currency and Finance*, 1970/71, p. 108.

In addition, India's exports of jute products may also have been restricted by commercial policies in the importing countries. Throughout the 1960s, imports of jute bags and fabrics were subject to a tariff of 23 per cent in the EEC countries.[42] Similarly, imports of jute cloth into Japan were liable to a tariff of 25 per cent.[43] Although imports into UK entered duty free on account of Commonwealth preferences, there were quantitative restrictions on the imports of jute manufactures. Most West European countries operated similar non-tariff barriers.[44] It is likely that these tariff and non-tariff barriers not only restricted world trade in jute products, but also provided a competitive edge to synthetic substitutes.

Summary

The main conclusions to emerge from our analysis in this chapter can be summed up as follows. The steady growth in the value and volume of India's exports of jute manufactures, during the first half of the 1960s, was made possible by two factors: a succession of good harvests which increased the availability of raw jute; and an expansion of world import demand, attributable largely to the American market. Although increasing competition from substitutes led to a stagnation in world jute consumption thereafter, it was not responsible for the decline in Indian exports during the latter half of the decade. In fact, India's dismal export performance after 1965/66 was largely the result of domestic factors and policies which affected the competitiveness of her jute industry. Shortages of raw jute, which lowered the total output, and the increasing pressure of domestic demand, both cut into the exportable surplus. Competitiveness was worsened further by the high prices of raw jute. The devaluation of the rupee in 1966 might have partially retrieved the situation, but it was neutralised by the levy of export duties. Towards the end of the decade, matters were made worse by non-price factors such as strikes, and the loss of a significant share of the American market for carpet backing, to synthetics. While the Indian jute manufacturing industry was faced with all these difficulties, its Pakistani counterpart pros-

---

[42] See *Industrial Fibres: A Review*, vols. 16 to 19. The Kennedy Round reductions on 1 January 1972 were minimal and the tariffs remained in the range 15–22 per cent; see vol. 20 (1973), p. 232.

[43] Ibid.

[44] Non-tariff barriers on the import of jute goods were employed by UK, Australia, France, Italy, West Germany, Netherlands, Switzerland and the Benelux countries. For details, see UNCTAD Secretariat Report, *Liberalization of Non-tariff Barriers*, TD/B/C.2/R.3 (Geneva, 30 December 1970), p. Annex 34.

pered. The latter benefited not only from the adequate availability of relatively better quality raw jute, but also from heavy subsidisation by the Government. It is no wonder that between 1965 and 1970, when India's share of the world market dropped from nearly 70 per cent to less than 50 per cent, Pakistan more than doubled its share from 20.7 per cent to 42.3 per cent.

4
Cotton textiles

Among the less developed countries, India was the first to export cotton textiles on a significant scale. As far back as 1948–1950, she accounted for more than 11 per cent of the world trade in cotton textiles. In the years that followed, the Indian textile industry was unable to maintain its level of exports, as a result of which its share of the world market registered a decline.[1] All the same, until 1960, cotton textiles were an important foreign exchange earner for the country. During the period 1950–1960, they contributed between 10 and 13 per cent of total export receipts each year.[2] In the 1960s, however, their relative importance in India's exports appears to have declined. The share of cotton textiles in export earnings fell from 7.7 per cent in the three-year period 1960/61–1962/63 to 6.3 per cent during 1968/69–1970/71.[3]

Table 4.1 outlines the main trends in India's exports of cotton textiles over the decade, and shows that: (a) exports of cotton yarn increased quite rapidly – particularly after 1967; (b) handloom cloth exports remained more or less unchanged except for the peak performance in 1965; and (c) in the first half of the 1960s exports of mill-made cloth declined both in value and in quantity. After 1966, however, rupee earnings from mill cloth exports increased rapidly, although the quantity seems to have remained more or less unchanged. This discrepancy can be explained partially by improved unit values and partially by the substantial devaluation of the rupee in June 1966. In terms of aggregate foreign exchange earnings, exports of

[1] For a detailed analysis of India's exports of cotton textiles during the 1950s, see Chapter V in M. Singh, *India's Export Trends* (Oxford, 1964). See also, A. Maizels, *Exports and Economic Growth of Developing Countries* (Cambridge, 1968), Appendix C, pp. 405–18.

[2] Singh, p. 73.

[3] Calculated from Table 2.6. It should be pointed out that we are using the term 'cotton textiles' in a somewhat restricted sense. It refers only to yarn and cloth and does not include clothing or cotton manufactures. Admittedly, this is a bit odd, but it is a direct consequence of a curious statistical practice in most countries whereby clothing is not included in the category of textiles. Even the Standard International Trade Classification follows this practice: cotton yarn and fabrics come under SITC 652, whereas clothing is SITC 841.

TABLE 4.1 India's exports of cotton textiles

Year	Cotton yarn		Handloom cloth		Mill-made cloth		Total export earnings in $ million
	Quantity in million kg	Value in million Rs	Quantity in million m	Value in million Rs	Quantity in million m	Value in million Rs	
1960	6.4	37.0	26.4	50.1	635.4	582.9	140.8
1961	6.9	37.6	25.9	47.9	525.1	461.7	115.0
1962	10.4	53.0	26.0	57.8	464.9	399.6	107.2
1963	13.6	62.1	33.2	77.3	485.7	410.2	115.5
1964	12.8	48.4	33.7	77.8	502.9	488.6	129.2
1965	12.8	60.4	39.7	95.3	506.9	472.5	132.0
1966	16.2	86.9	37.0	67.3	424.3	491.2	110.9
1967	12.4	81.5	31.9	68.5	409.6	593.7	99.2
1968	16.7	109.2	18.6	45.9	475.1	667.6	109.7
1969	33.0	237.4	26.3	71.5	418.5	630.9	125.3
1970	30.5	268.8	27.5	74.2	413.4	656.6	133.3

Source: Textile Commissioner, Government of India, Indian Textile Bulletin (May 1971).
Note:
(a) After April 1965, the quantity of mill cloth is in million square metres. This change in the unit of measurement introduces a downward bias of about 10 per cent in the statistics, and therefore partially accounts for the fall in the quantity of mill cloth exported between 1965 and 1966.
(b) With effect from June 1966, the value figures are in post-devaluation rupees.
(c) The last column on total exchange earnings has been computed by converting the rupee figures into dollars.

TABLE 4.2   *World consumption of fibres*

Annual average for the period	Consumption in million tons		Share in total fibre consumption: in per cent		Consumption per caput: in kg	
	Cotton	Man-made fibres	Cotton	Man-made fibres	Gotton	Man-made fibres
1960–1962	10.11	3.58	63.4	22.7	3.20	1.17
1963–1966	10.68	5.15	58.9	28.3	3.27	1.53
1967–1969	11.43	7.20	54.5	34.3	3.20	2.00

Source: FAO, 'World Fibre Consumption in the Sixties', *Monthly Bulletin of Agricultural Economics and Statistics* (March 1970).

Note: In each period, the third and fourth columns together do not add up to 100 per cent owing to the consumption of other natural fibres such as silk, flax and wool.

cotton textiles from India were quite stagnant throughout the decade; export receipts barely changed from an annual average of $121 million in the period 1960–1962 to $122.7 million in 1968–1970.

In order to assess this export performance of the Indian cotton textile industry, it is necessary to put it in the context of trends in world demand and the performance of competing countries.

World trade in cotton textiles

The world demand for cotton textiles grew very slowly during the decade under study. This is clearly reflected in the fact that world exports, which were 945.4 million kg during 1960–1962, increased only slightly to 1059.7 million kg in the period 1967–1969.[4] The relative stagnation in world import demand for cotton textiles can be explained in terms of the following factors.

(*a*) In recent years, one of the most important developments in world textile production has been the growing importance of man-made fibres.[5] Table 4.2, which outlines the changing composition of world fibre consumption, confirms this trend. We find that between 1960–1962 and 1967–1969, cotton consumption was quite stagnant, whereas the consumption of man-made fibres doubled. As a result, the

---

[4] See Table 4.3.

[5] The man-made fibres competing with cotton fall broadly into two categories. First, the artificial cellulose fibres like rayon which are cheap chemical copies of the basic cotton fibre. More recently, it is the development of non-cellulosic fibres like polyester which has led to increasing competition for cotton in the fibre market.

share of cotton in total fibre consumption declined from 63.4 to 54.5 per cent. The gains made by synthetic fibres appear to be quite substantial and therefore need some explanation. The obvious advantages of man-made fibres lie in their stable prices and quality, but they have also benefited from being product innovations. The drip-dry and permanent-press characteristics of their final output has made them appropriate in the context of changing consumer preferences.[6]

(*b*) The increased availability of synthetic fibres and the shift in tastes has led to a spreading use of synthetic and cotton blends. This has resulted in a replacement of 'pure cotton' by 'blended' textiles.[7] Although the yarn and fabric is produced by the cotton industry, the output can no longer be classified as cotton textiles because it has a synthetic content.

(*c*) The third factor responsible for the near stagnation in world import demand has been the restrictions on international trade in cotton textiles. The rapid expansion of cotton textile exports from LDCs, during the late 1950s, threatened not only the exports, but also the domestic markets of North American and West European countries. This threat of disruption prompted the developed countries to negotiate a trading arrangement with the less developed exporting countries, in order to regulate the expansion of trade in cotton textiles. The Long Term Arrangement (LTA) was established through GATT in 1962 and has been operative continuously since then. Most developed countries have invoked the LTA provisions to impose quantitative restrictions on imports of cotton textiles from LDCs. Obviously, these policies have restricted the growth of world trade in cotton textiles.[8]

Table 4.3 shows the world exports of cotton textiles during the 1960s and brings out the changes in relative shares of the main exporting countries. We find that India's share of the world market remained unchanged at about 8 per cent throughout the decade. However, when we look at the changing relative shares of other competing

[6] All these natural advantages have been supplemented by the price competitiveness of the synthetic fibres industry. For example, between 1960 and 1970, the list prices of branded polyester were reduced by more than 50 per cent, whereas cotton prices declined by only 5–8 per cent over the same period. See FAO, *Agricultural Commodity Projections 1970–1980*, vol. I (Rome, 1971), p. 239.

[7] See ibid. p. 241; and *A Study on Cotton Textiles* by GATT (Geneva, 1966), p. 11. According to the latter, about one-fourth the total mill-consumption of man-made fibres is processed by the cotton industry. This practice of blending is particularly common in the developed countries.

[8] The impact of the LTA on exports of cotton textiles from the LDCs in general, and from India in particular, will be discussed in detail later in the chapter.

TABLE 4.3   Exports of cotton textiles from main exporting countries: Yarn and cloth (in million kg)

	1960	1961	1962	1963	1964	1965	1966	1967	1968	1969	1970
India	89.0	73.2	71.4	78.4	79.5	85.2	80.3	70.8	83.8	94.2	90.8
Japan	190.8	171.8	179.5	163.5	151.7	145.2	139.3	106.9	94.2	83.3	67.6
USA	59.9	62.4	55.6	49.0	52.6	41.5	44.9	38.5	36.1	52.6	42.8
UK	50.3	43.6	38.3	35.7	36.8	32.9	29.2	24.8	28.2	28.3	26.2
Hong Kong	49.9	57.9	50.0	54.0	56.1	66.6	73.0	72.3	69.3	70.9	78.5
Taiwan	9.8	16.3	17.5	21.0	18.4	21.4	47.3	36.8	34.5	43.2	57.3
Pakistan	49.5	12.8	11.6	31.0	46.2	46.7	53.1	66.5	100.9	113.0	135.4
UAR	32.5	27.7	34.4	43.3	40.9	55.7	55.3	54.9	67.2	67.6	62.8
China	60.0	51.0	63.0	47.0	63.0	62.0	88.0	77.0	70.0	n.a.	n.a.
South Korea	3.9	1.0	2.2	5.1	26.6	11.0	11.6	18.8	14.3	14.9	17.7
World total including others	1006.4	924.2	905.7	935.8	1002.6	1002.3	1082.4	1002.2	1057.8	1120.0	1102.0

Relative shares: in percentages

	1960	1961	1962	1963	1964	1965	1966	1967	1968	1969	1970
India	8.8	7.9	7.9	8.4	7.9	8.5	7.4	7.1	7.9	8.4	8.2
Japan	19.0	18.5	19.8	17.4	15.1	14.4	12.8	10.7	8.9	7.4	6.1
USA	6.0	6.8	6.1	5.2	5.2	4.1	4.1	3.8	3.8	1.7	3.9
UK	5.0	4.7	4.2	3.8	3.7	3.3	2.7	2.5	2.7	2.5	2.4
Hong Kong	5.0	6.3	5.5	5.8	5.6	6.6	6.7	7.2	6.6	6.3	7.1
Taiwan	1.0	1.8	1.9	2.2	1.8	2.1	4.4	3.7	3.3	3.9	5.2
Pakistan	4.9	1.4	1.2	3.3	4.6	4.7	4.9	6.6	9.5	10.1	12.3
UAR	3.2	2.9	3.8	4.6	4.1	5.6	5.1	5.4	6.4	6.0	5.7
China	5.9	5.5	7.0	5.0	6.3	6.2	8.1	7.7	6.6	n.a.	n.a.
Total including others	100.0	100.0	100.0	100.0	100.0	100.0	100.0	100.0	100.0	100.0	100.0

Source: International Cotton Advisory Committee, Washington, *Cotton – World Statistics* (July 1970), vol. 23, no. 12, Part II; and (April 1972), vol. 25, no. 9, Part II, a quarterly publication.

Note:

(a) Exports of yarn and cloth have been added together for all countries except South Korea, which exports only cloth. (b) The figure for total world exports in 1970 is only an estimate since data are not available for all countries. (c) The above statistics relate only to cotton yarn and *pure* cotton fabrics.

countries, India's export performance is certainly disappointing. The share of the traditionally important exporters, viz. Japan, UK and USA, dropped sharply from 30 per cent in 1960 to about 11 per cent in 1970. But India failed to take advantage of this situation,[9] and it was countries like Pakistan, Hong Kong, Taiwan, South Korea and the UAR which seized this opportunity to expand their exports of cotton textiles. The extent of this success can be measured in terms of the change in their relative shares of the world market. Between 1960 and 1970, Hong Kong increased her share from 5.0 to 7.1 per cent, Taiwan from 1.0 to 5.5 per cent, and Pakistan from 4.9 to 12.3 per cent. It is interesting to note that in the 1950s, countries like Pakistan, Taiwan and UAR were net importers, and by 1960 had barely achieved self-sufficiency in cotton textiles through their programmes of import substitution.[10]

Given the fact that these Asian countries increased their exports even in the face of a stagnant world demand, how can we account for the poor export performance of the Indian textile industry? At least a part of the answer must lie in its competitiveness.

Competitiveness of Indian textiles

In order to analyse the competitiveness of India's cotton textile exports, it is necessary to (a) compare the cost structure of the textile industry in India with that in some successful exporting countries; (b) quantify the pressure of domestic demand; and (c) examine exchange rate policies. As for the first, a detailed comparison is clearly beyond the scope of our work. However, in the following section we shall attempt a brief comparison with the textile industry in some Asian exporting countries, viz. Hong Kong, Pakistan, Taiwan and South Korea.

On comparing costs

In the cotton textile industry the main constituents of the cost of production are: the costs of raw materials, the labour employed and the capital equipment installed. In fact, the price paid for raw cotton

---

[9] This was nothing but a repetition of the past. In the 1950s, when the UK and USA witnessed a fall in their shares of world exports, it was Japan, and not India, that seized the opportunity and increased her exports of cotton textiles at a phenomenal pace. For details, see Singh, p. 77.

[10] See *A Study on Cotton Textiles*, p. 25.

is the single most important element in the total costs of yarn and fabrics. On the average, raw cotton accounts for about 50 per cent of the cost of production of cloth.[11] In order of magnitude, labour costs are next and constitute approximately 18–20 per cent of the total.[12] As would be expected, capital costs are relatively difficult to quantify and are related to output per machine year, which in turn depends upon the productivity of the machinery and the number of shifts worked.[13]

Raw material costs: Raw cotton is freely available on the world market so that textile industries in all countries can purchase it on equal terms. However, cotton producing countries like India and Pakistan need not procure their raw material supplies in the world market. Although India's imports of raw cotton are considerable, its textile industry relies on domestic production for the bulk of its requirements.[14] There is no such problem in the case of Pakistan, which is a net exporter of raw cotton and can meet the entire demand of the cotton manufacturing sector itself. Therefore, it is quite obvious that in India and Pakistan, the domestic prices of cotton are a good index of changes in the cost of raw cotton used by their textile industries. However, this reasoning cannot be extended to countries like Hong Kong, Taiwan and South Korea, which do not grow any cotton and have to rely on imports to meet all their requirements. In such cases, the change in the average unit value of raw cotton imports is the appropriate index of changing raw material costs incurred by their textile industries.

In order to compare raw material costs, we have constructed indices of the cost of raw cotton to the cotton textile industries in these

[11] According to production cost estimates made by the Textile Council, Manchester, on the average, raw cotton constitutes a little over 70 per cent of the total yarn cost and yarn accounts for two-thirds the cost of woven cloth. Therefore, raw cotton constitutes about half the cost of production of cloth. See *Cotton and Allied Textiles*, vol. 1, a report by the Textile Council (Manchester, 1969), pp. 37 and 40.

[12] Ibid. Calculated from the same set of figures. It should be pointed out that labour costs constitute a higher proportion of total costs in the developed countries. The average figure of 18–20 per cent relates to India and Hong Kong.

[13] Ibid. p. 34.

[14] In the period 1965/66–1970/71, on the average, only 11 per cent of the domestic requirements of raw cotton were met by imports. Calculated from statistics published by the Reserve Bank of India; see *Report on Currency and Finance*, 1970/71, p. 83.

TABLE 4.4   *Indices of the cost of raw cotton to the cotton textile industries in some exporting countries*

Year	(1) India	(2) Pakistan	(3) Hong Kong	(4) South Korea	(5) Taiwan
1961	100	100	100	100	100
1962	104	97	99	91	97
1963	111	97	98	97	100
1964	117	114	97	96	95
1965	119	108	95	95	93
1966	127	96	91	95	90
1967	142	96	89	90	84
1968	155	110	96	94	86
1969	171	114	98	87	85

Source: For India: RBI, Bombay, *Report on Currency and Finance 1969/70*, pp. S30–1. For Pakistan: CSO Karachi, *Monthly Statistical Bulletin*. For Hong Kong, South Korea and Taiwan: UN *Yearbook of International Trade Statistics, 1962, 1963, 1965* and *1969*.

Note:

(a) The data for India and Pakistan relate to fiscal years beginning 1 April and 1 July respectively; column (1) is the wholesale price index for cotton in India with 1961/2 = 100, and column (2) is the wholesale price index for raw cotton in Pakistan in which series 1959/60 is the base year, but the index for 1961/2 happens to be 100.

(b) Columns (3), (4) and (5) have been arrived at as follows: the average unit value of raw cotton imports has been calculated from data on the quantity and value of imports, and these figures have been computed into an index with 1961 as base year.

countries.[15] Table 4.4 shows that the cost of raw cotton remained more or less constant in Hong Kong and Pakistan, while it registered a downward trend in Taiwan and South Korea. In sharp contrast, prices of cotton rose continuously in India and increased by more than 70 per cent between 1961 and 1969.[16] The rapid increase in domestic prices was a direct result of shortfalls in supply, and therefore, could have been prevented by allowing additional imports of raw cotton. However, this was not possible because of import restrictions.[17]

[15] It is necessary to note that the indices are based on the domestic currency costs of raw cotton to the textile industry in each of these countries. This is quite adequate for our purpose because we are interested in comparing the *change* in raw material costs *within* each country during the period under study, and *not* the absolute levels as *between* the countries.

[16] This sharp increase should have been at least partially neutralised by the devaluation of the rupee in 1966, but it did not actually happen for the reasons outlined on pp. 74–6.

[17] It is difficult to say whether India saved or lost foreign exchange through this policy. Access to imports of raw cotton would certainly have improved the price competitiveness of the Indian textiles industry, but *by itself*, it may not have led to an adequate increase in exports because of the other inhibiting factors and policies discussed in the following sections.

Clearly, the marked upward trend in raw cotton prices must have affected the competitiveness of Indian textiles quite adversely.

Labour costs: These costs derive directly from the wages paid to workers. However, an inter-country comparison of trends in money wages runs up against some conceptual problems. Low money wages do not necessarily imply low wage costs because the latter are partially determined by the output per man. Therefore, any meaningful comparison must relate to wage costs per unit of output. It is not difficult to find statistics on the changes in money wages paid to textile workers in different countries, but it is nearly impossible to obtain an index of labour productivity in different countries over a period of time. Given all the data limitations, we have attempted to compute a crude productivity index. Table 4.5 outlines the trends in money wages and labour productivity in the cotton textile industry of selected countries, during the 1960s.

We see that between 1960 and 1969 wage costs per unit of output increased by 36.1 per cent in India, 23 per cent in Hong Kong, and decreased slightly in the case of Taiwan and Pakistan. Although the above statistical exercise has many conceptual limitations, it does suggest that labour costs in the Indian textile industry increased more than in competing countries during the period under study.

Capital costs: It is quite natural that costs of production are at least partially determined by the type of capital equipment employed. In fact, given a certain level of machine utilisation, output per machine year depends entirely on the output per machine hour. As between countries, differences in the latter arise from the quality of the machinery used. Obviously, it is difficult to find an appropriate index for the quality of capital equipment. However, in the cotton weaving industry, the proportion of automatic looms in the total loomage does indicate roughly the degree of modernisation,[18] and to some extent the quality of the machinery. This reasoning is supported by findings of the GATT study, according to which the low level of cloth output per loom hour in LDCs was attributable (among other factors) to the relatively low percentage of automatic looms in these countries.[19]

---

[18] Any comment on the extent of modernisation must take into account the type and age of the automatic looms installed, as well as the quality of the cloth woven. The higher productivity of automatic as compared to ordinary looms arises from the fact that the former operate at much higher speeds.

[19] *A Study on Cotton Textiles*, p. 52.

TABLE 4.5 *A comparison of the change in money wages and labour productivity in the cotton industries of selected exporting countries*

(1960 = 100)	1960	1963	1966	1969	Percentage change in wage costs per unit of output between 1960 and 1969
India:					
Money wage index	100	111.8	137.9	164.4	+36.1
Productivity index	100	109.8	111.0	120.8	
Hong Kong:					
Money wage index	100	111.9	148.5	176.2	+23.0
Productivity index	100	125.3	141.0	143.3	
Pakistan:					
Money wage index	100	113.2	141.0	140.8	−4.0
Productivity index	100	112.0	146.7	n.a.	
Taiwan:					
Money wage index	100	116.9	139.1	153.1	−3.3
Productivity index	100	89.2	129.1	158.4	

Method and sources: The index of money wages for all countries has been derived from data on the average money earnings of workers in the textile industry. However, the computation of the crude productivity index is slightly more complex. In the case of India, Pakistan and Hong Kong we have calculated the output per employee to obtain the index of labour productivity. This ratio was arrived at by using a very simple method of dividing the country's total output of cotton yarn and cloth by the number of people employed in its cotton textile industry. For all three countries the production figures have been taken from statistics published by the International Cotton Advisory Committee, Washington, in its quarterly publication *Cotton – World Statistics* (July 1970) and (January 1972).

The other statistical sources for each of the countries are listed below:

(*a*) *India*: For the years 1960, 1963, 1966 and 1969, the per capita annual money earnings of workers in the cotton textile industry were Rs1555, 1740, 2145 and 2558 respectively: see *Indian Labour Statistics, 1967* and *1971*, published by the Labour Bureau, Government of India. Total production of yarn and cloth was 1548.0, 1780.9, 1786.7 and 1879.7 million kg. The employment figures in the cotton textile industry for these years were 895 000, 938 000, 931 000 and 899 000; see *Indian Textile Bulletin*, annual numbers for 1967, 1968 and 1969.

(*b*) *Hong Kong*: The index of money wages in Hong Kong's cotton spinning industry for the years 1960, 1963, 1966 and 1969 was 101, 113, 150 and 178, with 1958 as base year: see *Annual Departmental Report of the Commissioner of Labour, 1968/69*, p. 105. Total production was 129.9, 172.3, 217.4 and 229.2 million kg respectively. Employment in the cotton spinning and weaving industries for these years was 43 326, 45 863, 51 378 and 53 246: see *Government Annual Report, 1961, 1964, 1966* and *1969* (Hong Kong).

(*c*) *Pakistan*: The money wages in the textiles industry of Pakistan for the years 1960, 1963, 1966 and 1968 were Rs87.5, 99.1, 123.4 and 140.8 per month: see ILO *Yearbook of Labour Statistics, 1969* and *1971*. We have assumed the 1969 wage rate to be the same as in 1968. Production of cotton yarn and cloth in the country was 256.7, 301.8, 314.5 and 389.2 million kg. Total employment in the cotton textiles industry in these years was 171 000, 179 937 and 142 648. The figure for 1969 is not available: see *Census of Manufacturing Industries, 1962/63–1965/66* and *1966/67* published by the CSO, Government of Pakistan. We have assumed that there was no improvement in average labour productivity between 1966 and 1969.

(*d*) *Taiwan*: The wage rate in the textile industry of Taiwan was NT $33.21, 38.81, 46.18 and 50.85 per day: see ILO *Yearbook of Labour Statistics, 1969* and *1971*. The productivity index for Taiwan is derived directly from statistics on value added per person employed in the textiles industry as quoted by Mo-Huan Hsing, in *Taiwan: Industrialization and Trade Policies*, OECD (Oxford, 1971), p. 302. For 1960, 1963, 1966 and 1968 these figures were NT $27 352, 24 397, 35 312 and 43 337 at 1964 prices. We have assumed that average labour productivity did not change between 1968 and 1969.

TABLE 4.6   *Proportion of automatic looms in total capacity* (in percentages)

	1960	1964	1967
India	8	12	13
Hong Kong	71	86	100
Pakistan	60	64	69
Taiwan	38	54	70
South Korea	23	26	32
Japan	n.a.	24	28
UK	28	37	42
USA	100	100	100

Source: For 1960 and 1964; GATT, *A Study on Cotton Textiles*, pp. 192–6. For 1967: ICAC, *Cotton – World Statistics* (July 1970), pp. 162–3.
Note: All figures have been rounded off, and those for Japan are not comparable owing to a stricter definition of automatic looms.

Table 4.6 highlights the changes in the proportion of automatic looms since 1960, and brings out the trend towards modernisation of the cotton textile industry in some selected countries. These statistics suggest that owing to the quality of its machinery, the Indian textile industry must have been at a considerable disadvantage vis-à-vis its main competitors. It is quite clear that the proportion of automatic looms in India's cotton industry was extremely low throughout the period under study, and increased only slightly from 8 per cent in 1960 to 13 per cent in 1967. In sharp contrast, we see that even in 1960, a very large proportion of the textile industry in Pakistan and Hong Kong was modernised. By 1967, the percentage of automatic looms in place was 100 in Hong Kong, 69 in Pakistan, 70 in Taiwan and 32 in South Korea. Among the developed country competitors, UK modernised its cotton industry at a fairly rapid rate.

For quite some time, both the Government and the exporters of Indian textiles have been fully aware of the competitive disadvantage arising from the use of relatively old and outmoded capital equipment.[20] Despite this knowledge, very little has been done towards a rationalisation of India's cotton textile industry. The explanation for this is quite straightforward. On its part, the Government has been reluctant to allow a full-scale complete mechanisation for two reasons.

[20] At least since the *Report of the Textile Enquiry Committee*, Government of India (New Delhi, 1958). For details, see Singh, *India's Export Trends*, pp. 91–2.

(*a*) Installation of automatic looms, *ceteris paribus*, would reduce employment in cotton mills by half.[21] In a labour abundant economy which already has a very high level of unemployment, any policy aimed at such modernisation requires careful consideration in view of its welfare implications.

(*b*) Replacement of old machinery by new requires considerable amounts of foreign exchange, and therefore poses another problem.[22] Following from this, in 1962, the Government permitted replacement of plain looms by automatic looms as an export promotion measure, subject to the condition that mills undertook to export 50 per cent of such production and gave a guarantee towards this obligation.[23] The response of the textile industry to this incentive was quite marginal because: (1) producers were not willing to guarantee such a high proportion of exports, and (2) they could not raise adequate financial resources necessary for the replacement of old machinery.[24] Apart from the intensely competitive nature of the world market, the incentive to export was impaired by the relative attractiveness of the home market.

Pressure of domestic demand

In India, the home market has always absorbed the bulk of the country's cotton textile output. In the 1960s, however, domestic demand pressure appears to have increased. Table 4.7 brings out the main trends in domestic consumption and exports of cotton cloth, and shows that the proportion of output exported registered a marked decline from 10.0 to 6.1 per cent. Over the same period of time, i.e. between 1960 and 1967–1969, domestic consumption increased by 20 per cent. It is interesting to note that per capita consumption of cotton cloth in the period 1967–1969 was the same as it was in 1960. This

[21] *Report of the Textile Enquiry Committee*, p. 25.

[22] See *A Study on Cotton Textiles*, p. 58. It has been shown that the imports of the Indian cotton textile industry far exceeded its exports in the first half of the 1960s; cf. J. M. Chona, 'Balance of Payments Position of the Cotton Textile Industry', *RBI Bulletin* (Bombay, June 1966), pp. 636–43. According to this article, the main reason for the foreign exchange deficit was the large imports of raw cotton. Because of this, the Government was probably cautious about adding to the import bill on account of replacement textile machinery.

[23] For details, see *Report on Currency and Finance* 1962/63, p. 18.

[24] In 1966 GATT estimated that a minimum investment of $190 million per annum was necessary for 6 years to replace old and obsolete machinery in the Indian cotton textile industry. However, owing to financial difficulties, the cotton industry had been investing only an estimated $84 million per annum (*A Study on Cotton Textiles*, p. 58).

TABLE 4.7   *Domestic consumption and exports of cotton cloth from India*

Year/annual average for the period	(1) Estimated home consumption in million metres	(2) Index of domestic consumption (1960 = 100)	(3) Per capita availability of cotton cloth in metres	(4) Proportion of output exported in per cent
1960	5971	100	13.8	10.0
1961–1963	6596	110	14.5	7.3
1964–1966	7050	118	14.5	6.8
1967–1969	7164	120	13.7	6.1

Source: Textile Commissioner, Government of India, *Indian Textile Bulletin* (May 1971): for columns (1) and (3), p. 15; and for column (4), pp. 4 and 6. The annual averages have been computed from data for individual years.

Note:

(a) Estimated home consumption is domestic production plus imports minus exports, where domestic production includes the cloth output of both the mill and handloom sectors; (b) it is not as if the proportion of output exported in 1960 was abnormally high; in the period 1958–1960 export–output ratio was 10.2 per cent.

suggests that the availability of cotton cloth has barely kept up with the growth in population. We must not forget that in a poor country like India cloth is a very basic necessity, so that at low consumption levels the income elasticity of demand for it is quite high. Available estimates suggest that it is well above unity.[25] Therefore, growing urban and rural incomes must have exerted additional pressures on the nearly stagnant output of the cotton textile industry.[26]

We have shown earlier that the half-hearted attempts of the Government at promoting exports did not succeed, partly because of inadequate response from the textile industry. Exporters of cotton textiles were somewhat deterred by the intense competition from the newly emerging Asian competitors in the world market. Had it not been for the large domestic market, they would probably have made efforts to compete effectively. As it happened, sales in the domestic

[25] According to a CSO study, the income elasticity of demand for cotton textiles is 1.4; see an article by B. R. M. Chatterjee in the *Monthly Abstract of Statistics*, Government of India (New Delhi; October 1960).

[26] Production of cloth in India increased very little from 6626 million metres in 1960 to 7623 million metres during 1967–1969; cf. *Indian Textile Bulletin* (1967–8–9).

TABLE 4.8 *Domestic and export prices of some cotton textile products in 1966/67*

Description of cloth	Domestic market price	f.o.b. export price	Percentage differential
Poplin – white ⎤ mercerised	100	79	21
Poplin – dyed ⎦ and	100	71	29
Sanforised			
Grey sheeting	100	84	16
Printed dress material	100	81	19

Source: S. Paul and V. L. Mote, 'Competitiveness of Exports – a micro level approach', *Economic Journal* (December 1970), p. 902.

market were much more lucrative. Table 4.8, which pinpoints the difference between the domestic and export prices of some selected cotton textile products, confirms this. The data on prices are based on information supplied by a limited number of manufacturers who were regarded as being the more efficient producers, and hence the potential or actual exporters. Unfortunately, owing to the lack of adequate data on export prices, it is not possible to make a detailed comparison over the entire period under study. However, some indirect evidence is available. In an analysis of the competitiveness of selected textile exports, Paul and Mote have found that the difference between domestic and export prices cannot be explained in terms of cost differentials. They go on to show that the pressure of internal demand reinforced by the higher relative profitability of the home market, adversely affected the competitiveness of some cotton textile exports.[27] Given the almost stagnant production and the trends in domestic consumption, it is not difficult to see how the home market must have eaten into a potential exportable surplus.

Trade policies

It might be argued that the substantial devaluation of the rupee in 1966 should have reduced the relative profitability of the domestic market and restored the incentive to export. But, owing to previously existing government policies, this did not actually happen. At the beginning of the decade, policy makers were quite aware of the importance of the textile industry and its problems. Consequently, in the early 1960s they attempted to promote the exports of cotton yarn

[27] See Paul and Mote, pp. 901–9.

TABLE 4.9   *Import entitlements in the cotton textile industry before devaluation*

Entitlement to import	As a percentage of f.o.b. export value
Coal-tar dyes and textile chemicals	4.0 to 15.0
Raw cotton	66.7
Textile machinery	20.0

Source: Bhagwati and Desai, *India: Planning for Industrialisation*, p. 410.

and cloth, through the operation of import entitlement schemes.[28] The system was quite complicated, but Table 4.9 gives us the basic information. Such import licences allotted to cotton textile exporters fetched them high premiums in the market, thereby constituting an effective subsidy. The extent of the subsidisation was limited by restrictions on the sale of these import entitlements, which had to be surrendered at fixed premiums in most cases.[29] As a result, the premiums on import licences varied considerably as between different inputs. Clearly, it is extremely difficult to extract an average figure from this complicated structure of incentives. However, on the basis of data obtained from *one* exporter in Ahmedabad, Bhagwati and Desai have estimated the average market premiums as a percentage of the f.o.b. value of exports.[30] According to this, in May 1965, the effective subsidy implicit in the import entitlement schemes varied between 28.3 and 65.7 per cent, depending on the category of the cloth and its destination.[31]

Devaluation of the rupee in June 1966 was accompanied by an abolition of these import entitlement schemes. Although it is not cor-

[28] For a detailed discussion on these schemes and their operation in the case of the cotton textile industry, see J. Bhagwati and P. Desai, *India: Planning for Industrialisation*, OECD (Oxford, 1970), pp. 417–22.

[29] For example, cotton textile exporters had to surrender (a) two-thirds of their coal-tar dye entitlement to dye manufacturers; and (b) four-fifths of their machinery entitlement to manufacturers of textile machinery, at fixed premiums. Raw cotton import licences also had to be surrendered at a fixed margin to the Textile Commissioner; see ibid. p. 422.

[30] Cf. Table 19.4, ibid. p. 419.

[31] Ibid. The effective subsidy was relatively low for the coarse and medium varieties of cloth, and tended to be high for the fine and superfine varieties. Within each category the subsidy increased with the degree of processing involved, i.e. bleached cloth was subsidised more than grey fabric. In the inferior categories of cloth, subsidisation appeared lowest on exports to UK and highest on exports to the USA and Western Europe.

rect to generalise on the basis of data obtained from one exporting mill (as Bhagwati and Desai have done), our calculations based on available evidence suggest that the net effect of devaluation on the exports of cotton yarn and cloth was relatively insignificant. In fact, the *net* devaluation for the cotton textiles industry works out at 14.2 per cent, as against the apparent depreciation of 57.5 per cent.[32]

In the post-devaluation period, the subsidisation implicit in trade policies was scaled down considerably. To begin with, the cotton textiles industry received some import facilities under the new import replenishment scheme, but the import licences issued to exporters amounted only to about 5 per cent of the f.o.b. value of exports.[33] However, with effect from 1 April 1968, the Government also provided cash assistance at a flat rate of 5 per cent on the f.o.b. value of all exports of cotton textiles. This subsidy was paid through the Indian Cotton Mills Federation, and was financed by a reimbursement of non-refundable taxes.[34]

The GATT Long Term Arrangement

During the 1950s, exports of cotton textiles from Japan, India and Hong Kong grew quite rapidly in conditions of unrestricted access to the British, American and Canadian markets.[35] In fact, between 1953 and 1964 cotton textile exports from the developing countries as a group increased by 130 per cent, whereas exports from the developed countries recorded a marginal increase of only 4 per cent.[36] Clearly, the latter suffered a loss of export markets. But this was not the only result of the growth of textile industries in LDCs. The rich countries also began to feel the impact of these exports in their domestic markets. Following this trend, several attempts were made by the industrialised nations to control the rapidly growing flow of imports from LDCs. The measures adopted varied from voluntary bilateral agreements to quantitative restrictions. However, such policies did not provide adequate restraint, and in 1961, through GATT, the USA

[32] For details, see Chapter 11; in particular Table 11.3.
[33] See Table 10.1.
[34] For details, see 'Fourteenth Report of the Fifth Lok Sabha's Estimates Committee', *Ministry of Foreign Trade: Export Promotion Measures*, Lok Sabha Secretariat (New Delhi, April 1972), p. 127.
[35] Cf. *A Study on Cotton Textiles*, p. 82. However, most European countries did impose quantitative restrictions on the imports of cotton textiles from LDCs (ibid.).
[36] Ibid. p. 22.

initiated a conference of the main exporting and importing countries, in order to work out a scheme for the regulation of international trade in cotton textiles.[37]

To begin with, the contracting parties signed a short term agreement which was to operate for one year. Following further negotiations, in October 1962, the countries concerned concluded a long term arrangement regarding international trade in cotton textiles which was to run for five years. Article 3 of this arrangement gave importing countries a unilateral right to impose quotas if increasing imports threatened to disrupt their domestic market or industry, and article 6 allowed for the possibility of bilateral trade agreements.[38] In theory, the Long Term Arrangement (LTA) aimed at an 'orderly' but steady expansion of trade in cotton textiles and therefore stipulated a 5 per cent annual increase in quotas. It was also made out to be a short term measure which would provide the developed countries with a little time to rationalise their textile industries. Under no circumstances was it meant to provide any permanent protection. However, in 1967 the less developed countries agreed to a three-year extension of the arrangement on the condition that importing countries undertook to liberalise trade. The LTA was extended for another three years in 1970.

In reality, the developing countries have had little choice about these extensions of the LTA. Effectively, they had only two alternatives open to them: to accept a multilateral agreement which allowed for a limited expansion of exports, or to swallow unilaterally imposed quantitative restrictions on their exports. As the Pearson Commission has correctly pointed out, the former was clearly a preferable course to adopt.[39] As it happened, the agreement did not even prevent the imposition of quotas. Since the arrangement came into being, article 3 (which was meant to be resorted to only 'sparingly') has been invoked on numerous occasions. The following evidence on policies adopted by the main importing countries seems to suggest that, contrary to its professed co-operative spirit, the LTA has actually been used to foster protectionist motives of the developed countries.

(a) Within three years of the LTA coming into force, the USA imposed quotas on imports from most LDCs including India, Hong Kong, Pakistan, Taiwan and the UAR.[40] In most cases, these quanti-

---

[37] *Cotton and Allied Textiles*, p. 20.
[38] For these and other details about the precise provisions of the LTA, see *Arrangement Regarding International Trade in Cotton Textiles*, GATT (Geneva, 1971).
[39] *Partners in Development* (London, 1969), p. 89.
[40] See *A Study on Cotton Textiles*, p. 83.

tative restrictions were followed up by bilateral agreements.[41] A study by the Economist Intelligence Unit suggests that 'invocation of Article 3 has been extensively used as a threat to induce the signing of a bilateral treaty ... under Article 4.'[42]

(b) Most West European countries had substantial quota barriers on imports of cotton textiles from LDCs even before the LTA came into existence. In view of this, the arrangement required the EEC countries to increase their imports from LDCs by 88 per cent within the first five years. But this stipulation means very little when we find that in 1967 only 3.3 per cent of the total EEC consumption of cotton cloth was met by imports from the developing countries *and* Japan.[43] Quite apart from this, Italy and West Germany invoked article 3 to restrict imports from some LDCs.[44]

(c) In the 1950s, the UK had adopted relatively liberal policies towards imports of cotton textiles from the developing countries. All the same, it operated voluntary trade agreements with India, Pakistan and Hong Kong. In 1966, however, Britain imposed a global quota on imports of cotton textiles from all developing countries. The objective of this quota was to limit the growth of imports to 1 per cent per annum over the average level in the period 1962–1964.[45] This was an extremely protective policy. The ostensible reason for it was that imports from LDCs, already constituted a relatively high proportion of the UK cotton textile consumption as compared with other developed countries.

All these restrictive policies adopted by European and North American importing countries were directed only against the exports of cotton textiles from LDCs. The protectionist nature of the discrimination is apparent from the implicit reason for it, i.e. cheap labour in the developing countries endowed their textile industries with a competitive advantage which had to be neutralised in some way. This type of argument is fairly common. An OECD special committee found that tariff barriers and quantitative restrictions in the developed countries were not high enough 'to afford their cotton industry

---

[41] The USA signed bilateral agreements with some twenty-two countries. See *Cotton and Allied Textiles*, p. 20.

[42] John L. Sinclair, *Production, Marketing and Consumption of Cotton* (New York, 1968), pp. 66–7.

[43] *Cotton and Allied Textiles*, p. 21.

[44] *A Study on Cotton Textiles*, p. 83.

[45] For details, see *Cotton and Allied Textiles*, p. 22. Hong Kong and India had individual quotas – each slightly higher than one-third of the total. The remainder was divided among other countries.

effective protection against imports from low-cost countries.'[46]
Prima facie, such reasoning might appear to be stating the obvious
but it needs to be examined carefully.

First, as pointed out earlier, low money wages do not necessarily
mean low wage costs in the developing countries. When we measure
wage costs per unit of output in the textile industry, the difference
between the poor and the rich countries is not so much, owing to the
much higher labour productivity in the developed countries. Available evidence seems to confirm this. A study by the US Department of
Commerce found that 'labour costs per unit of cotton fabric in
India were substantially higher than in Japan, although still below
the United States level'.[47] However, India's competitive advantage
vis-à-vis the US was almost entirely offset by higher costs of other
factors of production. Second, it is now generally accepted that the
cotton textile industry is a capital intensive one, so that the main
cost savings would accrue from the use of modern machinery rather
than cheap labour.[48]

In addition to the quantitative restrictions applied through the
LTA, textile exporters in Asian countries also had to face tariff barriers
in most of the developed countries. Table 4.10 illustrates the extent of
restriction through tariffs.

Irrespective of the motives behind the GATT LTA, its direct
impact was to limit the expansion of international trade in cotton
textiles.

---

[46] *Modern Cotton Industry – A Capital-Intensive Industry*, Report of an OECD Special
Committee on Textiles (Paris, 1965), p. 131.

[47] The Report was entitled 'Comparative Fabric Production Costs in the US
and Four Other Countries' (1961), quoted in *A Study on Cotton Textiles*, p. 68.
Production costs in US cents per unit of cotton sheetings were as follows:

	US	Japan	India
Labour	3.9	1.7	2.5
Other	2.3	1.9	3.2

(The costs of raw cotton are excluded from this estimate.)

[48] According to the GATT study (ibid. p. 55) '... a modern cotton industry is among
the most highly capital-intensive of the manufacturing industries'. This is re-
affirmed by the Report of the OECD Special Committee (p. 95), according to
which, the cotton textile industry has become increasingly capital intensive with
investment amounting to $20 000 per work place. There is no doubt that, tradi-
tionally, cotton textiles was a labour-intensive industry. In the 1960s, however,
there was a technological transformation. It is quite possible that this technical
progress was stimulated by the rapid growth of exports from the LDCs. Cf. H. B.
Lary, *Imports of Manufactures from the Less Developed Countries* (New York, 1968),
p. 81.

TABLE 4.10 *Tariffs on textile imports in 1969* (in percentages)

	Cotton yarn	Woven cotton fabric
UK	7.5	17.5
EEC countries	6.4 to 8.0	13.3 to 16.3
USA	4.5 to 21.2	7.4 to 32.8 (average 16.4)
Canada	17.5 to 19.5	19.5 to 22.0

Source: Textile Council, Manchester, *Cotton and Allied Textiles*, p. 161.
Note: Exports from Commonwealth countries entered the UK market duty free. However, quite recently a tariff of 15 per cent has been introduced even on Commonwealth imports. All other rates have been reduced a little with effect from 1 January 1972 as a result of the Kennedy Round negotiations.

However, even in the face of all these restrictions, countries like Hong Kong, Pakistan, Taiwan, South Korea and the UAR increased their exports and raised their share of world trade. Pakistan's export performance is indeed most impressive. Between 1966 and 1970 its exports of cotton yarn and cloth increased from 53.1 to 131.2 million kg; as a result, her share in world exports rose from 4.9 to 12.3 per cent. This rapid growth can be explained in terms of the following factors: (*a*) The bulk of Pakistan's cotton textile exports consisted of yarn,[49] which is subject to fewer restrictions, particularly in other developing countries attempting to set up their own textile industries. This is so because yarn involves only some degree of processing and is not protected as much as the final cloth output. (*b*) Pakistan was not allotted an individual quota in the UK market, but it managed to increase its share of the global quota substantially.[50] Such expansion was possible owing to the bonus voucher scheme and the heavy subsidisation of cotton textile exports.[51] These policies raised the domestic currency returns of cotton textile exports so much, that the entrepreneurs were almost bound to respond to the incentive of high profits. However, the Pakistan Government's method of export promotion imposed 'very real costs in terms of domestic and imported

[49] See *Cotton – World Statistics* (July 1970), pp. 50–1.
[50] *Cotton and Allied Textiles*, pp. 22–3; India and Hong Kong were the only countries which were allotted individual quotas in the UK market.
[51] For a detailed discussion on the subject, see S. R. Lewis, *Pakistan: Industrialization and Trade Policies*, OECD (Oxford, 1971), pp. 80, 96 and 130–1. These heavy subsidies on the export of cotton manufactures were accompanied by a tax on the exports of raw cotton. Thus the effective protection afforded to the cotton textile industry was much higher than that apparent in the market premium on bonus vouchers. As Lewis and many others have argued, the net foreign exchange earnings from these exports were probably very little.

TABLE 4.11 *India's actual exports to the UK and the cotton quota* (in million square yards)

Year	Quota	Actual exports	Percentage filled
1968	n.a.	n.a.	108.5
1969	195.7	154.4	79.0
1970	202.9	77.1	38.0

Source: *Annual Report*, Government of India, Ministry of Foreign Trade, 1969/70, p. 82; and 1970/71, p. 100.
Note: Figures relate to quota years beginning 1 December and ending 30 November.

factors of production that have a positive opportunity cost'[52] on the economy, without adding significantly to the *net* foreign exchange earnings.

In sharp contrast, India's exports of cotton yarn and cloth remained quite stagnant throughout the period under study. Given the fact that, in the 1960s, a little over 40 per cent of India's cotton textile exports were sold to the UK, USA, Canada and EEC countries,[53] it might be argued that the LTA was at least partially responsible for India's poor export performance. Of the remaining 60 per cent, the bulk of India's cotton textile exports were absorbed by other LDCs in Asia and Africa. Although these developing countries did not restrict imports through the LTA, many of them did protect their 'infant' cotton textile industries through tariffs and import quotas. This factor must also have had a restrictive impact on India's exports.

In the case of the UK market, however, the quota restriction does not appear to have been the operative constraint towards the end of the decade. Until 1968, India had managed to export sufficiently to fulfil all quotas. In that year she exceeded her UK quota by 8.5 per cent, thereby using up a part of the 1969 allotment.[54] But in the next two years her exports to Britain dropped sharply, as is evident from Table 4.11. There were several reasons for this drastic fall.[55]

(*a*) In 1969 the UK Government introduced the import deposit

---

[52] Ibid. p. 131.

[53] Calculated from statistics published by the RBI in *Report on Currency and Finance 1970/71*, p. S153. During the period 1965/66 to 1970/71, the average share of the UK market was 24.2 per cent, of the North American market 13.7 per cent, and of EEC 2.9 per cent.

[54] See *Annual Report* of the Ministry of Foreign Trade and Supply, 1968/69, Government of India (New Delhi), pp. 70–1.

[55] For details, see *Annual Report*, Ministry of Foreign Trade, 1969/70, p. 82; and 1970/71, p. 100.

scheme making it obligatory for cotton textile importers to deposit 50 per cent of the import cost with the customs for six months. This policy almost certainly discouraged the import of cotton textiles in the years that followed.[56]

(*b*) In April 1969 a purchase tax of 13.75 per cent was imposed on household textiles in the UK market. This taxation definitely curbed consumption,[57] and thereby adversely affected India's cotton textile exports, in which household textiles were an important item.

Policies adopted by the UK Government may have adversely affected India's exports of cotton textiles, but the main reason for failure to fill her quota was the acute shortage of raw cotton during 1969 and 1970. The output of raw cotton fell substantially during the 1969/70 and 1970/71 seasons, as a result of which prices soared. In 1969/70 the availability of raw cotton fell short of the expected mill consumption,[58] and in 1970/71 production of cotton was 13.3 per cent lower than the previous year.[59] Consequently, the wholesale price index of raw cotton in India rose from 154.6 in 1968/69 to 170.9 in 1969/70 and 209.1 in 1970/71.[60] In view of these shortages and price movements, it is not surprising that the Indian textile industry could not even maintain its exports in a guaranteed market.

Non-price factors

So far we have considered the impact of world demand, competitiveness, and the LTA on India's exports of cotton textiles. There remain some factors which had an important bearing on the export perform-

---

[56] This reasoning is confirmed by the stagnation or decline of imports from most countries into UK after the introduction of the import deposit scheme:

Imports of woven cotton piece goods into the UK
(in million square yards)

	India	Pakistan	Hong Kong	Japan	UAR	China	South Korea
1968	203.4	81.2	119.8	11.7	5.7	51.2	10.6
1969	118.9	76.0	97.0	10.4	4.6	47.6	7.5
1970	98.4	82.4	108.2	6.4	5.2	20.1	5.0

Source: Textile Council, Manchester, *Quarterly Statistical Review* (Spring 1971), p. 19.

[57] See *Quarterly Statistical Review*: 'Sales of household textiles suffered an inevitable reaction from ... the imposition of purchase tax in May. Traders reduced their stocks to a minimum' (Winter 1969), and 'consumer expenditure on household textiles fell sharply in the latter half of 1969 (Spring 1970), p. 2.

[58] See *Annual Report*, Ministry of Foreign Trade, 1970/71, p. 101.

[59] *Report on Currency and Finance*, 1970/71, p. 83.

[60] Ibid. p. S30.

TABLE 4.12   *Exports of clothing from selected LDCs*
(in $ million)

	1963	1967	1968	1969	1970
India	10	12	20	29	40
Hong Kong	243	416	483	613	716
South Korea	5	59	112	161	214
Taiwan	10	47	97	128	199
Pakistan	n.a.	2	6	5	n.a.

Source: For 1963, 1968–1970: Hong Kong, Taiwan, and South Korea,
    GATT *International Trade, 1970*, p. 83. India and Pakistan, UN
    Yearbook of International Trade Statistics, 1964 and *1969*.
Note: The 1970 figure for India has been obtained from statistics pub-
    lished by the DGCIS, Calcutta.

ance of the Indian textile industry, and therefore need to be examined.
(*a*) *Clothing – the missed opportunity*:   We have shown that world
trade in cotton yarn and cloth was relatively stagnant. However, the
world demand for clothing grew very rapidly in the 1960s. This
growth is directly reflected in the fact that total world exports of
clothing increased from $1743 million in 1963 to $4878 million in
1970.[61] Such expansion was possible partially because the LTA did
not extend its application to cotton manufactures and clothing. In
fact, apart from the usual tariffs, there were no restrictions on trade
in clothing. Therefore, the developing countries could have raised
their cotton textile exports by changing the composition in favour
of cloth manufactures – particularly in view of the fact that the
clothing industry is much more labour intensive than the textiles
sector. It is obvious from Table 4.12[62] that Hong Kong, South Korea
and Taiwan did just this. It is also patently clear that India completely
failed to cash in on a promising opportunity. At the beginning of the
decade, its exports of clothing were virtually the same as Taiwan and
South Korea. However, by 1970, India had been left far behind by
its Asian competitors in the exports of clothing. Had India managed
to exploit the growth potential of the relatively unrestricted market
for clothing, its exports of cotton textiles in 1970 would have been
much higher than they actually were.

It is not as if the clothing industry was neglected in the Govern-

---

[61] See *International Trade, 1970*, GATT (Geneva), p. 83.
[62] These statistics relate to all clothing rather than just cotton clothing. Separate
data for the latter is not readily available.

TABLE 4.13   *Quality of fabrics produced in Indian cotton mills* (in percentages)

Year	Coarse	Medium	Fine and superfine	Total production in million metres
1960	14.0	75.5	10.5	4616.2
1965	17.5	70.7	11.8	4587.5
1970	13.9	71.5	14.6	4517.1

Source: Textile Commissioner, Bombay, *Indian Textile Bulletin* (May 1971), p. 55.
Note: The percentages have been calculated from the absolute figures in million metres.

ment's export promotion programme. Until the devaluation in 1966, exporters of readymade garments received exactly the same import entitlement facilities as the rest of the cotton textile industry.[63] Even in the post-devaluation period, they continued to benefit from import replenishments which ranged from 9 per cent to as much as 52 per cent of the f.o.b. value of exports.[64] There were two principal reasons why the Indian clothing industry was not sufficiently competitive in the world market.[65] In the first place, the rising costs of cotton fabrics pushed up its prices.[66] Second, by and large, the quality and designs of its products were not up to the mark. Both these factors constituted a serious constraint on export performance.

(b) *The quality factor*:   An important non-price factor that affected India's export performance in cotton textiles was the relatively poor quality of cloth produced in the country. In both the mill and handloom sectors, production tended to be concentrated in coarse and medium varieties of cloth. Table 4.13 shows that there was no change in this composition even during the 1960s. Less than one-seventh of the cloth produced in the cotton mills of India can be classified as the fine or superfine variety. Clearly, the quality of the cotton fabrics produced is determined by the nature of domestic demand. In a country where the bulk of the population lives at a bare subsistence level, the demand for fine cloth is naturally quite limited. Unfortunately, this domestic market orientation of the Indian cotton textile

[63] Bhagwati and Desai, *India: Planning for Industrialisation*, p. 410.
[64] See Table 10.1.
[65] For a detailed discussion of these factors, see 'Fourteenth Report of the Fifth Lok Sabha's Estimates Committee', *Ministry of Foreign Trade: Export Promotion Measures*, pp. 134–6.
[66] It has been estimated that prices of cotton fabrics in India were 20 to 30 per cent higher than international prices (ibid. p. 135).

industry has affected its export performance adversely in two ways:
(1) coarse and medium varieties of cloth are relatively unsuitable for
foreign markets; and (2) exports of poor quality and relatively unprocessed cloth are most vulnerable to programmes of import substitution in other developing countries.[67]

(c) *The dilemma of modernisation*: It was recognised long ago
that 'preference in the markets overseas is definitely for flawless cloth
which can be produced only on automatic looms'.[68] However, we have
shown that attempts to modernise the textile industry in India have not
been very successful. The reluctance of the industry is attributable to
the relative attractiveness of the home market. The Government's
efforts have also been quite half-hearted because of the extent of
unemployment that would be generated with the introduction of automatic looms.[69]

Clearly, the welfare implications of modernisation need to be
evaluated carefully. In a labour abundant economy like India where
employment is an important objective of policy, and where the bulk
of the demand is for coarse cloth, there is no case for modernising
the *whole* industry. On the other hand, this failure to modernise adversely affected India's export performance. An answer to the dilemma
might have been found in appropriate policies which aided, rather
than hindered, the development of an export sector within the cotton
textile industry.

Summary

The main conclusion emerging from the above analysis can be summed up as follows. The extremely slow growth in world demand for
cotton textiles does not explain the stagnation in India's textile exports
during the 1960s, because over the same period, other competing
countries like Pakistan, Hong Kong, UAR and Taiwan increased their
exports rapidly. The restrictions on international trade in cotton
textiles did have some adverse effects, but the main reasons for the

---

[67] The setting up of a cotton textile industry marks the beginning of import
substitution and industrialisation programmes in most developing countries.
This is a pretty natural development for two reasons. The textile industry requires
relatively low skills, and has access to a readily available domestic market.

[68] *Report of the Textile Enquiry Committee*, p. 25.

[69] In the early 1960s, it was the employment objective that prompted the Government to promote the growth of the handloom sector, and to impose restrictions
on the redeployment of labour in the mill sector. However, in the latter half of
the decade, emphasis shifted to export promotion and these restrictions were
relaxed. For details, see Maizels, *Exports and Economic Growth*, p. 408.

relatively poor export performance of the Indian cotton textile industry are to be found in domestic factors and policies. In the first place, price competitiveness was seriously affected by sharp increases in the cost of raw cotton, rising labour costs, and relatively old capital equipment. Second, the pressure of domestic demand coupled with the relative attractiveness of the home market reduced the exportable surplus. The devaluation of the rupee in June 1966 did little to improve competitiveness or make exports more attractive because, given the previous export incentives, its net effect was very small. Apart from these price factors, Indian textiles were not sufficiently competitive in the world market owing to their relatively poor quality. Although modernisation of the textile industry would have led to the requisite quality improvement, it would have resulted in a considerable reduction in employment. The introduction of automatic looms on a wide scale was therefore not possible in view of the welfare implications of such a policy. The development of a clothing industry would have provided a solution to this dilemma not only by increasing exports but also by adding to employment.

5
Tea

For many decades, India was the most important tea producing and exporting country in the world. In the late 1960s, however, she was replaced by Ceylon as the world's largest exporter of tea.[1] But that was not all. While in the past, along with jute manufactures, tea had been one of the two main sources of foreign exchange for India, its importance diminished rapidly during the period under study. The contribution of tea to the country's total export earnings dropped sharply from 19.1 per cent in 1960/61 to 9.5 per cent in 1970/71.[2] This chapter is devoted to an analysis of these striking developments in the export performance of the Indian tea industry.

Table 5.1 which outlines the changes in the value and volume of exports, from 1960 to 1970, reveals that exports of tea attained a peak level in 1963, and, except for some fluctuations, registered a downward trend thereafter. Over the decade as a whole, the average annual quantity of tea exported fell from 203.7 million kg in the three-year period 1960–1962 to 192.4 million kg during 1968–1970. As compared to the marked decline in export earnings, this fall of 5 per cent or so was relatively mild. The average annual value of exports fell by a little more than 25 per cent, from $257.9 million in 1960–1962 to $192.6 million in 1968–1970. This wide disparity between trends in volume and value can be explained in terms of the steadily falling average unit value of tea exports. It is worth noting that the fall in prices was not unique to Indian tea, but, as shown in Table 5.2, was merely a reflection of the more or less continuous decline in world prices of tea.[3] Therefore, in order to examine the trend in India's

---

[1] See Table 5.3 below. Although India continues to be the largest producer, her average annual share in world production fell from 33.6 per cent in the three-year period 1960–1962 to 31.8 per cent during 1968–1970; calculated from FAO, *Production Yearbook*, *1963*, p. 135 and *1970*, pp. 270–1.

[2] Table 2.6.

[3] Although the Calcutta and Colombo auctions became equally important in the last decade, a significant proportion of the total world output of tea is still marketed at the London auctions. What is more, tea from all the different producing regions turns up for sale in London. Thus, the average annual price of tea at London auctions is a reasonable approximation of the world price.

TABLE 5.1   *Exports of tea from India*

Year	Volume in million kg	Value in $ million	Average unit value in $ per kg
1960	193.1	252.6	1.31
1961	206.3	261.6	1.27
1962	211.8	259.4	1.22
1963	223.6	278.0	1.24
1964	210.5	262.3	1.25
1965	199.4	241.4	1.21
1966	179.2	207.6	1.16
1967	213.7	252.1	1.18
1968	208.4	221.9	1.06
1969	168.7	160.3	0.95
1970	200.2	195.7	0.98

Source: International Tea Committee, London, *Annual Bulletin of Statistics, 1971*, pp. 12 and 13.
Note: The average unit value has been computed from the data on value and volume.

TABLE 5.2   *Average annual price of all teas at London auctions* (in new pence per kg)

Year	1960	1961	1962	1963	1964	1965	1966	1967	1968	1969	1970
Price	50.7	48.6	49.0	46.5	47.2	46.0	44.8	45.7	43.5	40.5	45.7

Source: International Tea Committee, London, *Annual Bulletin of Statistics, 1971*, p. 48.

exports of tea, as a first step, it is necessary to consider the trends in world demand, as well as other factors that might have influenced the world market price of tea.

World demand for tea and India's exports

We shall begin with a look at India's export performance in the context of trends in world trade, and then go on to analyse the factors underlying the changes in world demand for tea.

Table 5.3 depicts the behaviour of exports of tea from the major producing countries and regions in the world, and brings out the changes in their relative shares. We find that between 1960–1962 and 1968–1970, the average annual volume of world exports increased very slowly from 547.2 million kg to 611.8 million kg. Thus,

TABLE 5.3 *Exports of tea from the major producing regions*
(in million kg)

	1960	1961	1962	1963	1964	1965	1966	1967	1968	1969	1970
India	193.1	206.1	211.8	223.6	210.5	199.4	179.2	213.7	208.4	168.7	200.2
Ceylon	185.9	193.1	204.9	206.8	206.5	224.2	200.1	216.5	208.7	201.4	208.3
East Africa	30.4	32.4	37.1	37.1	41.1	41.9	54.8	53.0	62.6	74.7	75.9
Indonesia	36.1	33.4	30.9	29.7	32.3	32.3	33.2	26.6	34.7	27.1	36.9
Rest of Africa	11.7	13.9	13.7	15.1	13.9	16.4	20.2	19.3	20.9	23.0	19.4
Far East	66.4	57.4	55.1	54.5	55.1	65.9	60.4	55.5	59.3	52.9	64.3
Latin America	3.8	6.6	7.9	9.0	10.3	14.5	15.9	14.6	17.8	17.4	23.1
Others	2.6	2.9	4.2	0.5	2.1	6.8	4.3	9.1	11.1	9.2	7.5
Total	530.0	545.8	565.6	576.3	571.8	601.4	568.1	608.3	623.5	574.4	635.6
Relative shares (in percentages)											
India	36.4	37.7	37.4	38.8	36.8	33.2	31.5	35.1	33.4	29.3	31.5
Ceylon	35.1	35.4	36.2	35.9	36.1	37.3	35.2	35.6	33.4	34.9	32.8
East Africa	5.7	5.9	6.6	6.4	7.2	7.0	9.6	8.7	10.0	13.0	11.9
Indonesia	6.8	6.1	5.5	5.2	5.6	5.4	5.8	1.4	5.6	4.7	5.8
Rest of Africa	2.2	2.5	2.4	2.6	2.4	2.7	3.6	3.2	3.4	4.0	3.1
Far East	12.5	10.5	9.7	9.5	9.6	11.0	10.6	9.1	9.5	9.2	10.1
Latin America	0.7	0.5	1.4	1.6	1.8	2.4	2.8	2.4	2.9	3.0	3.6
Others	0.6	1.4	0.8	0	0.5	1.0	0.9	4.5	1.8	1.9	1.2
Total	100.0	100.0	100.0	100.0	100.0	100.0	100.0	100.0	100.0	100.0	100.0

Source: International Tea Committee, London, *Annual Bulletin of Statistics*, for 1960–1969: 1971, p. 11; and for 1970: 1972, p. 11.
Note: The data for some individual countries have been grouped into regions. East Africa includes Kenya, Uganda, Tanzania and Malawi. Most of the exports from the Far East countries originated from China and Taiwan, but Japan, Malaysia, North Vietnam and South Vietnam are also included in the group. Rest of Africa includes Mauritius, Congo, Ruanda and Mozambique. Latin America includes Argentina, Brazil and Peru.

TABLE 5.4   *Net imports of tea for consumption: by regions*
(annual averages in million kg)

	1960–1962	1964–1966	1968–1970
UK and Ireland	243.2	235.3	236.1
Western Europe	26.6	31.0	32.3
USSR and Eastern Europe	21.6	35.6	28.7
North America	73.6	80.4	86.3
Latin America	6.0	7.4	9.5
Asia	59.4	64.5	78.3
Africa	76.9	88.5	103.2
Oceania	36.4	37.3	35.9
Total including others	547.6	584.5	621.8

Source: International Tea Committee, London, *Annual Bulletin of Statistics*, *1971*,
   p. 27, and *1972*, p. 27.
Note: The annual averages have been computed from data for individual years.

in a period when India's exports fell by about 5 per cent, world exports rose by nearly 12 per cent. As a result, India's relative share of the world market contracted from 37.2 per cent in 1960–1962 to 31.4 per cent in 1968–1970. Although Ceylon took India's place as the largest exporter, its average annual relative share also declined marginally from 35.6 per cent in 1960–1962 to 33.7 per cent in 1968–1970. Indonesia and the Far East countries experienced similar, albeit smaller, losses in their relative market shares. The markets lost by all these traditional exporters of tea were captured by the new tea exporting countries of Africa. This is evident from the fact that the East African countries increased their share of the world market from 6.1 per cent in 1960–1962 to 11.6 per cent in 1968–1970, and over the same period, the other African countries increased their average annual share from 2.4 per cent to 3.5 per cent. From the magnitude of the changes in relative shares it appears that India was the main loser, and that its tea exports bore the brunt of increased competition from the African tea industry. A little later in the chapter, we will go into the reasons for it. But, before doing that, it might be worthwhile to examine the factors responsible for the near stagnation in world demand for, and trade in, tea, during the 1960s.

Tea is a commodity which is re-exported to a considerable extent. As such, net imports, which almost certainly enter into consumption, are a better index of changes in demand in different parts of the world than the trends in export trade. However, Table 5.4 shows that between 1960–1962 and 1968–1970, total world net imports of tea increased by 13.6 per cent, which was only slightly more than the expansion in world exports. It is noticeable that the bulk of this increase was made possible by the rapid growth in net imports of the Asian and African countries. Net imports of the traditional consumers such as UK, Ireland and the Oceanic countries were quite stagnant throughout the 1960s. The net imports of tea into the USSR and East European countries increased considerably in the first half of the decade, but dropped off to a lower level thereafter. As for Western Europe and North America, there was a slow but continuous increase in net imports. The main inference that can be drawn from these trends is that the demand for tea did not increase very much in the high income countries, but revealed a marked growth in the low income countries.

Given the responsiveness of the demand for tea to changes in the level of income, this is hardly surprising. A few years ago, the FAO estimated the income elasticity of demand for tea to be: (*a*) negligible in UK and USA, (*b*) 0.3 to 0.4 in Western Europe and Japan, and (*c*) 0.6 to 1.0 in most developing countries of Asia and Africa.[4] Thus, the rising import demand for tea in the LDCs was probably a result of the relatively high income elasticity of demand and the rapid population growth in these areas. However, during the period under study, the LDCs constituted only a small portion of the world market for tea, and approximately three-fourths of the world net imports of tea were absorbed by the high income countries. One does not have to look very far to find reasons for the sluggish import demand and almost stagnant consumption in the latter group of countries. It is a well established fact that consumption of tea in developed countries is largely a matter of custom or habit, and as such, not very responsive to changes in income or price.[5] All available estimates confirm that the income and price elasticities of demand for tea in these countries are

---

[4] *Agricultural Commodities: Projections for 1975 and 1985*, FAO (Rome, 1967), pp. 29–31.

[5] See for example, FAO, *Tea – Trends and Prospects* (Rome, 1960), Commodity Bulletin Series no. 30, p. 11; and V. N. Murti, *An Econometric Study of the World Tea Economy: 1948–1961*, unpublished Ph.D. dissertation (University of Pennsylvania, 1966). Murti found that the demand for tea was distinctly price inelastic in UK, USA, Canada, Australia and Western Europe. Although there was some substitution between tea and coffee owing to changes in relative prices, on the whole, the relationship was rather weak. Following from this, one of the main conclusions of the study was that the level of tea consumption in any country is determined largely by habit.

extremely low.[6] Therefore, the demand for tea in Europe and North America could not have grown any faster than population growth.

Apart from its direct impact on import demand, this stagnation of consumption, in such a large segment of the world tea market, may also have had its effect on the price level. In fact, it is quite likely that, coupled with the price inelastic demand and the steady increase in export supplies of tea entering the world market,[7] it was responsible for the decline in world tea prices during the 1960s. Table 5.2 brings out the fact that between 1960–1962 and 1968–1970, the average annual price of tea at the London auctions fell by 12.6 per cent. The slump was particularly bad in 1969, when prices were 20 per cent lower than in 1960. This had the immediate effect of reviving the efforts at securing an international agreement, among the principal exporting and importing countries, in order to stabilise the prices of tea. In 1969, a series of meetings were held which culminated in the formation of an FAO Consultative Committee on Tea. Under its auspices, in December 1969, the exporting countries settled on an interim arrangement to regulate exports of tea, in 1970. It was decided to restrict exports to 595 million kg, thereby removing about 40 million kg of exportable tea from the world market.[8] For this purpose, each country was allotted an export quota for 1970.[9] That this makeshift agreement did have a favourable effect is obvious from the significant recovery of world tea prices in 1970. Clearly, it would be in the interest of all tea exporting countries to negotiate a more permanent agreement which would stabilise the world price of tea and guarantee their foreign exchange earnings.[10] In the long run, of

---

[6] For an exhaustive review of the elasticity estimates available, see *Tea – Trends and Prospects*, pp. 11–14 and 32–4; and G. K. Sarkar, *The World Tea Economy* (Calcutta, 1972), pp. 72–5. In view of the fact that UK is an extremely important market for Indian tea, it might be worth citing a more recent study of the British market which used 1960–1965 data. According to it, the income elasticity of the quantity of tea consumed and the expenditure on tea was practically zero. The price elasticity of demand, which related the quantity of tea consumed not just to tea prices, but also to coffee prices, worked out at −0.41. These unpublished estimates were made available by Robert Bacon.

[7] The 'overproduction', similar to that in coffee and cocoa, was a result of improving yields in the older producing countries such as India and Ceylon, and expanding production in the new tea producing countries of Africa. For details, see Sarkar, pp. 131–3.

[8] For details see, FAO, *Report of the First Session of the Consultative Committee on Tea*, CCP 70/3 (Rome, 8 December 1969).

[9] *Ibid.* p. xii; Ceylon and India were allotted a joint export quota of 421 million kg. Among the other major exporters, Indonesia received a quota of 35 million kg, and Kenya one of 34.5 million kg.

[10] A long-term international tea agreement would require the concurrence of all

course, an international tea agreement may not be sufficient to attain an overall balance between world supply and demand at the desired prices. In addition, it may be necessary to promote the demand for tea and to control the expansion in production.

Market distribution of exports

We have shown above that the demand for tea grew rapidly in some parts of the world, while it was virtually stagnant in some other parts. Hence, it is quite possible that the export performance of the Indian tea industry was influenced by shifts in its markets. Table 5.5 outlines the market distribution of India's tea exports and highlights the changes in relative shares of different markets. The most striking trend to emerge from these figures is the rapidly declining importance of the British market. The average annual volume of exports to UK fell from 121.3 million kg in 1960–1962 to 85.8 million kg in 1968–1970. Consequently, the share of the UK market, in India's exports of tea, dropped from nearly 60 per cent to 44 per cent. Exports to the North American countries also fell slightly, whereas exports to the West European and Oceanic countries were more or less unchanged. However, the losses in these traditional high income markets were made up by substantially increased exports to USSR, Eastern Europe, Asia and Africa. The average annual share of the USSR and and East European countries in India's total exports of tea rose from 6 per cent in 1960–1962 to 15 per cent in 1968–1970. Over the same period, the share of Asian countries increased from 8 per cent to 12.9 per cent, and that of the African countries from 10.6 per cent to 13 per cent.

To a large extent, this rapid increase in the share of relatively new markets was attributable to India's bilateral trade agreements with USSR, UAR, Afghanistan, Iraq, Jordan, Sudan, Tunisia and the East European countries.[11] Table 5.6 reveals that the average annual

the exporting and importing countries. So far, however, the negotiations have been confined only to the exporting countries. Although India, Ceylon and Indonesia, were very much in favour of such an arrangement, some of the African exporting countries were reluctant to commit themselves until their tea production plans crystallised. Therefore, the prospects of an international tea agreement remain uncertain. According to FAO press releases, exports of tea in 1971 were also regulated by a temporary arrangement among the exporting countries.

[11] For a brief description of the agreements under which tea was exported to these countries, see the Appendix on Trade Agreements in RBI Bombay, *Report on Currency and Finance*; several annual issues.

TABLE 5.5   *Market distribution of India's tea exports* (in million kg)

	1960	1961	1962	1963	1964	1965	1966	1967	1968	1969	1970
UK	120.8	123.2	119.9	135.6	119.7	104.2	87.2	116.1	102.0	59.9	95.6
Western Europe	9.9	10.3	13.0	12.3	8.0	9.1	7.5	10.1	12.2	8.4	9.6
North America	15.6	17.1	17.8	15.4	15.1	12.6	11.5	12.1	12.7	10.9	10.2
USSR	10.2	11.9	12.4	16.6	21.1	26.2	16.9	20.1	22.4	25.0	28.0
East Europe	0.2	0.4	1.5	2.0	3.5	2.7	5.1	4.2	3.5	3.8	3.2
Asia	14.3	17.7	17.1	14.3	13.5	12.9	15.2	14.0	25.1	27.9	20.3
Africa	18.2	22.7	23.9	23.2	21.2	24.0	28.0	28.3	20.7	26.7	26.5
Oceania	3.1	2.4	5.8	4.0	5.7	5.0	5.9	6.1	7.2	4.1	4.0
Total	193.1	206.3	211.8	223.5	210.5	199.4	179.2	213.7	208.4	168.7	200.2
Relative shares (in percentages)											
UK	62.6	59.7	56.6	60.7	56.9	52.3	48.7	54.3	48.9	35.5	47.8
Western Europe	5.1	5.0	6.1	5.5	3.8	4.6	4.2	4.7	5.9	5.0	4.8
North America	8.1	8.3	8.4	6.9	7.2	6.3	6.4	5.7	6.1	6.5	5.1
USSR and East Europe	5.4	6.0	6.6	8.3	11.7	14.5	12.3	11.4	12.4	17.1	15.6
Asia	7.4	8.6	8.1	6.4	6.4	6.5	8.5	6.6	12.0	16.5	10.1
Africa	9.4	11.0	11.3	10.4	10.1	12.0	15.6	13.2	9.9	15.8	13.2
Oceania	1.6	1.2	2.7	1.8	2.7	2.5	3.3	2.9	3.5	2.4	2.6

Source: International Tea Committee, London, *Annual Bulletin of Statistics*, *1971*, p. 13.

Note: The West European markets were primarily Ireland, West Germany and Netherlands. The markets in Africa were Sudan, UAR and Tunisia.

TABLE 5.6 *India's tea exports to bilateral agreement markets* (in million kg)

	1960	1961	1962	1963	1964	1965	1966	1967	1968	1969	1970
USSR	10.2	11.9	12.4	16.6	21.1	26.2	16.9	20.1	22.4	25.0	28.0
UAR	14.1	15.6	18.5	17.1	15.9	18.0	18.8	18.3	8.9	14.3	11.6
Afghanistan	3.4	3.3	4.5	4.2	4.8	3.7	6.7	5.1	9.2	13.5	10.7
Iraq	2.1	2.1	2.8	2.7	2.0	1.5	1.7	2.2	6.8	4.4	0.8
Jordan	0.2	1.2	1.0	0.8	1.2	1.6	1.7	1.2	1.9	2.7	2.0
Sudan	3.9	6.7	5.3	3.6	3.7	3.6	6.4	7.9	10.5	7.4	11.8
Tunisia	0.4	0.3	—	2.4	1.5	2.4	2.7	4.0	1.0	4.1	2.2
East Europe	0.2	0.4	1.5	2.0	3.5	2.7	5.1	4.2	3.5	3.8	3.2
Total	34.5	41.5	46.0	49.4	53.7	58.7	60.0	61.0	64.2	75.2	70.3
Percentage of all tea exports	17.9	20.1	21.7	22.1	25.2	29.4	33.5	28.5	30.8	44.6	35.1

Source: International Tea Committee, London, *Annual Bulletin of Statistics, 1971*, p. 13.

TABLE 5.7   *UK imports of tea by origin* (in million kg)

Year	India	Ceylon	East Africa	Total
1960	116.8	68.2	20.5	238.5
1965	114.4	79.6	23.4	253.4
1970	82.9	70.8	54.1	252.7

Source: International Tea Committee, London, *Annual Bulletin of Statistics, 1971*, p. 28.

quantity of tea exported to these markets rose from 40.7 million kg in 1960–1962 to 69.9 million kg in 1968–1970. As a result, their share in the total went up from 19.7 per cent to 36.8 per cent.[12]

If we compare the changes in market distribution with the trends in net import demand, we find that India's exports of tea shifted from the relatively stagnant markets to the markets which were growing faster. Had India been able to maintain the absolute level of her exports to the traditional markets, this shift would certainly have helped export growth. However, as it happened, the growth made possible by expansion in the new markets was neutralised by the steep fall in exports to the overwhelmingly important UK market.

Saturated demand and stagnant consumption may have prevented any increase in exports of tea to UK, but it certainly does not account for India's dismal export performance in that market. A mere glance at Table 5.7 shows that India lost a significant proportion of the UK market to the East African countries. Between 1960 and 1970, while total imports into UK increased slightly, imports from India fell by nearly 34 million kg and imports from East Africa increased by approximately that amount. Clearly, this poor export performance of the Indian tea industry cannot be explained in terms of changes in demand, and must therefore be analysed in terms of the factors that might have affected its competitiveness.

[12] It is sometimes argued that the continuous growth in India's exports of tea to these new markets, particularly the socialist countries of Eastern Europe, may not have been a net addition to India's exports, as it may have meant a mere diversion of export supplies away from the traditional markets. Indeed, it might even be suggested that India's relatively poor performance in the older markets was attributable to such displacement. We shall analyse this possibility of diversion in detail, whilst discussing India's bilateral rupee trade in Chapter 12. At this stage, it is sufficient to note that whereas between 1960–1962 and 1968–1970, the average annual volume of India's exports to the UK fell by 35.5 million kg, exports to USSR and Eastern Europe increased by only 16.4 million kg.

Competitiveness

Nearly 85 per cent of the total world output of tea is sold through auctions.[13] It follows that the world price of tea is determined not by producers on a cost plus basis, but by the adjustment of supply and demand in the international market. In these circumstances, the competitiveness of an individual tea producing area depends on its profitability, because the difference between its costs and the world price is an index of the extent to which it can survive lower world prices and increasing competition. Therefore, the competitiveness of the Indian tea industry could have been influenced by (a) its costs of production, (b) the pressure of domestic demand, and (c) the fiscal or trade policies adopted by the Government, all of which must have affected its profitability. In addition, there may also have been some non-price factors. We now turn to an analysis of these determinants of competitiveness, and their impact on export performance in the 1960s.

Costs of production

A detailed examination of the cost structure of the Indian tea industry is beyond the scope of our work. However, over a period of time, changes in factor prices and productivity are a good index of changes in cost efficiency. Thus, the competitiveness of the tea industry in India, relative to that in Ceylon and East Africa, can be assessed in terms of the trend in factor costs and productivity. In making this comparision, we shall rely on such evidence as is available.

Labour costs constitute a high proportion of the total costs of production in the tea industry.[14] As such, changes in the money wage rates provide a reasonably good indicator of changes in production costs. It would certainly be preferable to compare wage costs per unit of output, but the lack of necessary data precludes that possibility. However, in view of the fact that techniques of production are quite similar in India, Ceylon and East Africa,[15] a comparison of the trend

[13] Sarkar, *World Tea Economy*, p. 199.

[14] In the 1950s, labour costs accounted for 38 to 45 per cent of the total costs of production on India tea plantations; see *Report of the Plantation Enquiry Commission* (New Delhi, 1956), vol. I, p. 99. There is no reason to believe that this proportion changed in the 1960s.

[15] The similarity in production methods is attributable to the British origin of the tea plantations in all these countries.

TABLE 5.8   *Wage rates on tea plantations in India, Ceylon and Kenya*

Year	India Average daily earnings of male workers on Assam tea plantations: in Rs	Ceylon Average daily earnings of male workers on tea plantations: in Rs	Kenya Average daily earnings of male workers on tea plantations: in shillings
1960	1.69	2.59	3.00
1970	2.65	3.40	4.15
Percentage increase	56.8	31.3	38.3

Source: For India; Labour Bureau, Simla, *Indian Labour Statistics, 1963*, p. 55, and Indian Tea Board, Calcutta, *Tea Statistics, 1969/70*, p. 123.

For Ceylon; ILO *Yearbook of Labour Statistics, 1969*, p. 638, and *1971*, p. 668.

For Kenya: Indian Tea Board, *Tea Statistics, 1965/66*, p. 176; and *1969/70*, p. 228.

Note:

(a) The average daily earnings for 1960 in India were computed by dividing the average monthly earnings of Rs50.77 by 30. The 1970 average daily earnings were obtained by averaging the basic wages in all tea districts of Assam as on 1 October 1969, and adding to that the daily allowance payable as well as the wage increase granted in 1970.

(b) The average daily earnings of a field worker on a Kenyan tea plantations, are the minimum wage stipulated. The 1970 figure is, in fact, the wage payable in 1968, as later figures are not available.

in money wage costs may not be far off the mark. Table 5.8 brings out the change in wage rates of workers on tea plantations in India, Ceylon and Kenya. Between 1960 and 1970, the average daily earnings of a male worker on a tea plantation rose by 31 per cent in Ceylon, 38 per cent in Kenya and nearly 57 per cent in India. These figures are not adjusted for exchange rate changes, but they do show that in terms of domestic currency, labour costs increased most rapidly in India, and this may have worsened its competitiveness.

Let us now compare the trends in productivity. The tea industry is essentially an agricultural undertaking, and according to one estimate, only 6 per cent of the man-days worked in a year are attributable to the processing of tea.[16] Hence, the yield per hectare would give us a fair idea of productivity.[17] Table 5.9 traces the changes in

[16] See V. I. Chacko, 'Tea in the Seventies', *Commerce* (Bombay, 1 March 1969), p. 58. According to this estimate, 55 per cent of the man-days are spent in crop gathering and 35 per cent in agricultural operations in the field.

[17] Again, it would be preferable to compare labour productivity per hectare, but owing to the seasonal employment fluctuations on tea estates, data on employment per hectare are not readily available.

TABLE 5.9   *Average annual yield on tea*
plantations (in kg per hectare)

	1960–1962	1963–1966	1967–1969
India	1028	1075	1125
Ceylon	864	927	917
East Africa	815	835	930

Source: Indian Tea Board, Calcutta, *Tea Statistics, 1969/70*, pp. 214–6.

Note: The averages have been computed from data for individual years.

yield per hectare in the main tea producing regions, during the 1960s. We find that land productivity was the highest in India throughout the period, and increased almost at the same pace as that in East Africa. Obviously, it is unlikely that the competitiveness of the Indian tea industry suffered owing to productivity.

Despite the higher productivity, however, Indian tea has always suffered from a cost disadvantage vis-à-vis its East African competitors. In the late 1950s, production costs per unit weight in East Africa were much lower than in India.[18] Available evidence suggests that the East African countries probably retained this competitive edge even in the 1960s.[19] Given the fact that about half of India's tea output is constituted by low grade and common teas, while only one-fourth of Ceylon's output is inferior quality tea,[20] increasing competition from the East African common teas was bound to affect India's export performance more than that of Ceylon. Indeed, this is what actually happened during the period under study.

[18] See *Tea – Trends and Prospects*, p. 44.

[19] A recent World Bank report found that in 1968, the costs of production on tea plantations were 28.5 US cents per lb in North India, 24 cents per lb in South India, 24.6 cents per lb in Kenya, 26.4 cents per lb in Uganda, 21.5 cents per lb in Malawi and 24.6 cents per lb in Tanzania. In the case of India, the average costs of production may, in fact, have been higher because these estimates were based on reports from the well managed and more efficient estates. For details, see *Review of the World Tea Economy* (Washington, April 1970), p. 5, available in mimeographed form at the Institute of Agricultural Economics, Oxford. In 1968, the average costs of production on tea estates in Ceylon were estimated to be 25 cents per lb; see *Report of the Tea Commission*, Government of Ceylon, Sessional Paper no. XVIII, 1968, p. 138. All these estimates should be treated only as an overall index, since average costs are extremely difficult to quantify, and inter-country comparisons of costs, using the official exchange rates, create a host of problems arising from overvaluation of currencies.

[20] Sarkar, *World Tea Economy*, p. 210.

TABLE 5.10   *Estimated internal consumption of tea*
in India (in million kg)

Year	Consump-tion	Year	Consump-tion
1960/61	126.8	1965/66	166.0
1961/62	139.6	1966/67	184.2
1962/63	135.7	1967/68	180.7
1963/64	140.7	1968/69	185.9
1964/65	149.0	1969/70	203.3

Source: Indian Tea Board, Calcutta, *Tea Statistics, 1969/70*, p. 79.
Note: Internal consumption is not just the difference between production and exports. It takes into account the opening stock and the
changes in stock level at the end of the year. Throughout this period,
stocks varied in the range 60–80 million kg.

Pressure of domestic demand

There is a huge domestic market for tea in India, which must have
affected not only the profitability of the industry, but also the availability of supplies for export. Table 5.10 illustrates the phenomenal
growth of the consumption of tea in India during the 1960s. This
rapid increase is attributable partially to population growth and
partially to higher consumption per head. The average annual per
capita consumption of tea in India increased from 0.31 kg in 1962–1964
to 0.35 kg in 1965–1967 and 0.40 kg in 1967–1969.[21] Although in
absolute terms, this may not have been much, given the size of the
country's population, it had a very noticeable effect on the level of
consumption in the home market. In view of the fact that the income
elasticity of demand for tea in India is fairly high,[22] the trend outlined above was only to be expected.

While domestic consumption increased at a compound rate of
5.4 per cent per annum, the total production of tea, in India, grew at
only 2.3 per cent per annum. Consequently, as brought out in Table
5.11, there was a steady decline in the proportion of total output
that was exported. Thus we see that the size and expansion of the
domestic market may have constrained the export performance of the
Indian tea industry. As against this, Ceylon and the East African
countries had no such problem, because, in relation to total production, their domestic markets were very small.[23]

[21] International Tea Committee, London, *Annual Bulletin of Statistics, 1971*, p. 56.
[22] It has been estimated that the income elasticity of demand for tea in India is
1.28 in the rural areas and 1.16 in the urban areas; N. S. Ayengar, 'Some Estimates
of Engel Elasticities based on National Sample Survey Data', *Journal of the Royal
Statistical Society, 1967*; quoted in Sarkar, *World Tea Economy*, p. 76.

TABLE 5.11   *India's production and exports of tea*
(in million kg)

Year	Production	Exports	Exports as a percentage of production
1960	321.1	193.1	60.1
1961	354.4	206.3	58.2
1962	346.7	211.8	61.1
1963	346.4	223.6	64.5
1964	372.5	210.5	56.5
1965	366.4	199.4	54.5
1966	376.0	179.2	47.7
1967	384.8	213.7	55.5
1968	402.5	208.4	51.8
1969	396.0	168.7	42.6
1970	422.4	200.2	47.4

Source: International Tea Committee, London, *Annual Bulletin of Statistics, 1971*, pp. 10–11.

Note: The percentages in the last column have been computed.

The evidence adduced so far leaves little room for doubt that increasing domestic demand must have exerted considerable pressure on export supplies of tea. The extent to which it actually reduced the exportable surplus would depend on the relative profitability of home sales as compared to exports. Table 5.12 outlines the trend in the price of North and South Indian teas, both in London and in India, during the 1960s.[24] We find that while the average annual price of North Indian tea increased by 21.1 per cent between 1960–1962 and 1968–1970, at the Calcutta auctions, it actually fell by 17.7 per cent in the London auctions. Over the same period, the average annual price of South Indian tea at the Cochin auctions rose by 22.9 per cent, whereas in the London auctions it fell by 12.8 per cent. In so far as these price trends are an index of the changing relative profitability of the foreign and domestic markets, the pressure of domestic demand

[23] In the period 1966–1970, on the average, 94 per cent of Ceylon's output of tea was exported; the figure was only slightly lower at 91 per cent for the East African countries: calculated from statistics published by the International Tea Committee, London, *Annual Bulletin of Statistics, 1971*, pp. 10–11.

[24] The prices at the London auctions are not strictly comparable with the prices at the Calcutta and Cochin auctions. There is no point in converting them into a common currency because the London prices include transport costs as well as the traders' profits. However, this does not affect our analysis because we are only interested in the price trend within each country, and not as between the two countries.

TABLE 5.12   *Average annual prices of Indian tea*

Year	North Indian tea		South Indian tea	
	Calcutta auction Rs/kg	London auction new pence/kg	Cochin auction Rs/kg	London auction new pence/kg
1960	5.27	54.4	4.50	43.8
1961	4.75	51.4	4.56	42.6
1962	5.08	55.7	4.16	40.5
1963	4.99	51.1	4.45	39.8
1964	4.83	50.1	4.59	42.1
1965	5.28	48.0	4.70	41.1
1966	5.51	47.9	4.69	37.7
1967	5.53	49.3	5.42	39.0
1968	5.31	44.7	5.00	38.8
1969	6.09	41.5	5.30	31.6
1970	6.86	46.7	5.97	40.4

Source: International Tea Committee, London *Annual Bulletin of Statistics, 1971*, pp. 48–50.

TABLE 5.13   *Average annual taxation of Indian tea exports* (in Rs per kg)

Year	Excise duty	Export cess	Export duty
1960	0.23	0.044	0.53
1961	0.23	0.044	0.44
1962	0.32	0.044	0.25
1963	0.38	0.044	—
1964	0.38	0.044	—
1965	0.38	0.044	—
1966	0.38	0.044	1.66
1967	0.57	0.04	1.39
1968	0.48	0.04	1.05
1969	0.48	0.04	0.47
1970	0.76	0.04	—

Source: Indian Tea Board, Calcutta, *Tea Statistics, 1963*, p. 64,
   1967/68, p. 85, and *1969/70*, pp. 57, 82–5, 91 and 92.
Note:
(a) Until 10 June 1967, the cess was imposed only on exports, but
   after that date it was levied on all tea produced in the country. At
   the same time, the rate of the cess was lowered marginally from
   Rs4.40 to Rs4.00 per 100 kg.
(b) The export duty was abolished on 1 March 1963, reintroduced on
   6 June 1966, and abolished once again on 1 March 1970.
(c) The average annual rate of export duty with effect from 1966
   relates to Indian fiscal years beginning 1 April, and has been
   computed using the simple method of dividing the total export
   duty revenue by the quantity of exports in that year.

must have attracted some exportable output into internal consumption. It should be pointed out that the devaluation of the rupee in June 1966 may well have improved the relative profitability of export sales. However, as we shall show in the next section, a significant proportion of the devaluation was neutralised by the imposition of export duties. This little net effect that it may have had was also cancelled by the British devaluation in 1967.

The relative attractiveness of the home market and increases in domestic demand are particularly important determinants of exports, because the supply of tea is inelastic. Production cannot be increased at will for the simple reason that tea is a tree crop, and yields from new plants can be expected only after six years or so.[25] Sometimes, the gestation lag is even longer. Nevertheless, in India, very little effort has been made to step up the long term rate of growth of output.[26]

Fiscal and trade policies

Until now, we have analysed the export performance of the Indian tea industry without any reference to government policy. In the 1960s, however, the fiscal and trade policies adopted by the Government of India were quite crucial to this performance. For the sake of analytical convenience, we shall divide these policies into two groups. We begin by considering the impact of the taxes levied on exports, and then go on to examine the effects of the devaluation of the rupee in 1966.

The taxation of exports: During the period under study, exports of tea from India were subject to three taxes: excise duty, export cess and export duty. It is quite difficult to discern the incidence of these taxes because of the sliding scales, selective taxation and constantly changing rates. Table 5.13 tries to overcome this difficulty by high-

---

[25] In the short run, it may be possible to increase output by resorting to coarser plucking of the tea leaves, but that inevitably leads to poorer quality.

[26] In 1963, the Tea Finance Committee found that more than half the tea bushes in India were over-aged and uneconomic. In the tea industry, it is widely known that it is difficult to extract a growing yield from over-aged bushes. Thus it was very necessary to replant these. In fact, however, the progress in replanting was extremely slow. On the average, in the 1960s, only 0.5 per cent of the total area under tea was replanted each year. With a view to stepping up the replanting, in 1968, the Government introduced a replanting subsidy of Rs3500 per hectare for gardens in the plains, and Rs4500 per hectare for gardens in the hill areas. Until 1971, the effects of this policy were not really felt. For a detailed discussion on the question of replanting in the Indian tea industry, see K. M. Mandavawalla, 'Problems and Prospects for Indian Tea Exports during the Fourth Plan', *RBI Bulletin* (Bombay, March 1971), pp. 343–4.

lighting the changes in the average annual rate of taxation. Let us now analyse the impact of each of these taxes on the profitability and competitiveness of exports.

(*a*) *Excise duty*: Tea was one of the few Indian export industries which was not exempted from domestic taxes on the output exported. Unlike most other exportable products, the excise duty paid on tea was not even refundable at the point of export.[27] Table 5.13 shows clearly that the average annual rate of excise duty increased continuously over the decade. This average provides us with a reasonably good index of the overall incidence of the excise tax, but conceals the fact that there were five excise zones for tea in India. The rates of excise duty differed as between these zones. Hence, it is quite possible that the zones which accounted for a greater proportion of exports may have been taxed at a higher rate.[28] Statistics are not easily available because tea from different zones is blended before sale. But, taking all the five zones together, it has been estimated that, in 1968/69, the effective excise duty on exports was Rs 0.51 per kg as compared to Rs 0.46 per kg on domestic consumption.[29] Although, in principle, domestic consumption and exports were taxed equally, we see that, in practice, the excise duty was higher on exports.

(*b*) *Export cess*: Until 1967, exporters of tea had to pay a cess of Rs 4.40 per hundred kg. This tax was imposed and collected for the development of the tea industry, and was spent on items such as market propaganda and research. In June 1967, the levy was removed, and replaced by a cess of Rs 4.00 per hundred kg on all tea produced in the country. In this case, it seems that the burden of tax shifted from exports alone, to fall equally on exports and domestic consumption.

(*c*) *Export duty*: Table 5.13 brings out the main changes in the average rate of export duty on tea, during the 1960s. It shows that the

[27] There were a few minor exceptions. In 1962, excise paid on a particular variety of tea was refundable. On exports of packaged tea, a refund of excise duty was always possible, but this concession was quite insignificant because packaged tea constituted only 2 per cent of India's tea exports during the 1960s. However, the budget of 1970/71 introduced some meaningful rebates of excise duty on exports of loose tea.

[28] This was actually the case. For example, Zone V, which accounted for 48 per cent of total exports, was liable for the highest rate of excise duty at 9.9 per cent. The excise duty in the other zones ranged from 4 to 8 per cent; for details, see Mandavawalla, 'Tea Exports during the Fourth Plan', pp. 340–1.

[29] Ibid. Further confirmation is provided by the fact that even though, in 1968/69, only half the total output of tea was exported, nearly three-fifths of the excise revenue collected came from exports.

export duty was reduced gradually in the first three years of the decade, until it was abolished in March 1963. However, along with the devaluation of the rupee in June 1966, a specific export duty of Rs2.00 per kg was reintroduced.[30] On the assumption that the world demand for tea is price inelastic, the objective of this duty was to maintain the foreign exchange price of tea. In other words, the volume of exports was not expected to rise as a result of devaluation, or fall as a result of imposition of the duty. Soon after, in November 1966, the flat rate was replaced by a sliding scale export duty ranging from Rs0.80 to Rs3.00 per kg. Superior quality teas were subject to the higher tax, so that this measure was intended to help the export of common teas. In May 1967, these specific duties were converted into ad valorem rates. Later that year, the British devaluation reduced the rupee returns from exports of tea, and the Ceylonese devaluation neutralised the cost advantage that the Indian tea industry may have gained through the devaluation of 1966. Following these major developments abroad, the Indian Government granted some reductions in export duty during 1968 and 1969, which are reflected in a lower average rate of duty. In March 1970, the export duty on tea was abolished altogether.[31]

The taxes discussed so far were imposed and collected by the Central Government. In addition, State Governments in tea producing areas such as Assam, Bengal and Kerala also levied taxes on tea.[32]

The structure and incidence of the taxes imposed on tea was indeed quite complex. All the same, our analysis in the preceding paragraphs does show that the tax burden on exports was much heavier than on domestic consumption. For instance, in the period 1966–1969, the tax payable per unit weight on exports was, on average, more than three times that payable on domestic consumption.[33] This

---

[30] All the changes in the rate of export duty described in this paragraph are systematically tabulated in *Tea Statistics, 1969/70*, pp. 82–9.

[31] The Government of India budget for 1970/71 introduced some very basic changes in the taxation of tea. Apart from the abolition of export duty it brought in rebates of excise duty on loose tea exported. In order to encourage exports of superior teas, the rebates granted were greater for better quality teas. Essentially, all these changes were designed to make exports more attractive than the domestic market. To offset the loss in revenue, excise duties were stepped up, which is expected to have had a restrictive effect on domestic consumption.

[32] For an enumeration of the taxes imposed by State Governments on tea, see several issues of *Tea Statistics* published by the Indian Tea Board, Calcutta. In general, these taxes were relatively small. Kerala imposed a sales tax of 5 per cent, whereas the state of West Bengal charged an entry tax of Rs0.14 per kg on all tea entering the province. This may have had a fairly widespread incidence, because a large proportion of the tea output was sold at the Calcutta auctions.

[33] Table 5.13.

was not only because exports of tea were subject to an export duty and cess through most of the 1960s, but also because the effective excise duty on exports was higher. The bias in the tax structure is likely to have affected export performance in two ways. In the first place, it must have reduced the competitiveness of the Indian tea industry by lowering the profitability of exports. Second, it must have reduced the exportable surplus by making the domestic market relatively more attractive.

The effect of devaluation: Other things being equal, the devaluation of the rupee by 57.5 per cent in June 1966 should have improved the relative profitability of exports vis-à-vis home sales. In fact, however, a large proportion of the devaluation was neutralised by the imposition of duty on exports of tea. We have estimated that the *net* devaluation experienced by the Indian tea industry on 6 June 1966 was only 20.6 per cent.[34] Even though this was far less than the apparent depreciation in the exchange rate, it must have improved the incentive to export by raising the domestic currency returns per unit of foreign exchange earned, by exporters. Unfortunately, the incentive arising out of devaluation did not last very long. Some of it was lost when the excise duty was stepped up in early 1967. The remainder was neutralised by the British and Ceylonese devaluations in November 1967.[35] Since UK was the largest and most important market for Indian tea, devaluation of the pound sterling once again reduced the domestic currency returns per unit of foreign exchange earned by exporters of tea, in India. At the same time, Ceylon, which was India's principal competitor in the world market for tea, also devalued its currency thereby eliminating any cost advantage that the Indian tea industry might have gained in June 1966. Thus, it seems that in the case of tea, the favourable effect of the devaluation was very short-lived. As such, it did little to alleviate the pressure of domestic demand and the relative attractiveness of the home market.

Non-price factors

A look back at Table 5.1 tells us that in 1966 and 1969, there was a sharp fall in the quantity of tea exported from India. To a great ex-

---

[34] For the method of calculation, see Chapter 11, especially Tables 11.2 and 11.3.
[35] It has been shown that although the devaluation of the rupee conferred a significant competitive advantage on the Indian tea industry (even after allowance was made for export duties), its impact was almost completely neutralised by the devaluations in UK and Ceylon. For a detailed analysis, see I. S. Gulati, 'Competitiveness of India's Tea Exports', *Economic and Political Weekly* (Bombay, 17 February 1968), pp. 325–32.

TABLE 5.14   *Stocks of tea in the UK* (January of each year: in million kg)

1961	1962	1963	1964	1965	1966	1967	1968	1969	1970
74.4	72.6	72.5	87.4	80.4	91.4	79.7	86.7	105.4	67.7

Source: International Tea Committee, London, *Annual Bulletin of Statistics, 1971*, p. 46.

tent, these sudden drops in the level of exports can be explained in terms of non-price factors. If we examine the position of stocks of tea in London warehouses at the beginning of each year, which is outlined in Table 5.14, we find that the stocks at the beginning of 1966 and 1969 were very high indeed. There were many reasons for this pile up of stocks, but more often than not, poor prices during the year meant that tea was held back from the auctions. The direct consequence of these large stocks in January 1966 and January 1969 was, of course, a cut down in imports of tea during those years.

Apart from the position of stocks, in 1966, the following occur-rences in India were also responsible for the reduction in exports that year:[36] (*a*) strikes in Calcutta port docks during August–September 1966; and (*b*) the devaluation, which disrupted the flow of trade between India and the socialist countries of Eastern Europe; exports were resumed only a few months later when the trade agreements had been revised to take account of the depreciation in the exchange rate.

The factors described above could only have affected exports of tea in the short run. One might ask if there were any non-price factors which could have influenced the long term trend in exports. Although it is extremely difficult to quantify, there is a possibility that the large proportion of British investment in the Indian, Ceylonese and East African tea industries was one such factor.

In India, foreign companies exercise considerable control over the production and marketing of tea. Of the 146 companies in the tea plantations industry, 109 are branches of foreign companies with control in the UK.[37] Not only that, a few British firms dominate the Calcutta and Cochin auctions.[38] The picture is much the same in Ceylon, where, at the end of the 1960s, nearly two-fifths of the total estate acreage was owned by British companies.[39] Information on the

[36] For details, see the annual review in Indian Tea Board, Calcutta, *Tea Statistics, 1966/67*.
[37] *RBI Bulletin* (August 1969), p. 1169; and (June 1970), p. 930.
[38] Mandavawalla, 'Tea Exports during the Fourth Plan', p. 344.
[39] *Report of the Ceylon Tea Commission* (1968), p. 21.

extent of foreign investment and control in the East African tea industry is not available. However, it is unlikely that the situation could have changed significantly since independence in the early 1960s, when most of the tea plantations in these countries were British owned.[40] The interesting fact is that British investment in all these tea producing countries is probably concentrated in the hands of a few companies. According to a recent report of the UK Government, approximately 85 per cent of the British market for tea is controlled by four companies, and among them, Brooke Bond alone accounted for 43 per cent.[41] Owing to a complete lack of information, it is not possible to quantify the extent of control exercised by these four companies in the major tea producing countries. However, the snippets of indirect evidence cited above do suggest that the world tea industry is dominated by a few large international firms. If this is actually the case, it might provide an explanation for India's loss of the UK market to the East African countries. Given the high taxation of exports, and the large as well as relatively attractive domestic market in India, the multinational tea firms might have found it profitable to sell exportable supplies within India, and make up the shortfall by increasing imports from the East African countries where the domestic market was small, and taxation of exports minimal.

Summary

Our analysis of the trends in exports of tea from India leads to the following main conclusions. Although world trade in tea was limited by the stagnant demand in high income countries, the demand for tea rose rapidly in the LDCs. Among the latter, the Indian tea industry found some new export markets, but, at the same time, lost its foothold in the traditional markets. As a result, India's share in world exports of tea dropped significantly, and the contribution of tea to the country's export earnings fell sharply in the 1960s. There were several reasons for this poor export performance. It is possible that the Indian tea industry suffered from deteriorating cost competitiveness, but the principal reason for the fall in exports was the increasing pres-

---

[40] It should be mentioned that the rapid development of small tea holdings in Kenya does not seriously affect our conclusion. For, as late as 1968, commercial tea estates i.e. plantations, accounted for more than 85 per cent of Kenya's total tea production; calculated from N. H. Stern, *An Appraisal of Tea Production on Small Holdings in Kenya*, OECD (Paris, 1972), p. 12.

[41] For details, see *Tea Prices*, Report no 154, National Board for Prices and Incomes, HMSO (London, 1970), p.8.

sure of domestic demand. This pressure was reinforced by the Government's fiscal and trade policies which gave rise to a tax structure that discriminated against exports, and in favour of domestic consumption, thereby lowering the profitability of exports and making the home market relatively more attractive.

6

Cashew and tobacco

I. CASHEW KERNELS

In 1960, India enjoyed a virtual monopoly in the world market for cashew nuts.[1] Although, during the 1960s, competition from other sources increased, it was still very limited. As such, India's exports of cashew kernels continued to grow rapidly, throughout the decade. This trend emerges quite clearly from Table 6.1. The average annual quantity exported rose from 44.6 million kg in the three-year period 1960/61–1962/63 to 58.2 million kg during 1968/69–1970/71. Over the same period, the average annual foreign exchange receipts from the export of cashew almost doubled, rising from $39.5 million to $75.7 million. The substantial difference between trends in value and volume can be explained in terms of the improvement in prices, which is reflected in the increasing average unit value. As a result, the average share of cashew kernels in the country's total export earnings increased from 2.8 per cent in 1960/61–1962/63 to 4.0 per cent in 1968/69–1970/71.[2]

Prima facie, this appears to be an impressive export performance. However, the above statistics do not show the real exchange earnings of the Indian cashew industry, which had to import approximately two-thirds of its raw nut requirements.[3] In Table 6.2 we have estimated the net foreign exchange earnings after allowing for the cost of importing raw cashew nuts. Such an adjustment reduces the magnitude of our earlier figures, but the growth in exports is still quite clear. We see that the average annual net foreign exchange earned by the cashew industry increased from $21.7 million to $36.5 million between 1960/61–1962/63 and 1968/69–1970/71.

[1] See Table 6.3. The basic value of the cashew nut lies in its kernel, which has to be extracted from the raw nut and then shelled. In India, processing of cashew on a commercial scale began nearly half a century ago. To start with, only domestically produced nuts were processed, but in response to increasing world demand India began importing raw nuts for processing.

[2] Table 2.6.

[3] See Table 6.6.

Cashew kernels

TABLE 6.1   *India's exports of cashew kernels*

Year	Volume in million kg	Value in $ million	Average unit value in $ per kg
1960/61	43.6	39.7	0.91
1961/62	41.8	38.1	0.91
1962/63	48.5	40.7	0.84
1963/64	51.5	45.0	0.87
1964/65	55.8	61.0	1.09
1965/66	51.3	57.6	1.12
1966/67	50.0	61.3	1.23
1967/68	51.0	57.4	1.13
1968/69	63.7	81.2	1.27
1969/70	60.6	76.6	1.26
1970/71	50.3	69.4	1.38

Source: Statistics published by DGCIS, Calcutta.
Note: Figures relate to Indian fiscal years beginning 1 April, and have been converted into US dollars.

TABLE 6.2   *Net foreign exchange earnings from cashew* (in $ million)

Year	Exports of cashew kernels	Imports of raw cashew nuts	Net foreign exchange earnings
1960/61	39.7	20.2	19.5
1961/62	38.1	14.1	24.0
1962/63	40.7	19.2	21.5
1963/64	45.0	23.0	22.0
1964/65	61.0	34.5	26.5
1965/66	57.6	31.6	26.0
1966/67	61.3	30.7	30.6
1967/68	57.4	33.4	24.0
1968/69	81.2	41.8	39.4
1969/70	76.6	36.8	39.8
1970/71	69.4	39.2	30.2

Source: Statistics published by DGCIS, Calcutta.
Note: The net exchange earnings have been calculated as the difference between the first two columns.

Given the fact that the domestic consumption of cashew kernels in India is extremely small,[4] it is only natural that the growth in exports must be related to changes in world trade and demand.

Trends in world trade and consumption

International trade in cashew kernels is characterised by India's monopolistic position in the world market. Table 6.3 outlines the changes in world exports during the 1960s, and brings out the relative importance of India as the main exporter. In the first half of the decade, India accounted for approximately 95 per cent of world exports. It is curious that although she had to import the bulk of her raw cashew nut needs, processing and export of kernels was a near monopoly. The main reason behind this dominance has been the labour skills available to the Indian cashew industry.[5] This endowment bestowed a distinct comparative advantage on India, because extraction of kernels from the raw nuts is an extremely intricate operation requiring very special manual skills.[6] Without these, it is most likely that the kernels would break in the process of extraction. The fact that whole kernels fetch much higher prices than broken grades,[7] must have added to India's advantage. And until quite recently, there was no substitute for the labour intensive method of processing employed in India.

However, a few years ago, an Italian company developed a mechanical processing method which could compete effectively with hand operated plants.[8] This development offered the East African countries an opportunity of processing their cashew crop at home, instead of exporting it to India. Cashew processing plants were set up quite promptly in Mozambique and Tanzania.[9] Installation of new capacity

---

[4] It has been estimated that domestic consumption in India and Brazil together amounts to about 6–7 million kg per annum; see *Cashew Marketing*, a study by the UNCTAD/GATT International Trade Centre (Geneva, 1968), p. 3.

[5] It is interesting to note that more than two-thirds of India's cashew industry is concentrated in one district of Kerala, viz. Quilon. Such localisation of the industry has meant a permanent access to labour skills which have become indigenous to that area.

[6] For details, see B. E. Olsen, 'Cashew', *Indian Cashew Journal*, vol. VI, no. 2, a quarterly publication of the Indian Cashew Export Promotion Council, Ernakulum.

[7] For example, in 1967, the New York prices of whole kernels were 60 cents/lb, whereas broken pieces fetched about 37–40 cents/lb; see *Cashew Marketing*, p. 27.

[8] A detailed analysis of this new processing method can be found in ibid. pp. 15–17.

[9] Ibid. p. 11.

TABLE 6.3   World exports of cashew kernels (in million kg)

Year	India	Mozambique	Brazil	Tanzania	Kenya	Others	Total world	India's percentage share
1960	43.6	1.3	0.6	—	—	—	45.5	95.8
1961	41.8	1.1	0.4	—	—	—	43.3	96.5
1962	48.5	1.9	0.6	—	—	—	51.0	95.1
1963	51.5	2.6	1.1	—	—	—	55.2	93.3
1964	55.8	3.5	1.1	—	0.1	—	60.5	92.2
1965	51.3	4.0	0.7	0.1	0.2	1.0	57.3	89.5
1966	50.0	5.7	2.0	0.6	0.2	1.0	59.5	84.0
1967	51.0	8.1	1.5	1.4	0.2	1.0	63.2	80.7
1968	63.7	10.4	3.3	1.4	0.2	1.0	80.0	79.6
1969	60.6	12.8	5.1	2.4	0.2	1.0	82.1	73.8

Source:

(a) For India: Table 6.1;

(b) For other countries, 1960–1966: UNCTAD/GATT International Trade Centre, *Cashew Marketing*, p. 22;

(c) For other countries, 1967–1969: Mozambique – UN Year-book of *International Trade Statistics, 1969*; Brazil – *Annuaro Estatistico de Brasil, 1970*; Kenya and Tanzania –

Annual Trade Reports of Tanzania, Uganda and Kenya, published by the East African Customs and Excise Department.

Note: Figures for India relate to fiscal years beginning 1 April, and the statistics for East African countries have been converted into metric weights.

is obvious from the rapid increase in cashew kernel exports of these countries in the latter half of the decade. Table 6.3 shows that between 1965 and 1969, Mozambique's exports increased from 4.0 to 12.8 million kg, Tanzanian exports from 0.1 to 2.4 million kg, and Brazilian exports from 0.7 to 5.1 million kg. As a result, India's share in world exports, which averaged 94.6 per cent during 1960–1964, declined to 81.5 per cent in the period 1965–1969.

Obviously, India's exports did not keep pace with the expansion in world trade. Between 1960–1962 and 1967–1969, the average annual volume of India's cashew exports increased by only 31 per cent, rising from 44.6 million kg to 58.4 million kg, whereas, the average annual volume of world exports increased by 61 per cent, rising from 46.6 million to 75.1 million kg. This rapid growth in world trade was the result of a growing demand for the commodity and increasing world consumption.[10]

Cashew nuts are grown and processed only in India, Brazil and East Africa, but the consumption of cashew kernels is concentrated in the USA, USSR, Australia, Canada, UK and, of late, Eastern Europe.[11] It follows that all the consuming countries have to rely on imports to meet their demand. Therefore, trends in world exports are an almost perfect index of trends in world demand and consumption.

World exports increased from 45.5 million kg in 1960 to 82.1 million kg in 1969. This suggests that, during the 1960s, world consumption of cashew kernels increased by a little more than 80 per cent. Interestingly enough, growth in consumption was accompanied by continuously rising prices.[12] A recent FAO study found that these price increases in the past were absorbed without any reduction in demand.[13] It is not as if there are no substitutes for cashew nuts. In fact, as a drink accessory, peanuts come quite close, and in confectionary-use, almonds can be a good replacement. However, for several reasons, the possibilities of substitution are limited,

---

[10] The consumption of cashew nut kernels takes primarily two forms. Generally, they are eaten as dessert nuts, e.g. as a snack with cocktails. But, sometimes, they are consumed indirectly through use in confectionary. Depending upon the end-use, the nature of demand varies as between countries. In the USA, where cashew is consumed essentially along with cocktails, the demand is for whole kernels. It has been estimated that 80–85 per cent of US imports are constituted by whole kernels (ibid. p. 24). On the other hand, in Europe and the USSR, where the origin of demand is confectionary-use, it is mostly broken grades and pieces that are imported.

[11] Ibid. p. 8.

[12] See ibid. pp. 27 and 64.

[13] C. E. Parry, *World Market Outlook for Cashew Nuts*, FAO (Rome, 1968), as summarised in the *Indian Cashew Journal*, vol. VIII, no. 1.

and in the long run, the demand for cashew nuts can be sustained.[14]

During the period under study, an important development in the world market for cashew kernels was the emergence of the USSR and Eastern Europe as important buyers. The additional demand created by these relatively new markets may have been an important factor behind the rapid increase in world consumption and the rising price level. It might therefore be interesting to examine the relative importance of these markets in world trade. In view of the fact that the socialist countries import cashew kernels only from India, under bilateral trade agreements, it would be sufficient to look at the changing market distribution of India's exports.

New markets for Indian cashew nuts

Traditionally, the USA has been the single most important market for cashew kernels, and, in the late 1950s, it accounted for more than 60 per cent of India's exports.[15] This is hardly surprising specially when we consider the fact that cashew processing for export began only in response to American demand.[16] In the 1960s, however, the picture changed substantially.

Table 6.4 shows the most important markets for India's cashew exports and brings out the changes in their relative shares. The rapidly growing importance of the USSR market is most striking. Between 1961/62–1963/64 and 1968/69–1970/71, the average annual value of exports to the USSR shot up from $5.8 million to $26.0 million. Over the same period, exports to the USA increased relatively moderately, rising from $23.3 million to $34.7 million. As a result, the share of the American market in India's exports declined from 56.3 to 45.8 per cent, whereas the Soviet market share increased from 14.0 to 34.3 per cent. Together, the USA and USSR absorbed nearly three-fourths of India's exports, throughout the decade. There was no significant change in exports to other markets, except for the steady decline in the relative shares of West Germany, UK and East Germany.

---

[14] In the short run, increased cashew prices may induce packers to put fewer cashews in their mixed nut packs. But this can be done only to a limited extent, and cannot be done at all when it comes to cashew nut packs themselves. Similarly, confectionary demand may be price sensitive, but it cannot completely eliminate cashews because they have a distinctive taste, which is not perfectly substitutable.

[15] M. Singh, *India's Export Trends* (Oxford, 1964), p. 213.

[16] See D. H. Joshi, 'Cashew Industry in India', *Indian Cashew Journal*, vol. VIII, no. 1.

TABLE 6.4 *Market distribution of India's cashew kernel exports* (annual averages: in $ million)

	1961/62–1963/64	1964/65–1967/68	1968/69–1970/71
USA	23.3	29.3	34.7
USSR	5.8	14.7	26.0
Canada	1.4	2.0	2.9
Australia	1.4	2.0	2.1
West Germany	1.0	0.6	0.6
UK	2.3	3.2	2.2
East Germany	2.4	2.7	2.4
Total including others	41.4	59.2	75.7
Relative shares (in percentages)			
USA	56.3	49.5	45.8
USSR	14.0	24.8	34.3
Canada	3.4	3.4	3.8
Australia	3.4	3.4	2.8
West Germany	2.4	1.0	0.8
UK	5.6	5.4	2.9
East Germany	5.8	4.6	3.2
Total including others	100.0	100.0	100.0

Source: Statistics published by DGCIS, Calcutta.
Note:
(a) Figures relate to Indian fiscal years beginning 1 April and have been converted into US dollars.
(b) The annual averages have been computed from data for individual years, and then calculated into percentages.

Table 6.5 outlines the levels of per capita consumption of cashew kernels, in selected markets, during the first half of the decade. Of India's principal markets, per capita consumption was higher than 100 grams only in the USA, East Germany and Australia. In most West European countries and Japan it was less than 25 grams. These figures suggest that there was ample room for promoting cashew consumption in almost all the markets. From 1968, the task may have been made easier by the Kennedy Round concessions, which removed almost all tariff barriers faced by cashew kernels.[17] However, promotion of exports did not turn out to be so simple for India, because of increasing competition, and a few other problems which are discussed below.

[17] For details, see *Cashew Marketing*, p. 29.

TABLE 6.5   *Per capita consumption of cashew
kernels in some countries* (average for
1962–1966)

	Grams/head		Grams/head
East Germany	217	Netherlands	42
USA	162	Sweden	24
Australia	147	West Germany	21
Canada	89	France	11
UK	59	Japan	5
USSR	46	Italy	3

Source: UNCTAD/GATT International Trade Centre, *Cashew Marketing*, p. 26.

Increasing competition

Until quite recently, the Indian cashew industry had been secure in its monopolistic position. After 1965, however, it faced increasing competition, as a result of which it started losing its share of the world market. This problem is not evident from the upward trend in the value and volume of cashew nut kernels exported from India. However, as we have shown, most of that increase was sustained by a rapid expansion of exports to the USSR. But India steadily lost her share of the American market. A recent study shows that this was due to competition from Brazil and Mozambique, both of whom raised their shares in the US market.[18]

The basic problem of the cashew kernel industry in India arises from the availability of raw nuts. Table 6.6 brings out the fact that domestic production of raw cashew nuts, which contributed less than one-third the total requirements of the processing industry, was totally inadequate. On the average, almost 70 per cent of the nuts processed had to be imported. The bulk of these imports came from Mozambique and Tanzania.[19] It was a fortunate coincidence that the harvest periods which were March to May in India, October to November in Tanzania, and November to January in Mozambique, fitted into a neat cycle, thereby enabling the cashew industry in India to minimise inventory costs and storage damage.[20] However, the setting up of processing

[18] A. B. L. Mathur, 'India's Cashew Exports', *Economic and Political Weekly* (Bombay, 14 March 1970), pp. 487–92.

[19] *Cashew Marketing*, p. 13.

[20] Ibid. p. 6.

TABLE 6.6   *Import requirements and the production of raw cashew nuts in India* (in million kg)

Year	Domestic production	Imports	Estimated processing	Percentage of requirement met by imports
1961	66.0	131.7	197.7	66.6
1962	66.0	131.1	197.1	66.5
1963	76.2	164.4	240.6	68.3
1964	81.3	170.3	251.6	67.7
1965	82.0	175.5	257.5	68.2
1966	65.0	140.7	205.7	68.4
1967	56.0	168.2	224.2	75.0
1968	71.0	195.5	266.5	73.4
1969	61.0	163.4	224.4	72.8
1970	71.0	169.4	240.4	70.5

Source:

For 1961–1966; UNCTAD/GATT International Trade Centre, *Cashew Marketing*, p. 13

For 1967–1970: domestic production – *Cashew Statistics*, published by the Indian Cashew Export Promotion Council; imports – statistics published by DGCIS, Calcutta.

Note:

(a) Estimated processing is just the sum of domestic production and imports

(b) Import figures from 1967 relate to Indian fiscal years beginning 1 April

(c) The percentages in the last column have been computed.

TABLE 6.7   *Average unit value of raw cashew nuts imported into India* (in $ per ton)

Year	From Mozambique	From Tanzania	From Kenya	From all sources
1962	121	130	129	124
1963	127	138	134	131
1964	167	172	181	169
1965	192	199	217	196
1966	219	199	242	206

Source: UNCTAD/GATT International Trade Centre, *Cashew Marketing*, p. 14.

plants in East Africa quite naturally restricted the raw cashew nut supplies available for export to India. As a result, prices of raw nuts rose. Table 6.7 highlights this trend and shows that the costs of importing raw cashew nuts into India shot up rapidly during the first half of the decade. Between 1962 and 1966, the average unit value of raw nuts imported from Mozambique rose by 81 per cent,

TABLE 6.8   *Trend in import costs per ton of raw cashew nuts*

	Unit	1962	1965	1967	1968	1969	1970
Average unit value of imports	$	124	196	199	214	225	231
Rupee cost of imports	Rs	590	933	1493	1605	1688	1736

Source: For 1962 and 1965: Table 6.7; for 1967–1970: statistics published by DGCIS, Calcutta.
Note: From 1967, the figures relate to Indian fiscal years beginning 1 April, and have been computed from data on the quantity and value of raw cashew nut imports. All figures have been rounded oft to the nearest dollar/rupee.

from Tanzania by 53 per cent and from Kenya by 88 per cent. Table 6.8 shows that the upward trend in import costs continued in the late 1960s. Owing to the devaluation of the rupee in June 1966, the domestic currency costs incurred by importers rose even more. Between 1962 and 1970, the average import price of raw cashew nuts increased from Rs590 to Rs1736 per ton. Clearly, this must have been partially neutralised by the increased rupee returns that accrued to exporters of cashew kernels, after devaluation.

It is most surprising that these rapidly rising import costs did not induce an increase in domestic production. On the contrary, it appears that very little effort was made to encourage and develop indigenous cultivation.[21] Table 6.6 shows that, between 1961 and 1970, the domestic output was more or less stagnant, whereas the dependence on imports increased.

It is fairly obvious that if India is to sustain her cashew kernel exports, it is imperative for her to step up raw nut production. This can be done either by increasing the area under cultivation, or by raising the yield of existing plants. By itself, the first alternative might be rather difficult for the following reason. At the moment cashew nuts are grown over an area of about 260 thousand hectares. If exports are to be maintained at a level of 65 million kg per annum, it has been estimated that an additional area of 240 thousand hectares would have to be brought under cultivation.[22] Although it might be possible to extend the acreage, it would be near impossible to double it

[21] In view of the fact that the cashew nut tree is fairly simple to grow, is drought resistant, and thrives under a variety of climatic conditions, this stagnation in production is hard to understand.

[22] See T. A. Sriram, 'Increased Production of Cashew Nuts', *Indian Cashew Journal*, vol. II, no. 2, pp. 16–17.

in a short period of time. On the other hand, an improvement in yield is quite feasible. Higher production per hectare would also reduce the extra area requirements. Evidently, appropriate agronomic practices have been developed by the Indian Council of Agricultural Research, which would ensure sufficiently high yields.[23] Thus, it appears that the best policy would be one which combines efforts at extending the area with new methods of improving yields.

If India's cashew industry can successfully raise the level of raw cashew nut production within the country, it will have solved its basic problem. Increasing competition could then be met by more effective marketing techniques.[24]

II. TOBACCO

India is the second largest producer of tobacco in the world. It is only in the USA that the output of tobacco is higher.[25] This importance is not reflected in the quantum of India's exports of the commodity, because a large proportion of the crop is consumed in the domestic market. During the 1960s, the proportion of tobacco output exported averaged about 16 per cent.[26] All the same, receipts from the export of tobacco constituted a little more than 2 per cent of the total export earnings.

Table 6.9 brings out the main trends in tobacco exports during the decade. A mere glance at the table reveals that the bulk of the exports was accounted for by unmanufactured tobacco.[27] The foreign exchange earnings derived from the export of manufactured tobacco products appear to have been relatively unimportant, and quite

[23] For details, see ibid. In the matter of yield, India is placed at a natural advantage vis-à-vis East African countries. According to the UNCTAD/GATT study, even at the moment, a good average crop for a mature plantation tree is around 10 kg in East Africa, and 30 kg in India; see *Cashew Marketing*, p. 6.

[24] The Cashew Export Promotion Council has made efforts to promote the 'cashew habit' in Europe and the USA, by advertising and by participating in world trade fairs. However, these efforts need to be extended and intensified.

[25] *The Major Markets for Unmanufactured Tobacco*, a study by the UNCTAD/GATT International Trade Centre (Geneva, 1968), p. 4. Output in China is also higher, but statistics are not available.

[26] Calculated from statistics published in the FAO, *Production and Trade Yearbooks*.

[27] It is important to note that even unmanufactured tobacco requires some processing before it can be exported. In fact, the harvested tobacco leaf becomes marketable only after it has been cured of its moisture. Processing is necessary in order to dry the leaf and then grade it. See *Tobacco Exports*, a report by the Indian Institute of Foreign Trade (New Delhi, 1967), p. 43.

TABLE 6.9   *Exports of tobacco from India*

Year	Unmanufactured tobacco			Manufactured tobacco products in $ million
	Volume in million kg	Value in $ million	Average unit value of $/kg	
1960	40.7	30.5	0.75	2.38
1961	48.2	31.2	0.65	1.92
1962	63.5	39.3	0.62	1.83
1963	67.9	47.8	0.70	1.39
1964	71.7	47.0	0.66	3.34
1965	62.0	45.5	0.73	3.32
1966	35.6	27.9	0.78	2.14
1967	55.7	43.6	0.78	1.55
1968	52.1	44.1	0.85	1.26
1969	54.7	44.4	0.81	1.26

Source: FAO Rome, *Trade Yearbooks*, *1966*, pp. 246–7, and *1970*, pp. 322–3.
Note: Figures for the last column on manufactured tobacco products have been taken from statistics published by DGCIS, Calcutta. They relate to Indian fiscal years beginning 1 April, and have been converted into US dollars.

stagnant throughout the period under study. Therefore, we will be concerned with analysing trends in the former.

Over the ten-year period, there was a moderate growth in exports of unmanufactured tobacco. The average annual value of exports increased from $33.7 million in the three-year period 1960–1962 to $44 million during 1967–1969. This 33 per cent increase in export earnings was not accompanied by a similar increase in export volume. Between 1960–1962 and 1967–1969, the average annual quantity exported rose only from 50.8 to 54.2 million kg. The fact that prices must have risen is reflected in the increase in average unit value, which was particularly marked towards the end of the decade.

Comparing terminal periods may serve to indicate the general trend, but conceals the fact that exports reached a peak in the mid-1960s. In 1964, India exported about 72 million kg of tobacco fetching $47 million in foreign exchange. This was the result of a very good harvest and an extraordinarily good year in the world tobacco market.[28] The boom was followed by a slump, when, in 1966, exports of tobacco declined to an all time low of 35.6 million kg and $27.9 million. Essentially, the sudden drop was a direct result of the sharp decline in tobacco output during the 1965/66 season, for which there were two reasons:[29] (*a*) acreage under tobacco was 12 per cent lower

[28] See *Plantation Crops*, no. 13, Commonwealth Secretariat (London, 1970), p. 169.
[29] For details, see RBI Bombay, *Report on Currency and Finance*, 1966/67, p. 47.

than in the previous year, and (b) the relatively poor season resulted in much lower yields. If we exclude this abnormal year, India's export performance in tobacco presents a fairly clear picture: exports increased rapidly from 1960 to 1964, after which they remained more or less stagnant, at a lower level. This corresponds quite closely to the trends in world demand.

The world market for tobacco

It is difficult to obtain estimates of world demand for tobacco. However, for our purpose, trends in world trade are a sufficient index of changes in world demand for tobacco. Table 6.10 shows the world exports of tobacco, during the 1960s, and brings out the changes in relative shares of the main exporting countries.

We see that world exports grew rapidly in the early 1960s, increasing from 806 million kg in 1960 to 1008 million kg in 1964, but they were virtually stagnant after that. To a great extent, this stagnation in world import demand is attributable to the widespread and growing belief about the correlation between cigarette smoking and health. Fears of ill health are likely to have affected the demand for tobacco adversely in two ways: first, by acting as a restraint on consumption, and second, by causing a shift in preference to filter tipped cigarettes, which have a lower tobacco content.[30]

In the early 1960s, when the tobacco trade was still expanding, India managed to increase her share in world exports from 5 per cent in 1960 to an average of 7.4 per cent in the period 1962–1964 In other words, exports of tobacco from India rose faster than world exports. It is therefore surprising that, after 1965, she could not even maintain the absolute level of exports, and her share in the world market declined to an average of 5.4 per cent in the period 1967–1969.

However, over the decade as a whole, India retained her share in the world tobacco trade. But so did most of the other main exporting countries. At this stage, it is necessary to point out that Bulgaria, Greece and Turkey produce and export primarily oriental leaf tobacco,[31] and as such, do not really compete with India, the bulk of

[30] FAO, *Agricultural Commodity Projections, 1970–80*, vol. I (Rome, 1971), p. 209. According to this study, the demand for raw leaf rose slower than cigarette output, and publicity about the health hazards of smoking restricted tobacco consumption in many countries. See also *Major Markets for Unmanufactured Tobacco*, p. 6.

[31] Ibid. p. 16. Although there may be some degree of substitutability between the two varieties of tobacco, owing to distinct consumer preferences, it is very limited.

TABLE 6.10 *World exports of tobacco* (in million kg)

	1960	1961	1962	1963	1964	1965	1966	1967	1968	1969
USA	224.6	227.2	212.7	229.3	231.5	212.3	250.0	259.3	271.6	261.8
India	40.7	48.2	63.5	67.9	71.7	62.0	35.6	55.7	52.1	54.7
Rhodesia	87.2	95.3	98.0	96.8	102.3	122.5	–	–	–	–
Greece	61.0	65.9	47.4	51.9	70.2	72.9	73.2	87.7	70.2	71.0
Brazil	31.6	48.8	41.8	44.3	60.3	55.3	46.6	45.3	38.6	48.2
Turkey	58.0	88.4	90.7	44.6	57.0	69.0	85.2	91.8	81.3	70.5
Bulgaria	70.8	64.7	58.6	86.1	90.2	82.0	73.7	77.6	69.4	60.5
China	23.3	10.3	3.8	14.1	4.7	6.6	7.7	11.4	22.8	27.3
Canada	16.9	17.3	22.1	17.8	23.8	18.8	17.2	19.5	21.5	23.8
South Korea	0.5	–	0.1	0.3	6.4	1.4	10.0	10.9	10.9	20.1
Total, including others	806.3	864.8	858.2	889.9	1008.0	969.0	922.7	1008.2	993.4	1000.0

Relative shares (in percentages)

	1960	1961	1962	1963	1964	1965	1966	1967	1968	1969
USA	27.9	26.3	24.8	25.8	23.0	21.9	27.1	25.7	27.3	26.2
India	5.0	5.6	7.4	7.6	7.1	6.4	3.9	5.5	5.2	5.5
Rhodesia	10.8	11.0	11.4	10.9	10.1	12.6	–	–	–	–
Greece	7.6	7.6	5.5	5.8	7.0	7.5	7.9	8.7	7.1	7.1
Brazil	3.9	5.6	4.9	5.0	6.0	5.7	5.1	4.5	3.9	4.8
Turkey	7.1	10.2	10.6	5.0	5.7	7.1	9.2	9.1	8.2	7.1
Bulgaria	8.8	7.5	6.8	9.7	8.9	8.5	8.0	7.7	7.0	6.1
Total including others	100.0	100.0	100.0	100.0	100.0	100.0	100.0	100.0	100.0	100.0

Source: FAO *Trade Yearbook*, *1966*, p. 247; and *1970*, pp. 322–3.
Note: From 1960 to 1963, Rhodesia refers to the Federation of Rhodesia and Nyasaland. The percentage shares have been computed.

whose exports consist of flue-cured Virginia tobacco. Throughout the 1960s, about 80 per cent of the tobacco exported from India was flue-cured.[32]

Apart from India, the other main exporters of flue-cured Virginia tobacco are the USA, Rhodesia, Brazil and, on a smaller scale, Canada and South Korea.[33] The imposition of sanctions against Rhodesia after the UDI in 1965 officially eliminated Rhodesian tobacco from the world market. *Prima facie*, its share of 12.6 per cent could have been taken over by any country that could compete and sell effectively. Given the fact that, until then, India's exports had been increasing faster than world exports, one would have expected her to do well out of the embargo on Rhodesian tobacco. In reality, however, this did not happen and India's share in the world market declined.

Two questions arise in this context: first, which country or countries replaced Rhodesia in the world market, and second, what were the reasons for India's poor export performance after 1965? We shall take up each of these in turn.

South Korea and the USA were the only countries which increased their exports of tobacco substantially after 1965; Brazil's exports actually fell and Canada just about maintained them. South Korea, which had exported a little over 1 million kg in 1965, raised its exports to more than 20 million kg in 1969, capturing 2 per cent of the world market. The USA, which had been losing its share of the world market in the first half of the decade (from 27.9 per cent in 1960 to 21.9 per cent in 1965), recovered significantly and brought its share back to the 1960 level.

This success in recapturing its lost markets can be explained in terms of deliberate policy measures adopted by the American Government. In 1966, it introduced a subsidy of 5 cents per lb on virtually all varieties of tobacco exports.[34] In addition, the US Government continued to support exports of tobacco, throughout the decade, by operating schemes like the PL480, AID, and effecting barter transactions. Table 6.11 makes clear that a substantial proportion of the American tobacco exports were effected through government schemes

[32] During the period 1960/61 to 1965/66, on the average, flue-cured Virginia accounted for 79.5 per cent of the volume of India's tobacco exports; calculated from *Tobacco Exports*, p. 73. In 1970, this ratio had hardly changed, and was 81.8 per cent; calculated from statistics published by the Commonwealth Secretariat, London, in *Tobacco Intelligence* (February 1972), p. 54.

[33] *Major Markets for Unmanufactured Tobacco*, p. 7.

[34] Ibid. p. 19. To begin with, this subsidy applied to the stocks of the 1960, 1961 and 1962 crops, but soon it was extended to almost all tobacco exports. At prices prevailing in 1966, this amounted to an ad valorem subsidy of about 7 per cent.

TABLE 6.11   *US tobacco exports: the extent of government support*
(in million kg)

Year/Annual average for period	Exports supported by government schemes	Total exports	Proportion of supported sales: in percentages
1961–1965	36.0	223.0	16.1
1966	60.3	250.0	24.1
1967	58.1	259.6	22.4
1968	61.6	271.6	22.7
1969	86.5	261.9	33.0
1970	92.3	231.5	39.9

Source: Commonwealth Secretariat, London, *Tobacco Intelligence*, Vol. 23, No. 5 (May 1971), p. 122.
Note:
(a) All figures have been converted into metric weights.
(b) The annual average for the period 1961–1965 has been calculated from data for individual years.

of one kind or another. Basically, they took the following forms:[35] (a) government-financed exports under the PL480, which included foreign currency sales and long term dollar credit sales; (b) barter transactions, which meant that tobacco was exchanged for materials and services used by US agencies abroad; and (c) sales by the Commodity Credit Corporation which extended short term credit to buyers. Most of these measures were aimed primarily at the developing countries, although there were some barter transactions with European countries.[36] All these support policies were successful, particularly as supplies were readily forthcoming from stocks accumulated in the past.

Thus we see that the USA and South Korea were the only two countries which managed to increase their exports of flue-cured tobacco after the embargo on Rhodesian trade. But it is curious that, between 1965 and 1969, these countries increased their exports by only 70 million kg, whereas in 1965, Rhodesian exports had been about 122 million kg. The discrepancy can easily be explained by the fact that a large proportion of the Rhodesian crop was marketed

[35] This description is based on statistical information published in *Tobacco Intelligence* (May 1971), see p. 122.
[36] Ibid. For example, sales in exchange for the local currencies of importing countries were made to South Vietnam and Taiwan. Long term dollar credit sales were made to the Philippines and the Congo. In addition to Taiwan, there were barter deals with Italy, Denmark and the UK.

TABLE 6.12   *Average unit value of tobacco exports: selected countries* (in $/kg)

Year	World	USA	Canada	Rhodesia	India	Brazil	South Korea
1960	1.23	1.69	1.55	1.20	0.75	0.59	0.50
1964	1.20	1.78	1.47	1.01	0.66	0.47	0.38
1969	1.31	2.06	2.30	–	0.81	0.55	0.67

Source: FAO, *Trade Yearbook, 1966* and *1970*.

Note: The average unit values have been calculated from data on the value and volume of exports from each country.

clandestinely. Precise data are obviously not available, but estimates suggest that Rhodesian exports averaged about 50 million kg per annum in the embargo years.[37]

Let us now turn to our second question. In view of the above discussion, India's relatively poor export performance after 1965 might be partially attributable to the effective subsidisation methods adopted by the US Government. Clearly, this is not the complete explanation. After all, even as a new entrant to the world market, South Korea managed to increase its exports significantly. An important part of the answer must, therefore, lie in the competitiveness of Indian tobacco.

India's competitiveness and the exportable surplus

The competitive position of Indian tobacco should be considered in relation to countries that export the flue-cured type of tobacco.[38] Table 6.12 outlines the changes in the average unit value of unmanufactured tobacco exported from such countries. It seems that the average price of South Korean tobacco was much lower than that of others, which partially explains its export success after 1965. With the exception of South Korea and Brazil, India also enjoyed a tremendous advantage in price competitiveness. We find that the average price of tobacco exported from India was substantially lower than that from the USA, Canada and Rhodesia, throughout the 1960s. How-

---

[37] FAO, *Commodity Review, 1968* (Rome), pp. 129–31.

[38] Flue-cure is the name given to a particular method of processing tobacco, in which the leaf is dried and cured by being heated in basins. The fuel used for this purpose is coal. The advantage of this particular process is that it takes only five to six days, which makes it the quickest method of curing tobacco; see *Tobacco Exports*, p. 43.

TABLE 6.13   *Average yield in countries exporting flue-cured*
Virginia tobacco (annual averages in kg per hectare)

Period	India	USA	Canada	Rhodesia	South Korea
1961–1965	820	2150	1870	1210	1420
1966–1970	840	2250	1870	n.a.	1790

Source: FAO, *Production Yearbook, 1966* and *1970*.
Note: The average yield has been calculated from data on the area under cultivation and total output of tobacco in each country.

ever, it is quite likely that this advantage was neutralised by the relatively poor quality of tobacco produced in India.[39]

Traditional methods of cultivation not only led to poor quality, but also resulted in relatively low productivity as compared with competing countries. Table 6.13 shows that the average yield in India was much lower than in other countries producing and exporting flue-cured Virginia tobacco. What is more, productivity was quite stagnant over the decade. Clearly, these factors must have reduced the competitive strength of India's exports. This need not have been the case had better methods of cultivation been employed.[40] The introduction of improved varieties, the correct application of fertiliser and the use of appropriate agronomic practices, would certainly have raised the average yield per acre and improved the quality of the tobacco leaf.

However, even if such production techniques had been adopted and Indian tobacco were competitive in quality,[41] it is not certain that the export performance would have been any better. In fact, it is doubtful

---

[39] It is now generally accepted that Indian Virginia tobacco is of relatively poor quality, specially as compared with the North American leaf. Its high dust content only makes matters worse; see A. Hone and V. K. Saxena, 'Exports in the Fourth Plan', *Economic and Political Weekly* (Special Number 1970), p. 1279. Moreover, many importing countries have complained about the quality of Indian tobacco. For a detailed discussion on this aspect of the problem, see *Export Prospects of Tobacco*, a study by the National Council of Applied Economic Research (NCAER) (New Delhi, 1966), pp. vi and 126.

[40] According to the NCAER study (ibid. p. 16) the principal reasons for the stagnant yield in India have been the shortage of improved inputs and the slow response of tobacco farmers (arising partially out of their resource limitations) to the new methods of cultivation.

[41] In the case of tobacco, unlike that of manufactured goods, low prices cannot be a substitute for quality because Indian tobacco is used in blends, and if it has a high dust content it has an adverse effect on the quality of the final product, i.e. cigarettes. Thus low prices could not have induced buyers to increase the proportion of Indian Virginia tobacco in the final blend, while relatively poor quality may have induced them to look elsewhere for supplies.

TABLE 6.14 *Production and consumption of flue-cured Virginia tobacco in India* (in million kg)

Year	Production	Domestic consumption
1961/62	77.1	24.2
1962/63	84.4	24.0
1963/64	114.3	23.3
1964/65	94.3	28.2
1965/66	78.0	33.6
1966/67	102.5	33.6
1967/68	105.2	35.9
1968/69	133.4	39.5
1969/70	89.8	40.1

Source:

(a) For production figures: Commonwealth Secretariat, London, *Tobacco Intelligence*, vol. 24, no. 3 (March 1972), p. 75.

(b) For consumption figures: 1961/62 to 1965/66, *Tobacco Exports*, p. 16; 1966/67 to 1969/70; *Tobacco Intelligence* (May 1971), p. 121.

Note:

(a) All figures from *Tobacco Intelligence* have been converted into metric weights.

(b) The difference between domestic production and consumption need not equal exports because of changes in the level of stocks, and variations in the weight of tobacco, resulting from the amount of moisture contained in it.

whether India could have generated an adequate exportable surplus in tobacco, to meet the shortfall in world supplies created by the imposition of sanctions against Rhodesia. Our hypothesis is based on two factors: (a) during the 1960s, the pressure of domestic demand increased considerably, and (b) supply conditions in the tobacco industry were not conducive to increases in output. Available evidence seems to confirm this reasoning.

Pressure of domestic demand

The bulk of India's exports consist of flue-cured Virginia tobacco. Therefore, in order to analyse the pressure of domestic demand, it is necessary to examine the trend in the home consumption of this variety of tobacco. Table 6.14, which outlines the trends in the production and consumption of flue-cured Virginia tobacco in India, clearly shows that domestic consumption grew very rapidly. In fact, between 1961/62 and 1969/70, it increased by almost 66 per cent, rising from 24.2 million kg to 40.1 million kg. The factors behind this rapid growth are not difficult to find. The income elasticity of demand for tobacco in India has been estimated at o.5, and given the relatively low per capita consumption, the demand for tobacco was bound to increase with rising incomes. However, Virginia tobacco, which is used primarily in the manufacture of cigarettes, is a special case, because the income elasticity of demand for cigarettes is much higher, and is estimated to be a little over 1.2.[42] The rapid growth of the Indian cigarette industry provides confirmation. During the 1960s, the output of cigarettes grew at a compound rate of 5.4 per cent per annum.[43] In view of this, it is not surprising that the home consumption of flue-cured Virginia tobacco increased as fast as it actually did.

Supply conditions

Apart from the rising trend in consumption, Table 6.14 also brings out the sharp fluctuations in the production of flue-cured tobacco. Clearly, these fluctuations in the level of output must have disrupted the steady supply of an exportable surplus. Hence, it is necessary to trace the roots of this problem. *Prima facie*, variations in output appear to be the direct result of fluctuations in the area under tobacco cultivation. In India, the production of flue-cured Virginia tobacco is concentrated almost entirely in Andhra Pradesh, and in this state, between 1961/62 and 1969/70, the area under tobacco fluctuated widely from 377 thousand to 568 thousand acres.[44] There could have been three possible reasons for such changes in the acreage from year to year: (*a*) uncertainty of demand and prices; (*b*) inadequate supply of necessary inputs; and (*c*) competition from other cash crops. Let us look into each of these.

As for the first, it may be argued that the introduction of minimum export prices for different grades of flue-cured tobacco, by the Government in 1963, would have eliminated the tobacco farmers' risk by ensuring a floor price return. In reality, however, the benefits of this policy did not accrue to the small farmers, because of their inability to sort the produce according to recognised grades.[45]

---

[42] For estimates of income elasticity, see *Export Prospects of Tobacco*, pp. 9 and 156.

[43] The production of cigarettes in India increased from 36,971 million pieces in 1960 to 59,714 million pieces in 1969; see *Tobacco: A Statistical Handbook*, Tobacco Export Promotion Council (Madras, 1970).

[44] *Tobacco Intelligence* (March 1972), vol. 24, no. 3, pp. 74–5. Throughout the decade, more than 90 per cent of India's flue-cured Virginia tobacco was harvested in Andhra Pradesh.

[45] For a detailed discussion of the reasons cited in this paragraph, see P. Ramaswamy and H. T. Sapra, 'Export Trade in Unmanufactured Tobacco', *Foreign Trade Review*, Indian Institute of Foreign Trade (New Delhi, April–June 1968), p. 98.

Generally, they resorted to some kind of makeshift grading which did not always conform to grades specified by the Government, thereby leaving the traders free to offer arbitrary prices. Quite often, the traders exploited the situation by paying prices which were much lower than the quality would have required. The farmers could not know the appropriate price because there was no open market for tobacco. They sold their output to buying depots of companies at whatever prices the latter offered. Given the fact that four companies purchase three-fourths of the total production,[46] the small farmer had little choice or bargaining power in the matter. Thus we see that the government price support policies did not really help eliminate the uncertainties faced by the farmer.

In principle, it is always possible for the tobacco grower to obtain the necessary inputs, provided he has access to adequate finances. In practice, however, availability of credit is a major problem and indirect evidence suggests that this is a strong constraint on potential tobacco supplies. Tobacco cultivation is estimated to cost Rs700–800 per acre,[47] but even in the most important tobacco growing areas, farmers can obtain barely Rs10 per acre in the form of co-operative credit.[48] It is obvious that tobacco growers would have had to resort to borrowing, unless they could raise their own resources. In rural areas, the main sources of finance are moneylenders or big farmers, all of whom charge exorbitant interest rates. Alternatively, tobacco trading companies supply credit in the form of inputs, in exchange for which the farmer is tied down to sell his produce to the same company, irrespective of the fact that he may have been able to obtain higher prices elsewhere.[49] In view of such high costs of credit, it is not surprising that the farmers were unable to use the necessary inputs.

As if this were not enough, cultivation of tobacco was also adversely affected by relatively favourable prices of competing cash crops. The main alternatives to tobacco are sugar cane, groundnut, chillies and turmeric. It appears that these crops offered increasing competition to tobacco, thereby lowering its relative profitability to the farmer. Let us take the example of chillies and turmeric, which are the main alternative cash crops in many tobacco growing areas of Andhra

[46] *Export Prospects of Tobacco*, pp. 74–5.

[47] Ibid. p. 81.

[48] Ramaswamy and Sapra (p. 98) estimate that, on the average, a tobacco cultivator can manage about Rs9.50 per acre of co-operative credit.

[49] For details, see *Export Prospects of Tobacco*, p. 81. It is estimated that 40 per cent of the credit extended to tobacco growers comes from local moneylenders, while another 10 per cent comes from the tobacco companies. The rest is raised by farmers themselves.

TABLE 6.15   *Wholesale price index of tobacco and competing crops*
(1961/2 = 100)

	1965/6	1966/7	1967/8	1968/9	1969/70	1970/1
Tobacco	134.7	127.7	134.2	201.0	190.2	154.6
Spices	135.4	183.2	178.9	205.5	340.8	333.1
Groundnuts	141.8	187.6	165.1	149.4	199.3	214.8

Source: RBI Bombay, *Report on Currence and Finance, 1970/71*, pp. S30–31.

Pradesh. If we take the wholesale price index of spices as an approximation of changes in the price of chillies and turmeric, the data in Table 6.15 show that, after 1965/66, their prices rose much faster than that of Virginia tobacco. In some years, groundnut prices also registered a greater increase. It is these relative price movements that resulted in the wide fluctuations of area under tobacco in Andhra Pradesh.

We have now shown how the uncertainty of prices, the lack of credit and the higher profitability of competing cash crops operated as constraints on the supply of tobacco. Export supplies did not even respond very well to improved prices because a large proportion of the profits in the industry were appropriated by traders and exporters. It has been estimated that a tobacco farmer's profit amounted to only 18.7 per cent of the export price, while 10.1 per cent accrued to the exporter as profit, and 8.5 per cent was the trader's margin.[50] This study of the cost structure was carried out in Guntur, which is one of the most important tobacco districts of Andhra Pradesh. Although it relates only to 1963/64, it does reveal that the marketing system must have been biased in favour of the trader. Higher returns to tobacco growers would certainly have provided an incentive for increasing output and yield.[51]

[50] Ibid. p. 28.
[51] Our point is proved by the success of a pilot project in Guntur, Andhra Pradesh. In 1964, the Government sponsored the setting up of a tobacco growers' co-operative society, which procured the tobacco, graded it, and then marketed it by an auction system – on the basis of parity prices fixed by Agmark grades; see *Tobacco Exports*, p. 55. This system was a tremendous success because it ensured that farmers were given prices commensurate with the quality of their output. In fact, prices realised through the co-operative were 16–31 per cent higher than what farmers normally received from the traders; see *Export Prospects for Tobacco*, p. 74. However, the Guntur co-operative remained only an isolated example. In fact, there was no open market for tobacco, and farmers had to sell to the trading company depots at prices fixed by the latter. It is pretty clear that the only way higher returns to growers can be ensured is if they grade and market their produce themselves through an auction system.

The effect of devaluation

To a large extent, the factors discussed above explain India's relatively poor export performance in tobacco during the latter half of the 1960s. However, it might well be argued that the 57.5 per cent devaluation of the rupee in 1966 should have helped tobacco exports by raising the relative profitability of exports, on the assumption that the foreign exchange price remained unchanged. In theory, this favourable impact is quite plausible, but in practice it did not happen for the following reasons.

In the first place, a significant proportion of the devaluation was neutralised by the imposition of a 20 per cent ad valorem duty on the exports of unmanufactured tobacco. This meant that the net devaluation of 26.1 per cent was only half the apparent depreciation in the exchange rate.[52] Second, the devaluation coincided with one of the poorest agricultural seasons for many years, as a result of which, exportable supplies were already at a very low level. Thus there was little possibility of increasing the volume of exports in the short run. The tobacco crop did recover in 1967, but by that time, the competitive advantage arising out of devaluation was almost neutralised. The closure of the Suez Canal in June 1967 pushed up the freight rates, while devaluation of the pound sterling in November 1967 eliminated the cost advantage that Indian tobacco might have gained in its principal market.[53] Thirdly, there was no improvement in the quality of the tobacco leaf produced in India, and competitiveness continued to suffer on this account.[54]

Summary

The main conclusions to emerge from this chapter can be summed up as follows.

(a) Although India's exports of cashew kernels increased rapidly throughout the 1960s, she lost her monopolistic position in the world market. Increasing competition from Mozambique, Brazil and

---

[52] For details of calculation, see Table 11.3.

[53] During the 1960s, the UK market absorbed nearly half of India's tobacco exports; an average figure calculated from statistics published by DGCIS, Calcutta.

[54] Personal discussion with the representative of a leading West German tobacco company revealed that India failed to increase her exports to the West European markets, because she could not meet the quality requirements in these countries. While the demand in Europe was for a low nicotine, thin leaf and neutral tasting tobacco, India could supply only a relatively high nicotine and strong Virginia tobacco. See also *Tobacco Exports*, pp. 49–50.

Summary

Tanzania was responsible for the decline in India's share of world exports, during the latter half of the decade. The principal reason why India failed to increase her exports faster than she actually did was the totally inadequate domestic production of raw cashew nuts. Surprisingly enough, very little was done to reduce the dependence on imports and step up cashew cultivation in India.

(b) There was an impressive growth in exports of tobacco from 1960 to 1964, in which period, India increased her share of world trade. Given this trend, as a large supplier of flue-cured Virginia tobacco, one would have expected India to do well out of the embargo on Rhodesian tobacco after 1965. In fact, however, India's exports of tobacco in the second half ot the 1960s declined, and stagnated at a lower level. This may have been partially attributable to the sale of large quantities of tobacco by USA on concessional terms, but the main explanation lies in domestic factors. While low yields and poor quality worsened the competitiveness, increasing domestic consumption and restrictive supply conditions reduced the quantities of Virginia tobacco available for export.

7
Minerals

Among the exports of unprocessed raw materials from India, mineral ores have always been quantitatively significant. Iron ore, manganese ore and mica, which together constitute the bulk of these exports, increased their share in total export earnings from a little over 6 per cent in 1960/61 to nearly 10 per cent in 1970/71. It is necessary to point out that this aggregate figure conceals the distinctly different export trends in each of these minerals. Whereas the exports of iron ore grew at a phenomenal pace during the ten-year period, the exports of mica were virtually stagnant and manganese ore exports actually declined. The following analysis attempts to examine the reasons underlying these trends.

I. IRON ORE

Table 7.1 brings out the striking growth in India's iron ore exports during the period under study. Export earnings increased more than four times, rising from $35.8 million in 1960 to $158.7 million in 1970. Over the same period of time, the quantity of ore exported increased even more, rising from 3.2 to 21.2 million tons – at a compound rate of 20.8 per cent per annum. As a result of this rapid growth, the share of iron ore in total export earnings increased from 2.7 per cent in 1960/61 to 7.6 per cent in 1970/71.[1] This share may have been higher if iron ore prices had stayed at their 1960 level. In reality, the prices declined, which is quite apparent from the downward trend in the average unit value of India's exports. Admittedly, it is difficult to make generalisations about iron ore prices, because of vast differences in the grade and quality of ores, but there is little doubt that the world price of iron ore fell steadily during the 1960s.[2] Notwithstanding the falling prices, India's foreign exchange earnings from iron ore grew at a phenomenal pace, the reasons for which are most likely to be found in the rapidly expanding world market for iron ore.

---

[1] Table 2.6.
[2] See a Report of the UNCTAD Secretariat on *Problems of the World Market for Iron Ore*, TD/B/C.1/104 (Geneva, 30 April 1971), p. 11.

TABLE 7.1   *India's exports of iron ore*

Year	Volume in million tons	Value in $ million	Average unit value in $ per ton
1960	3.2	35.8	11.19
1961	3.3	37.6	11.39
1962	8.8	70.4	8.00
1963	9.3	74.4	8.00
1964	10.0	74.4	7.44
1965	11.3	82.8	7.33
1966	13.3	96.8	7.28
1967	13.5	100.8	7.47
1968	15.6	115.3	7.39
1969	15.1	117.3	7.77
1970	21.2	158.7	7.49

Source: RBI Bombay, *Report on Currency and Finance, 1969/70*, p. 79, and *1970/71*, p. 97.

Note: All figures relate to calendar years, except the one for 1960, which is taken from DGCIS statistics and relates to the fiscal year beginning 1 April. Export earnings have been converted into US dollars, and the average unit value has been calculated.

World demand for iron ore

The demand for iron ore derives from the requirements of the world iron and steel industry. More than 90 per cent of the iron ore mined is used in the manufacture of pig iron, and the remainder is consumed directly in steel furnaces.[3] In turn, pig iron is consumed mostly in the production of steel. It is quite obvious that the demand for iron ore would be closely related to the production of pig iron, and hence, the world steel output.

In the 1960s, the world iron and steel industry grew very rapidly. Between 1960 and 1969, world production of pig iron rose by 80 per cent and the world output of crude steel increased by 75 per cent.[4] This expansion of the steel industry is reflected in the world consump-

[3] UNCTAD, *Commodity Survey, 1966* (New York, 1966), p. 169. It is necessary to remember that steel production does not rely entirely on the use of ore. Nearly 40 per cent of the steel produced in the world comes from scrap, i.e. metal recovered from steel plants, other manufacturing units, and the disposal of obsolete machinery and equipment.

[4] World production of pig iron increased from 231.3 million tons in 1960 to 417.2 million tons in 1969; over the same period, the world output of crude steel increased from 327.6 million tons to 572.3 million tons. See UN *Statistical Yearbook, 1966*, pp. 300–1; and *1970*, pp. 307–8.

TABLE 7.2   *Apparent world consumption of iron ore* (in million tons)

Year	USSR	EEC	USA	Japan	Eastern Europe	UK	Total world
1960	90	123	119	17	28	35	455
1969	152	147	126	85	46	31	678

Source: UNCTAD, Report on *Iron Ore*, p. 7.

Note: Apparent consumption denotes production within the country plus imports, net of any exports of iron ore. It is a reasonable index of actual consumption, from which it differs only due to changes in stock.

tion of iron ore, which, as brought out in Table 7.2, increased from 455 million tons in 1960 to 678 million tons in 1969. In fact, such gross weight statistics understate the growth in demand for iron-in-ore, because the average iron content of the ore marketed increased continuously during the 1960s.[5]

World import requirements more than matched this substantial rise in demand. The primary reason was the declining self-sufficiency of the main iron-ore-consumption areas. For example, between 1960 and 1969, the self-sufficiency ratio declined from 74.9 to 71.3 per cent in the USA, from 11.3 to 2.2 per cent in Japan, from 49.7 to 39.9 per cent in the UK, from 29.8 to 14.3 per cent in West Germany, and from 33.3 to 10.2 per cent in Italy.[6] As a result, although world consumption grew by only 50 per cent, world exports of iron ore increased by 80 per cent.

Table 7.3 outlines the trend in world exports of iron ore and highlights the changes in relative shares of the main exporting countries. We find that world exports increased from 155.4 million tons in 1960 to 280.5 million tons in 1969. At the same time, India's exports rose somewhat faster, and increased from 3.2 to 15.1 million tons. Consequently, India's share in world exports more than doubled, from 2.1 per cent in 1960 to 5.4 per cent in 1969. It is necessary to note that India's exports did not increase faster than world exports throughout the decade. In fact, as is apparent from the above table, by 1964, India's share in the world total was already 5.1 per cent. This sharp increase in such a short time is to a large extent attributable to the inclusion of Goa in the Indian Union. Although separate export figures are not available, production statistics do indicate Goa's output of iron ore. Between 1964 and 1969 the production of iron ore in

[5] Cf. *World Market for Iron Ore*, United Nations (New York, 1968).

[6] UNCTAD, Report on *Iron Ore*, statistical annex, p. 3. The self-sufficiency ratio is simply the production of iron ore expressed as a percentage of apparent consumption.

TABLE 7.3   *World exports of iron ore* (in million tons)

	1960	1964	1967	1969
India	3.2	10.1	13.6	15.1
Brazil	5.2	9.3	14.3	21.7
Chile	5.2	9.1	9.9	9.9
Liberia	3.0	11.9	17.3	20.7
Peru	5.2	6.3	7.9	9.8
Venezuela	19.3	14.6	16.5	19.0
Sweden	19.7	24.2	23.4	32.0
USSR	15.2	22.6	28.9	34.0
Canada	17.2	31.0	35.7	28.4
Australia	–	–	9.2	26.9
World total including others	155.4	198.4	232.5	280.5
Relative shares (in percentages)				
India	2.1	5.1	5.8	5.4
Brazil	5.3	4.7	6.1	7.7
Liberia	1.9	6.0	7.4	7.4
Venezuela	12.4	7.4	7.1	6.7
Sweden	12.7	12.2	10.1	11.4
USSR	9.8	11.4	12.4	12.1
Canada	11.1	15.6	15.4	10.1
Australia	–	–	4.0	9.6

Source: For 1960, 1967 and 1969: UNCTAD, Report on *Iron Ore*, Annex p. 5. For 1964: *World Market for Iron Ore*, United Nations, pp. 60–5.

Goa averaged about 7 million tons per annum.[7] In order to estimate the proportion of this output exported, we have to resort to an indirect method. According to statistics published in 1964, India's exports of iron ore in 1962 were 3.8 million tons;[8] subsequently this figure was revised to 8.8 million tons.[9] It is justifiable to conclude that the inclusion of Goa in the Indian Union added to the country's iron ore exports by approximately 5 million tons in 1962. Thereafter, although India's exports increased continuously, iron ore production in Goa remained more or less stagnant. Clearly, the subsequent increase in exports originated from other areas in the country.

All said and done, by itself, India's export performance in the world iron ore market appears quite impressive. But the performance of

[7] RBI Bombay, *Report on Currency and Finance*, 1969/70, p. 79.
[8] Cf. RBI Bombay, *Report on Currency and Finance*, 1963/64, p. 37.
[9] See Table 7.1.

TABLE 7.4   *The principal markets for Indian iron ore* (in $ million)

	1961/62–1963/64 Annual average	1965/66	1968/69–1970/71 Annual average
Japan	44.1	62.9	105.6
Czechoslovakia	8.9	6.4	6.1
Rumania	3.9	4.7	8.5
Yugoslavia	2.3	3.3	1.3
West Germany	4.8	4.1	2.2
Italy	4.8	0.8	–
Total including others	75.0	88.4	132.3
Relative shares (in percentages)			
Japan	58.8	71.2	79.8
Czechoslovakia	11.9	7.2	4.6
Rumania	5.2	5.3	6.4
Yugoslavia	3.1	3.7	1.0
West Germany	6.4	4.6	1.7
Italy	6.4	0.9	–

Source: Statistics published by DGCIS, Calcutta.
Note: Figures relate to Indian fiscal years beginning 1 April, and have been converted into US dollars. The annual averages have been computed from data for individual years.

many other countries, e.g. Brazil, Liberia and Australia, was even better. Between 1960 and 1969, Brazil increased her share of world exports from 3.3 to 7.7 per cent, and Liberia increased her share from 1.9 to 7.4 per cent. Australia, which started exporting only in the late 1960s, managed to capture almost 10 per cent of the world market by 1969.[10]

Market distribution of India's iron ore exports

Apart from world demand, an important factor behind the rapid expansion of India's iron ore exports was the nature of the markets. Table 7.4 outlines the trend in exports to the country's principal markets for iron ore, and shows the overwhelming importance of the Japanese market. We find that the average annual proportion of

[10] This late entry of Australia into the world market is explained by the twenty-two year embargo on iron ore exports, which was lifted only in 1960. Prospecting began soon after, and it was only a few years before Australian exports entered the world market in a big way.

TABLE 7.5   *World imports of iron ore by origin*
(in million tons)

Year	EEC	Japan	USA	East Europe	UK	Total world
1960	62	15	35	19	18	156
	(40)	(10)	(23)	(12)	(11)	
1969	96	83	41	33	19	280
	(34)	(30)	(15)	(12)	(7)	

Source: UNCTAD, Report on *Iron Ore*, p. 8.
Note: Figures in brackets denote percentage shares.

exports going to Japan increased from 58.8 per cent in the three-year period 1961/62–1963/64 to 79.8 per cent during 1968/69–1970/71. Export earnings from this market also increased greatly, and shot up from $44.1 million to $105.6 million over the same period. On the other hand, the share of East European countries, viz. Czechoslovakia, Rumania and Yugoslavia fell from 20.2 per cent in 1961/62–1963/64 to 12 per cent in 1968/69–1970/71, while the share of West Germany and Italy fell even more drastically from 12.8 to 1.7 per cent. There are two basic trends underlying these statistics: (*a*) during the 1960s, an increasing proportion of India's iron ore exports found its way into the Japanese market; and (*b*) apart from East European countries, the rest of the markets became increasingly insignificant; in fact, at the end of the decade, Japan and Eastern Europe together absorbed nearly 92 per cent of India's exports. Both these trends favoured a rapid export growth owing to the continuous expansion in import requirements of these countries. Table 7.5, which outlines the changes in the world import demand for iron ore, shows quite clearly that Japan was the most dynamic and fastest growing market in the world. Of the other iron-ore-consuming regions, Eastern Europe was the only one that maintained its share in world imports. It is quite obvious how the shifts in market distribution, during the 1960s, aided India's export performance in this commodity. However, the resulting concentration of exports in virtually one market is likely to have important implications for the future prospects. Let us explore the possibilities.

Table 7.6, which gives a break-up of Japan's imports of iron ore from important sources, reveals that between 1960 and 1969, India's exports to Japan trebled, but at the same time, Japan's imports increased more than five times. With the exception of Malaysia, the export performance of all the other competing countries appears to

TABLE 7.6   *Japan's imports of iron ore from important sources*
(in million tons)

Year	From India	From Malaysia	From Chile	From Peru	From Australia	Total imports
1960	4.4	5.4	0.2	0.6	–	14.9
1961	4.9	6.6	2.2	2.4	–	20.9
1962	4.5	6.5	3.0	2.5	–	22.1
1963	5.8	6.7	3.3	2.9	–	26.0
1964	6.8	6.6	5.4	3.5	0.1	31.2
1965	7.9	7.0	6.9	4.5	0.2	39.0
1966	10.2	5.8	7.6	5.1	2.0	46.1
1967	10.8	5.2	8.1	6.8	8.3	56.7
1968	12.8	5.1	8.7	7.4	13.8	68.2
1969	13.6	5.4	7.8	8.6	23.2	83.2

Source: British Steel Corporation, *Annual Statistical Handbook*, vol. I, several issues.
Note: The 1960 and 1961 figures on the imports from India include imports from Goa, and
therefore do not tally with India's export statistics in Table 7.1.

have been better than that of India. From virtually nothing in 1960,
imports from Chile and Peru rose to 7.8 and 8.6 million tons respectively, in 1969. Australia, which emerged as a producer only after
1965, captured more than a quarter of the Japanese market by 1969,
whereas India's share contracted from 30 per cent in 1960 to 16 per
cent in 1969. Thus we see that India steadily lost her share in the
Japanese market. If this trend continues, in the long run it might have
an adverse effect on exports of iron ore from India.

The boom in the Japanese steel industry during the period under
study is definite evidence in support of the proposition that demand
was no constraint. In fact, it is generally accepted that supply conditions in the Indian iron ore industry constituted a bottleneck, thereby
preventing export performance from being better than it actually was.

Supply constraints in India

In the 1960s, the production of iron ore in India grew quite rapidly.
The amount of iron ore mined in the country increased by about 150
per cent. Table 7.7 brings out the trends in domestic production and
exports. We find that exports increased much faster than production.
While the country's iron ore output rose from 12.3 million tons in
1961 to 30.8 million tons in 1970, exports increased from 3.3 to 21.2

TABLE 7.7   *Domestic production and exports of iron ore from India* (in million tons)

Year	Production	Exports	Year-end stocks	Export–output percentage ratio
1961	12.3	3.3	3.4	26.8
1964	21.4	10.0	1.4	46.7
1967	25.8	13.5	3.8	52.3
1970	30.8	21.2	1.7	68.8

Source: RBI Bombay, *Report on Currency and Finance, 1969/70*, p. 79 and *1970/71*, p. 97.
Note: The output of Goa is included in the production figures with effect from 1964.

million tons. Consequently, the proportion of output exported increased steadily throughout. It is only reasonable to infer that the pressure of domestic demand did not cut into the potential exportable surplus. Thus, it seems certain that India's exports could not keep pace with the growth of the Japanese market because the increase in output was relatively slow. In order to analyse the supply conditions which led to this, it would be useful to begin with a brief description of the structure of India's iron ore industry.[11]

India's iron ore resources are scattered all over the country.[12] The ownership of the industry is equally widely dispersed. In 1966, there were 450 mines in the country and most of them were operated by small entrepreneurs in the private sector. Until the mid-1960s, iron ore mining was conducted essentially on a small scale, employing traditional (sometimes primitive) techniques.[13] Large scale mechanised mining was first attempted in the early 1960s, when the Government set up a National Mineral Development Corporation. Towards the end of the decade this corporation had already developed some, and

[11] The following description of the iron ore industry has been drawn from several issues of the *Report on Currency and Finance*, published annually by RBI Bombay; and an article by G. Narain, 'Exports of Mineral Ores', *Foreign Trade Review*, quarterly journal of the Indian Institute of Foreign Trade (New Delhi, July–September 1966).

[12] The states of Orissa, Goa and Madhya Pradesh are the main producers of iron ore and account for 65 per cent of the country's output. Bihar and Mysore come next, contributing 25 per cent of the total production; see *Report on Currency and Finance, 1969/70*, p. 78.

[13] According to the UNCTAD Report on *Iron Ore*, p. 26, even now, small-scale primitively equipped mines account for a significant proporition of total output.

was working on a few more, large mines in order to meet export commitments.[14] Export trade in iron ore throughout the country is conducted solely by the state-owned Minerals and Metals Trading Corporation, except in Goa where private traders are allowed to compete with it.

In any country, a rapidly growing iron ore industry must have its basis in efficient large scale mining, and, in view of the bulky nature of the product, must be endowed with a suitable transportation network to the point of export, and adequate port and shipping facilities thereafter. The Indian iron ore industry suffered from bottlenecks on all these counts. Its problems, which are generally recognised, can be summed up as follows.

(*a*) For many decades, iron ore mining in India has been conducted on a small scale, so that traditional labour intensive techniques are almost a natural corollary. It was difficult for such mines to raise the quantity and quality of their output significantly. They could not afford crushing or screening plants, and as such, had the practical difficulty of being unable to guarantee size specifications required in an increasingly competitive world market.

(*b*) Second, most of India's iron ore deposits are a considerable distance away from the coast. Hence, there was a need not only for better feeder and link roads from mines to loading stations, but also for adequate railway facilities from loading points to ports. Bottlenecks at different points in this transport network held up supplies and the development of new mines.

(*c*) Finally, port facilities in India were generally inadequate. This was so for two reasons: (1) most Indian ports could not accommodate ships of a large tonnage; and (2) the loading of the ore on to ships was done manually, and as such, it was very slow.

In the 1960s, there were many improvements in the infra-structure for the iron ore industry. The Kiruburu, Bailadila, Bellary and Hospet mine regions were all connected by railway to the nearest port. The port of Visakhapatnam was developed so as to accommodate larger

---

[14] The Kiruburu project located on the Bihar–Orissa border has an export capacity of 2 million tons per annum and has been operative since 1966. More recently, work has also been completed on the Bailadila (Madhya Pradesh) and Daitari (Orissa) mines with estimated annual export capacities of 4 and 2 million tons respectively. Apart from these, fairly substantial investments in export capacity were planned in the Bellary–Hospet area of Mysore, both in the public sector and in collaboration with the private sector, see G. Narain, *Foreign Trade Review* (July–September 1966), p. 137, and several issues of the *Report on Currency and Finance*.

ships. To some extent, loading was mechanised, as a result of which the rates of loading did improve.[15] In fact, it was only these developments that made possible the rapid growth in India's iron ore exports. But the moment we make some international comparisons it becomes clear that India faced substantial supply constraints, which put her at a disadvantage vis-à-vis the new but increasingly important exporting countries like Australia and Brazil. Let us take two examples.

(i) The transportation of iron ore from Bailadila, the largest mine in India, to the port of Visakhapatnam involves a rail journey of 475 km, over what has been described as some of the most difficult terrain in India. On the other hand, iron ore from Mt Tom Price in Australia is transported to the port of Dampier by a 290 km railway over flat and unencumbered terrain.[16]

(ii) In 1966, no port in India could handle ships of more than 25 000 tons, and loading rates averaged about 2000 tons per day. At that time, the port of Tubarao in Brazil could handle ships of up to 100 000 tons capacity and averaged a loading rate of about 6000 tons per hour.[17]

The most important difference was that, in sharp contrast to India's traditional mines, the new iron ore producing-exporting countries employed all the modern production techniques. Consequently, the projects in Brazil and Australia were planned and worked on a very large scale as fully integrated operations with mining, transportation and shipping all managed by a single agency,[18] thereby deriving many economies of scale. Production efficiency was aided further by the fact of large foreign investments in some of these projects, which guaranteed exports. In 1966, a UN study

---

[15] Exact information about the position at the time of writing is not available. However, according to the report of UNCTAD on *Iron Ore*, p. 29, the Vizag and Madras ports can take larger ships, but still not exceeding 55 000 tons. The extent of mechanisation in loading is not quantified. But it is reported that mechanical ore-handling facilities are under construction in the Vizag and Madras outer harbours. In a few years, the Government expects that the Vizag harbour will be able to accommodate 100 000-ton ships, whereas the Paradip and Marmugao harbours will be able to take 60 000-ton ore-carriers. For details, see 'Fourteenth Report of the Fifth Lok Sabha's Estimates Committee', *Ministry of Foreign Trade: Export Promotion Measures* (New Delhi, April 1972), pp. 149–50.

[16] UNCTAD, Report on *Iron Ore*, p. 29.

[17] G. Narain, *Foreign Trade Review* (July–September 1966), p. 136.

[18] Some of these massive investments were foreign in origin. Although precise data are not available, it is believed that there are substantial American investments in Brazil and Japanese investments in Australia.

found that a significant part of international trade in iron ore was between 'captive-mines' and the steel companies which controlled them.[19] India's exports of iron ore were not guaranteed by foreign capital in this manner.

The export potential

India's measured reserves of iron ore amount to approximately 8600 million tons, in addition to which there is a potential of another 20 400 million tons. A total of 29 000 million tons places India amongst the world's major potential sources of iron ore.[20] However, the mere existence of these reserves is no index of the export potential. A successful export effort has to be based on an economically viable exploitation of natural resources. But in India, the development of these resources raises immense problems. Unlike in Australia and Brazil, ore deposits are not concentrated in one district, but occur in widely separated areas.[21] This creates the very basic problem that each area has to develop independently with its own infra-structure. In an economy where resources are scarce, it may not be easy.

The problem might be compounded by the fact that nearly all large-scale investment in iron ore is linked with substantial marketing arrangements of one kind or another, so as to provide an assured outlet for most of the mined output in the principal ore-exporting countries. Long term contracts and supplying to parent companies are the most common arrangements. The proportion of the world market not covered by such arrangements is only one-third the total, and, according to some sources, this proportion is likely to decline.[22]

Towards the end of the decade under review, India signed long term supply agreements with some buyers, probably with the objective of securing future markets for its iron ore industry. The Minerals and Metals Trading Corporation of India contracted three long term agreements, one with Rumania and two with Japan, to supply about 155 million tons of iron ore in the 1970s.[23] This might have appeared to be a sound policy decision at the time, but subsequent developments

[19] UNCTAD, *Commodity Survey, 1966*, p. 180.
[20] *Survey of World Iron Ore Resources*, United Nations (New York, 1970).
[21] See *World Market for Iron Ore*, United Nations, p. 37.
[22] Cf. UNCTAD, Report on *Iron Ore*, p. 32.
[23] The agreements are: (*a*) with Rumania to supply 23.4 million tons of iron ore between 1970 and 1980; (*b*) with eight Japanese steel mills to supply 71.5 million tons of ore by 1979; cf. *Report on Currency and Finance, 1969/70*, p. 79, and (*c*) with some other Japanese steel companies to supply 61.3 million tons over nine years; cf. *Report on Currency and Finance, 1970/71*, p. 98.

TABLE 7.8   *India's exports of manganese ore*

Year	Volume in million tons	Value in $ million	Average unit value in $ per ton
1960	1.34	30.8	23.00
1961	1.00	23.1	23.10
1962	0.91	18.8	20.66
1963	0.93	17.0	18.28
1964	1.57	28.7	18.34
1965	1.13	19.5	17.26
1966	1.25	21.1	16.88
1967	1.10	16.7	15.18
1968	1.19	16.0	13.45
1969	1.34	18.1	13.51
1970	1.70	18.6	10.94

Source: For 1961–1966: RBI Bombay, *Report on Currency and Finance, 1967/68*, p. 50. For 1960 and 1967–1969: UNCTAD Secretariat, *Report on Problems of the World Market for Manganese Ore*, TD/B/C.1/105 (Geneva, May 1971), pp. 54 and 62. For 1970; statistics published by DGCIS, Calcutta.

Note: Figures of export earnings for the years 1961–1966 have been converted into US dollars. The 1970 figure relates to the fiscal year beginning 1 April. The rest relate to calendar years.

in the world market for iron ore should lead one to seriously question the wisdom of entering into such long term contractual arrangements. During the recent commodities boom, the world prices of iron ore registered a substantial increase, but India had to forgo some of the potential terms of trade gain because the contractually tied exports could not benefit from the higher prices. The Minerals and Metals Trading Corporation of India has been attempting to negotiate an increase in price for the iron ore sold through long term agreements, but has met with only limited success so far.[24]

II.   MANGANESE ORE

The success story of iron ore was not repeated in this industry. In fact, during the period under review, India's export performance in manganese ore appears quite disappointing. The falling trend in exports is brought out quite clearly by Table 7.8. Export earnings declined from $30.8 million in 1960 to $18.6 million in 1970. As a result, the share of manganese in the country's total exports fell from 2.2 to 0.9 per cent. In 1964, export receipts recovered tempor-

[24] For further discussion of this problem, see the Postscript.

TABLE 7.9 *Quality of India's manganese exports*
(in million tons)

Manganese content of ore	1960	1969
More than 35 per cent	1.1	0.5
Less than 35 per cent	0.2	0.8

Source: UNCTAD, Report on *Manganese Ore*, p. 13.

arily, almost reaching their 1960 level, but this jump was due to special circumstances in that year,[25] and not a part of the general trend which continued downward.

It is difficult to discern a definite trend in export volume as the quantity exported fluctuated widely. However, it is pretty clear that it did not decline. In fact, the average annual export volume increased from 1.08 million tons in 1960–1962 to 1.41 million tons in 1968–1970. It is obvious that the prices of manganese ore must have fallen substantially. We find that the average unit value declined continuously through the decade, falling by more than half from $23.00 per ton in 1960 to $10.94 per ton in 1970.

This drastic fall is attributable to: (*a*) the general fall in world prices of manganese ore, and (b) a deterioration in the quality of ore exported from India. It is now generally accepted that there was a marked decline in manganese ore prices during the 1960s.[26] The decline in the unit value of India's exports was even more marked because of a structural shift in its production towards lower grade ores. The expanding domestic steel industry absorbed an increasing amount of high grade ore, so that this shift had its impact on the quality of exports. Table 7.9 reveals that the proportion of high grade ore in total exports fell from 85 per cent in 1960 to 38 per cent in 1969.

It is necessary to point out that India's export performance in

[25] Private barter arrangements were largely responsible for this sharp increase in exports, so much so that, in 1964, exports exceeded production. Stocks accumulated over the past few years were disposed of. Incentives in the form of import entitlements which had induced exporters, were not possible once the state-owned MMTC took control of export trade in 1965; see G. Narain, *Foreign Trade Review* (July–September 1966), p. 138.

[26] For a detailed discussion, see Chapter V in the UNCTAD Report on *Manganese Ore*. According to this report, c.i.f. prices of manganese ore at European and US ports fell continuously through the decade (see p. 69), and the average unit value of world exports of manganese ore declined from $28.2 per ton in 1960 to $17.9 per ton in 1969 (cf. p. 64).

TABLE 7.10   *Ferro-manganese exports from India*

Year	Quantity in thousand tons	Value in $ million
1960	47.8	8.9
1961	56.3	10.6
1962	12.3	1.9
1963	21.9	3.5
1964	87.6	12.6
1965	56.4	8.0
1966	10.3	1.7
1967	29.3	3.2
1968	70.3	5.2
1969	115.4	11.3

Source: UNCTAD, Report on *Manganese Ore*, p. 57.

manganese was actually better than it appears on the surface. This is so because, during the 1960s, India began producing and exporting substantial quantities of ferro-manganese. It is interesting that with the exception of small quantities exported from Chile, India was the only developing country to export processed ore. Table 7.10, which brings out the main trends in India's exports of ferro-manganese, shows that these exports fluctuated very widely, dropping to extremely low levels in 1962 and 1966, as compared with peak performances in other years.[27] These erratic fluctuations are explained by the fact that until a few years ago, a significant proportion of ferro-manganese exports were a result of barter agreements with the US Commodity Credit Corporation in exchange for surplus agricultural products.[28] Consequently, exports of processed ore were dependent on imports of food. However, in the last three years of the decade, exports of ferro-manganese found markets without the aid of barter arrangements. *Prima facie*, such a shift towards processing appears to be a very attractive proposition. Let us take the example of 1969 to illustrate this. We know that the production of 1 ton of ferro-manganese requires 2 tons of ore.[29] Therefore, if the manganese ore used

[27] Clearly, production did not fluctuate as much. The surplus during the slack export years was easily absorbed by the expanding domestic steel industry. In 1968, domestic consumption of ferro-manganese was approximately 80 000 tons out of a total production of 160 000 tons; see *Minerals Yearbook, 1969*, vols. I–II, US Bureau of Mines (Washington), p. 682.

[28] Cf. UNCTAD, *Commodity Survey, 1966*, p. 204.

[29] UNCTAD, Report on *Manganese Ore*, p. 20.

in manufactured exports during 1969 had been exported in its unprocessed form, the volume of India's exports would have been 20 per cent higher than it was. However, processing of the ore added to export earnings by 62 per cent in the same year.

Given the much higher unit value of ferro-manganese this is hardly surprising, but it is unlikely that exports of processed ore can provide a long term solution because: (*a*) Until the mid-1960s, the cost of production of ferro-manganese in India was higher than elsewhere, basically because of the relatively higher costs of raw materials, viz. electricity and coke.[30] (*b*) Even if improved cost efficiency eliminates the divergence between domestic and world prices, exports may not be possible because imports of ferro-manganese are subject to tariffs in all importing countries.[31]

Taking exports of manganese ore and ferro-manganese together, we find that export receipts in 1969 were still 25 per cent lower than in 1960. In the following sections, we shall try and determine whether this relatively poor export performance was a result of trends in world demand or of domestic supply conditions.

World trade in manganese ore

Although precise data is not available, it has been estimated that over 90 per cent of the world output of manganese is consumed by the steel industry. The remainder is used in the manufacture of chemicals and dry-cell batteries.[32] Thus one would expect the world demand for manganese ore to be closely related to world steel output. Owing to the extremely low ratio of manganese consumption to steel production, this demand is also likely to be inelastic.[33]

A fair idea of the trends in world demand can be obtained by looking at world imports, because, apart from USSR and Japan, none of the important steel producing countries have any resources of manganese ore. Table 7.11 shows that, between 1960 and 1969, world

---

[30] For more details, see G. Narain, *Foreign Trade Review* (July–September 1966), p. 141–2.

[31] Despite reductions under the Kennedy Round in 1972, tariffs in the main importing countries were as follows:

	EEC	Japan	UK	USA
Rates of tariff	4–8%	12–15%	0–8%	7–39%

Source: UNCTAD, Report on *Manganese Ore*, p. 30.

[32] UNCTAD, *Commodity Survey, 1966*, p. 203, and *1968*, p. 84.

[33] According to the UNCTAD Report on *Manganese Ore*, p. 8, on the average, only 6.8 kg of manganese is required in the production of one ton of steel, and this ratio has remained unchanged over the last two decades.

TABLE 7.11 *World imports of manganese ore by origin*
(actual weight in thousand tons)

Year	EEC	Japan	UK	USA	East Europe	Others	World total
1960	1658	242	531	2307	732	574	6054
1969	2247	2025	438	1783	945	1186	8634

Source: UNCTAD, Report on *Manganese Ore*, p. 59.

imports of manganese ore increased by approximately 40 per cent, which was significantly less than the increase in steel production. This lag in import demand for manganese is explained by two special factors: (*a*) Japan, which had the fastest growing and most dynamic steel industry, used a relatively smaller quantity of manganese per ton of steel.[34] (*b*) The US, which as the largest importer of manganese ore in the world in 1960, reduced its imports substantially during the latter half of the 1960s, and met its needs by running down the huge stockpile which had been accumulated over the years.[35]

Despite these slowing down factors, world trade in manganese ore did grow at a reasonable rate. Table 7.12 outlines the trend in world exports of manganese ore and brings out the changing relative shares of the main exporting countries. We find that between 1960 and 1969, world exports increased from 6.1 to 8.5 million tons, but India's exports remained stagnant at about 1.3 million tons. Consequently, India lost her position as the leading exporter, and her share in world exports fell from 21.9 per cent to 15.8 per cent. Other traditional exporters, such as Congo, Ghana, and Brazil also lost their share in the world market. However, over the same period of time, Gabon (which started exporting only in 1962) and Australia greatly increased their shares in the world market, and by 1969, had captured a quarter of it. Among the other main exporting countries, USSR and South Africa increased their exports substantially. Given the fact that there were no commercial policy impediments to trade in manganese ore, how can one account for these sharply divergent performances of different exporting countries?

One possible explanation lies in the structure of the world market for manganese ore. Although there were no trade barriers, a fairly large proportion of the world market was restricted and not accessible to all exporters. This was so for two reasons:[36] (*a*) about 15 per cent of

---

[34] Ibid. p. 8.

[35] Ibid. p. 33.

[36] The following discussion is based on the findings of the UNCTAD Secretariat. For details, see the Report on *Manganese Ore*, pp. 27–9.

TABLE 7.12 *World exports of manganese ore* (actual weight in thousand tons)

Year	India	Brazil	Congo	Gabon	Ghana	USSR	South Africa	Australia	World total
1960	1342	866	305	–	555	973	881	47	6126
1969	1340	872	245	1549	329	1197	1821	653	8475
				Relative shares (in percentages)					
1960	21.9	14.1	5.0	–	9.1	15.9	14.4	0.8	100.0
1969	15.8	10.3	2.9	18.3	3.9	14.1	21.5	7.7	100.0

Source: UNCTAD, Report on *Manganese Ore*, p. 54.
Note: The percentage relative shares have been computed.

world exports – almost the entire USSR trade – were contracted under inter-governmental agreements; and (*b*) roughly 20 per cent of world exports were accounted for by 'captive mines', i.e. mines generally located in developing countries but owned or controlled by manganese consumers in the importing countries, e.g. steel companies and mineral trading agencies.[37] The UNCTAD Report cites Brazil and Gabon as the main examples of close links between mines and consuming interests, where parent companies made purchases corresponding to the extent of their financial participation in the enterprise. Quite often, they also arranged for sales of ore to manganese alloy plants in other parts of the world, in which they had financial or other interest.

Although detailed information is not available, the extent of foreign investment is relatively high in Brazil, Gabon, Australia and South Africa. For example, in Gabon, which itself accounted for 18 per cent of world exports in 1969, the most important manganese company, COMILOG, is controlled effectively by the US Steel Corporation which has a 49 per cent interest in it.[38] Clearly, no part of India's exports was guaranteed in this manner, and they had to be sold on a competitive basis in the unrestricted sections of the world market.

Market distribution

It is possible that the market distribution may have been responsible for the relative stagnation in India's manganese ore exports. However, Table 7.13, which shows the important markets for Indian manganese and outlines the changes in relative shares over time, clearly repudiates that possibility. In the period 1961/62–1963/64, Japan, USA and UK were the most important markets which, between them, absorbed nearly two-thirds of total exports. By the end of the decade, the UK and US shares had fallen drastically, whereas Japan's share had risen sharply to 69.6 per cent. On comparing this trend with Table 7.11, we see that India's exports shifted increasingly to the most dynamic market. Despite that, however, exports remained stagnant.

[37] A word about the historical origin of captive mines might be useful. The shortage of manganese after the Second World War, when it was regarded as a strategic material, induced several American steel companies to explore for possible deposits. Gradually, these were discovered in many parts of the world, and the controlling interest was almost naturally taken by the prospectors. So emerged the phenomenon of captive mines in the late 1950s and early 1960s.

[38] *Mineral Yearbook, 1968*, vol. IV, US Bureau of Mines (Washington, 1970), p. 270.

TABLE 7.13   *The main export markets for Indian manganese*
(annual averages)

	Export earnings in $ million		Relative shares in percentages	
	1961/62– 1963/64	1968/69– 1970/71	1961/62– 1963/64	1968/69– 1970/71
Japan	4.9	11.9	26.3	69.6
USA	3.8	1.4	20.4	8.2
UK	2.5	0.1	13.4	0.6
Czechoslovakia	1.4	1.5	7.5	8.8
West Germany	1.0	–	5.4	–
Belgium	0.6	0.5	3.2	2.3
Netherlands	0.4	0.3	2.2	1.8
Yugoslavia	0.8	–	4.3	–
Total including others	18.6	17.1	100.0	100.0

Source: Statistics published by DGCIS, Calcutta.
Note: Earnings have been converted into US dollars, and figures relate to Indian fiscal years beginning 1 April.

The story is somewhat more painful if we examine India's export performance in its three main markets. Table 7.14 illustrates how India steadily lost her share in the US, UK and Japanese markets. In the case of the American market, it may be argued that total imports declined continuously and consumption needs were met by running down the stockpile. However, India's exports fell much faster. To a great extent, this is accounted for by the substantial increase in exports from Gabon (imports from Brazil also fell), which was a direct consequence of US investment in that country's mining industry.[39] However, no such explanation is possible in the case of the UK market, wherein manganese consumption declined only slightly over the decade. But imports from India fell drastically and its share of the market declined from over 25 per cent in 1960 to less than 4 per cent in 1969.[40]

As for the Japanese market, the iron ore story was repeated. Between 1961 and 1969, India's exports to Japan trebled, but Japan's imports increased much faster so that India's share of the market fell from 63.6 to 33.2 per cent. Over the same period, imports from

[39] According to statistics published by the British Steel Corporation, US imports from Gabon rose from 77.9 million kg in 1963 to 231.7 million kg in 1969.

[40] At the same time, Brazil's exports of manganese ore to the UK rose from 24 to 78 thousand tons; see British Steel Corporation, *Annual Statistical Handbooks*.

TABLE 7.14 *Imports of manganese ore by the US, Japan and the UK*
(in thousand tons and percentages)

Year	US			Japan			UK		
	Total imports	From India	India's share	Total imports	From India	India's share	Total imports	From India	India's share
1961	1926.8	230.2	12.0	368.6	234.6	63.6	471.0	125.6	26.6
1965	1666.5	124.5	7.5	1064.8	466.2	43.8	502.4	49.4	9.8
1969	901.8	27.7	3.1	2025.0	672.1	33.2	438.2	17.3	3.9

Source: British Steel Corporation, *Annual Statistical Handbook, 1966 and 1969*.

South Africa and Australia increased at phenomenal rates.[41] Clearly, demand was no constraint in the Japanese market. There must have been domestic factors which prevented India's exports to Japan increasing faster than they actually did.

Domestic cost and supply conditions

Given the foreign demand for a commodity, a country's relative export performance as compared to its competitors is determined by domestic cost and supply conditions. In a mining industry like manganese, the main determinants of costs of production and elasticity of supply are: (a) availability of deposits, (b) scale and degree of mechanisation in mining operations, (c) internal transport network, (d) port facilities, and (e) transport costs to destination.

Manganese mines have been operated in India for a long time. The method of production is therefore very traditional. Moreover, mining operations are conducted on a very small scale – the production being spread over approximately 300 mines.[42] The labour intensive nature of the techniques employed is obvious from the following comparison. In 1969, production of manganese ore in Gabon and India was virtually the same. The Gabon industry employed only 1697 workers as compared to its counterpart in India, which employed 45 000 workers.[43] This vast difference is easily explained by the abundance of labour in India, which makes employment objectives an important consideration. However, given the present structure of the industry in India – small mines and primitive techniques – modernisation or mechanisation is difficult, as a result of which, it may not be possible to benefit from economies of scale.

The transport bottlenecks faced by the manganese industry in India were exactly the same as those faced by the iron ore industry, so that there is no need for extensive discussion. All the same, one comparison about port facilities may be illuminating. Loading capacity at most Indian ports during 1969 averaged 1700–3000 tons per day; in other countries, including Gabon, the minimum loading rate was 1200 tons per hour.[44]

Thus we see that export supplies from India's traditional manganese industry may have been limited by its production structure,

---

[41] Between 1961 and 1969, imports into Japan from Australia and South Africa increased as follows: (a) Australia: 53.6 to 416.1 thousand tons; (b) South Africa: 18.6 to 599.7 thousand tons; cf. *Annual Statistical Handbooks*, ibid.

[42] In 1968 there were 295 manganese mines in India. Cf. US *Minerals Yearbook, 1968*, vol. IV, p. 336.

[43] UNCTAD, Report on *Manganese Ore*, p. 25.

[44] Ibid., p. 26.

and by bottlenecks in transport and port facilities. In contrast, the new mining industries of Brazil, Gabon and Australia were equipped with large scale mechanised mines, efficient production methods and adequate transport, as well as port facilities.

The following non-price factors must also have had an adverse effect on the competitiveness of the manganese mining industry in India.

(*a*) The closure of the Suez Canal in 1967 resulted in a substantial increase in freight cost to Europe and America. This factor may have been particularly important because transport costs of shipment constitute a significant proportion of total costs for a bulky product like manganese ore.[45]

(*b*) A structural shift in production towards lower grade ores reduced the market potential for Indian manganese.[46] Not only that, it also reduced the profitability of mining. The reason is simple. Although costs of mining and internal transport are the same for all qualities of ore, prices vary greatly according to quality. In September 1970, f.o.b. prices of manganese ore in India varied from $28 to $10 per ton depending upon the percentage of manganese content.[47] Clearly, a deterioration in the quality of exports must also have reduced the competitiveness of the industry.

III. MICA

India is by far the largest producer and exporter of mica in the world. In 1965/66, its share in world exports was about 82 per cent, and approximately the same proportion of world output was mined in India.[48] Most of the remaining world supplies originated from Brazil and Madagascar.

[45] *Report on Currency and Finance, 1967/68*, p. 59.

[46] As we have shown earlier, in Table 7.9, this shift in production was reflected in exports. That was bound to be so because most of the output was exported, and during the 1960s, production only marginally exceeded exports.

[47] The f.o.b. prices of manganese ore as reported in the *Indian Mining and Engineering Journal* (Bombay, September 1970) were:

Manganese content	Price in $/ton
46–48%	28
38–40%	17
30–32%	10

[48] According to a note issued by the UNCTAD Secretariat, *World Trade in Mica, Problems and Possible Remedial Policies*, TD/B/C.1/SYN/14 (Geneva, 9 October 1968), India contributed 9559 tons of sheet mica to an estimated world output of 11 710 tons; cf. p. 4. For the year 1966, the UNCTAD, *Commodity Survey, 1968*, p. 88, estimated world exports at 9990 tons, of which, India contributed 8170 tons.

TABLE 7.15   *India's mica exports*

| Year | Unmanufactured mica including scrap and waste | | | Mica manufactures in $m. |
	Volume in million kg	Value in $ million	Average unit value in $/kg	
1960/61	28.4	21.3	0.75	0.2
1961/62	28.3	20.3	0.72	0.2
1962/63	34.3	21.8	0.64	0.2
1963/64	29.7	19.3	0.65	0.3
1964/65	31.2	20.5	0.66	0.7
1965/66	43.3	23.7	0.55	0.9
1966/67	18.6	19.1	1.03	2.2
1967/68	22.9	20.1	0.88	1.5
1968/69	20.8	18.0	0.87	2.6
1969/70	24.0	20.3	0.84	3.0
1970/71	24.0	20.8	0.87	2.1

Source: Statistics published by DGCIS, Calcutta.

Note: Figures related to Indian fiscal years beginning 1 April, and have been converted into US dollars.

Over the decade as a whole, India's dominant position in the world market did not change much. This was so because (a) it had a virtual monopoly in deposits of high grade mica, and (b) mica mining and processing is a highly labour intensive activity with little or no scope for mechanised capital intensive methods.[49] The relatively abundant supplies of labour in India therefore gave it an overwhelming comparative advantage.

Table 7.15 brings out the main trends in mica exports during the 1960s. It shows that export receipts from unmanufactured mica[50] were more or less stagnant throughout the decade, fluctuating around a level of $20 million. Earnings derived from exports of mica manufactures were negligible in the earlier years but increased after 1965/66. In the latter half of the decade they averaged $2.3

[49] This is so because mica deposits are generally very small, and the crystalline structure of mica requires many operations to be done by hand. For a detailed discussion of the production process in the mica industry, see Commonwealth Secretariat, *Non-Metallic Minerals*, no. 2 (London, 1967), pp. 139–40.

[50] It is important to note that mica blocks and splittings account for roughly 90 per cent of export receipts, although they constitute only one-third the total export volume. A significant proportion of the weight is that of waste and scrap mica which has a very low price, as compared to blocks and splittings. During the 1960s, the volume of blocks and splittings exported from India varied between 8 and 10 million kg.

TABLE 7.16   *Unit values of India's mica exports: 1966/67* (in $ per kg)

Type of mica	Unit value
Block	4.50
Splittings	1.40
Film	14.70
Manufactures	13.60
Scrap and waste	0.04

Source: UNCTAD, *World Trade in Mica*, p. 2.

million per annum. Despite this, the share of mica in total export earnings fell from 1.6 per cent in 1960/61 to 1.0 per cent in 1970/71.

Two clear trends are discernible in the quantity of unmanufactured mica exported. Export volume rose steadily until 1965/66, when it attained a peak of 43.3 million kg, as a result of which the average unit value declined from $0.75 to $0.55 per kg. After that year, the quantity exported decreased substantially – by about half – so that there was a significant recovery in unit value.

At this stage, it is necessary to point out that there are many different qualities of mica fetching widely divergent prices. Therefore, generalisations about unit values and price changes are not very meaningful. In fact, the average unit value computed above might well have been influenced by changes in the quality composition of exports.

Broadly speaking, there are two categories of mica: sheet and scrap. Sheet mica fetches relatively high prices, and in turn consists of block, film and splittings which are differentiated essentially by thickness.[51] These varieties of sheet mica are then processed for use in electrical industries. The relatively cheaper scrap mica is obtained from substandard newly mined mica, and the waste generated in the mica processing industry. This is used primarily as a filler in products like paint, rubber, plastics, etc. A small proportion of high-grade scrap is processed into sheet mica, and is termed 'reconstituted mica'. It can be a substitute for natural sheet mica in some applications. Table 7.16 shows clearly the sharp differences in the prices of different varieties of mica which we have elaborated upon above.

[51] The thickness corresponds broadly to certain end-uses. Block mica sheets are used as spacers in electronic tubes; film mica is used almost entirely for making dielectrics used in condensers; and splittings are used in the production of micanite, which is in turn used as an insulator in electrical appliances. See UNCTAD, *Commodity Survey, 1968*, p. 87.

TABLE 7.17   *World exports of mica*
(in million kg)

	1960	1964	1969
India	28.4	31.2	24.0
Madagascar	1.0	1.0	2.3
Brazil	0.7	1.7	1.8
Total	30.1	33.9	28.1

Source: For India and Madagascar: several issues of the UN *Yearbook of International Trade Statistics*; for Brazil: *Annuaro Estatistico do Brasil*, 1963, 1966 and 1970.

The demand for mica derives from its physical properties, which are: high resistance to heat, perfect cleavage and dielectric strength, i.e. the ability to stand high voltages without puncturing. These attributes make mica ideal for use as an insulator in the electronics industry. Therefore, one would expect the world demand for mica to grow along with the output of electrical industries.

World demand and trends in consumption

It is quite difficult to analyse trends in world demand for mica because statistics on world trade and consumption are not readily obtainable. All the same, Table 7.17 which shows the exports of the three main mica producing countries, does give us some idea of the trend in world exports. We find that the world trade in mica increased slightly in the first half of the decade, after which it declined. This trend was certainly not in keeping with the growth in the output of electrical industries. Although there is no index of the production of electrical appliances, production of electricity (which can be used as a suitable approximation) in the world doubled between 1960 and 1969.[52]

The fact that the world demand for mica did not keep pace with the production of goods in which the mineral is traditionally utilised, suggests that the marginal propensity to consume mica must have fallen. Although developed countries are the principal consumers of mica, it is almost impossible to get statistics on its consumption. Only the US Government publishes data on the actual consumption of sheet mica within the country.

For the period 1960 to 1965, however, there is an estimate of

[52] According to figures published in the UN *Statistical Yearbooks*, world electricity production increased from 2 303 600 million kWh in 1960 to 4 567 900 million kWh in 1969.

TABLE 7.18   *The American market for mica* (in million kg)

Year/annual averages	Total consumption of sheet mica	Consumption of splittings	Imports of splittings from India
1960–1962	4.02	n.a.	n.a.
1963–1965	4.54	3.40	3.27
1966	4.49	3.22	3.04
1967	3.72	2.81	2.68
1968	2.90	2.18	2.09
1969	2.99	2.31	2.18

Source: US Bureau of Mines, *Minerals Yearbook*, several issues.
Note: All figures have been converted into metric weights, and the annual averages have been computed from data on individual years.

apparent consumption in some mica importing countries. According to this, during the first half of the 1960s, the consumption of sheet mica in Australia, Canada, Japan and UK was more or less stagnant, but there was a steady increase in American consumption.[53] For the latter half of the decade, data is available only for the US market. Table 7.18 reveals that consumption of sheet mica in the US increased slightly in the period 1960–1965, and decreased rapidly after that. In fact, between 1966 and 1969 the total consumption of sheet mica fell by over 33 per cent. The bulk of this fall was in the consumption of splittings, which is directly reflected in reduced imports from India.

Two major factors were responsible for this decline in demand in the late 1960s: (a) A shift in the pattern of electronics output towards products that use relatively little or no mica, reduced the demand for mica in many industries. For example, the decline in demand for block and film mica was a direct consequence of the trend towards miniaturisation of electronic equipment and the replacement of electronic tubes and valves by transistors.[54] (b) In 1962, the US Government stopped purchases of mica for the stockpile. In view of the new technological developments, mica was no longer a strategic material.[55] The cessation of stockpile imports was followed by a running down of stocks, so that American import demand fell faster than consumption.

To some extent, the demand for mica was also affected by the growth of substitutes. In some industries, sheet mica was replaced by reconstituted mica, although the number of end-uses where this was possible were very few.[56] Contrary to commonly expressed opinion,

[53] Cf. *Non-Metallic Minerals*, no. 2, p. 148.
[54] See UNCTAD, *Commodity Survey, 1968*, p. 190.
[55] UNCTAD, *World Trade in Mica*, p. 13.
[56] Ibid.

synthetics did not pose any serious threat to mica.[57] Early successes like ceramic spark plugs, and synthetics research programmes financed by the American Government had given rise to this fear. However, since the strategic needs have been revised, the US Government has ceased financing research on synthetics to replace mica. So far, the development of synthetic mica has not been possible because of the unique combination of qualities possessed by natural mica, which makes it indispensable in most of its end-uses.[58]

In terms of foreign exchange earnings, the aforesaid decline in demand was partially offset by increased exports of mica manufactures. However, these manufactures constituted a very small proportion of total mica exports. The substantial tariff barriers in the main importing countries may, in fact, have held back their growth.[59] But as we have shown, the bulk of the earnings came from exports of unmanufactured mica. In this case, it was increased unit values that were responsible for the maintenance of foreign exchange earnings, despite the drop in quantity exported after 1965. Given the sluggishness of world demand, the factors underlying this rise in prices are most likely to be found in domestic policy.

Domestic policies

Although exports of mica were quite stagnant in the period 1960/61 to 1963/64, there was a marked decline in the average unit value. To combat this, and many other problems of the mica industry, the Government adopted the following policy measures with the objective of supporting mica exports.[60]

(*a*) The first measure was the introduction of a minimum price policy for exports. In February 1964, the Government fixed minimum f.o.b. prices for certain grades of splittings, a measure which was extended to all forms of splittings a few months later, and virtually

---

[57] Ibid.

[58] Ibid. p. 14.

[59] Tariffs like the ones listed below must certainly have affected the competitiveness of India's exports of mica manufactures. The rates prevailing in the late 1960s were:

	Australia	EEC	Japan	UK	USA
Rates of tariff	$12\frac{1}{2}\%$	5–10%	5%	10%	$22\frac{1}{2}$–25%

Source: Ibid. p. 8.

[60] The following description of government policies is based on information published annually by the Reserve Bank of India. See *Report on Currency and Finance*, *1964/65*, p. 44, *1965/66*, p. 49; and *1967/68*, p. 59.

all mica exports by the end of the year. The large number of entre-preneurs in the mica industry[61] had led to a great deal of price-cutting and uneconomic competition between exporters at home. A fixation of floor prices was meant to eliminate the waste arising from it.

(b) Price support measures were accompanied by a ban on exports on a consignment basis. It was stipulated that foreign buyers must furnish an irrevocable letter of credit for their purchases. It was argued that this would prevent buyers abroad from rejecting consign-ments as of inferior quality with the purpose of extracting a lower price. Soon after its introduction, all exports came under this scheme.

(c) In order to guarantee quality to buyers of Indian mica, the Government introduced a compulsory pre-shipment quality inspec-tion, which was conducted by a government agency. This measure was also designed to stabilise prices vis-à-vis quality.

Two years later, when the rupee was devalued by 57.5 per cent, the Government followed up these policies by measures to maintain the foreign exchange price of mica. The minimum rupee prices were raised across the board by 10 per cent, and an ad valorem export duty of 40 per cent was imposed. The net devaluation was, in fact, negative.[62]

Three factors made it possible for the Government to adopt the policies described in the preceding paragraphs. In the first place, India's near-monopoly position in the world mica trade meant that buyers had little choice in the matter. Second, mica usually accounts for a very small proportion of the total cost of the end-product, so that an increase in its price could be absorbed, by the users, without much difficulty. Third, there are no synthetic or other substitutes for high grade sheet mica. Hence, to the extent that mica is indispensable in its use in the electronics industry, price increases were unlikely to affect the quantity demanded.

In the case of mica, the average unit value is a far from perfect index of price, but it does provide a broad indication of the trend. A look back at Table 7.15 reveals that the minimum price policies adopted by the Government did succeed in arresting the decline in the average unit value, and stabilised prices at a higher level, which may have prevailed before. It should be pointed out that the minimum prices fixed were well above the market prices ruling at the time of

---

[61] In 1968 there were 605 mica mines in India, cf. US *Minerals Yearbook, 1968*, vol. IV, p. 336. Apart from these mining companies there were a large number of small traders.

[62] For details of the calculation and method, see Table 11.3.

their imposition, and were reported to be based on price levels in 1950/51.

However, in the long run, it would be difficult to repeat this success or bring about a further improvement in terms of trade, because, despite the special factors outlined above, price is important for an individual importing country to the extent that some degree of substitution is always possible as between different sources of supply. Admittedly, at present, India has an effective monopoly in resources of high-grade sheet mica. But there is some evidence of a trend to substitute low-grade mica for high grade mica.[63] Clearly, this possibility is very relevant to the formulation of future mica export policy.

Summary

Our analysis of India's exports of mineral ores, during the period 1960 to 1970, leads to the following main conclusions.

(a) The remarkable growth in India's exports of iron ore was made possible by the rapid expansion in world import demand and the increasing concentration of Indian exports in the Japanese market. However, compared to other competing countries such as Australia, Chile and Peru, India's export performance in Japan was not as impressive as it appears on surface. Available evidence suggests that relatively inefficient mining methods, inadequate transport networks and poor port facilities in India acted as constraints on potential export supplies of iron ore, thereby preventing exports from increasing faster than they actually did.

(b) Although world demand grew at a reasonable pace, exports of manganese ore from India fell steadily throughout the decade. Consequently, India lost her position as the leading manganese exporter in the world. The fall in foreign exchange earnings was accentuated by a general decline in world prices of manganese ore, and a marked shift in the composition of India's exports towards lower grade ores. We found that there were two principal reasons for this poor export performance. First, a considerable proportion of the world market was restricted by trade originating from captive mines. Second, the Indian manganese industry suffered from much the same supply constraints as the iron ore industry.

(c) Foreign exchange earnings from exports of mica were quite stagnant throughout the period under study. However, in the late

---

[63] According to UNCTAD, *World Trade in Mica*, p. 11, in the US there has been a trend for consumption to shift from high quality block mica to lower quality block mica.

1960s, the world demand for mica registered a marked decline because of a change in the pattern of electronics production and a decumulation of stocks by the USA. In the face of these circumstances, India used her near-monopoly position in world mica trade to stabilise export prices.

8

Leather and chemicals

I. MANUFACTURED LEATHER

India has been a leading exporter of leather for almost a hundred years. Table 8.1 sums up the export performance of the Indian leather industry during the 1960s. It shows that in the first half of the decade, exports of leather and leather manufactures grew very slowly, if at all.[1] After 1965/66, however, the growth was extremely rapid. The average annual value of manufactured leather exported rose from $50.5 million in the three-year period 1960/61–1962/63 to $100.6 million during 1968/69–1970/71. As a result, the share of leather and leather manufactures in the country's total export earnings increased from 3.6 per cent to 5.3 per cent.[2] Thus we see that, over the decade as a whole, the Indian leather industry nearly doubled its exports. A detailed look at the composition of these exports might help us analyse this rapid growth.

So far, the word leather has been used in a rather general sense to include tanned leather, finished leather, leather goods and leather manufactures.[3] Table 8.2 traces the trend in the exports of each of these separately, and shows that: (*a*) exports of semi-finished leather, which were virtually stagnant until 1965/66, grew rapidly thereafter; (*b*) exports of finished leather fluctuated considerably but registered a decline over the decade as a whole; (*c*) exports of leather goods and manufactures rose moderately, particularly in the late 1960s; and (*d*) leather footwear exports increased markedly rising from $4.7 million in 1960/61–1962/63 to $10.3 million during 1968/69–

---

[1] This was really a continuation of the long-term trend, for exports of manufactured leather were virtually stagnant throughout the 1950s; cf. M. Singh, *India's Export Trends* (Oxford, 1964), p. 15.

[2] Table 2.6.

[3] Hides and skins are manufactured into leather by a process called tanning. There are two basic tanning processes: vegetable tanning and mineral tanning, leading to vegetable tanned and chrome tanned leather respectively. Such tanned leather has to be treated before it becomes finished leather, and can be used in the manufacture of various end-products like footwear and other leather goods.

TABLE 8.1   *India's exports of leather and leather manufactures*

Year	Value in $ million	Value index 1960/61 = 100
1960/61	52.5	100
1961/62	51.4	98
1962/63	47.5	90
1963/64	55.4	106
1964/65	57.5	110
1965/66	59.3	113
1966/67	82.7	158
1967/68	71.3	136
1968/69	96.9	185
1969/70	108.7	207
1970/71	96.2	183

Source: Statistics published by DGCIS, Calcutta.
Note: All figures relate to Indian fiscal years beginning 1 April, and have been converted into US dollars.

TABLE 8.2   *Composition of Indian leather exports* (in $ million)

Year	Semi-finished leather		Finished leather	Leather goods and manufactures	Leather footwear
	Vegetable tanned	Chrome tanned			
1960/61	n.a.	—	3.86	0.32	5.54
1961/62	47.00	—	3.60	0.34	3.90
1962/63	44.30	—	2.42	0.45	4.65
1963/64	50.60	—	3.30	0.46	6.16
1964/65	50.90	—	4.27	0.54	7.32
1965/66	53.20	1.05	3.17	0.65	9.03
1966/67	55.00	18.34	2.82	0.47	9.24
1967/68	46.40	17.70	2.12	0.47	10.02
1968/69	66.00	24.16	2.17	0.94	9.47
1969/70	66.20	36.27	2.97	1.67	9.38
1970/71	59.20	32.66	2.57	1.81	12.12

Source: Ministry of Foreign Trade, Government of India, Export Promotion Council for. Finished Leather and Leather Manufactures, Kanpur, Mimeographed Export Statistics, 1971. However, for the years 1960/61 to 1964/65, figures for finished leather, leather footwear and leather goods and manufactures have been taken from *Report on Leather and Allied Industries of India*, Ministry of Commerce, Government of India (New Delhi, 1966), pp. 156–9.
Note:
(a) All figures relate to Indian fiscal years beginning 1 April, and have been converted into US dollars.
(b) The total of the above columns is larger than the figures for leather exports in Table 8.1, because in the trade statistics classification, leather footwear comes under a separate category. Similarly these figures on footwear exports do not tally with those in Table 2.3, because rubber, canvas, and non-leather soled footwear have been excluded here.

1970/71.[4] It is striking that finished leather and leather products, other than footwear, constituted less than 10 per cent of the total leather exports, throughout the period under study. In fact, the bulk of these exports was constituted by semi-finished tanned leather, whether vegetable tanned or chrome tanned. Traditionally, India has always exported vegetable tanned hides and skins, and in the first half of the 1960s, these accounted for about 90 per cent of leather exports. But this process of manufacturing leather was not without its problems. There was a serious shortage of vegetable tanning materials, imports of which amounted to a little over $4 million per annum during the period 1962–1965.[5] Therefore, the development of the chrome tanning process in India's leather industry was inevitable, specially in view of the fact that the tanning materials necessary for it were indigenously available in sufficient quantities.[6] Chrome tanned leather was first exported in 1965/66, and after that, there was an extremely rapid expansion in these exports, which averaged over $30 million per annum during 1968/69–1970/71. In fact, this increase accounted for most of the growth in leather exports during the latter half of the decade.[7] Having reviewed the overall trends, let us now consider India's export performance in the context of the growth in world demand.

World trade in leather

Table 8.3 outlines the trend in world exports of leather, and brings out the changes in relative shares of the main exporting countries. It shows that the world import demand for leather increased by a little more than 60 per cent between 1961–1963 and 1968. During this period, India's exports kept pace with the increase in demand, so that she maintained her share in the value of world exports. However, these figures conceal the long term trend which is rather important. It is necessary to note that India's share in the world leather trade had fallen from 29 per cent in 1951 to 19 per cent in 1960.[8] During

[4] It should be noted that this does not explain the increase in exports of leather and leather manufactures, because the latter figure does not include footwear, for reasons set out in the note to Table 8.2.

[5] *Foreign Trade of India*, a journal published periodically by the Ministry of Commerce (New Delhi): special issue on the leather industry (January 1966), p. 13.

[6] Ibid. p. 14, 15 and 39.

[7] It is for this reason that we have included leather and leather manufactures among non-traditional exports.

[8] Benjamin Cohen: 'Stagnation of Indian Exports: 1951–1961', *Quarterly Journal of Economics* (November 1964), p. 615.

TABLE 8.3   *World exports of leather* (in $ million)

	1961–1963 Annual average	1964	1965	1966	1967	1968
India	50.6	50.5	70.1	78.0	69.3	82.3
France	52.7	55.7	66.6	79.9	67.5	83.7
UK	51.4	56.8	59.7	64.4	51.4	64.3
West Germany	34.1	38.4	43.7	52.8	52.7	52.7
USA	30.2	26.3	28.8	30.6	30.8	32.3
Pakistan	5.9	7.8	12.1	20.8	26.3	26.4
Argentina	3.5	6.9	5.0	8.5	11.0	14.0
Total includ- ing others	315.7	339.5	398.1	481.5	437.7	510.8
Relative shares (in percentages)						
India	16.0	14.9	17.6	16.2	15.8	16.1
France	16.7	16.4	16.7	16.6	15.4	16.4
UK	16.3	16.7	15.0	13.4	11.7	12.6
West Germany	10.8	11.3	11.0	11.0	12.0	10.3
USA	9.6	7.7	7.2	6.4	7.0	6.3
Pakistan	1.9	2.3	3.0	4.3	6.0	5.2
Argentina	1.1	2.0	1.3	1.8	2.5	2.7
Total includ- ing others	100.0	100.0	100.0	100.0	100.0	100.0

Source: FAO, *The World Hides, Skins, Leather and Footwear Economy*, Commodity Bulletin Series no. 48 (Rome, 1970), p. 77.

Note:

(a) The percentage shares have been calculated.

(b) In the period 1955–1957, India's exports were $46 million out of a world total of $209.8 million – about 22 per cent.

(c) The above statistics relate only to trade in semi-finished and finished leather.

the years 1961–1963, it fell further to an average level of 16 per cent.

Although India continued to be the world's leading exporter of leather, along with France, her performance does not compare well with that of other developing countries. We only have to look at the changes in relative shares of some competing countires to confirm that leather exports of developed countries like the UK and USA did not increase as rapidly as world exports. The markets lost by them were captured by other competitors, e.g. Pakistan and Argentina, both of whom increased their exports significantly. Between 1961–1963 and 1968, the value of leather exports from developing countries, as a group, increased by about 108 per cent, an expansion which far exceeded the growth in India's exports.[9]

Given the facts that: (*a*) India has the largest cattle population in the world; (*b*) the leather industry is distinctly labour intensive, with low skill requirements; and (*c*) there are no substantial economies of scale,[10] the relatively poor export performance seems surprising. In view of the most favourable factor endowments, both in raw materials and in the manufacturing process, one would expect the Indian leather industry to have an overwhelming comparative advantage. In fact, with very similar factor endowments, Pakistan's leather exports did grow at a phenomenal pace. There were three main reasons why India's export performance in leather was not as good as it could have been, and these are to be found in domestic supply conditions, the market distribution of her exports, and non-price factors such as tariff barriers in the developed country markets. Let us examine each of them in turn.

Domestic supply conditions

It is now generally accepted that an inelastic supply of hides and a slow rate of growth in the supply of skins, reinforced by increasing pressure of domestic demand, were the main constraints on the exportable surplus of leather in India.[11]

Normally, hides and skins are a by-product of meat production. In India, however, the supply of hides is rather inelastic because of the legislation against cattle slaughter. According to one estimate, about 96 per cent of the cattle die from natural causes, i.e. disease, starvation and old age.[12] This raises two basic problems for the leather manufacturing industry. First, where cattle are diseased, the hides cannot be used to yield high quality leather. Second, to prevent any

---

[9] *FAO, World Hides, Skins, Leather and Footwear Economy*, p. 77. Exports of leather from developing countries increased from $65.5 million in 1960–1963 to $136.6 million in 1968. The picture is no different if we look at the volume of trade. Between 1955–1957 and 1968, the quantity of leather exported from developing countries grew by an estimated 150 per cent whereas India's shipments rose by only 40 per cent; ibid. p. 79.

[10] Cf. a study by the UNCTAD Secretariat, *Leather and Leather Products: a summary report*, TD/B/C.2/101 (Geneva, 19 January 1970), pp. 1 and 23.

[11] In 1966, a government-appointed committee recognised these factors as the main bottlenecks confronting leather export promotion; see *Report on Leather and Allied Industries of India*, pp. 123–4.

[12] *Survey of India's Export Potential in Leather and Leather Products*, vol. 1 (October 1969), a study by the Gokhale Institute of Politics and Economics, Poona, and the Central Leather Research Institute, Madras; cf. p. 36.

kind of decay, hides need to be processed immediately after the death of the animal.[13] The latter is well nigh impossible in India because most of the hides have to be recovered from dead animals, wherever they might be.

However, the scarcity of good quality leather was not the only bottleneck in supply. In the 1960s, tanning materials were also not available in adequate quantities.[14] In the case of vegetable tanning materials, this may have been largely due to the shortage of foreign exchange and hence import restrictions,[15] but it appears that chrome salts, said to be in adequate supply, were also not available to tanners for some time.[16] Similarly, exports of finished leather were greatly restricted by the problems of procuring auxiliary raw materials necessary for finishing.[17]

In any country, the increase in demand for leather and leather goods depends upon the existing level of development, the growth in population, and the rise in per capita incomes. It is quite difficult to obtain statistics on the demand for leather and leather goods in India. However, in view of the fact that the main consumer of leather is usually the footwear industry,[18] we can use the footwear output in India as an approximate index of the trend in domestic demand for leather. Table 8.4 shows that, between 1960/61 and 1967/68, footwear consumption in India increased by more than 75 per cent. In view of the rapid population growth and some increase in per capita income, this was bound to happen, particularly because at low consumption levels the income elasticity of demand for footwear is likely to be high. While consumption registered a marked increase, available evidence suggests that the production of leather increased relatively slowly. For instance, the quantity of cattle and buffalo hides processed by the tanning industry in India rose by about 30 per cent in the

[13] For a detailed discussion on these aspects of the problem, see UNCTAD, *Leather and Leather Products*, p. 23.

[14] *Report on Leather and Allied Industries of India*, p. 111.

[15] In order to overcome the shortage of tanning materials such as wattle bark, these items have recently been placed under the open-general-licence scheme, which means that they can be imported without special permission.

[16] See Y. Nayudamma, 'Research for Leather Industry', *Foreign Trade of India* (January 1966), p. 39.

[17] Ibid.

[18] Although no separate figures are available for India, it has been estimated that more than two-thirds of the leather output in developed countries is utilised by the footwear industry; see a study by the UNCTAD–GATT International Trade Centre, *Hides, Skins and Leather – Major Markets in Western Europe* (Geneva, 1968). There is no reason why this proportion should be very much different in India.

TABLE 8.4   *Production and exports of footwear in India*
(in million pairs)

	1960/61	1965/66	1967/68
Production	102.0	153.0	182.0
Exports	4.9	9.4	10.8
Apparent domestic consumption	97.1	143.6	171.2

Source:

(*a*) For production, 1960/61 and 1965/66: FAO, *World Hides, Skins, Leather and Footwear Economy*, p. 88; 1967/68: Export Promotion Council for Finished Leather and Leather Manufactures, Kanpur, letter to author dated 12 August 1970.

(*b*) For exports, statistics published by DGCIS, Calcutta.

Note: Apparent domestic consumption is the difference between production and exports.

early 1960s, and declined thereafter.[19] Clearly, the pressure of domestic demand must have restricted the exportable surplus which was already constrained by difficult supply conditions.

Market distribution

Another possible explanation for India's export performance might be found in the market distribution of its leather exports. According to an UNCTAD report, the concentration of Indian exports in the UK market probably curbed their growth owing to the relatively slow growth of the British economy and the declining importance of its leather industry.[20] This conclusion certainly looks plausible in the context of Table 8.5 which shows the important markets for Indian leather, and the changes in their relative shares during the 1960s. We find that in the earlier years of the decade, more than half of India's leather exports were concentrated in the UK market. This might well have been one of the reasons for stagnation during that period. However, by 1965/66, a diversification of markets is discernible and this trend continued in the late 1960s. A shift away from

[19] The quantity of cattle and buffalo hides processed by the Indian tanning industry, during the 1960s, was as follows: (in thousand tons, wet-salted weight)

1961–1963	1964	1965	1966	1967	1968
36.5	46.5	42.1	37.0	35.8	33.0

Source: FAO, *World Hides, Skins, Leather and Footwear Economy*, p. 50–1.

[20] *Leather and Leather Products*, p. 51. In the first place, this concentration must have come about for two reasons: (a) the traditional importance of UK as India's largest trading partner, and (b) the Commonwealth preferences offered by the UK market.

TABLE 8.5 *Market distribution of India's leather exports*

| | 1961/62–1963/64 Annual average | | 1965/6 | | 1967/68–1969/70 Annual average | |
	in $ million	in %	in $ million	in %	in $ million	in %
UK	27.0	52.5	22.8	38.4	22.9	24.8
West Germany	5.5	10.7	6.7	11.3	5.0	5.4
Italy	2.7	5.3	4.4	7.4	8.6	9.3
France	3.1	6.0	5.3	8.9	5.8	6.3
USA	4.0	7.8	8.5	14.3	5.3	5.7
Japan	3.0	5.8	2.7	4.6	4.3	4.7
USSR and Eastern Europe	3.1	6.0	3.9	6.6	31.9	34.6
Total including others	51.4	100.0	59.3	100.0	92.3	100.0

Source: Statistics published by DGCIS, Calcutta.

Note: All figures relate to Indian fiscal years beginning 1 April, and have been converted into US dollars. The percentages have been calculated.

the relatively stagnant UK market, in favour of some rapidly expanding ones, at least partially explains the accelerated growth in leather exports after 1965/66.

Non-price factors

We have shown how domestic supply conditions operated as a constraint on the exportable surplus. Consequently, there were only two ways in which the Indian leather industry could have increased its foreign exchange earnings faster than it actually did.

First, it could have sought to improve the quality of leather,[21] but the main hurdle confronting this possibility was extremely difficult to overcome. It has already been pointed out that unless a hide is processed immediately after the animal's death, some putrefaction and decay is always likely, thereby affecting the quality of the

[21] According to the UNCTAD Report on *Leather and Leather Products*, p. 58: 'There is little or no demand for inferior leather in the developed countries ... so that ... the importance of achieving a high enough quality seems to over-ride price factors'. It is correctly argued that a reduction in leather prices is most unlikely to have any impact on demand because of the relatively high manufacturing costs which have to be incurred subsequently, irrespective of the quality of leather.

leather. In India, strong sentiments and legislation against cattle slaughter prevent a direct solution to this problem.[22]

The second alternative was to increase the share of finished leather and leather manufactures in total exports. This would not only have raised the gross foreign exchange earnings,[23] but would have also created additional employment in the economy. Therefore, it is clear that it would have been beneficial for India to process hides and skins as much as economically possible, so as to maximise the value added before export. Such reasoning was widely accepted and generally recognised,[24] and yet finished leather and leather manufactures constituted less than 5 per cent of total leather exports in 1970/71. Apart from the supply constraints discussed above, the main reason for this export pattern is to be found in the substantial tariff barriers maintained by developed countries.

Tariff structures in the developed countries have always been such as to encourage the import of raw materials (i.e. raw hides and skins), and to protect their domestic industry by imposing tariffs on processed and manufactured goods (i.e. finished leather and leather products). Although, in the 1960s, there was a tendency for importers in developed countries to import semi-processed rather than raw hides,[25] the tariff barriers remained substantial. Table 8.6 highlights the fact that, until 1967, tariffs on the imports of finished leather and leather products in most developed country markets were quite high. It is apparent that the tariff rates increased with the degree of processing involved, thereby discouraging the exports of leather manufactures from developing countries.

It has been shown that, in such escalated tariff structures, the effective protection[26] is always higher than the nominal protection,

---

[22] Another factor which hindered quality improvement was that a large proportion of the machinery in the Indian leather industry was quite old, and not suitable for the production of high quality leather. It is for this reason that the Government Committee in 1966 strongly recommended modernisation of the export units; cf. *Report on Leather and Allied Industries*, p. 124.

[23] 'the value of pickled skins is generally some 10–15 per cent higher, the value of wet-in-the-blue leather is 35–40 per cent higher, and that of rough vegetable tanned leather is 40 per cent higher than the value of corresponding unprocessed hides and skins.... Crust ready-to-finish leather may fetch up to 60 per cent more, and finished leather up to 100 per cent more than raw hides and skins'; FAO, *World Hides, Skins, Leather and Footwear Economy*, p. 92:'

[24] See for example, *Report on Leather and Allied Industries of India*, p. 124.

[25] This trend can be explained almost entirely in terms of the fact that in the developed countries it was increasingly difficult to obtain labour for the earlier unpleasant stages of the tanning process; see UNCTAD, *Leather and Leather Products*, p. 50.

[26] The effective rate of protection can be defined as the incremental value added

TABLE 8.6   *Tariffs on imports of leather and leather products in selected developed countries until 1967*
(ad valorem percentages)

	EEC	Japan	Sweden	UK	USA
Raw hides & skins	–	–	–	0–10	0–4
Rough tanned leather	0–9	15	0–7	10–20	8–10
Finished leather	10	15–20	7	10–20	8–12.5
Leather travel goods	15	20–40	13–20	15–20	16–20
Footwear	16	27–30	14–18	13.5–30	5–20

Source: FAO, *World Hides, Skins, Leather and Footwear Economy*, p. 94.
Note: The above tariff rates for UK do not take into account the Commonwealth preferences.

and increases with every stage of processing.[27] The reasoning is quite simple. Tariffs on final outputs constitute an effective subsidy on production within the importing country, whereas tariffs on inputs used in that particular industry are, in effect, a tax. Therefore, the effective protective rate coincides with the nominal tariff rate only if tariffs on inputs and outputs are equal. If the tariff on the final output is higher than that on the intermediate product or raw material, effective protection is higher than the apparent protection visible in the nominal tariff rates. Therefore, although nominal tariffs were reduced in the Kennedy Round negotiations, the effective protection afforded to the leather industry in developed countries continued to be high. Table 8.7 shows that, at the end of the 1960s, effective tariff rates for finished leather were higher than 30 per cent in UK and Japan, and ranged from 10–22 per cent for leather goods, and 19–36 per cent for footwear, in most developed countries. In such a context, it is hardly surprising that India failed to increase her exports of finished leather and leather manufactures.

II.   CHEMICALS AND ALLIED PRODUCTS

India's exports of chemical and allied products increased substantially during the period under study. The average annual foreign exchange earnings of this group of industries rose from $16 million in the three-year period 1960/61–1962/63 to $40.3 million during 1968/69–

obtainable by imposing tariffs, expressed as a percentage of value added at world prices, given a constant exchange rate.
[27] W. M. Corden, *The Theory of Protection* (Oxford, 1971), pp. 59–60.

TABLE 8.7   *Effective protection for leather manufactures after 1967*
(in percentages)

	Finished leather		Leather goods		Leather footwear	
	Nominal tariff	Effective rate	Nominal tariff	Effective rate	Nominal tariff	Effective rate
EEC	4.8	12.3	7.3	10.4	11.9	19.3
Japan	11.6	34.7	11.8	15.0	22.9	36.5
Sweden	1.7	4.3	10.4	22.1	11.9	22.8
UK	11.4	30.4	9.3	18.1	20.4	32.7
USA	4.7	12.0	7.7	11.4	14.9	26.3

Source: FAO, *World Hides, Skins, Leather and Footwear Economy*, p. 95.
Note: The nominal tariff rates are lower than in Table 8.6 because of the Kennedy Round
reductions in 1967. Here again, the UK rates do not include Commonwealth preferences.

1970/71.[28] Over the same period of time, the share of chemicals in the
country's total exports increased from 1.2 to 2.1 per cent.[29] These
figures seem to suggest a continuously rising trend, but that was not
the case. In fact, to begin with, exports of chemicals and related
products increased very little. In the mid-1960s, they fluctuated
around a level of $20 million, and it was only after 1967/68 that there
was a marked increase. In order to analyse this trend, as a first step, it
is necessary to consider the commodity composition of these exports so
as to identify the dynamic export sectors within the chemical industry.

Commodity composition

The group of chemical and allied industries manufactures a wide
variety of products. All the same, it is possible to classify its exports
according to the following broad categories:[30] (*a*) chemicals – elements
and compounds; (*b*) crude chemicals manufactured from coal,
petroleum and natural gas; (*c*) dyeing, tanning and colouring
materials; (*d*) medicinal and pharmaceutical products; (*e*) perfume
materials, soaps, cosmetics, toilet and polishing preparations, etc.;
(*f*) plastic materials; and (*g*) other chemical materials and products.
Table 8.8 traces the trends in foreign exchange earnings of each of
these export groups.

[28] See Table 8.8.
[29] Table 2.6.
[30] These categories correspond roughly to the SITC grouping. Most of them are
self explanatory. The first includes largely organic and inorganic chemicals,
whereas the last category is constituted by products like disinfectants and
insecticides.

TABLE 8.8   *Exports of chemicals and allied products from India* (in $ million)

	1960/61	1961/62	1962/63	1963/64	1964/65	1965/66	1966/67	1967/68	1968/69	1969/70	1970/71
Chemicals: elements and compounds	1.75	2.71	2.81	2.38	3.77	3.99	2.59	2.95	4.39	5.90	10.45
Crude chemicals	0.22	0.25	0.24	0.48	0.37	1.16	2.00	2.29	3.56	5.02	1.51
Dyeing and tanning materials	0.93	0.67	0.70	1.19	1.36	2.52	1.75	2.73	4.88	5.37	9.68
Medicinal and pharmaceutical products	2.07	2.06	2.24	2.20	4.43	5.53	5.03	4.44	5.33	7.97	11.29
Perfumes, oils, soap and toilet goods	8.69	9.55	9.04	6.06	6.87	4.88	4.96	4.99	5.84	9.49	9.50
Plastic materials	0.02	0.03	0.13	0.13	0.63	1.01	0.39	0.19	2.42	5.05	4.26
Chemical materials and products	0.40	0.29	0.43	0.56	1.64	1.48	0.93	1.16	1.80	1.57	1.63
Total including others	15.1	16.4	16.5	14.5	21.6	23.3	20.0	21.0	31.8	40.5	48.5

Source: Statistics published by DGCIS, Calcutta.

Note: All figures relate to Indian fiscal years beginning 1 April, and have been converted into US dollars.

TABLE 8.9   *Percentage composition of chemical exports*

Industrial groups	1960/61–1962/63 Annual average	1965/66	1968/69–1970/71 Annual average
Chemicals	15.1	17.1	17.2
Crude chemicals	1.5	5.0	8.3
Dyeing and tanning materials	4.8	10.8	16.5
Medicinal and pharmaceutical products	13.3	23.7	20.3
Perfumes, oils, soaps, etc.	56.8	20.9	20.6
Plastic materials	1.1	4.3	9.7
Chemical materials and products	2.3	6.4	4.1
Total	100.0	100.0	100.0

Source: Table 8.8.

Note: The percentages have been computed, and the annual averages obtained from data for individual years.

A careful study of this table reveals that the bulk of the rapid growth towards the end of the decade was due to a sharp increase in exports of chemicals, dyeing and tanning materials, and medicinal and pharmaceutical products. Taken together, the exports of these three industries more than trebled, rising from $10.1 million in 1967/68 to $31.4 million in 1970/71. At the same time, plastic materials acquired significance as exportables, and their exports jumped from $0.2 million to $4.3 million. Clearly, these were the dynamic export industries in the chemicals sector, which is confirmed further by the changes in their relative shares of total chemical exports over the decade as a whole. Table 8.9 shows that, between 1960/61–1962/63 and 1968/69–1970/71, their shares in total foreign exchange receipts changed as follows: (*a*) chemicals – 15.1 to 17.2 per cent; (*b*) dyeing and tanning materials – 4.8 to 16.5 per cent; (*c*) medicinal and pharmaceutical products – 13.3 to 20.3 per cent; and (*d*) plastic materials – 1.1 to 9.7 per cent. On the other hand, exports of perfume materials, soaps, cosmetics, etc., which had been the mainstay in 1960/61, declined and stagnated; over the decade, their share fell from 56.8 per cent to 20.6 per cent. Exports of crude chemicals and chemical materials increased faster than the total, thereby resulting in increased shares, but their contribution remained relatively small.

The above export performance of the Indian chemical industry is not surprising if we place it in the context of trends in world trade. World exports of chemicals increased by about 160 per cent rising from $7450 million in 1960 to $19420 million in 1970.[31] Although

[31] UN *Monthly Bulletin of Statistics* (New York, March 1966 and April 1972).

India's exports increased slightly faster and her share in world trade rose from 0.20 to 0.24 per cent, she remained a marginal exporter in the world market. Effectively, therefore, India's export trends can be explained only in terms of price competitiveness and the elasticity of supply in her chemicals industry.[32]

Competitiveness

The ability of the Indian chemical industry to compete in the world market must have been affected by (*a*) its cost structure, (*b*) domestic supply and demand conditions, and (*c*) the Government's trade policies. We shall consider the possible effect of each of these factors.

Comparative costs

One of the main determinants of price competitiveness is the cost of raw materials and intermediate products that are used up in the production process. In the chemicals industry, hydrocarbons are the basis of the major chemical intermediates which in turn are necessary for the manufacture of chemicals, fertilisers, plastics, synthetics, etc.[33] These hydrocarbons can be obtained either from coal and alcohol, or from naphtha which emerges as a by-product of petroleum refining. It is now widely known that naphtha is a very rich source of hydrocarbons, and therefore, a much cheaper raw material than coal and alcohol.[34] However, until the end of 1966, the Indian chemical industry obtained all its hydrocarbons from coal and alcohol. It was only in 1967/68 that two naphtha cracker plants were set up, and petrochemicals were manufactured in India for the first time.[35] It is not certain to what extent the absence of a significant petrochemicals base adversely affected the cost competitiveness of Indian chemical industries. The sudden jump in exports of chemicals and plastics

---

[32] In theory, a marginal supplier can increase sales significantly at the prevailing price, without upsetting the market.

[33] The following description of the cost-structure and production-structure in the chemicals industry is drawn from R.H. Patil, 'Exports of Chemicals and Allied Products: Problems and Prospects', *RBI Bulletin* (Bombay, July 1971), pp. 985–7.

[34] Ibid. pp. 986–7. This is perhaps the main reason why chemical industries all over the world have been shifting from coal-based to petroleum-based chemicals. Moreover, petrochemicals are amenable to processes of production which yield much higher economies of scale. According to an estimate made by *The Economist* (London, 3 October 1970) in 1970, more than two-thirds of the chemical industry in developed countries was based on petrochemicals (quoted in ibid.) It is necessary to note that there is no reason for the Indian chemical industry to shift to petrochemicals so completely, because India has vast resources of coal available at low costs, whereas naphtha production is relatively import intensive. This argument is greatly strengthened because of the recent increase in oil prices.

[35] Ibid.

after 1967/68 might be explainable in terms of the new petrochemicals base, the output of which became available in the late 1960s.[36]

Elasticity of supply

The availability of an adequate and increasing exportable surplus depends upon the pressure of domestic demand and the supply conditions. Owing to the paucity of data, it is not possible to quantify the trend in domestic demand, but the following indirect evidence seems to suggest increasing pressure. First, production in the chemicals industry began essentially to meet import substitution objectives; therefore, it is not surprising that an overwhelming proportion of the output was consumed in the home market. Second, it is generally accepted that scarcities in the domestic market kept internal prices of chemicals consistently higher than world prices.[37] These shortages were evidently due to a combination of excess demand and inadequate domestic production; and the production was not sufficient because of a shortfall in the supply of intermediates and basic raw materials.[38] Thus it becomes clear how shortages of inputs coupled with increasing domestic demand must have operated as a constraint on export supplies.

Trade policies

Given the relative attractiveness of the home market, the scarcities, and the high costs,[39] it is quite obvious that exports could only have been sustained with the help of trade policies. Therefore, it is not surprising that even before devaluation, exporters of chemicals and allied products were subsidised heavily through: (a) import entitlements which varied from 40 to 75 per cent; (b) refund of excise or import duties paid on any of the inputs used in the exported product; (c) income tax concessions; (d) export credit facilities; and (e) preferential supply of certain raw materials.[40] As we shall show later, by far the greatest element of subsidisation was implicit in the import

---

[36] Starting in 1967/68, the output of petrochemicals reached a level of 0.23 million tons in 1970. It has been reported that this led to a distinct burst of activity in the plastics industry. cf. RBI Bombay, *Report on Currency and Finance, 1970/71*, p. 114.

[37] Patil, *RBI Bulletin* (July 1971), pp. 985–6.

[38] See *Report on Currency and Finance, 1969/70*, p. 93.

[39] It has been shown that, in the early 1960s, Indian prices of some chemicals and related products were much higher than world prices; cf. R. K. Singh, *Prosperity Through Export* (Calcutta, 1965), pp. 216–21.

[40] For a description of the pre-devaluation and post-devaluation incentives provided to the chemicals industry, see Patil, pp. 984–5. We shall undertake a detailed analysis of all these export promotion policies in Chapter 10.

entitlement schemes. However, these import entitlements were withdrawn at the time of the devaluation of the rupee. Therefore, the *net* devaluation in June 1966 was much less than the apparent depreciation in the exchange rate, and worked out at only 14.9 per cent for the chemicals industry.[41] If this was the case, how can we account for the rapid growth in exports of chemicals and related products after 1967/68? The following three factors might provide the explanation.

(*a*) First, the chemicals industry continued to benefit from export incentives even after the devaluation of the rupee. Subsidisation now took the form of: (1) cash subsidies ranging from 10 to 25 per cent of the f.o.b. value of exports,[42] (2) customs and excise duty refunds; (3) export credit concessions, and (4) import replenishment schemes.[43]

(*b*) Second, the liberalisation of imports that accompanied devaluation in 1966,[44] helped the exporters of chemical and allied products considerably, by removing serious bottlenecks in the supply of raw materials and intermediates. The improvement in the supply situation is reflected in the marked increase in imports of chemicals after 1966.[45]

(*c*) Third, in April 1968, the drugs and pharmaceuticals industry was brought under the export obligation scheme of the Government. It was stipulated that every pharmaceuticals firm had to export at least 5 per cent of its output, failing which, it was liable to cuts in its import privileges.[46] In view of this compulsory export scheme, it is not surprising that, between 1967/68 and 1970/71, exports of medicinal and pharmaceutical products more than doubled.

---

[41] For method of calculation, see Table 11.1 and 11.3.

[42] Patil, *RBI Bulletin* (July 1971), p. 985.

[43] These were merely a revised version of the earlier entitlement schemes. In 1970/71, import replenishment rates varied from 5 per cent for some chemicals, to 20 per cent for drugs and pharmaceuticals, and 60 per cent for some synthetics and dyes; cf. *Import Trade Control Policy, 1970/71*, vol. II, Ministry of Foreign Trade, Government of India (New Delhi). For a discussion on the incentive implicit in this scheme, see Chapter 10, pp. 232–6.

[44] For details of the import liberalisation that accompanied devaluation, see J. Bhagwati and P. Desai, *India: Planning for Industrialisation*, OECD (Oxford, 1970), pp. 483–6.

[45] In the latter half of the 1960s, India's imports of chemicals *excluding* manufactured fertilisers were as follows: (in $ million).

1965/66	1966/67	1967/68	1968/69	1969/70	1970/71
138.7	141.7	178.2	192.6	157.3	174.8

Source: RBI Bombay, *Report on Currency and Finance*, 1970/71, p. S144.
Imports increased substantially after the devaluation, but fell back in 1969/70 because of the return of import restrictions. At the same time, domestic production of chemical intermediates also increased, thereby adding to their availability; cf. Patil, *RBI Bulletin* (July 1971), p. 986.

[46] *Import Trade Control Policy, 1968/69*, vol. I, pp. 7 and 158. Small scale units, and units which had been in production for less than five years, were exempt from this obligation.

TABLE 8.10 *Market distribution of India's exports of chemicals*
(relative shares: in percentages)

	1960/61–1962/63 Annual average	1967/68–1969/70 Annual average
South East Asia	31.6	32.2
West Asia	4.5	8.5
Africa	5.7	15.6
Eastern Europe	5.2	17.6
Western Europe	32.0	14.8
North America	12.4	6.5
Total including others	100.0	100.0

Source: Patil, *RBI Bulletin* (July 1971), pp. 991.
Note:

(a) The percentage shares have been calculated from statistics tabulated in the article cited above. It is necessary to note that these include many more manufactures as 'allied products', as compared to the SITC definition which we have been using so far. However, reducing the figures to percentages partially eliminates the problem and makes them quite adequate for our purpose of studying the changes in relative shares of different markets.

(b) The regional groupings need a little more explanation. India's main markets in South East Asia were Japan, Nepal, Ceylon, Burma and Hong Kong; in West Asia, Iraq; in Africa, UAR; in Eastern Europe, USSR, Yugoslavia and Czechoslovakia; in Western Europe, UK, Netherlands and West Germany; and in North America, USA.

Market distribution

It is possible that some part of the increase in exports of chemicals and allied products was due to shifts in the market distribution. Table 8.10 brings out the change in relative shares of different markets during the 1960s. We find that there was a clear and marked shift away from Western Europe and North America whose combined share fell from 44.4 per cent in 1960/61–1962/63 to 21.3 per cent in 1967/68–1969/70. Over the same period of time, the share of West Asia rose from 4.5 to 8.5 per cent, of Africa from 5.7 to 15.6 per cent, and of Eastern Europe from 5.2 to 17.6 per cent. South East Asia continued to be the largest market and retained its share in the total at about 32 per cent. In absolute terms, foreign exchange receipts from exports of chemicals and allied products to Western Europe and North America remained quite stagnant. In fact, most of the increase in Indian chemical exports, during the 1960s, is attributable to the expansion of trade with the developing countries and the socialist countries of Eastern Europe.[47]

The decline in the relative importance of developed country

[47] For data on the foreign exchange receipts from exports to different countries see Patil, *RBI Bulletin* (July 1971), pp. 991.

TABLE 8.11   *Number of foreign collaboration agreements in the*
Indian chemicals industry with restrictions on exports

Industrial group	Up to 1960	1961–1965	1964–1970	Total
Basic chemical industries	10(41)	13(43)	7(23)	30(107)
Medicines and pharmaceuticals	15(30)	11(22)	4(14)	30(66)
Others	10(21)	4(20)	3(17)	17(58)
Total chemical and allied products	35(92)	28(85)	14(54)	77(231)

Source: UNCTAD, *Restrictions on Exports in Foreign Collaboration Agreements in India*, p. 9.
Note: Figures in brackets indicate the total number of effective agreements. Exports restrictions
were of the following types:
(a) permission of collaborators for exporting;
(b) prohibition on exports to certain countries;
(c) exports allowed only to certain countries;
(d) total ban on exports;
(e) need to channel exports through collaborator's agents;
(f) restriction or prohibition on the use of the trade mark; and
(g) others.

markets does need to be explained. Available evidence suggests that
restrictions on exports in foreign collaboration agreements may have
been partially responsible. Given the high incidence of foreign
investment in the Indian chemicals industry, it also seems quite
plausible. A recent UNCTAD study found that in the manufacturing
sector of the Indian economy, the chemical industry had the largest
number of companies with foreign capital participation.[48] Table 8.11
outlines the number of such foreign collaboration agreements which
restricted exports. It shows that, on the average, about one-third of
the foreign collaborations imposed some kind of restriction on
exports. In the medicines and pharmaceuticals industry, the proportion was much higher, and about half the agreements restricted
exports. A prohibition of exports to the collaborator's own country,
and wherever it had branch affiliates, was a fairly common restriction.[49] Given the fact that the bulk of the foreign investment in the
Indian chemicals industry was West European or American,[50] it is

[48] *Restrictions on Exports in Foreign Collaboration Agreements in India*, a study
carried out by the India Investment Centre, New Delhi, for UNCTAD, United
Nations, TD/B/389 (New York, 1971), p. 7.   [49] Ibid. p. 8.
[50] During the period 1960/61 to 1963/64, a little more than 85 per cent of the
minority foreign capital participation in the Indian chemicals and allied products
industry originated from the UK, USA and West Germany; cf. RBI, *Foreign
Collaboration in Indian Industry* (Bombay, 1968), p. 121.

only obvious that exports to these countries could not have increased. The protective nature of these restrictive arrangements by foreign investors becomes clearer when we find that imports of chemicals by the USA and West European countries more than trebled between 1960 and 1970.[51]

Summary

The salient points to emerge from the discussion on India's exports of leather and chemicals can be summarised as follows.

(*a*) Exports of manufactured leather from India were virtually stagnant until 1965/66, but grew very rapidly thereafter. This growth was attributable to the rising trend in world import demand and the establishment of a chrome tanning industry in India. In fact, exports of chrome tanned semi-finished leather accounted for the bulk of the increase in India's foreign exchange receipts from leather. Although India maintained her share of world exports, her performance did not compare well with that of other developing countries which increased their share of the world leather market. Had it not been for the inelastic supply of hides and the increasing pressure of domestic demand, exports would certainly have done better. Export earnings could also have been increased by expanding the exports of finished leather and leather manufactures, but that was prevented by substantial tariff barriers in the developed countries, as a result of which, finished products constituted a very small proportion of leather exports throughout the period under study.

(*b*) India's exports of chemicals and allied products increased very slowly until 1967/68, but grew at a remarkable pace in the last three years of the decade. We found that exports of chemicals were constrained by a variety of factors such as relatively high costs of production, shortages of inputs, increasing domestic demand, and restrictions on exports in foreign collaboration agreements. In the late 1960s, however, exports were boosted by the import liberalisation for inputs, heavy subsidisation, and the compulsory export obligation scheme.

[51] The following figures bring out the trends in the imports of chemicals by selected developed countries during the 1960s:

(in $ million)	1960	1970
Western Europe	3 237	11 460
USA	481	1 450

Source: OECD, Paris, *The Chemical Industry*, *1960/61*, p. 103; and *1970/71*, p. 57.

9
Engineering goods

Products of engineering industries acquired importance in India's exports during the 1960s. Among the non-traditional exports, these 'new manufactures' experienced the most rapid growth. Table 9.1 highlights these trends and shows that exports of engineering goods which were only $14.1 million in 1960/61 rose to $155.5 million in 1970/71; a tenfold increase, at a compound rate of growth of 27 per cent per annum. As a result, their share in total exports jumped from 1.0 to 7.6 per cent.

This substantial increase in India's exports was quite consistent with the rapid expansion in world trade. Between 1960 and 1970, world exports of engineering products more than trebled, rising from $31 100 million to $95 500 million.[1] However, the bulk of this trade originated from the developed countries,[2] and although India's share in world exports rose from 0.05 to 0.16 per cent, it remained a very tiny fraction of the total. Therefore, it would be appropriate to compare India's export performance in engineering goods with that of other LDCs, rather than the main developed country exporters.

Table 9.2 outlines the trends in the exports of engineering goods from India, Argentina, Brazil, Mexico, Hong Kong, Taiwan and South Korea during the 1960s. Taken together, these countries supplied the bulk of engineering products exported by the developing countries as a group.[3] We find that the growth in India's exports of engineering goods compares quite favourably with the performance of other developing countries, except for Hong Kong and Taiwan

---

[1] Cf. GATT, *International Trade, 1967* (Geneva), p. 35 and *1970*, pp. 22–3. The 1970 figure includes road motor vehicles in order to make it comparable with the 1960 data.

[2] Ibid. The share of the industrialised countries was a little higher than 87 per cent throughout the decade. The developing countries increased their share slightly from 0.6 in 1960 to 1.3 per cent in 1970, at the expense of the socialist countries, whose share declined marginally.

[3] See 'Exports of Engineering Products from Selected Industrializing Countries', a special article in GATT, *International Trade, 1968*, p. 61.

TABLE 9.1   *India's exports of engineering goods*

Year	(1) Value in $ million	(2) Value index 1970/71 = 100	(3) Percentage share in total exports
1960/61	14.1	9	1.0
1961/62	16.4	11	1.2
1962/63	19.8	13	1.4
1963/64	28.2	18	1.7
1964/65	35.3	23	2.1
1965/66	39.7	26	2.4
1966/67	41.5	27	2.7
1967/68	55.3	36	3.5
1968/69	113.3	73	6.3
1969/70	141.8	91	7.5
1970/71	155.5	100	7.6

Source: For column (1): Table 2.3; and for column (3): Table 2.6.
Note: The value index has been computed. All figures relate to Indian fiscal years beginning 1 April.

which benefited from special circumstances.[4] In proportionate terms, exports from South Korea, Argentina and Brazil also increased much faster, but that was because they started from a very small base in 1960. In absolute terms, India's exports grew to a much higher level at the end of the decade.

[4] Both were island economies whose export expansion was based on exports of processed imported materials. Among other things, Taiwan's export effort was boosted by: (*a*) the Vietnam war, which created a demand for its non-traditional exports; (*b*) large amounts of technical and financial aid. The development of the Hong Kong economy was greatly aided by an influx of foreign capital. Although precise data is not available, foreign investment did play an important part in some export industries, e.g. electronics. Given the tiny domestic markets, in both cases, a large part of the output was exported. For these and other details of Taiwan's and Hong Kong's export performance, see Ian Little, T. Scitovsky and Maurice Scott, *Industry and Trade in Some Developing Countries* (Oxford, 1970), pp. 254–60. The case of India and the three Latin American countries is vastly different. In these economies, imports were generally restricted, industries were based on domestic materials and inputs, and exports of engineering products were a very small proportion of the total output. It has been estimated that only 1–3 per cent of the domestic production of engineering goods in India, Argentina, Brazil and Mexico was exported; cf. GATT, *International Trade, 1968*, p. 88.

From the above discussion, it is quite clear that it would be more appropriate to compare India's performance with that of the Latin American countries, rather than Hong Kong and Taiwan.

TABLE 9.2   *Exports of engineering goods from selected LDCs* (in $ million)

	1960	1965	1969
India	14.1	39.7	141.8
Argentina	3.5	19.6	63.8
Brazil	2.0	30.6	65.5
Mexico	8.7	21.9	97.7
Hong Kong	54.2	118.2	333.5
Taiwan	1.8*	24.7	175.9
South Korea	0.1	7.7	63.0

Source: UN *Yearbook of International Trade Statistics, 1960, 1966* and *1969*, except for India, which figures are taken from Table 9.1, and relate to fiscal years beginning 1 April.

Note:

(*a*) In this table, engineering goods have been defined to include: (1) machinery and transport equipment: SITC Section 7; (2) metal manufactures: SITC 69; and (3) scientific instruments, watches, clocks, etc: SITC 861 and 864. In cases where exports under the third category have been negligible (and as such do not appear in UN statistics) they have been ignored. In others, exports under SITC 86 have been taken as a suitable approximation.

(*b*) It is necessary to note that in the case of India, engineering goods include some items in addition to our above definition. This would tend to overstate India's performance in comparison, but only marginally.

(*c*) The export figures for Mexico, Hong Kong, and Taiwan have been converted into US dollars from domestic currencies. The exchange rates used are 1 US dollar as equal to: (1) 12.49 Mexican pesos; (2) 5.71 HK dollars for 1960 and 1965, and 6.06 HK dollars for 1969; (3) 40.10 NT dollars.

* Taiwan's exports of engineering products in 1959; cf. GATT, *International Trade, 1968*, p. 64.

So far, we have referred to engineering goods as an aggregate. However, in order to analyse the export growth, it is necessary to consider their commodity composition and the changes in it.

Changing commodity composition

The striking fact about India's exports of engineering goods is their highly diversified composition, ranging from simple consumer goods and metal manufactures on the one hand, to industrial machinery and transport equipment on the other. This is amply illustrated by Table 9.3, which lists the important engineering exports.

In order to examine the factors behind the rapid export growth,

TABLE 9.3 *Important engineering export industries in India*

Steel pipes, tubes and fittings	Sewing machines and parts
Automobile and auto parts	Structural steel fabrications
Electric wires and cables	Electrical accessories
Bicycles and parts	and appliances
Jute, textile and knitting	Radios and components
machinery	Builders' hardware
Hand tools and small tools	including locks
Iron and steel castings	Water and sanitary fittings
Transmission line towers	Steel bars and shaftings
Railway coaches and wagons	Telephonic and telegraphic
Electric fans and parts	equipment
Diesel engines and parts	Railway track materials
Machine tools	EPNS wares
Dry and storage batteries	Airconditioners, refrigerators,
Electric motors, switchgear,	water coolers, etc.
transformers, etc.	Bolts, nuts, rivets and washers
Aluminium ingots, sheets,	Mechanical pumps
foils, etc.	Agricultural implements
Wire ropes and wire products	Electric lamps
Office machinery,	Steel furniture
typewriters, etc.	Air compressors

Source: Engineering Export Promotion Council, Calcutta, *Home Bulletin*, 12 August 1971.
Note: Except for sewing machines and the last seven industries, exports of each of the others were greater than one million dollars per annum during the period 1969/70–1970/71.

we have selected the first twenty industries in the list for a detailed analysis. Together they constituted about half the total engineering goods exports in 1960/61, two-thirds in 1965/66, and three-fourths in 1970/71.

Table 9.4 traces the changes in export earnings from each of the selected industries during the period under study, and reveals the following trends.

(*a*) Exports of some products like automobiles and parts, electric wires and cables, bicycles and parts, hand tools and small tools, and iron and steel castings increased continuously throughout the decade, and at a particularly rapid rate after 1965/66. Consequently, in 1970/71, the foreign exchange earnings of each of these industries exceeded $5 million. Much the same is true for steel pipes and tubes and jute and textile machinery, but for the fact that their exports fell in 1970/71.

(*b*) There were other engineering goods like transmission line towers, diesel engines, machine tools, electric motors, office machinery,

TABLE 9.4 *Exports of selected engineering goods from India: a detailed breakdown (in $ million)*

	1960/61	1961/62	1962/63	1963/64	1964/65	1965/66	1966/67	1967/68	1968/69	1969/70	1970/71
Steel pipes, tubes and fittings	0.37	0.26	0.13	0.79	1.75	4.41	6.03	6.55	13.65	15.04	9.58
Automobile and auto parts	0.24	0.27	0.28	1.22	2.33	2.46	2.86	3.31	7.92	19.13	28.36
Electric wires and cables	0.04	0.01	0.19	0.33	1.23	1.56	1.60	2.24	10.32	14.88	15.09
Bicycles and parts	0.13	0.39	0.29	0.90	1.67	2.41	1.91	2.97	5.09	6.22	9.21
Jute, textile and knitting machinery	0.35	0.84	7.80	0.85	1.02	0.93	0.73	1.22	2.43	9.61	7.95
Hand tools and small tools	0.08	0.15	0.13	0.23	0.52	1.08	1.35	2.86	3.72	3.56	5.84
Iron and steel castings	0.51	0.74	0.75	1.09	1.13	1.48	1.53	2.35	3.28	3.92	6.05
Transmission line towers	0.02	0.47	0.61	0.17	0.72	0.23	0.74	1.67	1.38	3.94	3.82
Railway coaches and wagons	—	0.05	0.09	0.03	0.09	0.02	1.28	3.01	11.08	0.70	2.81
Electric fans and parts	1.95	1.62	2.11	1.20	2.07	2.20	2.18	2.26	2.49	2.85	1.92
Diesel engines and parts	0.53	1.00	1.14	1.37	2.66	2.65	1.88	1.67	2.80	3.35	3.64
Machine tools	0.09	0.20	0.13	0.22	0.35	0.75	0.88	0.91	2.51	3.94	3.78
Dry and storage batteries	0.25	0.34	0.48	1.38	0.98	2.11	2.19	1.92	2.69	2.37	2.89
Electric motors, switchgear, transformers	0.04	0.06	0.05	0.07	0.12	0.19	0.35	0.37	1.55	3.38	2.99
Aluminium ingots, sheets and other manufactures	0.59	0.75	0.78	0.92	1.19	1.11	0.74	2.02	10.86	6.34	3.06
Wire ropes and wire products	0.04	0.08	0.07	0.06	0.11	0.29	0.95	0.97	1.76	2.94	3.93
Office machinery typewriters, data processing machines	—	0.07	0.12	0.05	0.75	1.00	0.60	1.87	1.86	2.64	2.57
Sewing machines and parts	1.16	0.95	1.09	0.55	0.99	0.66	0.71	0.75	0.72	1.14	0.21
Structural steel fabrications	0.04	0.07	0.10	0.13	0.14	0.30	0.38	0.59	1.14	2.52	1.89
Electrical accessories and appliances	0.21	0.22	0.17	0.25	0.58	0.68	0.64	0.80	1.38	1.12	1.38
Total including others	14.06	16.42	19.79	28.18	35.30	39.69	41.51	55.30	113.30	141.82	155.45

Source: Engineering Export Promotion Council, Calcutta, *Home Bulletin*, 12 September 1968, 30 July 1970 and 12 August 1971.

Note: All figures relate to Indian fiscal years beginning 1 April, and have been converted into US dollars.

TABLE 9.5   *The trend in exports of simple engineering products* (in $ million)

Industry	1960/61	1965/66	1970/71
Electric fans	1.95	2.20	1.92
Sewing machines	1.16	0.66	0.21
Steel furniture	0.30	0.59	0.77
Steel trunks	0.51	0.51	0.44
Brass and copper utensils	0.23	0.30	0.29
Stainless steel utensils	0.11	0.44	0.57
Umbrellas	0.13	0.52	0.40
Cutlery	0.28	0.22	0.27
Total of above	4.67	5.63	4.87
As a percentage of engineering exports	33.1	14.2	3.1

Source: Engineering Export Promotion Council, Calcutta, *Home Bulletin*, 12 September 1968 and 12 August 1971.

Note: All figures relate to Indian fiscal years beginning 1 April, and have been converted into US dollars.

electrical appliances and wire and wire products, the exports of which grew steadily, but less rapidly than the first group.

(*c*) Exports of a few products like electric fans, batteries and sewing machines were virtually stagnant.

(*d*) Finally, exports of railway wagons, aluminium manufactures and structural steel fabrications fluctuated so widely that no distinct trend is discernible.

Although these trends highlight the commodity composition of engineering exports, they provide no index of the changes in it. During the period 1960–1970, one important change in composition was the rapidly declining importance of simple manufactures, which constituted a large proportion of the engineering products exported at the beginning of the decade. It might be worthwhile to investigate the factors underlying this change.

To begin with, the slender industrial base allowed only for products that could be manufactured economically with relatively simple technology, and on a small scale. Therefore, it is not surprising that the earliest engineering products exported from India were consumer goods that were either metal manufactures or simple machinery, e.g. utensils, steel trunks, sewing machines, etc. We have selected eight such products, which together accounted for 33.1 per cent of total engineering exports in 1960/61. Table 9.5 outlines the export trend in

TABLE 9.6   *Composition of India's engineering goods exports*

	1961/62		1965/66		1970/71	
Industrial group	in $m	in %	in $m	in %	in $m	in %
Manufactures of nonferrous metals	0.36	2.2	1.49	3.8	6.94	4.5
Iron and steel manufactures	1.93	11.8	5.78	14.6	39.54	25.4
Other metal manufactures	3.70	22.5	7.05	17.8	3.64	2.3
Non-electrical machinery	4.97	30.3	10.00	25.2	27.48	17.7
Electrical apparatus and appliances	2.14	13.0	6.70	16.9	28.39	18.3
Transport equipment	1.01	6.2	5.23	13.2	40.06	25.8
Miscellaneous manufactured articles	0.99	6.0	1.91	4.8	5.63	3.6
Total	16.42	100.0	39.69	100.0	155.45	100.0

Source: For 1961/62 and 1965/66: Ministry of Commerce, Government of India, *Brochure of Statistics of Imports and Exports* (New Delhi, September 1966). The figures have been computed from the data in this brochure. For 1970/71: Engineering Export Promotion Council, Calcutta, *Home Bulletin*, 12 August 1971.

each of these and shows that foreign exchange earnings from the group of industries as a whole remained more or less stagnant throughout the 1960s. However, given the rapid growth in the total exports of engineering goods, the share of this group fell drastically to a mere 3.1 per cent in 1970/71.

There were two basic reasons for such a contraction in the relative share of the aforesaid group of industries. First, in the early 1960s, the bulk of these exports were directed to other LDCs,[5] and being relatively simple manufactures, they were most vulnerable to import substitution programmes in their main markets. Second, to some extent, the diversification in the industrial production base was bound to be reflected in the composition of exports. This factor emerges clearly if we look at the changes in the industrial group composition of India's engineering goods exports over the decade.

Table 9.6 shows that exports of metal manufactures rose in the early 1960s but declined thereafter, as a result of which, their share in total engineering exports fell dramatically from 22.5 per cent in

[5] In 1960/61, about 90 per cent of India's engineering exports were marketed in the developing countries of Asia and Africa; cf. Table 9.7.

1961/62 to 2.3 per cent in 1970/71. Over the same period, the share of non-electrical machinery fell from 30.3 to 17.7 per cent, although, in absolute terms, these exports rose from $4.97 million to $27.48 million. On the other hand, exports of transport equipment, iron and steel manufactures and electrical apparatus and appliances increased much faster than total exports, rising from 1.01, 1.93 and 2.14 million dollars respectively in 1961/62 to 40.06, 39.54 and 28.39 million dollars in 1970/71. Consequently, their combined share in the total exports of engineering goods more than doubled, increasing from 31 per cent to almost 70 per cent.

It is apparent that the commodity composition changed markedly during the 1960s. It would also be interesting to analyse whether there were any changes in the markets for these exports, and if so, how did they affect the export growth?

Changes in market distribution

As was to be expected, a large proportion of Indian engineering goods were marketed in other developing countries. This fact is borne out by Table 9.7 which outlines the market distribution of these exports, and brings out the changes in relative shares of different regions. The trends emerging from these statistics can be summed up as follows.

(a) Although the developing countries of Asia and Africa were the main markets throughout the 1960s, their share in the total declined from an average of 88.1 per cent in the three-year period 1960/61–1962/63 to 73.6 per cent during 1968/69–1970/71. But there were considerable changes in proportional shares within this group: (1) South East Asian countries absorbed more than 40 per cent of the total exports until 1962/63, but after that, their share declined continuously and fell to 22.3 per cent in 1970/71; (2) the importance of the West Asian countries remained unchanged, with their share ranging from 20 to 25 per cent during the 1960s; (3) the share of African countries also fluctuated around one-fifth the total until 1968/69, after which it increased suddenly and grew to 29.6 per cent in 1970/71. In absolute terms, of course, exports to all these markets increased substantially.

(b) Over the decade, the average annual share of developed countries in India's exports showed a marked increase, rising from 8.2 per cent in 1960/61–1962/63 to 22.7 per cent during 1968/69–

TABLE 9.7   Market distribution of Indian engineering goods exports: by regions (in $ million)

	1960/61	1961/62	1962/63	1963/64	1964/65	1965/66	1966/67	1967/68	1968/69	1969/70	1970/71
South East Asia	5.92	7.19	8.28	10.97	13.99	13.10	11.51	14.21	32.83	32.95	34.60
West Asia	3.85	3.91	5.49	6.73	9.26	9.61	8.97	11.64	29.75	31.31	33.80
Africa	2.67	3.28	3.69	4.12	5.87	7.68	8.37	9.59	21.38	39.30	46.07
Eastern Europe	0.01	0.07	0.18	0.47	1.19	2.98	3.99	8.79	11.97	14.22	16.42
Western Europe	0.81	0.72	1.13	4.04	2.60	3.90	3.82	4.27	5.51	12.18	13.55
North America	0.33	0.49	0.49	0.93	1.33	1.28	3.17	3.96	6.45	7.01	6.47
Total, including others	14.07	16.42	19.79	28.18	35.30	39.69	41.51	55.30	113.30	141.82	155.45

Relative shares (in percentages)

	1960/61	1961/62	1962/63	1963/64	1964/65	1965/66	1966/67	1967/68	1968/69	1969/70	1970/71
South East Asia	42.1	43.8	41.8	38.9	39.6	33.0	27.7	25.7	29.0	23.2	22.3
West Asia	27.4	23.8	27.7	23.9	26.2	24.2	21.6	21.0	26.3	22.1	21.7
Africa	19.0	20.0	18.6	14.6	16.6	19.3	20.2	17.3	18.9	27.7	29.6
Eastern Europe		–	0.9	1.7	3.4	7.5	9.6	15.9	10.6	10.0	10.6
Western Europe	5.8	4.4	5.7	14.3	7.4	9.8	9.2	7.7	4.9	8.6	8.7
North America	2.3	3.0	2.5	3.3	3.8	3.2	7.6	7.2	5.7	4.9	4.2
Total, including others	100.0	100.0	100.0	100.0	100.0	100.0	100.0	100.0	100.0	100.0	100.0

Source: Engineering Export Promotion Council, Calcutta; statistics reproduced in R. K. Singh, *Changing Horizon* (Bombay, 1970), p. 92.
Note: All figures relate to Indian fiscal years beginning 1 April, and have been converted into US dollars. The percentage shares have been computed.

1970/71. Most of this is attributable to the rapid expansion of trade with the socialist countries of Eastern Europe, whose share increased from virtually zero in 1960/61 to 10.6 per cent in 1970/71. To begin with, West European countries were the main developed economy markets, but in the late 1960s, there was an appreciable increase in exports to North America. Although the relative shares of both these regions fluctuated widely, in absolute terms, exports registered a rising trend.

The extent of the absolute increase in foreign exchange earnings is brought out clearly in Table 9.8, which shows the main markets for Indian engineering goods. It is clear that India's principal markets in Africa were UAR, Sudan, Nigeria and Kenya. In West Asia they were Iran, Iraq and Kuwait, and in South East Asia, Ceylon and Malaysia. Among the developed countries, UK, USA and West Germany were the main buyers. The one trend which emerges clearly is that exports to each of these fourteen main markets[6] increased most rapidly in the latter half of the 1960s. The growth was particularly marked in the case of UAR, Iran, Ceylon, Yugoslavia, Malaysia, Nigeria and Sudan.[7] It is interesting that during this period India operated trade agreements with three of these countries. Obviously, bilateral trade arrangements played an important part in the growth of engineering exports from India. We shall make an attempt to quantify their impact.

In the second half of the 1960s, India had bilateral trade agreements with the socialist countries of East Europe, UAR, Sudan and Afghanistan.[8] Table 9.9 outlines the trends in exports to these countries. We find that between 1966/67 and 1970/71, exports of engineering products to the trade agreement countries increased at a phenomenal pace; in fact, until 1969/70 they virtually doubled each year. In these five years, while engineering exports to this group of countries increased by $38.4 million, total engineering exports increased by $113.9 million. Therefore, a little over one-third the growth in India's exports of engineering goods, during the latter half

[6] These fourteen countries accounted for nearly half of India's engineering exports in 1960/61, and more than two-thirds in 1970/71.

[7] The sudden increase in imports by UAR, Nigeria and Sudan during 1969/70 and 1970/71 accounts for the sharp increase in the share of African countries during those years.

[8] Some of these arrangements specifically included exports of engineering goods from India; cf. RBI Bombay, *Report on Currency and Finance, 1966/67* to *1970/71*. See in particular the Appendix on India's Trade and Payments Arrangements in each issue.

TABLE 9.8 *Main importers of Indian engineering goods* (in $ million)

	Annual average 1961/62–1965/66	1966/67	1967/68	1968/69	1969/70	1970/71
UAR	1.17	1.29	1.43	6.27	20.99	21.55
Iran	1.73	3.00	4.50	10.97	10.58	14.00
Ceylon	1.42	1.60	1.84	5.43	9.35	8.63
Yugoslavia	0.12	0.89	0.68	2.78	5.64	8.22
Malaysia	2.30	2.62	3.66	4.22	5.90	8.00
Nigeria	0.71	1.79	2.06	1.50	2.27	7.18
Sudan	0.79	0.43	1.20	2.63	6.27	5.81
USA	0.83	2.81	3.39	4.84	6.24	5.72
Iraq	1.74	1.30	1.04	3.10	4.10	5.69
UK	1.77	2.45	1.83	2.62	6.83	5.52
Kuwait	1.35	2.32	2.67	8.53	6.93	4.21
West Germany	0.36	0.35	0.54	0.99	2.76	4.18
Thailand	0.91	0.68	1.93	2.46	3.29	3.91
Kenya	1.12	2.96	2.25	5.74	3.83	3.78

Source: Engineering Export Promotion Council, Calcutta, *Home Bulletin*, 12 September 1968, 30 July 1970, and 12 August 1971.

Note: All figures relate to Indian fiscal years beginning 1 April, and have been converted into US dollars. The statistics for the period 1961/62–1965/66 include some steel products which were subsequently excluded from the category of engineering goods. The Malaysia figures include Singapore.

TABLE 9.9   *Engineering exports to bilateral trade agreement markets*
(in $ million)

	1966/67	1967/68	1968/69	1969/70	1970/71
Eastern Europe	3.99	8.79	11.97	14.22	16.42
UAR	1.29	1.43	6.27	20.99	21.55
Sudan	0.43	1.20	2.63	6.27	5.81
Afghanistan	0.33	0.25	0.45	0.72	0.68
Total of above	6.04	11.67	21.32	42.20	44.46
As percentage of total engineering exports	14.6	21.1	18.8	29.8	28.6

Source: Tables 9.7 and 9.8, except for Afghanistan, which figures are taken from the statistical appendix in Singh, *Changing Horizon*, p. 93.
Note: The percentages in the last row have been calculated as a proportion of the totals in Table 9.4.

of the decade, is attributable to bilateral trade agreements. This figure is a slight underestimate because it does not take into account the short term arrangements with Iran, Ceylon and Indonesia.[9]

Competitiveness

In the long run, the single most important factor underlying the export trends discussed above is the competitiveness of Indian engineering goods in the world market. As shown earlier, over a period of time, changes in competitiveness depend upon: (*a*) changes in relative export prices; (*b*) changes in exchange rate and trade policies; and (*c*) non-price factors. We shall analyse how each of these factors affected the exports of engineering goods from India during the period 1960–1970.

Relative prices
India is only a marginal supplier of engineering products in the world market. Therefore, price competitiveness is a necessary condition for export. But it is not a sufficient condition because non-price

[9] It was not possible to include these short term agreements in our calculations because the necessary statistics were not available. However, we do know that India had a trade agreement with Iran for the period 13 November 1967 to 10 March 1970 in which some engineering goods were specially mentioned (cf. *Report on Currency and Finance, 1967/68*, p. 177). In addition, India extended a credit of Rs50 million to Ceylon for the import of manufactures from India during 1967/68 (ibid. p. 174). Indonesia received a similar credit of Rs100 million during 1966/67 (See *Report on Currency and Finance, 1966/67*, p. 168).

factors like quality and marketing methods are also extremely crucial. A country's ability to sell at competitive prices, and hence its export performance, is determined by domestic demand and supply conditions. Supply factors directly influence the costs of production and through it, price competitiveness. On the other hand, demand conditions at home determine the relative profitability of exports. Our preceding analysis of the trends in traditional exports has clearly shown that the increasing pressure of domestic demand reduced the availability of exportable surpluses. One would expect this to be true of engineering industries, particularly in view of the fact that most of them were originally established to meet import-substitution objectives, and as such, an overwhelming proportion of their output was consumed domestically. In reality, however, the situation turned out to be completely different. Starting in 1965, the Indian economy suffered a severe industrial recession which lasted about three years. It is thus important to analyse how this change in domestic demand conditions affected the export performance of the country's engineering industry.

Impact of the recession: The factors leading to the widespread recession in the Indian economy during the period 1965 to 1967 are fairly well known, and have been analysed in detail.[10] Basically, it began with the sharp fall in agricultural output in 1965/66. This reduced the supply of certain industrial raw materials. At the same time, lower farm incomes meant a fall in the demand for consumer goods. But owing to shortages, the prices of food and some other consumer necessities rose sharply.[11] In order to hold such inflation, the Government did two things. First, it adopted restrictive monetary and fiscal policies which curbed private investment. Second, it reduced public outlays. And so the circle was complete. Quite soon, recessionary conditions prevailed in a majority of the engineering industries, the demand for whose products was cut off for two reasons: (a) lower production in the consumer goods sector; and (b) reduction

---

[10] For a brief diagnosis of the recession see Government of India, New Delhi, *Economic Survey, 1967/68*, pp. 10–14, and *1968/69*, p. 11. A more detailed analysis can be found in A. M. Khusro, 'Recession, Inflation and Economic Policy', *Economic and Political Weekly* (14 October 1967), pp. 1857–62.

[11] It is curious that the recession co-existed with inflation in some sectors of the economy. This apparent contradiction is explained quite well by A. M. Khusro (ibid). Because of the sharp increase in prices of some commodities, the impact of the recession was not felt at all by a few industries. For example, all industries catering to the demand of the agricultural sector continued to operate full capacity.

TABLE 9.10 *Annual percentage underutilisation of capacity in engineering industries*

Industry	1965	1966	1967	Annual average during recession
1. Steel pipes and tubes	13.6	17.2	46.2	25.7
2. Automobiles and parts	2.3	2.6	5.3	3.4
3. Electric wires and cables	38.8	51.6	56.9	49.1
4. Bicycles and parts	8.3	0.5	−3.9	1.6
5. Jute, textiles and knitting machinery	50.2	34.6	18.0	34.3
6. Hand tools and small tools	14.6	31.9	40.7	29.1
7. Iron and steel castings	32.5	51.0	59.5	47.7
8. Transmission line towers	14.8	29.1	32.6	25.5
9. Railway coaches and wagons	14.7	44.2	57.8	38.9
10. Electric fans and parts	4.7	15.0	12.6	10.8
11. Diesel engines	–	–	–	–
12. Machine tools	24.9	18.8	37.0	26.9
13. Dry and storage batteries	–	–	–	–
14. Electric motors, transformers, etc.	–	–	–	–
15. Aluminium manufactures	30.0	21.1	8.3	19.8
16. Wire ropes and wire products	41.1	38.8	65.7	48.5
17. Office machinery	n.a.	n.a.	n.a.	n.a.
18. Sewing machines	4.7	12.6	22.2	13.2
19. Structural steel fabrications	23.7	33.1	60.0	38.9
20. Electrical accessories and appliances	–	–	–	–

Source: *RBI Bulletin* (April 1969), pp. 487–8, except for industries 5, 8 and 9. For nos. 5 and 8: D.Trehan 'Exports of Engineering Goods – Recent Boom and the Causes', *Economic and Political Weekly* (4 July 1970), p. 1054; for no. 9: *RBI Bulletin* (July 1968), p. 871.

Notes:

(a) Excess capacity in the rubber and plastic insulated cables industry has been taken as an index for item no. 3, and excess capacity in the lathe tools industry as an approximation for item no. 6.

(b) For no. 15, excess capacity has been calculated as a simple arithmetic average of underutilisation in the aluminium ingots and the aluminium sheets and foils industries.

(c) For no. 5, the figures are a simple arithmetic average of underutilisation in the jute machinery and the textile machinery industries.

(d) Industries nos. 11, 13, 14 and 20 operated at full capacity during the recession. The proportion of production to capacity during 1965–67 was 1.45, 1.09, 1.39 and 1.13 respectively in these industries. (Calculated from the above sources.)

in public sector investment outlays.[12] This fact is borne out by Table 9.10, which shows the extent of underutilisation of capacity in the selected engineering industries during the period of recession.[13]

It is clear from these figures that there was substantial excess capacity in all engineering industries except for those manufacturing automobiles and parts, bicycles, diesel engines, batteries, electric motors and electrical accessories. However, the extent of underutilisation varied during the recession years. In order to obtain a general index of underutilisation in the period 1965–1967, we have calculated the annual average excess capacity in each engineering industry, and this is shown in the last column of Table 9.10.

In order to analyse the impact of recession, let us begin by tracing its effect on exports at the theoretical level. To begin with, reduced domestic demand would make for a larger exportable surplus. But that would happen even at given prices, whereas recessionary conditions also lead to a fall in the prices of inputs and outputs. *Ceteris paribus*, lower prices in the domestic market would lead to an increase in exports for three reasons. First, if domestic output prices fall to a level below world prices, it would make exports more attractive than domestic sales. Second, lower input prices would improve the cost competitiveness of exports. And third, when no domestic sales are possible at the margin, producers would be willing to export at prices lower than average costs (in order to recover at least a part of the fixed costs), thereby improving their price competitiveness in the world market. So much for the theoretical argument, but did it actually happen in reality?

Table 9.11 outlines the export trends in the selected engineering industries during the period 1964/65 to 1967/68. The choice of years is determined by the following facts: (a) 1964/65 was the last year of normal economic activity before the recession set in; and (b) the economy began to recover from the recession in 1968/69.[14] We have

---

[12] Cf. *Report on Currency and Finance, 1967/68*, p. 62. Although the recession in some consumer goods industries like cotton textiles and jute goods (which relied on agricultural cash crops for the basic raw material) originated in supply factors, the consequent recession in the engineering industries was entirely because of a lack of demand.

[13] The underutilisation of capacity was nothing new. In the early 1960s, some degree of excess capacity had existed in almost all engineering industries. However, as we shall show later in the chapter, this was basically due to a shortage of raw materials, spares, components and foreign exchange. But our concern here is the underutilisation during 1965–1967, which arose out of a lack of demand, and *not* supply factors. It is worth noting that the underutilisation in the recession years was much higher than in the early 1960s; cf. *RBI Bulletin* (Bombay, April 1969), pp. 487–8.

[14] See Government of India, *Economic Survey, 1968–69*, p. 10 and *1969–70*, p. 13.

TABLE 9.11   *Impact of the recession on engineering exports from India*

Industrial groups	Average excess capacity in the recession (in percentages)	Value of exports in $ million			
		1964/ 65	1965/ 66	1966/ 67	1967/ 68
I. *More than 25% excess capacity*					
Electric wires and cables	49.1	1.23	1.56	1.60	2.24
Wire ropes and products	48.5	0.11	0.29	0.95	0.97
Iron and steel castings	47.7	1.13	1.48	1.53	2.35
Railway coaches and wagons	38.9	0.09	0.02	1.28	3.01
Structural steel fabrications	38.9	0.14	0.30	0.38	0.59
Jute and textile machinery	34.3	1.02	0.93	0.73	1.22
Hand tools and small tools	29.1	0.52	1.08	1.35	2.86
Machine tools	26.9	0.35	0.75	0.88	0.91
Steel pipes and tubes	25.7	1.75	4.41	6.03	6.55
Transmission towers	25.5	0.72	0.23	0.74	1.67
Total of I		7.06	11.05	15.47	22.37
II. *Less than 25% excess capacity*					
Aluminium manufactures	19.8	1.19	1.11	0.74	2.02
Sewing machines and parts	13.2	0.99	0.66	0.71	0.75
Electric fans and parts	10.8	2.07	2.20	2.18	2.26
Automobiles and parts	3.4	2.33	2.46	2.86	3.31
Bicycles and parts	1.6	1.67	2.41	1.91	2.97
Total of II		8.25	8.84	8.40	11.31
III. *Full capacity operating industries*					
Dry and storage batteries	–	0.98	2.11	2.19	1.92
Electrical accessories	–	0.58	0.68	0.64	0.80
Electrical motors, etc.	–	0.12	0.19	0.35	0.37
Diesel engines	–	2.66	2.65	1.88	1.67
Total of III		4.34	5.63	5.06	4.76

Source: Tables 9.4 and 9.10.
Note: Industries in this table are listed in descending order of underutilisation.

classified the industries into three groups according to the degree of underutilisation. The ten industries in Group I had an excess capacity of more than 25 per cent. Underutilisation was much less in the five industries of Group II, whereas the four industries in Group III operated at full capacity or more. An aggregation of the export performance of these groups produces striking results.

Between 1964/65 and 1967/68, exports of the engineering industries which had an excess capacity higher than 25 per cent increased by 217 per cent. In sharp contrast, the exports of industries with a lower excess capacity, i.e. less than 25 per cent, increased by just 37 per cent, and the exports of industries operating at full capacity rose by only 10 per cent. A statistical calculation provides further evidence of a significant correlation. The coefficient of rank correlation between the degree of underutilisation and the percentage increase in exports from 1964/65 to 1967/68 works out at 0.52.[15]

Although the above figures suggest a strong correlation between the recession and export growth, no unequivocal sanctity can be attached to them. Clearly, a recession in the home market is not always a sufficient condition for an increase in exports. This is obvious from a few trends in Table 9.11 itself. For example, there was no significant increase in the exports of jute and textile machinery although more than one-third the capacity in the industry was idle; at the same time, exports of automobiles and parts increased steadily despite the fact that the industry was operating near full capacity.

All the same, we have shown that the recession in the mid-1960s, in general, did have a favourable effect on the exports of engineering goods from India. Therefore, we can say that it was *one* of the factors underlying the acceleration in export growth after 1965/66.[16]

Little statistical evidence is available to support the causation of this impact, but it is known that domestic prices of some engineering goods registered a marked decline during the recession. A survey by the Indian Engineering Association revealed that between 1965/66 and 1967, prices of structural steel fabrications fell by 20 to 45

---

[15] For twenty pairs of observations the crucial value of Spearman's rank correlation coefficient is 0.377 at 95 per cent level of significance.

[16] This favourable impact of domestic recession on exports was not unique to India. A special study by GATT found that exports of engineering products showed accelerated growth in Argentina from 1963, and in Brazil during 1963–1965, which coincided with periods of reduced internal demand in these countries; cf. GATT, *International Trade, 1968*, p. 88. Further confirmation is provided by Little, Scitovsky and Scott who found that in Brazil 'During the period of industrial recession there was a marked increase in the exports of non-traditional goods, including manufactures' (*Industry and Trade in some Developing Countries*, p. 380).

per cent, of steel castings by 20 per cent, of electric transformers and switchgear by 20 to 25 per cent, of welding electrodes by 15 to 30 per cent, of industrial fans by 10 to 12 per cent, and of water coolers by 9 to 15 per cent.[17] Clearly, this must have reduced the relative attractiveness of the home market and improved the price competitiveness of exports.

From an analysis of the demand factors which aided export growth after 1965, let us now turn to the supply conditions during the decade under study.

Bottlenecks in supply: In the first half of the 1960s, almost all the engineering industries suffered from serious supply constraints. It has been shown that during this period industries manufacturing metal products, machinery, electrical appliances and transport equipment were handicapped by shortages of raw materials.[18] This naturally led to an underutilisation of capacity and higher unit costs of production.

The scarcity of foreign exchange and the consequent import restrictions were the most usual bottlenecks in material supplies. Matters were made worse by the fact that sometimes no domestic substitutes were available. And in cases where the necessary raw materials or intermediates were indigenously produced, they were often in short supply, were of unreliable quality, and sold at high prices.[19] Supply conditions were particularly bad in the case of basic industrial materials like iron and steel, copper, aluminium and zinc. In fact, acute shortages of alloy steel, spring steel and specially shaped steels adversely affected production in a majority of the engineering industries.[20]

In the absence of any special support, all these factors must have reduced the competitiveness of exports. However, the supply constraints on engineering exporters were relaxed to some extent through two of the export promotion policies adopted by the Government:[21] (*a*) import entitlement schemes made exporters eligible for import licences; and (*b*) the preferential supply of certain raw materials to exporters helped them directly.[22] But neither of these measures

[17] See *Eastern Economist* (New Delhi, 22 September 1967), pp. 547–8.
[18] For details, see a study by the National Council of Applied Economic Research (NCAER), *Underutilization of Industrial Capacity* (New Delhi, October 1966), pp. 44–9. The description of supply bottlenecks in the first half of the 1960s is based on this work.
[19] Ibid. pp. 45–6.   [20] Ibid. p. 47.
[21] Both these policies are discussed in detail later in this chapter.
[22] Exporters of engineering goods were granted a 133 per cent replenishment quota for indigenous raw materials, such as steel plates; cf. *RBI Bulletin* (October 1970), p. 1715.

ensured the quality or prices of domestic raw materials, and supply conditions continued to be difficult, even for exporters in the engineering industry. It was the import liberalisation that accompanied devaluation which removed a large proportion of the supply bottlenecks – at least in the short run. The priority industries, which included most of the engineering ones, were given almost complete freedom to import the raw materials, spares and components necessary for full capacity production.[23] At the same time, the scheme for the preferential supply of indigenous raw materials to exporters was continued.[24] This relaxation of the supply constraints in 1966/67 may well have reinforced the favourable impact of the recession, which was discussed earlier.

However, the liberal import policy was shortlived and the principle of 'indigenous availability' became operative in the sanction of import licences once again.[25] Gradually, import restrictions returned. Therefore, it is not surprising that towards the end of the 1960s acute shortages of certain indigenous raw materials, particularly steel, created serious problems for exports of engineering goods.[26]

Export promotion policies

It is generally accepted that domestic prices of Indian engineering goods are much higher than world prices. Estimates of the price differential vary but it can safely be put at about 50 per cent.[27] Clearly, these products could not have been competitive in the world market

---

[23] For details, see *Annual Report* of the Ministry of Commerce, 1966/67, Government of India (New Delhi), p. 22.   [24] Ibid. p. 23.

[25] Cf. J. Bhagwati and P. Desai, *India: Planning for Industrialisation*, OECD (Oxford, 1970), pp. 484–6. In real terms, this meant that an import licence could *only* be issued if the particular item was *not* domestically produced or available. In fact, importers had to obtain 'regret letters' from the domestic producers.

[26] For a detailed report, see Singh, *Changing Horizon*, p. 25.

[27] (a) An official report by the Directorate General of Technical Development (DGTD), Government of India, suggests that during the period 1960–1967, domestic prices of engineering goods were 30–40 per cent higher than c.i.f. import prices; see 'Import Substitution and its Impact' extracts from which are reproduced in *Eastern Economist* (19 September 1969), pp. 565–70.

(b) According to another estimate, domestic prices were 40–60 per cent higher than international prices in the case of most engineering goods. See R. H. Patil 'Exports of Engineering Goods: Problems and Prospects' in *RBI Bulletin* (Bombay, October 1970), p. 1715.

(c) A study by the Engineering Export Promotion Council showed even more startling results (quoted in Patil, p. 1716). In 1965, a fan which sold for Rs147 at home had to be priced at Rs63 to sell competitively in Australia. Similarly, a 5/6 h.p. diesel engine selling in India for Rs1930, had to be priced at Rs1001 in Australia.

without subsidisation; and, in fact, this has been the rationale underlying all the incentives provided to exporters of engineering products.

During the 1960s, export promotion policies took a variety of forms.[28] For our purpose, it might be useful to trace the changes in incentives through the decade. In doing so we shall use the devaluation of the rupee as a point of reference.

Before June 1966, exports were subsidised through the following measures:

(*a*) *Import entitlement schemes*, in which exporters were allowed to retain a certain proportion of the foreign exchange earned in the form of import licences. The stated objective of this scheme was to enable exporters to import their requirements of components and raw materials, but the import entitlement granted to each exporter was *twice* his estimated import content.[29] Implicit in this surplus foreign exchange allotment was a subsidy, because the import licences fetched high premiums in the market.

(*b*) *Customs and excise duty drawbacks*, which led to a refund of taxes paid on any of the inputs used in the exported output.

(*c*) *Income tax concessions*, which meant that profits from exports were taxed at a lower rate than domestic sales.

(*d*) *Railway freight concessions* saved on internal transport costs and were particularly beneficial to exports of non-traditional manufactures.

(*e*) *Preferential supply* of indigenous raw materials, which meant that exporters were given a priority in the allocation of scarce raw materials like steel.

(*f*) *Compensatory support*, which was merely direct cash subsidies for some selected engineering industries.

Apart from the import entitlement schemes, most of these incentives were retained even after the devaluation of the rupee in June 1966. Exporters of engineering goods continued to benefit from customs and excise duty drawbacks, income tax concessions, railway freight concessions and a preferential supply of raw materials.[30] The main changes in export policy were the following:

(*a*) First, the import entitlement schemes were abolished. However, in August 1966, the Government announced the introduction of import replenishment schemes.[31] These replenishments were much

---

[28] The actual working and the economic implications of all these export promotion policies are discussed in detail in the next chapter.

[29] Cf. *Annual Report* of the Ministry of Commerce, 1963/64, Government of India, p. 14.

[30] Patil, *RBI Bulletin* (October 1970), p. 1716.

[31] *Report on Currency and Finance*, 1966/67, p. 159.

the same as the earlier entitlements, i.e. exporters were allowed to retain a specified percentage of their foreign exchange earnings in the form of import licences. The only difference was that the replenishment proportion was meant to be *equal* to the import content, whereas the *entitlement* had been *twice* estimated import requirement.[32]

(*b*) Second, the scheme of compensatory support, i.e. direct subsidies, was extended to almost all engineering goods industries. With effect from August 1966, exporters received cash subsidies as a specified proportion of their export earnings.[33] When this measure was first introduced the rates of subsidy varied between 10 and 20 per cent of the f.o.b. value of exports.[34] Gradually, however, these rates were increased and some of them were much higher in 1969/70.

(*c*) Third, the Government introduced a scheme for supplying steel at international prices to engineering exporters. With effect from May 1967, exporters of engineering goods were reimbursed to the extent of the difference between the domestic and international prices of steel used in the export shipments.[35]

(*d*) Fourth, in April 1968, the Government announced a compulsory export obligation scheme. Although this was not a positive incentive like the others, it did amount to an export promotion measure. It was stipulated that firms manufacturing bicycles, stationary diesel engines, wire ropes, batteries, small tools and automobile ancillaries had to export at least 5 per cent of their total production, failing which, they were liable to cuts in their import licence privileges.[36]

Clearly, it would be extremely difficult to assess the net impact of this whole complex of export promotion policies. All the same, it is necessary to have some idea of the degree of subsidisation implicit in these measures. In the following analysis, we will attempt to quantify the subsidy equivalent of the import entitlement, import replenishment and compensatory support schemes. However, in our calculations we do not take into account customs and excise duty drawbacks, income tax concessions, railway freight concessions and preferential

---

[32] See Chapter 10, p. 232.

[33] The rates of subsidy under the compensatory support scheme are not published anywhere by the Government. Circulars and orders are issued from time to time by the Ministry of Foreign Trade, and this information is passed on by the Engineering Export Promotion Council to its members. As such, we had to resort to secondary sources for these figures.

[34] Patil, *RBI Bulletin* (October 1970), pp. 1715–16.

[35] Cf. *Report on Currency and Finance, 1966/67*, p. 159.

[36] See *Import Trade Control Policy, 1968/69*, vol. I, Ministry of Commerce, Government of India (New Delhi), pp. 7 and 158.

supply of raw materials. Although these measures were positive incentives to exporters, non-availability of the necessary data makes it almost impossible to estimate their subsidy equivalent. This omission does not seriously affect the validity of our estimates, for two reasons. In the first place, most of the effective subsidisation was provided through import entitlement/replenishment schemes and cash incentives.[37] And second, because these incentives remained unchanged despite the devaluation, their net effect was more or less constant throughout the period under study.

Table 9.12 highlights the changes in export incentives provided to selected engineering industries during the 1960s.[38] It is interesting that before the devaluation, import entitlement schemes were the major incentive. Cash subsidies were given to only three industries, and that too, in only 1965/66. On the other hand, in the post-devaluation period, the emphasis shifted to direct cash subsidies.

Given the data in Table 9.12, we have tried to calculate the changes in net rupee returns per dollar of foreign exchange earned by exporters in each of these engineering industries. The exercise assumes that:

(a) in the pre-devaluation period, import entitlements were just twice the actual import content, so that only *half* the foreign exchange allotment was sold by exporters in the open market for a premium;

(b) after devaluation, in cases where the import replenishment was half or less than half the earlier entitlement, there was no marketable surplus of foreign exchange available to the exporters. However, wherever the replenishment was more than half the entitlement, the excess was marketable, and therefore had a subsidy implicit in it; and

(c) in the post-devaluation period, actual imports of exporters were equal to the replenishment wherever the latter was half or less than half the previous entitlement. However, in cases where surplus foreign exchange was allotted to exporters, it was sold, and their actual imports were just half the earlier entitlement.[39]

In addition to the above, it is also necessary to make some assumptions about the market premium on import licences sold by exporters.

[37] According to Bhagwati and Desai, *India: Planning for Industrialisation*, p. 406, the effective subsidy implicit in the import entitlement schemes significantly exceeded the subsidy flowing from all other measures of export promotion.

[38] It should be noted that we have selected only twelve of the twenty industries analysed so far. This is because of the inadequacy of data. But the sample is still fairly representative of the engineering industries.

[39] These three assumptions are simply the Government's definition of import entitlement/replenishment schemes. In reality, the element of surplus foreign exchange allotted may have been higher, but the unavailability of precise data and information about it prevents an alternative set of assumptions.

TABLE 9.12 ... value of exports)

| Industry | Pre-devaluation | | Post-devaluation | | |
| | | | Cash subsidies | | |
	(1) Import entitlements operative from 1964	(2) Cash subsidies in 1965/66 only	(3) 1966/67	(4) 1969/70	(5) Import replenishment licences
Steel pipes and tubes	40	20	20	30	15
Automobiles and parts	75	–	10	10	20
Bicycles and parts	40	33	20	30	27
Jute and textile machinery	40	–	10	10	17
Hand tools and small tools	75	–	15	15	50
Iron and steel castings	40	4	20	25	5
Electric fans and parts	40	–	10	20	20
Diesel engines	75	–	10	20	20
Machine tools	40	–	10	25	20
Dry and storage batteries	60	–	10	10	40
Electric motors, transformers, etc.	40	–	15	21	40
Aluminium manufactures	75	–	10	10	10

Source: For columns (1), (4) and (5): RBI Bulletin (October 1970), p. 1715. For columns (2) and (3) M. Frankena, Exports of Engineering Goods from India, unpublished Ph. D. thesis, MIT 1971, pp. 154–8.
Note:
(a) The rate of subsidy on bicycles in 1965/66 is a weighted average of that on cycles and parts.
(b) Cash subsidy rates in column (3) relate to the period August 1966 to August 1967.

TABLE 9.13   *Cash subsidy equivalents of the main export incentives* (in rupees per dollar of exports)

Industry	Pre-devaluation			Post-devaluation			
	(1) At 75% premium on import entitlements 1964/65	(2) At 100% premium on import entitlements 1965/66	(3) Cash subsidies at $1 = Rs4.76 1965/66	(4) At 50% premium on import replenishment 1969/70	(5) Cash subsidies at $1 = Rs7.50 1966/67	(6) Cash subsidies at $1 = Rs7.50 1969/70	(7) Increase in import costs after devaluation 1966–1970
Steel pipes and tubes	0.71	0.95	0.95	—	1.50	2.25	0.41
Automobiles and parts	1.34	1.79	—	—	0.75	0.75	0.55
Bicycles and parts	0.71	0.95	1.59	0.26	1.50	2.25	0.55
Jute and textile machinery	0.71	0.95	—	—	0.75	0.75	0.47
Hand tools and small tools	1.34	1.79	—	0.47	1.13	1.13	1.03
Iron and steel castings	0.71	0.95	0.19	—	1.50	1.88	0.14
Electric fans and parts	0.71	0.95	—	—	0.75	1.50	0.55
Diesel engines	1.34	1.79	—	—	0.75	1.50	0.55
Machine tools	0.71	0.95	—	—	0.75	1.88	0.55
Dry and storage batteries	1.07	1.43	—	0.38	0.75	0.75	0.82
Electric motors, etc.	0.71	0.95	—	0.75	1.13	1.58	0.55
Aluminium manufactures	1.34	1.79	—	—	0.75	0.75	0.27

Note: Calculated from the data in Table 9.12 using the assumptions made about the market premiums and imports.

The rates of premium used are based on available evidence. We assume that the market premium was 75 per cent in 1964/65, but it rose to 100 per cent in 1965/66.[40] Immediately after the devaluation, in 1966/67, there was no market premium on import licences. This is a very plausible assumption in view of the nearly complete liberalisation of imports in August 1966. However, with the gradual return of import restrictions, the surplus import replenishment licences also began to fetch market premiums.[41] We have assumed that this premium was 50 per cent in 1969/70. Finally, it is also assumed that in each year, the premium on the import licences marketed was the same (across the board) for all the twelve industries. This may not be strictly true because in reality, import licences were specific, so that the market premiums may have varied as between industries. However, our assumption is certainly a reasonable approximation since most engineering industries have roughly similar imported inputs.

Table 9.13 shows the cash subsidy equivalents of the export incentives in Table 9.12, in terms of rupees per dollar of exports. The method of calculation used is straightforward. Taking one dollar as equal to Rs4.76 before June 1966, and Rs7.50 after that, the direct subsidies are worked out simply as the specified proportion of Rs4.76 or 7.50. In the case of import entitlements and replenishments, the subsidy equivalent is just the surplus foreign exchange allotted times the prevailing market premium. The last column in the Table 9.13 shows the increase in rupee import costs borne by exporters as a result of the devaluation; this increase has been calculated on the basis of assumption (c) on page 204.

Table 9.14 outlines the changes in the net rupee returns per dollar of engineering exports. It is derived directly from the cash subsidy equivalents of the main export incentives, net of the increase in import costs after devaluation. A careful study of these figures reveals the following facts.

(a) First, in the middle and late 1960s, exporters of most engineering goods benefited from continuously increasing rupee returns per unit of foreign exchange earned. Throughout this period, export promotion policies kept the effective exchange rate for engineering exports much higher than the official rate. Some industries like the

---

[40] According to Bhagwati and Desai, *India: Planning for Industrialisation*, p. 418, the average market premium for the engineering industry import licences was 70 to 80% in 1964/65. They go on to say that the premiums increased markedly in 1965/66, particularly in the months before devaluation.

[41] Cf. N. Pant, 'What Sort of Incentives for Exports', *Economic and Political Weekly* (19 February 1972), p. 467.

TABLE 9.14   *Net rupee returns to one dollar of engineering exports*

Industry	(A) 1964/65	(B) 1965/66	(C) 1966/67	(D) 1969/70
Steel pipes and tubes	5.47	6.66	8.59	9.34
Automobiles and parts	6.10	6.55	7.70	7.70
Bicycles and parts	5.47	7.30	8.45	9.46
Jute and textile machinery	5.47	5.71	7.78	7.78
Hand tools and small tools	6.10	6.55	7.60	8.07
Iron and steel castings	5.47	5.90	8.86	9.24
Electric fans and parts	5.47	5.71	7.70	8.45
Diesel engines	6.10	6.55	7.70	8.45
Machine tools	5.47	5.71	7.70	8.83
Dry and storage batteries	5.83	6.19	7.43	7.81
Electric motors, transformers, etc.	5.47	5.71	8.08	9.28
Aluminium manufactures	6.10	6.55	7.98	7.98
Simple average of above	5.71	6.25	7.96	8.53
Weighted average of above	5.76	6.41	8.04	8.46

Source: Table 9.13.
Method: (A) = Rs4.76 + (1); (B) = Rs4.76 + (2) + (3); (C) = Rs7.50 + (5) − (7); and (D) = Rs7.50 + (4) + (6) − (7) where the numbers in brackets denote the columns in Table 9.13.
Note: Column (C) relates to the financial year 1966/67 *after* 6 June 1966, *and* includes the export incentives announced after devaluation. By itself, the devaluation raised the net rupee returns equally in all in industries to Rs7.50. In computing the weighted average, we have used the relative share of each industry in total engineering exports as the weight in that particular year.

ones manufacturing steel pipes and tubes, bicycles, iron and steel castings, machine tools, and electric motors and transformers, gained more than the others.

(*b*) Second, it is clear that the *net* devaluation in June 1966 was nowhere near 57.5 per cent, because in 1965/66, exports in the selected engineering industries were on the average receiving Rs6.25 (as against the official Rs4.76) per dollar of foreign exchange earned. To the extent that we have not taken income tax, railway freight and other tax concessions into account, our calculations underestimate the actual net rupee returns.[42] Therefore, it is likely that the final impact

[42] It is necessary to point out that for this very reason, our figures also understate the domestic resource cost of earning foreign exchange through the engineering industry. But this downward bias does not affect our comparison of pre- and post-devaluation export incentives, because the effect of tax and freight concessions remained quite unchanged even after June 1966, i.e. more or less throughout the period under consideration.

of devaluation on the domestic currency returns of engineering exporters was almost negligible.

(c) Third, subsidisation continued even after devaluation. The net rupee returns to exporters increased from an average of Rs5.71 per dollar in 1964/65 to Rs8.53 per dollar in 1969/70; a jump of nearly 50 per cent. These figures become even more significant when we consider the fact that in 1960/61, there were no entitlement schemes, and virtually no other export promotion measures. Therefore, over the decade as a whole, the rupee returns of engineering goods exporters increased by almost 80 per cent.

Despite all its limitations of data and assumptions, the above statistical exercise does show that the export promotion policies continuously improved the incentive to export. The effective subsidisation implicit in these policies certainly must have had a favourable impact on the exports of engineering goods, simply by boosting their price competitiveness in the world market and by improving the relative profitability of exports.

Non-price factors

So far, our analysis has been concerned with the factors and policies which affected the price competitiveness of Indian engineering goods. In the 1960s, however, there were several non-price factors which had a significant impact on the export performance of India's engineering industries. We shall discuss four of them briefly.

Closure of the Suez Canal: This occurrence in June 1967 had a marked effect on India's exports of engineering goods, for the simple reason that the costs of shipping them constitute a significant proportion of their f.o.b. value. Available evidence on the incidence of freight charges seems to provide confirmation. Take for example the data in Table 9.15 which show that in five of our selected engineering industries freight constituted 16.5 to 38.0 per cent of the value of exports. A study by the Indian Institute of Foreign Trade[43] revealed that the incidence of freight costs on most exports of non-traditional manufactures was much higher than the usual 10 per cent, and, in some cases, even equal to the value of exports.

The Suez closure increased the shipping distance between Asia and East Africa on the one hand, and West Africa, Europe and America on the other. The resulting increase in freight costs had two direct effects. First, it improved India's competitiveness in the East African, West Asian and South East Asian markets vis-à-vis her European and

---

[43] *Ocean Freight Rates and India's Exports* quoted in Trehan, *Economic and Political Weekly* (4 July 1970).

TABLE 9.15   *Ocean freight costs for selected engineering exports in 1965*

Weighted average for all destinations	As a percentage of f.o.b. value of exports
Steel tubes	16.5
Iron and steel bars	17.3
Bicycles	38.0
Electric fans	23.8
Sewing machines	34.6
Cast iron pipes	21.2
Centrifugal pumps	74.7

Source: T. K. Sarangan, *Liner Shipping in India's Overseas Trade*, United Nations (New York, 1967), p. 64.

American competitors. Second, it put Indian engineering goods at a disadvantage in the West European and North American markets. In order to quantify the net benefits or costs of these effects, it is necessary to examine the changes in the market composition of India's exports since 1967/68.

A careful study of Tables 9.7 and 9.8 reveals the following marked changes between 1967/68 and 1968/69.

(*a*) Exports to South East Asian countries suddenly increased from $14.2 million to $32.8 million, and exports to West Asia shot up from $11.6 million to $29.8 million. This was a complete break from the near stagnation in exports to these regions since 1964/65.

(*b*) Whereas total engineering exports increased by almost 100 per cent, exports to Western Europe and North America increased relatively little from 4.27 and 3.96 million dollars respectively to 5.51 and 6.45 million dollars.

(*c*) Exports to Africa increased from $9.6 million to $21.4 million; most of this $11.3 million increase was attributable to increased imports by east of Suez countries – exports to UAR, Sudan and Kenya increased by $9.8 million.

It is interesting that the export levels attained because of the sudden increase in 1968/69 were maintained, if not raised in the remaining years of the decade. And if we consider the whole period between 1967/68 and 1970/71, we find that India's engineering exports increased most rapidly to the UAR, Iran, Ceylon, Malaysia, Sudan and Iraq, in all of which countries India's competitiveness must have improved as a result of the Suez closure. It is necessary to point out that India's exports to Yugoslavia also grew rapidly, but that was largely because of the bilateral trade agreement.

From the above trends it might appear that India's engineering exports benefited greatly from the stoppage of shipping through the Suez in June 1967. On the other hand, it could be argued that her exports to Europe, West Africa and North America must have suffered as a result of it. This is undoubtedly true, but it is likely that the benefits were much greater than the costs because: (a) exports to Eastern Europe were under trade agreements, and as such, not crucially affected by an increase in transport costs; (b) the bulk of the exports to Africa went to countries east of Suez; and (c) Western Europe and North America absorbed only a small proportion – less than 15 per cent – of India's exports throughout the 1960s.

Therefore, on balance, it can be inferred that the political factors which led to the closure of the Suez Canal in 1967 had a distinctly favourable effect on India's exports of engineering goods during the late 1960s.

The quality factor: India is a marginal supplier of engineering products in the world market. In theory, therefore, she faces a perfectly elastic foreign demand curve and should be able to increase her exports indefinitely as long as she can sell at the given world prices. In practice, however, this was not the case, and India's export performance was constrained by non-price factors like quality and marketing efficiency.

Consider first, the importance of quality. Generally, it was extremely difficult for Indian exporters to procure orders at prices quoted by other competitors from developed countries because: (a) India was not known in the world market for the quality of its industrial production; (b) the past performance of Indian exporters had been poor and did not inspire confidence.

The first of these reasons is easy to explain. In most markets there is a natural hesitation about the quality of industrial products from developing countries,[44] and buyers are very 'brand-conscious'. In the case of Indian products, available evidence tends to confirm this. For instance, a survey of India's export prospects in Asia and East Africa found that the quality competitiveness of most engineering goods

---

[44] Interviews with several exporters of engineering goods revealed that this was a major obstacle in their search for new markets. I was told by one particular firm that it started exporting agricultural implements to East Africa as 'Made in Germany'. It was only after a few years when the quality of its brand became generally accepted that it inscribed 'Made in India' upon its products.

from India was poor.[45] It is plausible that in an economy where the bulk of domestic production is oriented to the home market, sufficient attention was not paid to designing and quality improvements. However, in markets abroad, there were also many other complaints about Indian engineering products. For example, in the past decade, there were innumerable instances where the final consignments were of poorer quality than the samples supplied.[46] Quite frequently, Indian exporters did not meet the promised delivery dates as well.[47] All these factors naturally led to a poor reputation for Indian products in many markets.

In view of the above, it is hardly surprising that Indian exporters found it difficult to procure orders at prevailing world prices, and therefore resorted to selling at lower prices. A NCAER study found definite evidence of such price cutting methods: 'Our basic competitive problems stem from the fact that we have to rely too much on low price quotations to make up for the poor reputation of our manufactured products, their deficiencies in quality, and unsatisfactory finish and packaging to match the standards of our competitors'.[48] Perhaps it was the heavy subsidisation from the Government which prevented the use of better marketing techniques.

Marketing efforts: It is generally accepted that the developed countries have distinct marketing advantages, e.g. long established sales agencies, market acceptance of their brands through advertising, export credit facilities and so on. It is therefore obvious that LDCs must develop better marketing techniques in order to counteract prevailing conditions. This is particularly necessary for increasing the non-traditional exports of manufactures, where product differentiation results in a much greater importance for brand names. It follows that engineering goods need a far more elaborate marketing network as compared with traditional exports of primary and processed products.

Although India's exports of engineering goods grew rapidly in the

---

[45] Cf. NCAER, *India's Export Potential in Selected Countries*, vol. I (New Delhi, August 1970), p. 219; quality was defined to include design, styling, etc.

[46] See ibid. p. 58. Although a few individuals or firms seeking quick short term profits may have been responsible for this, they did adversely affect the general reputation of Indian products.

[47] This fact is generally known and also emerged in discussion with a few Indian Embassies in Europe. The inability to keep to the promised delivery dates may well have been a direct result of the raw material shortages and supply bottlenecks discussed earlier in the chapter.

[48] Ibid. p. 26.

1960s, the resources devoted to marketing were far from adequate. Only three firms in the entire engineering industry set up their own marketing units abroad.[49] A few others relied on export houses,[50] while the companies with foreign collaboration relied on their parent for export marketing. However, a majority of the firms based their exports on individual ad hoc efforts,[51] e.g. appointing local sales agents in different countries. But individual firms spent much less than was actually necessary on marketing, partially because of a scarcity of financial resources, and partially because of difficulties in procuring foreign exchange.

The Government attempted to supplement the marketing efforts by participation in trade fairs and by setting up commercial sections in their missions abroad. However, a NCAER study found that: 'there were glaring shortcomings in India's organisation and manner of its participation in trade shows'; and 'none of the trade missions abroad were equipped with extensive information on Indian producers and their products'.[52]

It is obvious from the above that the sales promotion efforts behind the engineering exports were far from adequate.

This relative neglect of non-price factors like quality and marketing perhaps stems from the domestic market orientation of industrial production in India. Given the import-substitution policies of the 1950s, the economy did not have any orientation towards exports. Manufacturers who were used to the sellers' market at home were not particular about improving the quality of their product or their sales techniques. Lessons were perhaps drawn from the traditional exports which did not need such intensive marketing efforts.

Restrictions on exports by foreign collaborators: It has been estimated that firms with foreign technical collaboration account for a significant proportion of India's engineering exports.[53] Such collaboration agreements, which usually run for five to ten years of production time,

---

[49] Frankena, *Exports of Engineering Goods from India*, p. 462. These firms were Tatas, Kirloskars and Jay Engineering.

[50] This method of marketing did not develop much in India, largely because exporters were reluctant to use the export houses that were there, for fear that it might cut into their profit margins. For a detailed discussion see 'Export Houses & World Trade', *Commerce* (Bombay, 1 March 1969), pp. 32–3.

[51] Ibid.

[52] NCAER, *India's Export Potential in Selected Countries*, vol. I, pp. 54 and 56.

[53] M. Frankena, 'Restrictions on Exports by Foreign Investors: The Case of India', *Journal of World Trade Law* (September/October 1972), pp. 575–93.

TABLE 9.16   *The proportion of foreign collaboration agreements in Indian engineering industries with restrictions on exports* (in numbers)

Industrial group	1961–1965		1964–1970	
	Agreements with export restrictions	Total number of agreements	Agreements with export restrictions	Total number of agreements
Transport equipment	32	57	17	32
Machinery and machine tools	74	149	69	129
Metals and metal products	21	66	7	18
Electrical goods and machinery	53	101	36	65
Total	180	373	129	244

Source: UNCTAD, *Restrictions on Exports in Foreign Collaboration Agreements in India*, New York, 1971, p. 9.

frequently carry export restrictive clauses. Table 9.16 reveals that, during the 1960s, more than half the foreign collaboration agreements in the Indian engineering industries restricted exports in one way or another. Typically, these restrictions took the form of: (*a*) a total ban on exports; (*b*) prohibition of exports to certain countries; (*c*) exports allowed only to certain countries; (*d*) permission of collaborator for exports; (*e*) requirement to channel exports through the collaborator's agents; (*f*) restrictions on the use of the collaborator's trade-mark for exports; (*g*) higher royalty rates on exports, and so on.[54] In general, foreign collaborators prohibited exports by the Indian licensee firm to their own country and wherever else they had branch affiliates. This meant that the North American and West European markets were often out of bounds for Indian engineering goods.[55] On the other

[54] Cf. UNCTAD, *Restrictions on Exports in Foreign Collaboration Agreements in India*, p. 7.

[55] See Frankena, pp. 579–82. For instance, as a result of such market restrictions, virtually all the relatively sophisticated machine tools produced with foreign technical collaboration in India, could not be exported except to developing countries where the demand was negligible. This was quite a constraint, because 65 per cent of India's machine tool production came from three firms which had technical collaboration agreements with foreign companies (ibid.).

hand, it was quite common for exports to be restricted to narrow regional markets such as Burma, Ceylon, Nepal and Afghanistan.[56] Such stipulations naturally limited the export prospects of several engineering products from India.[57] On the basis of information gathered from individual Indian engineering firms, Frankena investigated all types of export restrictions[58] and found that, 'discrimination against exports by foreign collaborators was a significant export barrier. . . . The barrier appears to have been greatest for exports to advanced Western countries and where foreign collaborators did not have a substantial investment in the Indian company'.[59] Thus we see that in addition to the problems arising out of uncompetitive quality and inadequate marketing efforts, exports of engineering goods may also have suffered on account of restrictive clauses in foreign collaboration agreements.

Summary

The important trends emerging from the above analysis can be summed up as follows:

India's exports of engineering goods grew very rapidly in the 1960s, and her performance compares quite well with that of other developing countries. Simple metal manufactures, which had constituted the bulk of these exports in 1960, declined in importance. In fact, most of the growth came from increased exports of electrical machinery, transport equipment and iron and steel products. Although other LDCs continued to be the main markets, the share of developed countries registered a marked increase. This was largely because of the expansion of trade with the socialist countries of Eastern Europe.

An analysis of the competitiveness of Indian engineering industries revealed that there were three main factors underlying the impressive

[56] Ibid. p. 579.
[57] A detailed industry-wise classification of export restrictions is not available, but the broad industrial groups in Table 9.16 would include most of the engineering industries discussed in this chapter.
[58] For details, see ibid. pp. 579–91.
[59] Ibid. p. 591. In cases where foreign collaborators had a substantial investment or a majority equity participation in the Indian company, the situation was somewhat different. Given the heavy subsidisation, exports might well have been a profitable proposition. Frankena (ibid. p. 589) cites a few cases where firms with a majority foreign capital participation received export orders from their parent companies, in response to the export incentives offered by the Indian Government. However, there were only eight such companies. The bulk of the foreign collaboration in Indian engineering industries was technical rather than financial, and the export incentives did not induce the collaborators to relax the restrictions on exports.

export performance: (*a*) the recession in the domestic market during the period 1965 to 1967; (*b*) heavy subsidisation by the Government; and (*c*) the closure of the Suez canal in June 1967. It is extremely difficult to quantify the effect of each of these factors separately, but it is clear that the recession and the Suez closure were directly responsible for the acceleration in export growth during the late 1960s. Of course, increasingly heavy subsidisation throughout the decade acted as a crucial prop to the export effort. Although the net impact of the rupee devaluation was almost negligible, domestic currency returns of engineering exporters continued to increase even after June 1966, owing to other export incentives. Perhaps this emphasis on price competitiveness resulted in the neglect of non-price factors like quality, delivery dates and marketing. Had adequate attention been paid to these aspects, it is likely that exports of engineering goods in 1970 would have been higher than they actually were. It is also clear that, in the long run, competitiveness cannot be maintained by continuing subsidisation – some amount of emphasis will need to be placed on non-price factors.

Part Three
Policy analysis: a macro economic view

10

Export policies in the 1960s

So far, we have been concerned mainly with an examination of the factors underlying the trends in India's exports from 1960 to 1970. In the last seven chapters, we made an attempt to analyse India's export performance in her major traditional and non-traditional exports, which, taken together, accounted for more than 60 per cent of the total export earnings during the 1960s. Given the diverse commodity composition, this micro approach was clearly essential, and we did find that the factors and policies affecting export trends varied considerably as between products. However, meaningful policy prescriptions must be based not only on lessons drawn from the export problems of individual commodities, but also on an evaluation of factors that influenced exports as a whole. Therefore, the following chapters, which are devoted to an analysis of policy, focus attention on the macro economic aspects of the problem.

This particular chapter considers the domestic policies towards exportables, except for the 1966 devaluation of the rupee, which is discussed in the next chapter. Thereafter, we go on to consider the effects of the policy of bilateral trade agreements on export growth.

It is striking that during the period under study, Indian export policy went through numerous modifications and reformulations. But all these changes did have the common objective of promoting export growth. The efforts at export promotion provided a sharp contrast with the pessimistic neglect of exports in the 1950s. Thus, before we analyse India's export policies since 1960 in detail, it will be useful to examine the factors which led to this change in attitude towards exports.

The outlook on exports

Successive stages in the evolution of India's export policy are quite clearly reflected in the Five Year Plan documents. As such, it might be instructive to consider the planners' outlook on exports. Given the relatively comfortable position of foreign exchange reserves immediately after the Korean War boom, the First Plan was largely indifferent to exports.[1] But the Second Five Year Plan went even further. It assumed that no significant increase in export earnings was possible.[2] This pessimism was based on two factors. In the first place, it sprang from the widespread belief that exports of primary products and raw materials were faced with unfavourable prospects in the world market.[3] Second, it was felt that non-traditional manufactures, which constituted a tiny proportion of the country's exports at that time, had little prospects of securing sizeable export markets until industrialisation was well under way.[4] The natural consequence of such export pessimism was a conviction that, in the long run, industrialisation could be consistent with a viable balance of payments position only if it was based on a programme which minimised imports. Thus, import substitution became the keystone of the development strategy in the late 1950s. As a result, exports were neglected by the Government. In fact, it has been shown that during this period some domestic and trade policies added up to a positive discrimination against exports.[5]

As it happened, the concentration on import-saving investment did not lead to all the desired results. It was discovered that the process of import substitution in the capital and intermediate goods sectors turned out to be far more difficult than import substitution in the consumer goods sector. What is more, it did not lead to the expected reduction in pressure on the balance of payments. In fact, increasing investment in the capital goods sector compounded import needs rapidly. Thus, in spite of the general sense of fatalism about exports and the actual stagnation of export earnings, there was a gradual realisation that if the Indian economy was ever to attain its objective of self-reliance, it was necessary that an increasing proportion of the external resources required to finance economic development be met

[1] The role of commercial policy was defined in very general terms, and although one of the aims was to maintain a high level of exports, the Plan also stated that 'in periods of relatively easy foreign exchange supplies, the need for export promotion would be less evident'. See *First Five Year Plan*, Government of India, Planning Commission (New Delhi, 1951), p. 453.

[2] See *Second Five Year Plan*, Government of India, Planning Commission (New Delhi, 1956), pp. 96–9.

[3] It is often alleged that the Mahalanobis model, which provided the framework for the Second Plan, was inspired by the autarkic pattern of Soviet development. However, it is necessary to point out that export pessimism was not unique to the Mahalanobis model. In that period, many Western economists also held out gloomy prospects for the exports of primary products. See for example, Ragnar Nurkse, *Patterns of Trade and Development* (Oxford, 1961).

[4] Cf. *Second Five Year Plan*, p. 99.

[5] For a detailed analysis of the domestic policies that had a restrictive effect on export growth, see M. Singh, *India's Export Trends* (Oxford, 1964), especially pp. 152–74.

out of foreign exchange receipts derived from exports. In other words, exports had to be increased simply to reduce the dependence on foreign aid. From being a neglected issue, this is how export growth came to be an imperative in Indian economic planning.

Consequently, the Third Five Year Plan showed a distinct change in the attitude of the planners towards exports, who now argued, 'one of the main drawbacks in the past has been that the programme for exports has not been regarded as an integral part of the country's development effort under the five year plans'.[6] And so it was finally recognised that export promotion was just as important as import substitution in the process of development. Exports were therefore given a high priority in the plan, and export promotion was envisaged as a major plank of economic policy.[7]

This radical shift in the role assigned to exports was followed by major changes in export policy. Export promotion measures were introduced on a wide scale. The subsidisation implicit in these measures was gradually escalated. The trend of growing subsidisation for exports culminated in the devaluation of the rupee in June 1966, which was accompanied by an attempt to rationalise export policy. However, the efforts at eliminating the excessive export subsidies were shortlived, as the whole gamut of incentives was revived soon after devaluation. In a nutshell, this was the broad sequence of developments in the policy towards exports. Let us now turn to a more detailed analysis and evaluation of export policies adopted by the Government in the period 1960 to 1970.

Export promotion policies

In a situation where policies were changed frequently, and the incentive schemes varied significantly as between commodity groups, it is extremely important to be clear about the facts. In other words, analysis must necessarily be preceded by a comprehensive statement of the policy in question. Therefore, our discussion of each of the export promotion measures employed by the Indian Government is conducted in three stages: first, a statement of its operational characteristics; second, an examination of its so called rationale; and third, an evaluation of its success and efficacy. In what follows, these export incentive schemes are not taken up in chronological order. For the sake of analytical convenience, we have instead classified them accord-

[6] *Third Five Year Plan*, Government of India, Planning Commission (New Delhi, 1961), p. 137.
[7] Ibid. pp. 138–41.

ing to the type of subsidisation involved, into five groups: (*a*) fiscal concessions, (*b*) incentives implicit in import policy, (*c*) subsidisation related explicitly to inputs, (*d*) direct financial incentives, and (*e*) marketing assistance from the Government. However, the sequence in which those policies were adopted, does emerge from our discussion.

At the outset, it is worth noting that export policy in India was a part of the overall framework of economic planning. As such, it was inevitably linked with policies towards production, consumption, investment and imports. A detailed consideration of all these policies would involve too much of a digression, but, wherever necessary, we shall refer to them and their impact on the export sector.[8]

Fiscal concessions

Special fiscal treatment granted to exporters gives rise to two kinds of concessions: those that relate to the payment of direct taxes, and those that relate to the payment of indirect taxes. Under the first type of concession, earnings from exports are either partially exempted from income tax, or are taxed at a lower rate. Such measures improve the incentive to export by increasing the total receipts from export sales. On the other hand, the second type of concession usually amounts to a remission of the taxes or tariffs paid on inputs used in the exported output. This reduces the prices of inputs and hence lowers the costs of exporters, thereby improving the incentive. During the period under study, both types of fiscal concessions were used in India to provide encouragement for exports.

Income tax rebates and credits: In the early 1960s, the Government experimented with a variety of concessional tax schemes for exporters.[9] The 1962 budget introduced a system whereby the income derived from exports was taxed at 45 per cent, rather than the usual 50 per cent. The tax liability was calculated on the assumption that the proportion of total profits attributable to exports was the same as the proportion of export earnings in the total sales proceeds of the firm. The next development was a new kind of tax rebate brought in by the Finance Act of 1963. Under this scheme, exporters in a large number of manufacturing industries were granted a rebate in income tax,

---

[8] For information on the investment licensing and import control policies adopted in India, Jagdish Bhagwati and Padma Desai, *India: Planning for Industrialisation*, OECD (Oxford, 1970), is a valuable reference.

[9] The operational details about these income tax concessions are reported in a study by the UNCTAD Secretariat, *Incentives for Industrial Exports*, TD/B/C.2/89/Rev. 1 (New York, 1970), pp. 36 and 38; see also Bhagwati and Desai, pp. 402–3 and 432–3.

calculated at the average rate of tax on 2 per cent of the export turn-over.[10] In other words, 2 per cent of the f.o.b. value of exports was taken off from the exporter's taxable income. The rebate was allowed to the manufacturer himself or to the first purchaser of the goods finally exported. Assuming that the average rate of corporate income tax was 50 per cent, this rebate must have amounted to an implicit cash subsidy equal to 1 per cent of the export sales.[11]

However, the most substantial tax incentive was introduced two years later by the Finance Act of 1965, in which, exporters of selected products were granted tax credit certificates as a specified percentage of the f.o.b. value of exports. The rate of tax credit ranged from 2 to 15 per cent depending upon the commodity exported.[12] The significance of the scheme is obvious from the fact that it covered twenty-nine commodities which accounted for 53 per cent of total exports.[13] These certificates could be used by an exporter either for adjusting his income tax liability, or for claiming a refund from the income tax authorities. Therefore, if the rate of tax credit was 2 per cent, which it was in most cases, the exporter was entitled to an income tax refund equal to 2 per cent of his export proceeds. In order to determine the cash subsidy implicit in this fiscal concession, it might be useful to illustrate our argument with a simple example. If a particular firm exported goods worth Rs1000, it could claim a tax refund of Rs20. Hence, the net gain accruing to the firm, expressed as a proportion of the f.o.b. value of exports, would have been 2 per cent. From this it could be inferred that the implicit cash subsidy was equal to the rate of tax credit. On the other hand, it might be argued that if the exporter's net income was increased by Rs20, given the income tax rate of 50 per cent, this amounted to increasing his gross pre-tax income by Rs40, i.e. an implicit subsidy of 4 per cent, which was twice the rate of the tax credit. The latter interpretation is correct if we

[10] A list of industries eligible for this rebate can be found in Bhagwati and Desai, pp. 432–3.

[11] A numerical example might serve to illustrate the point. Let us suppose that an exporter's taxable income is RsX. Hence the tax that he pays is Rs$X/2$. If his exports are Rs500, then, at a tax concession of 2 per cent, the tax that he pays is reduced to Rs$(X-10)/2$, i.e. Rs$X/2$–Rs5. It is clear that the *net* gain of the exporter and, therefore, the subsidy is Rs5, which is 1 per cent of the f.o.b. value of exports.

[12] Cf. ibid. Table 19.8, p. 433. It is necessary to point out that the tax credits of 10 and 15 per cent were extended to commodities like minerals and fresh fruits which accounted for a relatively small proportion of total export earnings. The important exports, such as jute manufactures, tea and cashew kernels received tax credits of only 2 per cent of the f.o.b. value.

[13] See UNCTAD, *Incentives for Industrial Exports*, p. 36.

want to measure the ad valorem cash subsidy equivalent of the tax credit defined with reference to the gross income of the exporter. However, if we are concerned with the net subsidy accruing to the exporter defined with reference to the f.o.b. value of exports, the first interpretation is the correct one. Our objective in this chapter is to determine the net subsidy equivalent of export incentives offered by the Government in relation to the value of exports. Therefore, we shall take the cash subsidy implicit in this particular fiscal concession as being equal to the rate of tax credit.

All these tax incentives discussed so far were withdrawn along with the devaluation of the rupee in June 1966. It was only two years later that the Finance Bill of 1968 revived the method of subsidising exports through income tax incentives. However, as compared with those described above, the new scheme was relatively mild. According to it, 133 per cent of the export promotional expenditure incurred by a firm in any given year, could be taken off its taxable income in the following year. Expenses incurred for the purpose of advertising outside India, maintaining a sales office abroad, conducting market research, etc. were eligible for a tax rebate under this scheme. In so far as it encouraged individual firms to incur export promotion expenditure, this concession constituted an indirect export incentive.

The device of income tax rebates has two features that make it an attractive policy alternative: (a) it is a method of subsidisation that does not lead to any apparent increase in government expenditure, although, in fact, it does involve revenue forgone; and (b) it is administratively feasible as well as practical, because it only makes use of the existing income tax system for implementation. At the same time, however, this device has certain limitations. In the first place, if the income tax relief is related to profits on exports, the incentive provided by it may not be significant, specially when profits account for a small proportion of the value of exports. Moreover, a tax rebate constitutes a relatively uncertain incentive for the simple reason that an exporter cannot normally predict the magnitude of profits at the time of accepting an export order. To an extent, these difficulties can be circumvented if the tax concession is related to export promotion expenditure or the value of exports, and is adjustable against the total tax liability of the exporter, rather than just the profits on exports.[14] Perhaps this was the rationale for the tax incentives introduced in India after 1963.

[14] Even such schemes are not free of problems; for if the profits on domestic sales are higher than on export sales, which was often the case in India, firms that specialise in exporting would be placed at a comparative disadvantage.

The question that arises is whether or not the three tax rebate schemes operative in India during the first half of the 1960s contributed to export growth in that period. In view of their relatively small magnitude, it is unlikely that the first two income tax concessions had any significant impact on export performance. This is confirmed by the findings of an NCAER study, according to which, 'the quantum of rebate was hardly adequate to have any promotional effect on exports'.[15] The third scheme of tax credit certificates did imply greater subsidisation, but it was in operation for too short a period.

Drawback of customs and excise duties: In India, fiscal concessions for exporters with respect to indirect taxes took the form of: (*a*) a drawback of tariffs paid on the imported raw materials and intermediates; (*b*) a refund of central excise duties paid on domestically produced inputs; and (*c*) an exemption from sales tax on the output sold abroad. Although some of these concessions were introduced as early as 1954 and 1956, their scope was enlarged only in the 1960s.[16]

Under the drawback system, 98 per cent of the customs duty paid on an imported article was refunded when it was re-exported as such without any processing. On the other hand, if the imported article was used as an input in manufacturing, the entire duty was refunded when the manufactured good was finally exported.[17] In addition to this remission of tariffs on inputs, any excise duties levied by the Central Government on indigenous materials used in the manufacture of export products were refunded to exporters. With the exception of salt, non-edible vegetable oils and tea, this refund facility also extended to excisable final products.[18] Furthermore, all State Governments exempted the final transaction relating to exports from the payment of sales tax. However, the sales tax levied on internal transactions at several points before the export was actually effected, could not be easily identified, and was therefore not exempted.[19]

The rationale for the refund of indirect taxes payable by exporters is quite straightforward. Any manufactured good which is a potential export uses a number of inputs. Customs duties or internal taxes on these inputs raise the cost of production in that particular export industry, and thereby affect its competitiveness in the world market.

[15] NCAER, *Export Strategy for India* (New Delhi, June 1969), p. 67.
[16] See Bhagwati and Desai, *India: Planning for Industrialisation*, p. 401.
[17] Cf. UNCTAD, *Incentives for Industrial Exports*, p. 43.
[18] Ibid. p. 34.
[19] NCAER, *Export Strategy for India*, p. 68.

Therefore, it is argued that policies aimed at promoting the export of manufactures must compensate exporters for the escalation in their costs attributable to domestic taxes.[20]

In theory, a system of refunds and drawbacks might well provide the necessary compensation, but in practice, it is fraught with a number of administrative difficulties. First, it is very hard to identify the import content in any consignment of exports. Second, even if that were possible, it is not easy to calculate the tariffs or other taxes actually paid on the inputs used, in order to refund the correct amount. These problems can only be overcome by laying down detailed rules governing the drawback and refund facilities made available to exporters. Such procedure inevitably leads to delays and uncertainties. The result is that if the profitability of an export order depends on a tax refund, which might not always materialise, manufacturers are reluctant to venture into exports.

In fact, it was precisely these types of problems that arose in India. The complicated structure of administrative rules made it extremely difficult for exporters to qualify for refunds of duties and exemption from sales tax, so that the incentive implicit in these measures was greatly reduced.[21] Several attempts were made at streamlining the bureaucratic procedures governing the drawback system. In one such effort, the customs duty drawback was merged with the excise duty refund, and for seventy-six selected export commodities, a combined refund of customs and excise duties was made at pre-specified rates.[22] It is obvious that this method eliminated the uncertainty for exporters of these 76 products; but for a large number of manufactured goods, the drawback was still calculated on an application made by the exporter, after the product had been exported.[23] Such product-wise determination of the drawback entitlement of exporters led to the usual delays, uncertainties and administrative complications. In addition, it did nothing to neutralise the incidence of taxes imposed by the State Governments and local authorities. For all these reasons, a recent study concluded that 'the present scheme of refund of

---

[20] Incidentally, this would also meet the objective of improving the relative profitability of exports as compared with home sales.

[21] For details of the difficulties faced by exporters claiming refunds of duties and/or exemption from sales tax, see extracts from the Report of the Central Excise Reorganisation Committee, Government of India (New Delhi, 1963), and Report of the Import and Export Policy Committee, Government of India (New Delhi, 1962), which are quoted in Bhagwati and Desai, *India: Planning for Industrialisation*, pp. 401–2.

[22] Cf. UNCTAD, *Incentives for Industrial Exports*, p. 43.

[23] Ibid. There were at least 265 such items.

customs and excise duties is restrictive, time consuming and does not compensate the exporter fully'.[24]

Given the piecemeal and ad hoc determination of tax refunds for exporters, it is virtually impossible to quantify the subsidisation implicit in these fiscal concessions. One can only say that the actual administrative problems probably reduced the incentive. A prompt and predictable system of drawbacks would have done better from the point of view of providing a stable incentive, although a liberalisation of the rules may well have led to misuse and corruption.[25]

Incentives implicit in import policy

In an economy where imports are regulated by quantitative restrictions, the domestic market price of an imported good far exceeds its c.i.f. import price, so that foreign exchange is at a premium. It is in such a situation that import policy can be used to subsidise exports. An obvious method of doing so is to allow exporters to retain some of their foreign exchange earnings. Such a scheme provides substantial encouragement to exports in the following way. First, it enables exporters to purchase importable inputs at world prices. This lowers the costs of production and thereby improves the incentive to export. Second, it makes it possible for exporters to sell their surplus foreign exchange in the open market at a premium. The resulting increase in total receipts from export sales makes for a further improvement in the incentive to export. The principal attraction of this method of subsidisation is that it does not impose any direct burden on the budgetary resources of the Government.

Thus, it is not surprising that the import policies adopted by the Indian Government have been a very important instrument of export

---

[24] NCAER, *Export Strategy for India*, p. 73.

[25] In view of the numerous administrative difficulties that arise in the efficient implementation of a drawback system, alternative methods of attaining the same objective might be suggested. One such method is the manufacture-in-bond or the free trade zone. Under this system, the problem of refunding import duties does not arise, because any article may be imported duty free into a physically delimited zone, as long as it is re-exported in a processed or manufactured form. Clearly, these manufacture-in-bond facilities are most suitable for countries with a significant entrepôt trade and for products which require relatively simple processing operations before re-export. Export processing zones are therefore not so appropriate for an economy like India, where industrial exports are based on a large number of domestically produced inputs which have to be procured from all over the country. But this does not mean that they are of no use. Indeed, they might well provide an effective base for exporting certain types of manufactures. However, they cannot be a complete substitute for the drawback system.

promotion ever since 1960. In fact, a large part of the export subsidisation programme was based on the principle of foreign exchange retention for exporters. Until 1966, import entitlement schemes were the main instrument of export policy. Although they were formally withdrawn at the time of devaluation, it was not long before they were reintroduced in the form of import replenishment schemes for exporters. We now turn to an analysis of the operation and efficiency of each of these exchange retention schemes. In addition, we will also consider the impact of the preferential treatment received by exporters with respect to import licensing.

Import entitlement schemes:[26]   Import entitlements for exporters were first introduced in 1957, but at that time, their scope was very limited, and their only objective was to ease the supply bottlenecks. It was only after 1960, when the Third Plan emphasised the importance of exports, that these schemes acquired importance as an export promotion policy. The change in objectives is obvious from the fact that the administration of import entitlements was gradually shifted from the Ministry of Commerce and Industry to the Export Promotion Councils.

Under the system of import entitlements, exporters were allowed to retain a certain proportion of their foreign exchange earnings in the form of import licences. According to the Government, the main objective of this scheme was to enable exporters to import their requirements of components and raw materials. However, the import entitlement granted to each exporter was twice his estimated import content.[27] Given the fact that import licences fetched high premiums in the open market, this surplus foreign exchange allotment amounted to an implicit cash subsidy, which was effectively financed by the buyers of these licences.

The Indian import entitlement schemes had two characteristics, which made them different from the usual exchange retention schemes. First, exporters were not free to import whatever they liked under these entitlements. In keeping with the overall tenor of import policy, consumer goods could not, of course, be imported. But that

[26] For a detailed discussion on the evolution, coverage, operation and effectiveness of the Indian import entitlement schemes, see Bhagwati and Desai, *India: Planning for Industrialisation*, Chapters 19 and 20, pp. 406–29 and 432–67. This section has benefited greatly from the aforesaid study, and in order to avoid unnecessary repetition, we shall focus attention on the salient features and problems.

[27] Cf. *Annual Report* of the Ministry of Commerce, 1963/64, Government of India (New Delhi), p. 14.

was not the sole restriction. In fact, the entitlements could only be used in accordance with the list of authorised imports issued for each export industry. Although there were stray exceptions, permissible imports under these lists generally consisted of direct inputs for the industries in question. Second, import licences earned by exporters could not be sold to just anybody. The transferability of import entitlements was limited to traders and manufactures covered by the same entitlement scheme. The alleged rationale was to ensure that the foreign exchange allotted to a particular industry was used within it. Such restrictions on the use and saleability of the import licences granted to exporters as an incentive, gave rise to a large number of segmented markets for foreign exchange.

Exports which benefited from the incentive provided by these entitlement schemes were: engineering goods, chemicals and allied products, plastic and linoleum goods, handicrafts, cotton textiles, tanned leather, finished leather and leather products, paper and paper products, fish and fish products, processed foods, jewellery and precious stones, coir manufactures, woollen carpets and rugs, wood manufactures, cinematographic films and vegetable oils.[28] The rates of entitlement varied considerably from product to product and industry to industry, ranging from 10 per cent to 100 per cent of the f.o.b. value of exports.[29] Similarly, the market premium on import licences also varied substantially as between industries. Therefore, it is extremely difficult to quantify precisely the extent of subsidisation implicit in this export promotion scheme. However, some aggregate figures do provide useful pointers. Bhagwati and Desai found that the average market premium on import licences issued to exporters under the entitlement scheme was around 70 to 80 per cent, and in the period just before the devaluation, it was even higher.[30] An illustration would highlight the subsidy effect of this premium. Consider a product for which the rate of entitlement was 50 per cent of the f.o.b. value of exports. That was, in fact, a fairly typical rate. If we assume that the import entitlement was just twice the actual import content, so that only half the foreign exchange allotment was

---

[28] Entitlements were also available for some other exports but their scope was a very limited one, both in terms of the rate of entitlement and in terms of the very specific imports that were permissible; cf. Bhagwati and Desai, *India: Planning for Industrialisation*, pp. 436–7. Thus, for all practical purposes, it was the above industries which were the principal beneficiaries of the exchange retention scheme.

[29] For more details on the rates of entitlement, see ibid. Table 19.9, pp. 435–7; Table 19.11, pp. 439–44; and Table 19.12, pp. 445–7.

[30] Ibid. p. 418.

sold in the open market, then, at a market premium equal to 80 per cent, this entitlement amounted to an implicit cash subsidy of 20 per cent of the f.o.b. value of exports. It is widely known that, in practice, the rule of twice-the-import-content was violated frequently, and the surplus foreign exchange was often greater than half the entitlement.[31] This means that the implicit subsidy was probably more than the 20 per cent of our example.[32]

Quite apart from such substantial incentives for individual export commodities, the subsidisation implicit in import entitlement schemes as a whole, increased steadily throughout the first half of the 1960s. The total annual value of import licences issued as an export promotion measure rose sharply from Rs268.7 million in 1961/62 to Rs648.5 million in 1963/64.[33] Although exact data for the later years are not available, it is most likely that the figure was even higher in 1965/66, simply because the export drive was intensified after 1963, and import entitlements were the main instruments of export promotion policy.[34]

It is generally accepted that the incentives provided by the import entitlement schemes for exporters had a distinctly favourable effect on export growth. Professor Bhagwati and Mrs Desai, who are otherwise extremely critical of this method of export promotion, found that 'these schemes were undoubtedly instrumental in sustaining the spurt in Indian export performance during the Third Plan'.[35] However, the fact that this policy actually led to an increase in exports does not mean that it was the most efficient method of doing so. The import entitlement schemes probably compensated exporters for the over-valued exchange rate, but they suffered from numerous limitations.[36]

(a) First, continuous changes in the coverage of the schemes, frequent alternations in the rates of entitlement, and fluctuations in the market premiums introduced an inherent instability into the incentive provided by these schemes. This is likely to have had an adverse effect on the long term planning for exports.

(b) Second, the heavy subsidisation implicit in the entitlements

---

[31] See ibid., pp. 411–13.

[32] Let us suppose that the actual import content was only 30 per cent of the entitlement, in which case 70 per cent of the foreign exchange allotment to the exporter constituted a surplus. In our hypothetical example, the import entitlement of 50 per cent would now imply a cash subsidy of 28 per cent.

[33] Ibid. p. 406.

[34] Cf. ibid. p. 414.

[35] Ibid. p. 429.

[36] The following paragraphs draw on the elaborate critique of import entitlement schemes set out by Bhagwati and Desai, ibid.

created an incentive to overinvoice exports, which sometimes encouraged traders in search of quick profits, with the sole objective of short run immediate profit maximisation, to export shoddy goods at fake high price declarations. Such practices probably led to a poor quality reputation for Indian goods, thereby harming India's long term prospects for exports of manufactures.

(c) Third, variations in the rates of entitlement and restrictions on the use of import licences so obtained, gave rise to a system of multiple exchange rates based on a complicated structure of incentives, which not only resulted in unpredictable resource allocation effects, but also created a situation where additions to gross foreign exchange earnings were no index of the net increase in foreign exchange earned from exports. The latter problem has been discussed extensively by economists. It is argued that in extreme situations, large subsidies may lead to 'negative value added' activities.[37] This means that the foreign exchange earned from the export of a particular product minus the subsidy, may be less than the cost of its inputs at world prices. In other words, an export which is profitable for the individual exporter owing to subsidisation, might constitute a social loss. Following such reasoning, Bhagwati and Desai suggest that the possibility of negative value added in India's export industries 'could not be dismissed as negligible.'[38] However, we cannot attach much weight to this inference because it is not supported by any empirical evidence. But it is certainly true that owing to the heavy subsidisation implicit in the entitlement schemes, the net increase in foreign exchange earnings was probably much less than that suggested by the apparent export growth.

(d) Fourth, as the subsidisation gathered momentum, the rules governing the rates, coverage and use of import entitlements grew increasingly complex. The natural consequence was that the administration of entitlement schemes became far too cumbersome, so much so that exporters who were meant to benefit from this policy, found it difficult to understand. These administrative difficulties, coupled with a general dissatisfaction about the efficacy of prevalent export promotion measures, were some of the problems which finally led to the devaluation of the rupee in June 1966.[39]

---

[37] See, for example, ibid. pp. 363–7.

[38] Ibid. p. 463.

[39] At the end of the Third Plan period, the Government felt that export promotion measures like the import entitlement schemes were not adequate to bring about the desired export growth, and this was one of the major factors underlying the devaluation of the rupee. See *Annual Report* of the Ministry of Commerce, 1966/67, Government of India, p. 22.

Import replenishment schemes: The import entitlement schemes were abolished along with the devaluation. However, in August 1966, the Government announced the introduction of import replenishment schemes.[40] In principle, this new import policy for registered exporters was much the same as the earlier entitlements, whereby exporters were allowed to retain a specific percentage of their foreign exchange earnings in the form of import licences. Its stated objective was just to enable exporters to meet their import requirements of inputs.[41] Therefore, the import replenishment proportion was meant to be *equal* to the import content,[42] whereas the entitlement had been *double* the estimated import requirement. The import contents were determined and certified by government-designated technical authorities.[43] Another distinguishing feature of the import replenishment policy was that exports to rupee payment countries were eligible for the grant of an import entitlement on a global basis, which was not the case in the pre-devaluation period.[44]

The rationale of this modified foreign exchange retention scheme, which is still in operation, was quite obvious. In an economy where quantitative import restrictions were widely used, no other export promotion measure could provide exporters with such a free access to imported inputs at world prices. And to the extent that replenishment licences lowered the costs of exporters, they constituted a subsidy which improved the incentive to export.

Having outlined the principles underlying this scheme, let us now turn to its operational details. In keeping with the overall objective, the imports permissible under the replenishment scheme were, in general, restricted to the raw materials, intermediates, spares and components required by that particular export industry.[45] The rules concerning the transferability of import licences were much the same as they were in the case of entitlement schemes. A replenishment licence earned by exporting a particular product, could be sold to manufacturers within the same product group.[46] Although a few traditional exports were eligible for import replenishment licences,

---

[40] See *Report on Currency and Finance, 1966/67*, p. 159.   [41] Ibid.

[42] Cf. 'Fourteenth Report of the Fifth Lok Sabha's Estimates Committee', *Ministry of Foreign Trade: Export Promotion Measures*, Lok Sabha Secretariat (New Delhi, April 1972), p. 225.

[43] See UNCTAD, *Incentives for Industrial Exports*, p. 31.

[44] Cf. NCAER, *Export Strategy for India*, p. 70.

[45] The materials that could be imported through an import replenishment licence were specified in great detail for every export product. See for example, *Import Trade Control Policy, 1970/71*, vol. II, Ministry of Foreign Trade, Government of India (New Delhi), pp. 41–221.   [46] Cf. ibid. p. 16.

the scheme was essentially meant for non-traditional exports of manufactures.

There were considerable variations in the rates of replenishment
not only as between broad categories of products, but also within each
category. This fact emerges quite clearly from Table 10.1, in which
we have compiled the information available about the coverage and
incidence of the import replenishment schemes. The rate of replenishment ranged from as little as 2 per cent to as much as 75 per cent of
the f.o.b. value of exports. Even within commodity groups, it varied
substantially. For example, in the case of engineering goods, it ranged
from 5 per cent to 75 per cent, whereas in chemical products it
ranged from 5 per cent to 60 per cent. Although to a lesser degree,
such a variation in the rates of replenishment was common to all
non-traditional exports of manufactures. To an extent, this was inevitable because the import content of each exported item was determined separately.

Given the high rates of replenishment for some manufactured exports, it is quite likely that the import licences received by exporters
of such products exceeded their average import content. Therefore,
in these exports, the replenishment scheme must have provided a
dual incentive by lowering costs of imported inputs and by enabling
exporters to sell some surplus foreign exchange in the open market at
a premium.[47] Available evidence suggests that exporters of engineering products such as hand tools, small tools, bicycles, dry and storage
batteries, electric motors and transformers certainly benefited from
surplus foreign exchange allotments. This is obvious from the fact
that the rate of replenishment for these export industries was more
than half the previous rate of entitlement.[48] In view of the large number of manufactured goods that were exported, it would be tedious to
undertake a similar exercise of comparing entitlement and replenishment rates for all exports. It is sufficient to note that, in some cases,
the replenishment scheme did lead to surplus foreign exchange allotments.

The widely dispersed replenishment rates make it difficult to discern the overall incentive effect of the scheme. In order to obtain some
idea, we have estimated the average rate of replenishment for each

[47] In view of the nearly complete import liberalisation for export industries
that was announced in August 1966, there may have been little premium on
foreign exchange at that time. However, this liberalisation was shortlived, and
with the gradual return of import restrictions, import licences once again began
to fetch a premium in the market.

[48] See Table 9.12. Our inference follows directly from the premise that the import
entitlement was meant to be twice the actual import content.

TABLE 10.1 *Import replenishment rates for exporters in the*
post-devaluation period (as a percentage of the f.o.b. value of exports)

Eligible export industries	(1) The range of announced import replenishment rates	(2) The actual average rate of import replenishment
Engineering goods	5 to 75	26.7
Chemical and allied products	5 to 60	24.0
Plastics	10 to 50	29.1
Leather and leather goods	3 to 15	5.9
Sports goods	10 to 40	15.9
Fish and fish products	10	6.3
Processed foods	2 to 20	10.4
Handicrafts	10 to 40	30.7
Cashew kernels	2	2.7
Tobacco unmanufactured	3	2.3
Woollen carpets	5 to 40	4.8
Woollen textiles	30 to 70	15.5
Coir products	5	5.1
Cotton textiles	6.5	5.4
Ready-made garments	9 to 52.5	6.9
Natural silk garments	5 to 50	27.7
Gems and jewellery	25 to 70	67.5
Cinematographic films	25 to 50	35.8

Source: For column (1): *Import Trade Control Policy, 1970/71*, vol. II, Ministry of Foreign Trade, Government of India, pp. 41–216. For column (2): 'Fourteenth Report of the Fifth Lok Sabha's Estimates Committee', Lok Sabha Secretariat, Appendix XXIX, pp. 354–6.

Note: The figures in column (1) are based on the announcement made in 1970/71, and represent an approximate range. For some stray items, the rate of replenishment may have been out of this range, but these were only exceptions. The data in column (2) has been computed by expressing the value of import replenishment licences *actually* issued to exporters in each industry as a percentage of the f.o.b. value of exports of that industry. These figures were available for the years 1968/69, 1969/70 and 1970/71, and our computation is an average for this period.

group of export industries, by expressing the total value of import replenishment licences actually issued to a industry as a percentage of the f.o.b. value of its exports. These figures, which are presented in Table 10.1, show that although some manufactured goods did benefit from very high replenishments, on the average, import replenishment licences did not exceed 30 per cent of the export value, even for non-traditional items. All the same, in absolute terms, the incentive implicit in the scheme as a whole increased steadily in the

TABLE 10.2   *Total issue of import replenishment licences*

In million rupees	1967/68	1968/69	1969/70	1970/71
Value of licences issued	428.7	613.9	859.2	947.4
Value of exports under the scheme	n.a.	3183.1	4994.7	5959.6

Source: 'Fourteenth Report of the Fifth Lok Sabha's Estimates Committee', Lok Sabha Secretariat, p. 356.
Note: All figures relate to Indian fiscal years beginning 1 April.

late 1960s. This is evident from Table 10.2, which reveals a marked growth in the total value of import replenishment licences granted to exporters, ever since the introduction of the scheme. We find that between 1967/68 and 1970/71, the value of import licences issued more than doubled rising from Rs428.7 million to Rs947.4 million, and in this period, the scheme extended to approximately one-third of India's total exports. Given these magnitudes, there can be little doubt that the import replenishment policy provided a significant export incentive.

One might ask whether this method of foreign exchange retention was an improvement over the previous entitlement schemes. A comparison of the two suggests that the import replenishment method was distinctly better for the following reasons. In the first place, the subsidisation implicit in it was not excessive, which reduced the possibility of overinvoicing and negative value added. Second, it eliminated some of the uncertainties inherent in the earlier entitlement schemes through specific measures: (*a*) the rates of replenishment were relatively stable; (*b*) as long as an exporter registered the export contract with the Government, irrespective of subsequent changes in replenishment rates, he received import licences in accordance with the rate prevalent at the time of obtaining the export order;[49] and (*c*) replenishment licences could be issued in advance either against firm export orders or on the basis of past export performance.[50] Despite these improvements, however, the import replenishment

[49] 'Estimates Committee Report', p. 217.
[50] This particular facility was introduced only in 1970/71. Under it, exporters who have secured firm orders from abroad can apply for the issue of import replenishment licences in advance. Large exporters whose foreign exchange earnings have exceeded one million rupees per annum in the past, can apply for replenishment licences in advance without any specific orders. All such licences, issued before the exports are actually effected, are adjusted against the exporters' entitlement at the end of the financial year. For more details of this new scheme, see *Import Trade Control Policy, 1970/71*, vol. II, pp. 23–4.

scheme suffered from numerous limitations. It gave rise to a large number of segmented markets for import licences. It did not preclude the possibility of some manufactured exports getting extraordinary incentives through replenishments far greater than their import content. And most important, it retained all the administrative complexity of the preceding import entitlement schemes, which made the system not only difficult to administer, but also susceptible to misuse.

Preferential import licensing: Yet another kind of export incentive implicit in import policy was the preferential treatment accorded to exporters in the normal allocation of foreign exchange. In April 1968, the Government announced that firms which exported more than 10 per cent of their total production would be eligible for preferential treatment,[51] both in the issue of capital-goods or actual-user import licences, and in permission to import from the cheapest source of supply, rather than from tied sources. This measure was supplementary to the import replenishment schemes already in operation, and was essentially aimed at benefiting non-traditional exports of manufactures.[52] In 1970/71, the policy went a step further, and the degree of preferential treatment was related to the proportion of output exported. Firms that exported more than 10 per cent of their production continued to receive preference, but those that exported more than 25 per cent of their production were eligible to purchase an even larger proportion of their import requirements from the cheapest source, against free foreign exchange.[53]

Since imports from tied sources are generally more expensive,[54] the allocation of free foreign exchange import licences must have lowered the costs of imported inputs for these exporters even further, thereby improving the incentive to export. The primary attraction of this method of subsidisation must have been that it involved no apparent costs for the Government exchequer, and only required a few changes in administrative rules.

It is most interesting that the policy of relating export performance and priorities in import licensing operated in the reverse direction as

---

[51] *Import Trade Control Policy, 1968/69*, vol. I, Ministry of Commerce, Government of India (New Delhi), pp. 6–7.

[52] Although tea, coffee, cotton textiles and jute manufactures were in the list of priority industries, they were not extended this special treatment; cf. ibid.

[53] See *Import Trade Control Policy, 1970/71*, vol. II, p. 6.

[54] For evidence on the fact that imports from tied sources usually cost more than competitive world prices, see Michael Kidron, *Foreign Investments in India* (London, 1965), pp. 122–3; and Jagdish Bhagwati, 'The Tying of Aid', in J. Bhagwati and R. Eckaus (ed.), *Foreign Aid* (Penguin, 1970), pp. 252–70.

well. In other words, not only did the Government's import policy give preference to firms with a good export performance, it also discriminated against firms with a relatively poor export performance. This was the essence of the export obligation scheme which was introduced in April 1968. Under it, every firm in a few selected industries had to export at least 5 per cent of its total output.[55] If it did not meet this minimum obligation, it was liable to be penalised through a reduction in its free foreign exchange, as well as overall import licence allocation. However, firms that could be classified as small scale units, or those which had not been in production for five years, were exempted from the obligation. The industries covered by this compulsory export scheme were: bicycles, bicycle parts, stationary diesel engines, small tools, dry and storage batteries, wire ropes, automobile ancillaries, drugs and pharmaceuticals, and paints, varnishes and enamels.[56] In 1970/71, the industries manufacturing transmission towers and steel pipes and tubes were added to this list.[57]

Considering that most of these manufacturing export industries were dependent upon imports for some of their crucial inputs, the scheme probably did have a favourable effect on export performance. In fact, we find that exports of the industries subject to compulsory export obligation did increase substantially after 1968/69.[58] But it is necessary to realise that such compulsory obligations cannot be the basis of a long term sustained export effort. In the short run, they might well lead to an increase in foreign exchange earnings. However, this would not ensure the competitiveness of exports, for it is quite possible that manufacturers in these industries export 5 per cent of their output and make up the losses on that transaction by putting up prices on domestic market sales.[59] Of course, to the extent that the selected industries had high profit margins and that

[55] Cf. *Import Trade Control Policy, 1968/69*, vol. I, p. 7.

[56] Ibid. p. 158.

[57] *Import Trade Control Policy, 1970/71*, vol. I, p. 187.

[58] See Tables 8.8 and 9.4. However, it is not possible to say what proportion of the export growth was directly attributable to the export obligation scheme. For at the same time, there were several other factors such as the heavy subsidisation by the Government which were also partially responsible for the increase in exports. As we have shown earlier, in the case of engineering goods, the closure of the Suez Canal was another important factor underlying the accelerated export growth in the late 1960s.

[59] A recent and similar government policy has been to permit the creation of new or additional capacity in industry under obligation to export 60 to 75 per cent of the output so generated. This preference for exporters in industrial licensing policy was introduced in the Export Policy Resolution of 1970. For details, see 'Estimates Committee Report', p. 31.

some of them were competitive export industries even before the introduction of the export obligation scheme, it could be argued that the non-exporting firms in these industries should have been able to compete in the world market, and export a small proportion of their total production.[60]

Subsidisation related explicitly to inputs

Sometimes, the inducement to export might be provided by subsidising the inputs entering into the production of exportables. Such indirect export promotion measures which aim at lowering the costs of specific inputs, constituted the third group of policies adopted in India. They were the supply of indigenous materials to exporters at world prices, preference to export industries in the allocation of scarce domestic inputs, railway freight concessions, and special export credit facilities. While the first two policies were directed towards inputs used in production, the third sought to lower transport costs, and the fourth attempted to reduce the capital costs involved in exporting. We shall discuss each of them in turn.

Supply of indigenous materials at world prices: Import substitution implemented through protection often creates capital and intermediate goods industries in which the costs of production are higher than international costs and prices. This worsens the competitiveness of export industries which use such manufactured goods and intermediates as inputs. An obvious way out of the problem is to allow exporters a free access to imports, but this solution suffers from two limitations. First, foreign exchange might be scarce. Second, the domestic intermediate goods industries might require a large market to benefit from economies of scale, without which it might not be possible to reduce the costs of production. In these circumstances, there might be a rationale for export industries being made to use the relatively high cost domestically produced inputs, but in order to ensure the competitiveness of exports, it is necessary that the inputs be made available to exporters at world prices.

It was with this end in mind that, on 2 May 1967, the Government introduced a scheme for the supply of steel at world prices.[61]

---

[60] Given the relative attractiveness of the home market, the purpose of the scheme was to extract an exportable surplus, which would not be forthcoming otherwise. Therefore, its impact depended on the choice of industries and the efficacy with which the penal clauses were invoked. Unfortunately, no information is available about the extent to which penalties were actually imposed on defaulting firms.

[61] For details of the scheme as it was announced then, see RBI Bombay, *Report on Currency and Finance, 1966/67*, p. 159.

Under this scheme, exporters of engineering goods were reimbursed to the extent of the difference between domestic and international prices of steel. The reimbursement was based on the amount of steel used in the manufactured export, and was granted after the export had been actually effected. However, interviews with several exporters in the engineering industry revealed that the incentive implicit in this measure was considerably reduced by the administrative delays involved in reimbursement.[62]

The scheme is still in existence, and it is worth quoting the following government statement on its operation:

> In the engineering industry steel is the most important raw material required for production. Presently two schemes are under operation for the supply of iron and steel to engineering exporters at international price viz. 'Joint Plant Committee Scheme' and 'Engineering Export Promotion Council Scheme'. The former is intended for the supply of indigenous iron and steel and the latter for supply of imported steel from 'off-the-shelf' for execution of outstanding export orders. Under both these schemes indigenous as well as the imported steel is supplied to the manufacturers of engineering goods at international price or the Joint Committee Price (this is announced from time to time by JPC) whichever is lower. This is an intra-industry arrangement without any expenditure from Government funds.[63]

It is striking that exporters of engineering products always pay the lower price for steel. This is quite understandable as a compensatory measure in a situation where domestic prices are higher than world prices. But even when domestic prices are lower, which was the case in India during 1969, exporters could effectively purchase their steel requirements at that lower price.

Apart from the above, there was almost no attempt to ensure that exporters could procure tradable inputs at world prices. There was a scheme under which domestic manufacturers of plastic raw materials supplied exporters of plastic goods with the basic inputs at international prices. However, this did not really constitute a net incentive, because the exporter had to transfer a part of his import replenishment licence to the manufacturer from whom he obtained the raw materials at world prices.[64]

---

[62] For example, a firm that exported agricultural implements had claimed a reimbursement of Rs65 000 under the steel scheme for the quarter April–June 1969, and one year later, it had received only Rs11000 against the entire claim. Interviews with several exporters of engineering goods revealed similar instances.

[63] 'Estimates Committee Report', p. 48.

[64] For details of the scheme, see ibid. pp. 48–9.

Preference in the allocation of scarce domestic inputs: Where quantitative controls are fairly common, subsidisation does not only consist of lower cost inputs. In situations of physical scarcity, the very fact that a scarce input is made available to exporters, constitutes an effective subsidy.

In such an effort to assist export industries, the Government decided to give them high priority in the allocation of scarce domestic materials. Starting in 1966/67, exporters in the engineering, chemicals, plastics, processed foods and garments industries were granted a 'green form' allotment of the necessary indigenous raw materials.[65] These allotments were made by the Director of Export Promotion and, in principle, were based on the actual raw material requirements of the export orders received.[66] Given the large number of supply bottlenecks that operated in the Indian economy, this measure probably had a favourable effect on export performance. However, owing to a complete lack of information, no further analysis is possible.

Railway freight concessions: In 1960, the Ministry of Railways introduced a reduction in the freight rates for a wide range of exports. The freight concessions were available from the place of production to the port of shipment. This measure was basically meant for the benefit of non-traditional exports of manufactures.[67] It was felt that since export consignments were only a small fraction of the total freight traffic carried by the railways, these concessions would not impose much of a burden on the overall budget of the railways.[68] On the other hand, given the large distances within India and the bulky nature of exportables like engineering goods, it was felt that lower transport costs would have a distinctly favourable effect on the incentive to export. The scheme was therefore in operation throughout the 1960s.

There might well be some justification for granting freight concessions to export items that are particularly bulky. However, such subsidisation must necessarily be selective. As it happened, freight concessions were extended to exports merely because of their inland location, and on a wide scale.[69] This tended to ignore the fact that transport facilities implied a social cost for the economy. What is more, the financial position of the Indian railways deteriorated steadily

[65] *Annual Report* of the Ministry of Commerce, *1966/67* Government of India, pp. 23–4.
[66] Ibid.
[67] See Bhagwati and Desai, *India: Planning for Industrialisation*, p. 404.
[68] See *Report of the Import and Export Policy Committee*, Ministry of Commerce, Government of India (New Delhi, 1962), p. 34.
[69] Bhagwati and Desai, p. 405.

after 1967. Clearly, the freight concessions for exporters were not the cause, but they did mean revenue forgone.

Export credit and insurance facilities: It is only recently that export credit has acquired increasing importance as an aspect of export promotion policy in India. This is hardly surprising, because until 1960 the bulk of India's exports consisted of primary products and traditional manufactures such as jute goods and cotton textiles. In the international market, these traditional products are normally sold for documentary bills of payment, or against letters of credit. In either case, the exporter receives payment without much of a time lag, so that the problem of seeking post-shipment credit does not arise. However, the world market for manufactured goods is another story altogether. It is quite usual for exporters in developed countries, who account for a large proportion of the world trade in manufactures, to offer long term credit to purchasers of capital goods, and short term or medium term credit in the case of other manufactured goods. Therefore, it is difficult for manufacturers in developing countries to export their products unless they can offer similar deferred payment facilities to buyers. This problem, coupled with the belief that long term export prospects lay in the non-traditional exports of manufactures, induced the Indian Government to do something about export credit facilities.

The obvious first step was to ensure the availability of credit to exporters, and if possible, on concessional terms. This method of export assistance was first introduced in March 1963, when the Reserve Bank of India instituted the export bill credit scheme, which provided commercial banks with refinance facilities for any lending to the export sector of the economy.[70] The scheme had one objective, and that was to encourage banks to extend export credit, for which purpose it contained two provisions: (*a*) it enabled commercial banks to borrow from the Reserve Bank sums equal to the export credit granted, at the bank rate, irrespective of the net liquidity ratio;[71] and (*b*) the refinance was provided at an interest rate of $4\frac{1}{2}$ per cent per annum, on the understanding that banks did not charge exporters a

---

[70] For an extensive discussion of the export credit facilities available in India, see S. K. Verghese, *Export Credit and Credit Insurance Policies in India and Abroad*, Indian Institute of Foreign Trade (New Delhi, 1970), pp. 23–106; and NCAER, *Export Strategy for India*, pp. 52–65. The following description of the operational details of the schemes in question is drawn from these two sources.

[71] This provision constituted an incentive in so far as, normally, if the liquidity ratio falls below a certain statutory level, commercial banks in India can borrow from the Reserve Bank only at a higher interest rate.

rate higher than 6 per cent. In 1968, the Reserve Bank introduced an additional incentive, whereby it granted commercial banks a subsidy equal to 25 per cent of the interest income accruing to them from export credits. At the ceiling interest rate of 6 per cent on export credit,[72] this amounted to a subsidy of 1.5 per cent per annum.[73]

In addition to these concessional refinance facilities offered by the central bank, there are two other institutions that support the programme of providing credit to the exporters. The first is the Industrial Development Bank of India (IDBI), which was established in 1964, with the primary objective of refinancing medium term export credits granted by commercial banks. The refinance was made available to the extent of 100 per cent, as an interest rate of $4\frac{1}{2}$ per cent, subject to the condition that, in turn, the banks did not charge more than 6 per cent. To be eligible, the credits had to be for a period longer than six months but not exceeding five years.[74] In 1968, the IDBI introduced an additional scheme of direct participation in the extension of medium term export credit. Although the scheme is administered in collaboration with commercial banks, through it, the IDBI extends credit to exporters of capital goods and engineering products at a concessional rate of $4\frac{1}{2}$ per cent, while for their contribution, the banks continue to charge 6 per cent.[75]

The second institution that supports the provision of export finance in India is the Export Credit and Guarantee Corporation (ECGC). Originally instituted in the form of an Export Risk Insurance Corporation, the ECGC came into being in 1964. Its primary function is to provide exporters with insurance facilities in order to eliminate the risks of marketing abroad. The policies issued by it generally cover 80 to 85 per cent of the value of export contracts against commercial and political risks. However, the cover does not extend to risks arising out of default by the exporter himself, or changes in the exchange

---

[72] The ceiling interest rate has recently been raised to 7 per cent per annum; see 'Estimates Committee Report', p. 218.

[73] Since the rate of interest in the domestic market was considerably higher than 6 per cent, the subsidy was designed to improve the relative profitability of extending export credit. For details, see Verghese, *Export Credit and Credit Insurance Policies*, p. 37.

[74] In August 1967, the IDBI extended the permissible period to seven years for 'deserving cases' and ten years for 'exceptionally deserving cases'. However, the credit actually advanced for these longer periods has been relatively meagre; see NCAER, *Export Strategy for India*, p. 55.

[75] The apparent reason for this new scheme was that in the case of large export contracts, commercial banks may not have been willing to undertake the risk despite the refinance facilities, whereas if a part of the credit itself was provided by IDBI, it was felt that the banks might also be induced to follow suit.

rate. For exports effected on deferred payment terms, the ECGC recently reduced its premium by $12\frac{1}{2}$ per cent.[76] Basically, this insurance facility provides a very useful supplement to the export credit system. It enhances the ability and willingness of commercial banks to provide export finance by removing the burden of risk from their shoulders. Thus, the possession of an export credit insurance policy greatly improves a manufacturer's chances of procuring export credit on reasonable terms, even if he is a small entrepreneur, or for that matter, new in the business.

The rationale of such export promotion measures is indeed quite obvious. It is widely known that exporters in the developed economies market their manufactured products by offering deferred payment facilities to buyers. What is more, a large number of developed countries subsidise the provision of export credit by charging low interest rates, and setting up government-supported export insurance corporations.[77] Therefore, if India had to break into the world market with new export products, it had no choice but to provide matching export credit and insurance facilities, merely in order to keep up with her competitors. And indeed, as we have seen, the Government attempted to do just that. The question that arises is whether or not the assistance was adequate.

Consider first, the availability of export finance. From the above discussion it is clear that the commercial banking system is the primary source of export credit in the Indian economy. Available evidence suggests that although the incentives provided by the RBI, IDBI and ECGC did increase the volume of export credit, the export finance actually made available by the banks was not adequate. For instance, a NCAER study found that 'for various reasons, the procedures adopted by the commercial banks are dilatory and time consuming. Also commercial banks are not sufficiently export-oriented, and they seem to be treating the export accounts like all the other accounts'.[78] A study by the Indian Institute of Foreign Trade arrived at a similar conclusion, and found that the traditional security-oriented approach of Indian banks which prompted them to ask for collateral, created obstacles in the way of several exporters seeking post-shipment credit.[79]

[76] 'Estimates Committee Report', p. 218.
[77] See UNCTAD, *Incentives for Industrial Exports*, pp. 19–20 and 47–54.
[78] NCAER, *Export Strategy for India*, p. 64.
[79] Verghese, *Export Credit and Credit Insurance Policies*, p. 56. It is because of these general problems of providing export credit through commercial banks that there has been a pressure to establish an Export Bank with the sole objective of providing export credit facilities, but the proposal is still being deliberated upon by the Government; cf. 'Estimates Committee Report', op. cit., p. 237.

The availability of export credit insurance facilities was also not sufficient, and although the value of export risks covered by the ECGC increased from Rs70 million in 1960 to Rs1103 million in 1970, these policies accounted for only 5 per cent of India's total exports.[80] Admittedly, traditional items which constitute about 55 per cent of Indian exports are sold through letters of credit, while some others are sold through established marketing channels, and as such, do not require export credit or insurance.[81] All the same, at the end of the 1960s, the ECGC extended its facilities to only 20 per cent of the insurable exports.[82]

It is obvious that the administration of export credit and insurance facilities in India needs substantial improvement. However, it is also necessary to point out that these schemes, and any improvements therein, have some very important economic implications. First, it is crucial to realise that when a country provides export credit, it is in effect exporting capital, because it markets the product and credit as a package deal. Second, in a capital scarce economy, the provision of such credit to the export sector on concessional terms constitutes an opportunity cost, in so far as that credit has alternative uses in domestic production. Third, when a country extends deferred payment facilities against its exports, it accentuates its current balance of payments difficulties. All these problems are of great relevance in a developing country like India where both capital and foreign exchange are relatively scarce. But if there are manufactured products in which India has a comparative advantage and cannot be sold without offering attractive credit terms to buyers, the provision of export credit is imperative. It is one of the ironies of inequality that poor countries wanting to develop their exports of manufactures must export capital in the form of credit, purely in order to compete with the rich countries who offer similar facilities to buyers. One can only say that while formulating incentives in the form of export credit and insurance facilities, the overall scarcity of capital must be kept in mind.

Direct financial incentives

Broadly speaking, there are two reasons why direct financial assistance may be introduced as an incentive to export. In the first place, its objective may be entirely compensatory. This is quite possible if past trade policies have placed an exclusive emphasis on import substitution through the use of protective tariffs and quotas. The

---

[80] 'Estimates Committee Report', pp. 239 and 241.

[81] Verghese, *Export Credit and Credit Insurance Policies*, p. 96.

[82] 'Estimates Committee Report', p. 241.

resulting situation of an overvalued exchange rate which discriminates against exports of manufactures, often necessitates export incentives purely as a compensatory measure. Under these circumstances, if indirect measures like tax refunds, tax exemptions and special import facilities for exporters do not completely offset the discrimination, direct financial assistance might be called for. Second, exporters may be offered financial assistance in the form of a net subsidy. The most common rationale for such subsidisation is that manufacturers in developing countries are 'infants' in exporting, and as such, need assistance while they are growing up.[83] In India, the direct financial incentives offered to exporters were probably prompted by both the reasons outlined above. They took the form of cash subsidies related to the value of exports and cash assistance for specific export promotion expenditures. We shall discuss each of them in turn.

Cash subsidies on export sales: Soon after the devaluation, in August 1966, the Government announced the compensatory support programme for exports. Under this scheme, exporters of selected non-traditional industrial products were granted cash subsidies specified as a fixed percentage of the f.o.b. value of exports.[84] The stated objective was to enable exporters 'to meet competition in foreign markets, to develop marketing competence, and to neutralise disadvantages inherent in the present stage of development of the economy'.[85] This method of subsidisation is still in operation. Table 10.3 lists the export industries which benefited from the scheme during the period 1966/67– 1970/71, and also shows the aggregate value of the cash subsidies dis-

---

[83] This reasoning is based on the popular infant industry argument for protection. Briefly, it can be stated as follows. The capturing of new export markets for manufactures calls for an additional investment in order to gather information, learn marketing methods, establish sales contacts, create goodwill and so on. The investment may need to be subsidised if the act of selling abroad gives rise to externalities which create a divergence between private and social costs. In other words, if the benefits accruing from such investment are external to the individual firm, and in fact benefit many more exporters in the economy, subsidisation on infant marketing grounds would be justified. External economies of this type are generated if the firms pioneering exports of manufactures improve the export consciousness in the economy as a whole, create marketing skills that may be used by others, or establish a good reputation abroad that would benefit other exporting firms.

[84] For a short period before the devaluation, a few exports of manufactures (less than 20 in number) received cash assistance, but this was on a very small scale and was withdrawn along with the devaluation; see NCAER, *Export Strategy for India*, p. 69.

[85] *Annual Report* of the Ministry of Commerce, *1967/68*, Government of India, p. 20.

TABLE 10.3   Cash subsidies received by export industries since 1966 (in million rupees)

Product group	1966/67		1967/68		1968/69		1969/70		1970/71	
	Value of exports	Amount of cash assistance paid	Value of exports	Amount of cash assistance paid	Value of exports	Amount of cash assistance paid	Value of exports	Amount of cash assistance paid	Value of exports	Amount of cash assistance paid
Engineering goods	133.3	16.0	336.5	49.5	668.6	89.4	722.9	102.2	1142.4	165.3
Chemicals and allied products	42.0	4.6	147.3	16.3	215.6	27.2	321.0	36.5	379.8	52.0
Plastic goods	4.9	0.5	18.0	1.8	17.4	1.7	52.1	8.5	51.4	4.8
Sports goods	3.2	0.3	8.5	0.8	8.6	0.9	14.8	2.1	21.5	3.1
Processed foods	5.3	0.3	16.1	1.0	10.8	0.6	18.3	1.1	28.6	2.5
Woollen carpets	29.5	3.0	14.0	1.4	1.2	0.1	0.8	0.1	–	–
Cottonseed cakes	–	–	93.0	22.1	32.5	4.3	40.2	5.0	58.6	7.4
Ferrous scrap	58.3	5.8	125.3	12.0	84.3	5.0	80.4	4.2	66.2	3.3
Groundnut extractions	–	–	–	–	–	–	83.9	2.1	34.2	1.1
Iron and steel	–	–	–	–	–	–	394.0	60.8	342.3	48.5
Total	276.5	30.5	758.8	104.8	1039.1	129.2	1728.3	222.4	2125.1	288.0

Source: 'Fourteenth Report of the Fifth Lok Sabha's Estimates Committee', Lok Sabha Secretariat, insertion between pp. 370 and 371.

Notes:

(a) Cash assistance on woollen carpets, rugs, etc., was discontinued from 1 January 1967; payments in the following years were for arrears.

(b) The cash assistance for cottonseed cakes was introduced on 14 June 1967, with retrospective effect from the devaluation, so that there was no payment in 1966/67, but a large sum was paid in 1967/68. The rate of assistance was reduced in 1969.

(c) The rate of cash assistance on ferrous scrap was reduced from 10 per cent to 5 per cent after 9 September 1967.

(d) The cash assistance for exports of groundnut extractions and iron and steel was introduced after the devaluation.

(e) A scheme for cash assistance on coir products was introduced in 1970/71. However, the magnitude of this subsidy was relatively small; the cash assistance paid was Rs12 000 on exports of Rs84 000; an average rate of 14.3 per cent.

(f) All figures have been rounded off to the nearest 100,000, and as such, the columns may not add up.

(g) The above data on the f.o.b. value of exports may not tally with statistics in earlier chapters because they are based on a different unspecified source and classification.

246

bursed to each industry every year. Although the rates of subsidy ranged from 3 per cent to 25 per cent of the f.o.b. value of exports,[86] details of these rates are not published by the Government. However, the aggregate data outlined in Table 10.3 do provide us with an overall idea. We computed the average rates of export subsidy for the individual industries, by adding up the cash assistance given to each industry over the entire period 1966/67–1970/71 and expressing that as a percentage of the f.o.b. value of its exports in the corresponding period. The results of the exercise are as follows: engineering goods, 14.1 per cent; chemicals and allied products, 12.4 per cent; plastic goods, 12.0 per cent; sports goods, 12.7 per cent; processed foods, 7.0 per cent; woollen carpets and rugs, 10.1 per cent; cottonseed cakes, 17.3 per cent; ferrous scrap, 7.3 per cent; groundnut extractions, 2.7 per cent; coir products, 14.3 per cent; and iron and steel, 14.8 per cent. The average rate of cash subsidy for all the export industries worked out at 13.1 per cent of the f.o.b. value of exports.

The overall importance of this particular incentive is obvious from the fact that these subsidies were extended to the bulk of the non-traditional exports of manufactures, and that the total disbursement increased rapidly from Rs30.5 million in 1966/67 to Rs288.0 million in 1970/71. The rationale for the cash subsidisation programme emerges clearly from a statement by the Government submitted to the Estimates Committee of the Lok Sabha, according to which, support is provided for:

> non-traditional and industrial products, particularly those with potential for growth on the basis of a broad judgment as to the need for assistance due to the lack of economies of scale inherent in nascent industries and factors like incidence of non-refundable taxes and levies all of which affect their competitiveness in international markets. Though the main responsibility for the task of further improving their competitive ability naturally rests with producing units Government had decided to provide the necessary assistance to build up efficient production and also, in the meanwhile, endeavour to compensate exports for the temporary handicaps that stem from transitional difficulties inherent in a developing economy and to alleviate the disadvantages arising from our domestic fiscal policies.[87]

Thus we see that the cash subsidies paid to exporters of selected products were designed to provide compensation for the relatively high cost of domestic tradable inputs, as well as subsidisation in the infant stages of export marketing. The rising trend in export earnings of all the subsidised industries, which is evident from Table 10.3,

[86] See 'Estimates Committee Report', p. 229.   [87] Ibid. pp. 228–9.

leaves little room for doubt that the cash subsidies did have a favourable effect on export performance.

In view of the fact that direct financial assistance increases the total receipts from export sales, its effectiveness as an export incentive is hardly surprising. But it is important to analyse how it compares with alternative export incentive schemes. As a method of subsidisation, ad valorem cash subsidies based on the f.o.b. value of exports have several distinct advantages. In the first place, they provide a stable and predictable incentive. Second, they are easily understood by commercial firms, and therefore, can be introduced readily into any calculation about the profitability of exports. Third, they have the virtue of being administratively simple with little room for discretion, which reduces not only the burden on the Government's managerial resources, but also the pressures that can be exerted on the decision makers by vested interest groups seeking to maximise their own receipts under the scheme. Fourth, they do not involve any foreign exchange expenditure.

Despite the obvious advantages, however, direct cash subsidies are only rarely used as a method of export assistance. The reasons for this are manifold and complex. A most important factor is that any programme of cash subsidies imposes a fiscal burden on the government, and in a situation where the mobilisation of financial resources raises several politico-economic problems, it can be a sufficient deterrent. Moreover, explicit cash subsidies for exports are a violation of GATT rules, and fear of consequent retaliation by the developed countries deters potential users. In addition, foreign buyers who are aware of the subsidies frequently offer prices lower than they would have otherwise, thereby neutralising the incentive effect. It is for such reasons that, in practice, developing countries are usually reluctant to use direct subsidies as a means of export promotion. Quite apart from these practical difficulties, subsidies related to the gross value of exports also suffer from another major drawback. Under such a scheme, a uniform nominal rate of subsidy related to gross export value provides a higher *effective* subsidy on domestic value added to products with a larger import content.[88] A simple example would illustrate this point. Take two manufactured exports, *A* and *B*. Sup-

[88] Our reasoning is based on the concept of effective protection, in which the rate of protection implicit in a tariff is related to the value added in an import competing industry rather than the gross value of its output. Although this concept was developed to analyse the effects of tariffs, it can also be applied to export subsidies. For a detailed theoretical analysis of such application, see W. M. Corden, 'The Structure of a Tariff System and the Effective Protective Rate', *Journal of Political Economy* (June 1966).

pose that the import content in *A* is 60 per cent, and in *B*, 20 per cent. If we assume that in both cases imports are obtained at world prices, then a uniform export subsidy of 10 per cent would provide an effective subsidy of 25 per cent in the case of *A*, and only 12.5 per cent in the case of *B*. Thus we see that a cash subsidy related to the gross value of exports gives rise to a situation where there is no incentive to reduce the import content of exports, and, in fact, products with a higher import content receive a greater effective subsidy. Moreover, in extreme cases, cash subsidies paid according to the f.o.b. value of exports may lead to negative value added activities. For example, consider a manufactured good priced at Rs1000, which has an import content of Rs900. In such a case, an ad valorem cash subsidy of 30 per cent may provide the manufacturer with an incentive to export it at a price of Rs800. Owing to the subsidy, the transaction would be privately profitable although it would constitute a social loss.[89]

Given the above limitations it is clear that a scheme of cash subsidies related to the gross f.o.b. value of exports is not the best policy. In fact, an alternative scheme of cash subsidies linked to the domestic value added in export activity would be preferable for two reasons. First, it would eliminate the bias in favour of high import contents as well as the possibilities of negative value added. Second, it would provide an incentive to increase the *net*, rather than the *gross* foreign exchange earnings from exports. However, this economically superior alternative also suffers from serious practical difficulties. In the absence of detailed statistical information, calculating the domestic value added for each manufactured export poses complex problems. Even if that were possible, it would lead to a situation where a uniform effective subsidy rate would mean that the apparent rates of subsidy on gross export value vary substantially from product to product depending upon the import content of different exports. It is not difficult to see how such a scheme might create the usual problems arising out of administrative complexity.

Financial assistance for export promotion: In July 1963, the Government instituted a Market Development Fund to finance the expenditure incurred in projects aimed at developing export markets for

---

[89] It is clear from our example that the possibility of negative value added arises either if the import content is very high, or if the subsidisation implicit in the incentive is heavy. Given these conditions, it is unlikely that the Indian cash subsidy scheme led to negative value added in export industries, simply because the rates of subsidy were generally low and the import content of India's manufactured exports was usually not that high.

Indian products. The fund was financed by budget allocations each year. Export promotion activities covered by this scheme were: market research and commodity surveys; export publicity and dissemination of information; participation in trade fairs and exhibitions abroad; exploration of foreign markets by trade delegations and study teams; establishment of overseas branches and offices; operation of export promotion councils and other similar organisations; quality control and pre-shipment inspection; and other selected export promotion measures.[90] However, in order to be eligible for financial assistance, such activities had to be sponsored by official organisations like export promotion councils and commodity boards, or approved by the export assistance directorate of the Government.

This scheme of direct financial assistance designed to encourage export promotion expenditure is still in operation. The rate of assistance, which is dependent on the nature of the activity and the type of sponsoring organisation, varies from 50 per cent to as much as 100 per cent of the total costs involved.[91] The total assistance disbursed under this scheme was Rs16.5 million in 1967/68, Rs13.9 million in 1968/69, Rs13.4 million in 1969/70 and Rs18.7 million in 1970/71.[92]

The rationale for such direct subsidisation of export promotion efforts is quite straightforward. As we have argued earlier, manufacturers who are infants in export marketing may be reluctant to undertake the initial investment necessary to open up new markets for exports of non-traditional products. What is more, investment of this type gives rise to external economies which might benefit the export trade of the country as a whole. Therein lies the case for subsidisation of such investment. As it happened, however, it is unlikely

---

[90] For these and other operational details of the scheme, see 'Estimates Committee Report', pp. 227–33 and 359–60. It is necessary to point out that although the market development fund was originally introduced to finance export promotion expenditures, in the post-devaluation period it has been increasingly utilised to finance other export incentive schemes as well. For example, the cash subsidies on exports discussed in the preceding section, and the interest subsidy paid to commercial banks for the purpose of providing export credit or concessional terms, are both financed from this fund (ibid. p. 228). In fact, the cash subsidies paid to the selected export industries account for the bulk of the expenditure from the market development fund (ibid. p. 359). Financial assistance for export promotion expenditure *per se* accounts for a very small proportion of the fund's disbursements. This is patently clear from the fact that in the period 1967/68–1970/71, the total financial assistance extended for export promotion expenses was only Rs62.5 million, whereas the total disbursements of the market development fund amounted to Rs1386.0 million (calculated from p. 359); a ratio of less than 5 per cent.

[91] See NCAER, *Export Strategy for India*, p. 69.

[92] 'Estimates Committee Report', p. 359.

that the scheme had much of an impact on export performance. In the first place, the magnitude of the financial assistance offered was extremely small. Second, 'procedural delays, specially at the stage of scrutiny of the proposals for promotional activities, largely limit[ed] the usefulness of the scheme'.[93]

Marketing assistance from the Government

So far, we have discussed the methods of subsidisation which provided an incentive to export either by increasing the total receipts from export sales or by reducing the costs of exporters. However, quite apart from financial inducements, the Government also provided marketing assistance and other related services in an effort to promote exports. These facilities took the form of collection and dissemination of market information, export publicity and exhibitions abroad, quality control and inspection, training towards the development of export skills, and assistance with designing, packaging, etc.[94] Even though such services did not directly increase the monetary returns of exporters, they did constitute an indirect subsidy in as much as most of the facilities were made available free, or on concessional terms.

The above measures, which amounted to direct entrepreneurial participation by the Government in export promotion, were prompted by several factors. Until 1960, exports had been almost completely neglected so that there was very little export consciousness in the economy. In this situation, the lack of information about foreign markets and underdeveloped marketing methods constituted a major constraint on the potential exports of manufactures. The manufacturing sector itself was reluctant to make the investment necessary to acquire the information and marketing expertise, primarily because of the risks involved in exporting, but also because such investment may not have been profitable for individual firms. For these reasons, it was felt that the Government could perform an important role by providing marketing assistance and other related services to the export sector. The fact that facilities like the gathering of market information and publicity for exports involved only a slight extension of the Government's existing activities abroad, added to the rationale.

Let us now consider briefly the marketing services and facilities that were made available by the Indian Government for exporters during the 1960s. In doing so, we shall also examine their impact. *Foreign market information*: Most Indian diplomatic missions abroad have a commercial attaché or trade representative, whose primary

[93] NCAER, *Export Strategy for India*, p. 69.
[94] See UNCTAD, *Incentives for Industrial Exports*, pp. 55–63.

function is the collection of foreign market information. These commercial officers perform the traditional duty of sending regular reports to the Government on the general economic conditions, commercial policy changes, trade regulations, and export prospects for Indian products in the countries where they are stationed.[95] This information is then passed on by the Ministry of Foreign Trade to export promotion councils, commodity boards, commercial export houses, chambers of commerce and other such organisations, from where it filters down to individual exporters.[96] Long delays are hence almost inevitable. But in addition to their routine duties, commercial officers are also expected to provide assistance to Indian exporters and export organisations, conduct market surveys, procure samples, settle trade disputes, explore new opportunities and so on.[97] In practice, however, such services are far from satisfactory. This is evident from a government statement submitted to a recent parliamentary committee: 'we entirely agree that there is need for a great deal of improvement in the services rendered by commercial sections of our missions abroad'.[98] The basic problem arises because the commerce officers are drawn from the diplomatic corps. They do not have any specialised knowledge of trade problems, and what is more, they do not stay in one place long enough to acquire the necessary expertise.[99]

Export publicity abroad: We have shown earlier that export promotion councils, commodity boards, and commercial export houses were given financial assistance to meet export promotion expenditures. In addition, the Ministry of Foreign Trade arranged participation in foreign trade fairs and exhibitions, through its Directorate of Exhibitions and the Council of Trade Fairs and Exhibitions.[100] Although India participated in a large number of international trade fairs, this method of publicity was not effective. In fact, a government spokesman admitted 'I do not think that we have been successful in arranging these fairs or exhibitions ... as satisfactorily as we should have'.[101]

Quality control and inspection: Competitive quality is an extremely important aspect of export marketing. The Export (Quality Control and Inspection) Act was introduced in 1963 with the objective of ensuring the quality of Indian exports.[102] This legislation empowered

---

[95] See ibid. p. 58.   [96] Ibid.   [97] 'Estimates Committee Report', p. 262.
[98] Ibid. p. 267.
[99] For a detailed discusssion of the problems relating to the export promotion functions of Indian missions abroad, see ibid. pp. 261–74.
[100] Ibid. p. 253.   [101] Ibid. p. 256.

the Government to subject exportable commodities to quality control as well as pre-shipment inspection, and to prohibit exports of products which did not meet the specified quality standards. The actual task of quality inspection was undertaken by both government and private agencies, all of which were supervised by a national Export Inspection Council. One estimate suggests that, by 1969, 85 per cent of India's exports were covered under some scheme of quality control and pre-shipment inspection.[103]

All the same, there have been persistent complaints about the quality of Indian products, and in many countries India does not have a reputation for being a supplier of good quality manufactures.[104] Available evidence suggests that the system of quality control is far from thorough, and leaves much to be desired.[105]

Improvements in administration are clearly necessary, but the most important lesson to be drawn from this experience is that although efficient pre-shipment inspection might be able to prevent the export of shoddy goods, in the long run, quality control must be introduced at every stage of the production process. Compulsory quality control is only a preliminary step, which should be followed by a quality consciousness on the part of exporters themselves.

Apart from the above efforts at collection of foreign market information, export publicity abroad and quality control, the Government set up special institutes for the purpose of: (a) training personnel in export marketing and management techniques; (b) evolving new designs to meet the requirements of different industries; and (c) developing packaging technology.[106] These aspects of export promotion acquired prominence only with the emergence of non-traditional exports of manufactures, in the marketing of which non-price factors play an important role. The traditional exports, which were sold through established marketing channels and were frequently shipped in unprocessed bulk, did not require such facilities. However, these institutes were set up quite recently and very little information is available on their operation. Therefore, it is not possible to comment on their effectiveness.

[102] For details about the administration of quality control, see NCAER, *Export Strategy for India*, pp. 36–9, and the 'Estimates Committee Report', pp. 242–6.

[103] NCAER, *Export Strategy for India*, p. 38.

[104] Ibid. For examples of poor quality Indian manufactures sold abroad, see also NCAER, *India's Export Potential in Selected Countries*, vol. I (New Delhi, 1970), pp. 150, 177 and 183.

[105] See NCAER, *Export Strategy for India*, p, 38.

[106] See UNCTAD, *Incentives for Industrial Exports*, pp. 62–3.

An evaluation of policy

The preceding discussion sought to provide a comprehensive and analytical description of export policies that were operative in India during the period 1960 to 1970. This detailed evaluation of each export promotion measure served a dual purpose: it revealed how far each policy was successful in attaining its objective; and it brought out the conceptual and administrative drawbacks of these export incentive schemes. However, such a partial-analysis-oriented approach is unlikely to tell the whole story. This does not mean that a careful examination of individual policies is unnecessary. It is certainly worthwhile insofar as it constitutes the basis for a more complete discussion. But export policies cannot be looked at in isolation, because their final impact also depends on import policies, domestic policies and other conditions prevalent in the economy. Therefore, the overall effect of the wide variety of export promotion measures adopted in India, on export performance, can best be assessed in terms of all the relevant factors and policies.

Clearly, such an exhaustive analysis would be beyond the scope of this work. Our objective is limited to an evaluation of Indian export policy in the context of a macro economic framework. Towards this end, the following pages seek to analyse the actual effect of export promotion policies on India's export trends. Before entering into such a discussion, however, it might be useful to outline very briefly the economic criteria on which the formulation of an export policy should, in theory, be based. Following from that, it may be possible to say something about the success or failure of Indian policies.

The economics of export promotion

Three considerations are relevant towards the determination of an appropriate export policy: the state of the balance of payments and exchange rate policy, the existing level of import restrictions, and the terms of trade.

(*a*) Consider an economy faced by a balance of payments deficit. In terms of orthodox trade theory, under certain assumptions, the first-best policy would be a combination of the devaluation necessary to restore equilibrium in the balance of payments, and the optimum set of trade taxes.[107] The assumptions under which this policy prescrip-

---

[107] Cf. W. M. Corden, *Trade Policy and Economic Welfare* (Clarendon Press, Oxford, 1974), Chapter 7.

tion is valid, are, to say the least, quite unrealistic. Therefore, it is perfectly possible that an exchange rate depreciation does not take place in countries which have balance of payments problems. The reasons for this are not far to seek: a devaluation may not be politically acceptable, or it may not be regarded as desirable on economic grounds.[108] In case of the former, a possible alternative would be a uniform tariff on all imports accompanied by an equivalent uniform subsidy on all exports adjusted for the necessary set of trade taxes. In case of the latter, there might be valid economic reasons for *selective* tariff protection and export subsidisation, rather than an across-the-board *general* exchange rate policy. Thus export subsidisation might be necessary as one part of the substitute for exchange rate adjustment.

(b) In fact, during the 1950s, India attempted to iron out balance of payments difficulties by the use of import restrictions alone; the emphasis was on import substitution rather than export promotion. The resulting overvalued exchange rate, supported by a regime of tariffs and import controls, created a systematic bias against exports. In the first place, it meant that the price paid by Indian exporters for imported, or domestically produced importable inputs, was higher than the world price so that they were placed at a disadvantage vis-à-vis their competitors. Such a 'tax' on inputs without any subsidy on the output also meant that the effective protection of export activities was negative. Second, the protection that supported the overvalued rupee raised further the relative profitability of producing importables as compared to exportables.

Under these circumstances, if the exchange rate remains unchanged, export subsidisation is necessary purely as a compensatory measure. *Ceteris paribus*, this subsidisation should be extended to all exports at a level equal to that of import restrictions, so as to completely offset the bias against exports. The justification is simply that an increase in exports would improve the balance of payments just as much as an equivalent reduction in imports. Hence India's export promotion policies in the 1960s must be seen in the context of the existing level of import restrictions.

[108] The political reluctance to devalue currencies is so widespread and well known that it needs no substantiation. The economic arguments against an exchange rate adjustment might be the: (a) adverse effects of a devaluation on internal income distribution; (b) low elasticities of foreign demand for exports and domestic demand for imports so that a devaluation might worsen the balance of payments and (c) destabilising short term capital movements and a discouragement of long term capital inflows that might result from a devaluation.

(c) A third consideration which must be taken into account while formulating policy is the terms of trade argument for taxes on exports. In its simplest form, the argument is that if the foreign elasticity of demand is less than infinite, a country can, by restricting the supply, obtain a higher foreign exchange price for its exports and, for the optimum restriction, higher foreign exchange earnings. For policy purposes, the important thing is to determine the degree of restriction on exports, which yields maximum benefit to the country concerned. There is a considerable amount of theoretical literature on the subject of the optimum rate of export tax, which we shall not go into here;[109] suffice it to say, that, in the absence of foreign retaliation, the higher the foreign elasticity of demand for exports the lower is the optimum tax rate. There are two reasons why this term of trade argument should be treated with caution in its application to policy decisions. First, in the short run, restricting export supplies through a tax on exports may yield a terms of trade gain, but it may be against the long term export interests of the country because alternative sources of supply are likely to be developed; these may take the form of synthetic substitutes or purchase of the same product from other countries.[110] Second, oligopolistic market situations, which was the case for two of India's principal exports, may be characterised by a kinky demand curve; so that an export duty which restricts the supply may not lead to any significant price gain, at any rate after a time, but may result in a substantial loss of the country's sales to the other oligopolists. There is no doubt that the foreign demand for many of India's traditional exports is less than infinitely elastic. However, there is a danger that export taxes may have been above the optimum, so that the policy towards these exports needs to be considered in the light of the above observations.

Having outlined the economic implications of export promotion, let us now turn our attention to the effect of export policies actually adopted in India, on export performance.

Promotion and export trends

In sharp contrast with the 1950s, the 1960s were a decade in which policy makers paid a great deal of attention to exports, and although

---

[109] For an extensive theoretical discussion on the optimum rate of export tax, see ibid.

[110] Restricted export supplies might also lead to greater economy in the use of the commodity concerned. For example, reduced supplies of a raw material might induce (a) technical change that economises on its use per unit of output, or (b) a switch to products that use less of it as an input.

the period under study witnessed only a moderate increase in the total value of exports, it was a definite break from the past stagnation in export earnings.[111] This section considers the effect of promotion policies, adopted by the Government, on the trends in India's principal exports. It will be convenient to take up traditional and non-traditional exports separately.

The most striking fact to emerge from the discussion is that the incentive schemes were almost exclusively aimed at non-traditional exports of manufactures. We found that very few traditional exports benefited from export promotion policies in the 1960s. Among the vast and complicated structure of export incentives that existed before the devaluation, only the following were available to traditional items: (a) substantial import entitlements were granted to exporters of cotton textiles and vegetable oils; (b) minor income tax concessions were extended to exporters of jute manufactures, tea, cashew kernels and mineral ores for a very short period before the devaluation. But that was all, and it was by no means sufficient to compensate for the overvalued exchange rate which continued to discriminate against these exports. The devaluation of the rupee did not much alter the situation, because, as far as traditional exports were concerned, a large part of it was neutralised by the imposition of export duties.[112] In the post-devaluation period, exports of cashew kernels, tobacco and coir products were eligible for small import replenishments, while exports of cottonseed oilcakes received cash subsidies, but none of these was very significant.

Thus it appears that, apart from a few exceptions, traditional exports were largely neglected by the policy makers. In fact, the Government's export promotion efforts did little to prevent or slow down the decline in India's relative share of the world market in commodities such as jute manufactures and tea, which, taken together, accounted for more than 35 per cent of the country's foreign exchange earnings until the mid-1960s. Other less important traditional exports suffered the same fate. Cotton textiles were perhaps

---

[111] The average annual value of exports increased from $1392 million in the three-year period 1960/61–1962/63 to $1914 million during 1968/69–1970/71 and the volume of exports increased roughly in the same proportion, (calculated from Table 2.1 p. 17). By contrast, there was no significant increase in exports during the 1950s. In fact the average annual value of exports fell slightly from $1280 million in 1951/52–1953/54 to $1238 million during 1957/58–1959/60 (calculated from Singh, p. 15) .

[112] For a detailed analysis of the impact of devaluation on export performance, see Chapter 11.

the solitary exception, where the heavy subsidisation probably enabled the industry to maintain its share of the world market.[113]

All this might seem somewhat paradoxical in a period when the vital importance of the export sector was widely accepted in government circles; as such, it needs explanation. One possible reason underlying the implicit bias of export promotion policies may have been the assumption that the foreign demand for most of India's traditional exports was less than infinitely elastic, and the consequent belief that an increase in such exports would only worsen the terms of trade. Thus the maintenance of an overvalued currency, accompanied by import restrictions and subsidisation of non-traditional exports, was effectively a way of taxing the traditional exports. It is perfectly true that the elasticity of foreign demand for many of India's traditional exports was less than infinite. However, it did not justify the extent of the discrimination implicit in the overvalued exchange rate, and the actual neglect of traditional items in export promotion. While this strategy may have given rise to a terms of trade gain in the short run, it was certainly not in India's long term export interests. For even at the end of the 1960s, traditional commodities which suffered on account of this policy made up a little more than two-thirds of the country's export earnings. What is more, in the period that policy makers were concerned with encouraging exports of non-traditional products, India steadily lost her share of the world market in many traditional exports.

To some extent, this loss was made up for by the growth in non-traditional exports of manufactures, the average annual value of which quadrupled over the decade. It rose from $146.8 million in the three-year period 1960/61–1962/63 to $580.2 million during 1968/69–1970/71.[114] There is no doubt that the export subsidisation programme adopted by the Government was one of the principal factors underlying this rapid expansion.[115] In other words, promotion policies of the 1960s had a distinctly favourable effect on the trend in exports of non-traditional products. However, this should

[113] It should be noted that even in this case India did not fare as well as her competitors, who managed to increase their relative shares.

[114] Calculated from Table 2.9. At the same time, the average annual value of traditional exports of manufactures fell from $411.4 million to $394.3 million (Table 2.3), while that of primary and semi-processed product exports, other than iron ore, declined slightly from $764.7 million to $760.6 million (calculated from Table 2.8).

[115] In evaluating the impact of import entitlement schemes on export performance, Bhagwati and Desai reached the same conclusion; *India: Planning for Industrialisation*, p. 429.

not be taken to mean that the policies actually adopted were the best way of obtaining the increase in exports. As a matter of fact, the subsidisation methods suffered from one serious defect.

The administrative complexity, the uncertainty and the bureaucratic delays inherent in most of the schemes must have almost certainly reduced the net incentive. This emerged quite clearly from our discussion in the last section. For example, the incentive implicit in fiscal concessions was significantly affected by the uncertainty of administrative decisions on the rate of tax refunds and by the delay in the actual payment of refunds. The financial inducement implicit in the import entitlement schemes was reduced by the instability and uncertainty of the incentive. While import replenishment schemes were an improvement in some respects, they continued to be problematic on account of administrative complexity.[116] In the case of subsidisation related explicitly to inputs, exporters faced similar problems. The scheme of direct cash subsidies was perhaps the only one which was relatively free of these limitations. In general, however, exporters could not be certain about their final cash receipts from the gamut of promotion policies, which not only reduced the value of the incentive but also made it difficult for firms to calculate the profitability of export orders.

It follows that defective methods of subsidisation probably reduced the potential impact of export promotion policies. In addition, the possible favourable effects of promotion were also counteracted by the sharp rise in India's relative cost and price level, as well as the higher relative profitability of selling exportables at home and of import substitution. Let us consider these factors in turn.

Table 10.4 outlines the movement in the general price level during the 1960s, as reflected in the all-India wholesale price index and consumer price index. Wholesale and retail prices increased steadily throughout the decade, although the rise was more pronounced around the mid-1960s because of the agricultural drought and the escalated defence expenditure following the war with Pakistan. In the period 1961/62–1970/71, the wholesale price index rose by 81 per cent at a compound rate of 6.8 per cent per annum, and the consumer price index registered an increase of 78 per cent at a compound rate of 6.6 per cent per annum. This inflation was quite substantial by Indian standards, and stands out in contrast with the 1950s. In fact, between 1951/52 and 1960/61, wholesale prices rose by only 5.8 per cent, or 0.7 per cent per annum, while the consumer price index increased by

---

[116] For example, the bureaucratic delays involved in obtaining import licences.

TABLE 10.4   *Indices of wholesale and retail prices in India*

Average of months in	Wholesale price index for all commodities 1961/62 = 100	Consumer price index for industrial workers 1949 = 100
1961/62	100	127
1962/63	103.8	131
1963/64	110.2	137
1964/65	122.3	157
1965/66	131.6	169
1966/67	149.9	191
1967/68	167.3	213
1968/69	165.4	212
1969/70	171.6	215
1970/71	181.1	226

Source: RBI Bombay, *Report on Currency and Finance, 1966/67, 1969/70* and *1970/71*.
Note: The series on the consumer price index for industrial workers with 1949 as base year was discontinued in 1968. The figures from 1968/69 onwards have been converted in order to make them comparable.

just 18 per cent, at a rate of 1.9 per cent per annum.[117] Therefore, even though exports were paid scant attention in the 1950s, the relative price stability prevented matters from being worse. On the other hand, it is possible that the sharp increase in relative costs and prices during the 1960s worsened the cost competitiveness of Indian exports. Although an overall inflation rate of 7 per cent per annum is by no means excessive when compared with inflation in the rest of the world, it was greater than the average rate of price increase in several countries,[118] and our earlier analysis revealed that this problem was quite serious for some export industries. In fact, the costs of exporters of jute manufactures, cotton textiles, and to some extent, tea, rose much faster than in competing countries. Moreover, insofar as the world prices of Indian exports did not rise as much, the inflation must have reduced the relative profitability of exports vis-à-vis sales in the

[117] Calculated from Singh, *India's Export Trends*, pp. 165–6.
[118] During the 1960s the average rate of inflation in the OECD countries was 3.6 per cent per annum (calculated from OECD, *Inflation: The Present Problem* (Paris, 1970), p. 15). Although comparable data are not available for developing countries, indirect evidence suggests that inflation in India was not excessive. For instance, in the period 1960–1965, the average annual rate of inflation in LDCs was 8 per cent, or, excluding the high inflation countries, 3.4 per cent, cf. J. O. Adekunle, 'Rates of Inflation: 1949–65', *IMF Staff Papers* (November 1968), p. 533.

domestic market, making the sale of exportables at home a more attractive proposition than before.

Clearly, the export promotion efforts were, to some extent, counteracted by rapidly rising costs and prices. In the case of non-traditional
exports of manufactures, the subsidisation was obviously large enough
to provide a net incentive despite these changes. However, most traditional exports did not benefit from a similar subsidisation, so that their
relative profitability in the 1960s was probably not significantly better
than in the 1950s. Indeed, for some commodities, such as jute manufactures, the position may have deteriorated towards the end of the
decade under study. Under normal circumstances, the devaluation of
57.5 per cent in June 1966 would have offset the inflation, but, as we
go on to show later, a large proportion of it was neutralised by the policy
changes that accompanied it.

The higher relative profitability of the import competing manufacturing sector was a direct consequence of the import substitution
policies based on protection and an overvalued exchange rate. This
meant that manufacturing production for the home market was encouraged relative to agriculture, and to manufacturing production
for export, which, in turn, had been a serious obstacle to export
growth in the 1950s. The shift in emphasis from import substitution
to export promotion, which started around 1960, was partially meant
to alter the relative incentives and to compensate the export sector of
the economy for the overvalued exchange rate. In the early 1960s,
the various subsidisation measures did contribute towards this objective, and that is borne out by the improvement in export performance. Owing to the complexity of measures involved it is difficult to
be precise, but it would not be far wrong to say that, as the subsidisation was gradually escalated, the compensation probably turned
into a net incentive for some exports.[119] In June 1966, the existing
incentives were replaced by the devaluation of the rupee, but as we
have seen, subsidisation continued even afterwards. However, it is
important to reiterate that, in general, the benefits from the export
incentive schemes or the devaluation did not accrue to traditional

---

[119] Ian Little, T. Scitovsky and Maurice Scott, *Industry and Trade in Some Developing Countries* (Oxford, 1970), p. 180, describe the situation as follows:
'India's export promotion has constituted such a bureaucratic tangle that it
is virtually impossible for a researcher to estimate, for any year in the 1960s,
the relative attraction of selling manufactures at home or for export. The
manufacturer himself probably had equal difficulties ... it seems probable that
for a year or two prior to the devaluation of 1966, ... the incentive to export
was as great for many industries as the incentive to sell at home.'

exports, which continued to be discriminated against throughout the decade.

Failures of export policy

Following from the above discussion, it may now be possible to say something towards an overall evaluation of the export policies that were actually adopted in India during the 1960s. Allegedly, a great deal of emphasis was placed on export promotion, and yet the increase in total export earnings brought about by the gamut of promotion policies was relatively modest. Even more significant is the fact that this increase was confined to a small range of exports. To what extent was this attributable to insufficient or inappropriate export promotion?

A straightforward answer to the question is difficult, owing to the complexity of the factors involved, but there is little doubt that the *modus operandi* of export promotion left much to be desired. Our analysis suggests that there were three basic failures of export policy in the 1960s: (*a*) the relative neglect of traditional exports which accounted for a large proportion of the country's foreign exchange earnings; (*b*) inappropriate, and perhaps excessive, subsidisation of a narrow range of non-traditional exports of manufactures; and (*c*) the inability to create, or develop, other new manufactured exports which may have had a large growth potential. This concluding section is concerned with a brief discussion of these so-called failures.

The near stagnation in foreign exchange earnings derived from traditional exports is as good an index as any of the relatively poor export performance in these commodities. While exports of iron ore, cashew kernels and oilcakes registered a substantial increase, such growth was only an exception to the overall picture of stagnation and was counteracted by a decline in the exports of other traditional items. That was not all. In the latter half of the 1960s, India steadily lost her relative share of the world market for a large number of these exports. One might argue that the maintenance of relative market shares is by no means mandatory, and by itself, may not even mean very much. As a matter of fact, insofar as India's agricultural production could not grow any faster than it did, a loss in the relative market share of agricultural and agro-based industrial exports was perhaps inevitable.

However, in cases where world import demand is nearly stagnant, as it was for some of India's principal exports, a loss in market shares implies a fall in the absolute value of exports. Such an outcome may be most undesirable in an economy where foreign exchange is scarce.

Nevertheless, promotion policies adopted by the Government largely neglected traditional exports[120] which, in absolute terms, continued to be rather important foreign exchange earners. Very little was done to prevent or slow down the decline in India's relative share of the world market for some of these commodities, whereas the discriminatory overvalued exchange rate continued to exist. The terms of trade argument was certainly no justification for the extent of discrimination against traditional exports. In a period when the importance of exports was widely stressed and talked about, this was surely a serious limitation of the policies that were pursued.

The second failure of export policy was one of excessive attention rather than of neglect. Export promotion efforts were concentrated on a few selected groups of non-traditional manufactured exports which were engineering goods, iron and steel and chemical products. There is little doubt that India should have increased its exports of these manufactures, as indeed it did, but that should not have led to a dictum of exports for the sake of exports. After all, maximisation of exports *per se* is not a desirable objective. Unfortunately, the policies that were adopted during the early 1960s did lead to indiscriminate export promotion.[121] Clearly, an appropriate export promotion policy must be based on some assessment of the real benefit derived from the additional exports. India exports in order to import goods that either could be obtained on more favourable terms through trade than if they had to be produced at home, or could not be produced at home at all. Therefore, exports should be increased when the extra imports obtained in exchange are worth more than the extra exports or the goods that could be produced instead of these extra exports. As it happened, the complex subsidisation measures concealed the domestic resource costs of the increase in exports.

Our previous discussion revealed that this was because the Government attempted to minimise the budgetary costs of export promotion, but in the process neglected the domestic resource costs of subsidisation. As far as public expenditure was concerned, the fiscal concessions merely called for some adjustments in the tax collection procedure, although, in fact, they meant revenue forgone. The incentives implicit in import policy only required a few changes in the rules governing the allocation of foreign exchange, but the market premium on import licences involved a transfer of financial resources to the exporter selling them. And as we have seen, the subsidisation re-

---

[120] With the important exception of cotton textiles.
[121] For an elaborate discussion on this point, see Bhagwati and Desai, *India: Planning for Industrialisation*, Chapter 20.

lated explicitly to inputs did not also require any expenditure from the exchequer, while the finance necessary for export credit was provided by commercial banks. It was only the direct financial assistance for exports that imposed a fiscal burden on the Government. In an economy where the mobilisation of financial resources always posed a problem, the emphasis on minimising budgetary costs was understandable. Unfortunately, however, this preoccupation led to a situation where domestic resource costs were left out of account.[122] As a result some exports were granted excessive and indiscriminate subsidisation.[123]

It need hardly be stressed that domestic resources which went into such subsidisation of exports had alternative uses, and therefore, constituted a cost to the economy even though this was not reflected in increased government expenditure. Thus, while formulating export promotion policies, in addition to budgetary costs, the Government should also have considered the domestic resource cost of earning foreign exchange through exports. That may have exposed the excessive and unnecessary subsidisation. Moreover, if an increase in exports was brought about at the cost of a resource shift from other sectors of the economy, the social opportunity cost of such a shift and of the export subsidisation that was instrumental in it, should have been assessed carefully.[124] Given the overvalued exchange rate and the import restrictions, export promotion was probably necessary as a compensatory measure; all we are saying is that it should have been based on a systematic evaluation of its costs and effectiveness.

Failure on the export front, however, did not only consist of the neglect of traditional exports and excessive subsidisation of a few,

---

[122] It is worth noting that this may not be a case of mere administrative expediency or misguided economic doctrine. In our opinion, it is quite likely that vested interests and pressure groups played a part in determining the structure of incentives that has been discussed at length. All said and done, budgets are scrutinised quite thoroughly in the Indian parliament and subsidies which show up as budgetary costs are not only subject to continuous review, but are also liable to be questioned. On the other hand, indirect and concealed subsidisation is perhaps the most secure form of protection, because the magnitude of the subsidy is not at all apparent. Thus, vested interests may have supported the continuation of these types of export promotion measures.

[123] This is confirmed by evidence examined earlier in the Chapter; see also Bhagwati and Desai, *India: Planning for Industrialisation*, Chapter 20.

[124] For example, it is perfectly possible that resources diverted into the production of non-traditional exports of manufactures came from the traditional export sector, or the agricultural sector, both of which were relatively underprotected; in either case it meant an opportunity cost in terms of the output forgone in those sectors.

select non-traditional exports; it also consisted of not exporting things which it would have been socially profitable to export. The inability to develop such new exports is attributable to the fact that the Government took its existing industrial base and subsidised heavily, without attempting to see what other sorts of industrial exports could have been developed. While the Government's export promotion efforts were essentially directed towards the engineering, chemical and iron and steel industries, there were several other non-traditional manufactured exports such as clothing, processed foods, leather manufactures, sports goods, toys, plastic goods, canned fish products, wood manufactures, electronics and precision instruments,[125] which could have been developed in India. Besides a tremendous potential in terms of growing world demand, these manufactures had a distinct advantage of being labour intensive in production.[126]

As far as the Indian economy is concerned, the new 'dynamic' commodity groups mentioned above can be divided into two categories: those that are based on the use of domestic resources and those that are not. Domestic resource based products, e.g. clothing, processed foods, leather manufactures, sports goods or fish products would have been particularly suitable for India as they would have resulted in high net foreign exchange earnings. This does not mean that industrial exports based on imported materials, e.g. plastic goods, toys, precision instruments or electronic equipment, did not hold out any promise. It might be argued that after all, Japan's and more recently, Hong Kong's success at exporting manufactures was partially based on the use of imported intermediates and raw materials. While, at a superficial level, it is perfectly true, one must be wary about such inter-country analysis, and careful thought must be given to the problem before recommending policies that were successful in other countries, for conditions in the country concerned might be substantially different.

In India, however, most of these industries escaped the extensive

---

[125] Some of these products were the basis of the rapid growth in exports of manufactures from the small South-East Asian countries. The point is *not* that India should have exported exactly what Hong Kong and Taiwan did, but that Indian policies should have provided some incentive for non-traditional exports that would have been socially profitable and would have benefited from a large and expanding foreign demand. In addition to the appropriate trade policies this would also have needed entrepreneurs who could identify the prospects and undertake such exports.

[126] Apart from the comparative advantage that India would have had in the export of labour intensive manufactures, the development of such new exports would also have lead to the creation of employment opportunities at home.

network of export promotion in the period before 1966, partially because some of them did not even exist as export industries. It was only the develuation of the rupee and the export subsidisation policies adopted thereafter that provided an incentive for such exports to be developed. As a result, towards the end of the 1960s, these items did begin to contribute something to India's foreign exchange earnings, but, in proportionate terms, they remained relatively insignificant.

Some of the main conclusions emerging from the discussion on evaluation of policies can be summed up as follows. During the 1960s, the Government placed a great deal of emphasis on the export sector of the economy, but the export promotion policies succeeded only in bringing about a modest increase in total export earnings. To a significant extent, this was a failure of export policy. We found that traditional exports, which accounted for a sizeable share of the country's foreign exchange receipts, were largely neglected. What is more, the subsidisation was concentrated on a small range of non-traditional manufactured exports, so that other new and dynamic exports were not even developed.

I I

The impact of devaluation

It is generally accepted that, besides the pressure from abroad, there were two basic policy objectives underlying the devaluation of the rupee in June 1966. In the first place, it sought to replace the administratively cumbersome structure of import restrictions and export subsidies by a straightforward exchange rate depreciation. At the same time, it aimed at improving the balance of payments position. In view of the first objective, it is hardly surprising that the devaluation was accompanied by an elimination of the prevalent export incentives and import controls, as a result of which, the effective devaluation was much less than that suggested by the apparent change in parity of the rupee. All the same, the devaluation was, at least partially, intended to stimulate exports, and it is important to examine whether or not it actually did.

This chapter attempts to analyse the impact of the Indian devaluation in 1966 on export performance in the subsequent years. The first section estimates the *net* devaluation as distinct from the apparent depreciation in the exchange value of the rupee. The section following that, examines the influence of certain exogenous factors, such as the two successive droughts, which coincided with the devaluation decision. Having thus determined the extent to which other changes in the economy interacted with the devaluation of the rupee, we shall then consider its effect on Indian exports during the period 1966 to 1970.

Estimates of net devaluation

The devaluation of the rupee in June 1966 was accompanied by several simultaneous changes in export policy. Along with the devaluation, the export promotion measures based on import entitlement schemes and tax credits were abolished.[1] At the same time, export duties were imposed on a number of traditional exports.[2] It

---

[1] Cf. *Annual Report* of the Ministry of Commerce, *1966/67*, Government of India (New Delhi), p. 22.

[2] See RBI Bombay, *Report on Currency and Finance*, *1966/67*, p. 124.

is clear that the *de facto* devaluation must have been quite different from the *de jure* one. Therefore, in order to make any proper assessment of the effect of the rupee devaluation on exports, it is necessary to make adjustments for the accompanying changes in export policy and estimate the *net* devaluation.

There were many more changes in export policy in the months following devaluation, but we shall only take into account the elimination of import entitlements and tax credits, and the imposition of export duties, i.e. policy changes which were announced simultaneously with the devaluation. Moreover, we shall confine our analysis to the following important exports: jute manufactures, tea, cotton textiles, cashew kernels, tobacco, iron ore, engineering goods, leather, manganese ore, mica, oilcakes, coffee, black pepper, chemicals and allied products, coir manufacturers and raw cotton. Taken together, these sixteen commodity groups constituted 74.2 per cent of India's total exports in 1965/66.[3]

In order to estimate the net devaluation, it is necessary to quantify the subsidy implicit in the import entitlement schemes and tax credits before June 1966, and the incidence of export duties after that date. Let us take up each one in turn.

(a) *Import entitlements*: Under this scheme, which we have discussed at length earlier, exporters were allowed to retain a specified proportion of their export earnings in the form of import licences, and the import entitlement granted to each exporter was twice his estimated import content. The surplus foreign exchange allotment constituted an effective subsidy because exporters received high premiums from the sale of import licences in the open market. Among the selected exports, only leather, cotton textiles, engineering goods and chemicals and allied products benefited from significant import entitlements.[4] The rates of entitlement varied considerably as between products in each of these industries, as did the market premium on each import licence. However, in order to make a rough estimate of the subsidisation implicit in these schemes, we have taken an average rate of entitlement and an average figure for the market premium on import licences, in the case of the leather, cotton textiles and chemicals industries. For engineering goods, we have relied on

---

[3] Calculated from Table 2.6. In that year, exports of black pepper (not included in the said table) constituted 1.3 per cent of India's total exports (computed from DGCIS statistics).

[4] See J. Bhagwati and P. Desai, *India: Planning for Industrialisation*, OECD (Oxford, 1970), Table 19.9, pp. 434–7.

TABLE 11.1   *Subsidy implicit in import entitlement schemes during 1965/66*

Export industry	(1) Rate of entitlement as a percentage of the f.o.b. value of exports	(2) Import entitlements in rupees per dollar of exports	(3) Average percentage market premium on import licences	(4) Cash subsidy equivalent of the import entitlement in rupees per dollar of exports
Leather	19	0.90	100	0.45
Cotton textiles	95.7	4.56	75	1.71
Chemicals and allied products	70	3.33	100	1.67
Engineering goods	20 to 100	—	100	1.65*

Source:

For column (1): Bhagwati and Desai, *India: Planning for Industrialisation*: (*a*) the total import entitlement on exports of tanned hides and skins was 19 per cent, cf. Table 19.9, p. 435; (*b*) the entitlements for engineering goods varied from 20 to 100 per cent, cf. Table 19.11, pp. 439–44; (*c*) the typical entitlements for exports of chemicals and allied products ranged from 50 to 75 per cent in early 1964, cf. Table 19.12, pp. 445–7; these rates were subsequently increased (p. 411) and as such, we have taken the average rate of entitlement to be 70 per cent just before the devaluation; (*d*) the cotton textile industry benefited from several entitlements which were 66.7 per cent for raw cotton, 20 per cent for machinery and an average of 9 per cent for coal-tar dyes and chemicals (cf. p. 410), adding up to 95.7 per cent of the f.o.b. value of exports.

For column (3): Bhagwati and Desai, p. 418, suggest that the premiums were normally 70 to 80 per cent on most import licences and somewhat less on cotton textiles. However, they go on to say that the market premiums rose sharply in the months before devaluation. As such, we have taken the average market premium at 100 per cent, except for cotton textiles which is assumed to be 75 per cent.

Note:

Column (2) has been computed simply as the percentage in column (1) times Rs4.76.

Column (4) has been calculated as half of column (2), (which was the surplus foreign exchange allotment) times the average market premium.

* This figure of the cash subsidy equivalent in the case of engineering goods is derived from Table 9.14, p. 208, which calculated the average net rupee returns per dollar of engineering goods exports at Rs6.41 to the dollar. Rs1.65 is just the difference between this and the official exchange rate of Rs4.76 to the dollar.

our earlier detailed calculations of the subsidy implicit in the import entitlement schemes. The average figures based on available evidence are entered in columns (1) and (3) of Table 11.1. We assume that the import entitlements were just twice the actual import content, so that only half the foreign exchange allotment was sold by exporters in the open market for a premium.[5] The cash subsidy equivalent in rupees per dollar of exports has been calculated simply as the surplus foreign exchange in the entitlement times the market premium available. However, owing to the very crude method of averaging the entitlements and premiums, the data computed should be treated as a rough approximation rather than a precise estimate.

(*b*) *Tax credits*: We have seen that fiscal concessions introduced in 1965 granted exporters in selected industries tax credit certificates ranging from 2 to 15 per cent of the f.o.b. value of exports.[6] These certificates could be used for getting income tax liabilities adjusted, or claiming a refund so that, as explained earlier, the effective subsidy on exports was equal to the rate of tax credit.[7] However, this incentive was withdrawn when the devaluation was announced. Hence, the subsidy implicit in such tax concessions for exporters ceased to exist after the devaluation of the rupee.

(*c*) *Export duties*: Along with the devaluation, the Government imposed duties on the exports of jute manufactures, tea, coffee, black pepper, unmanufactured tobacco, raw wool, raw cotton, hides and skins, leather, coir manufactures, oilcakes, manganese ore, iron ore and some other minerals.[8] The importance of this measure is obvious from the fact that the aforesaid 'traditional' exports accounted for nearly 60 per cent of India's total exports in the year 1965/66.[9] It would be quite straightforward to estimate the incidence of these duties if they were fixed ad valorem. Actually, however, except in the case of mica, leather and coir manufactures,[10] all duties imposed were specific, i.e. in rupees per unit weight. Starting from these specific rates, in Table 11.2, we have calculated their ad valorem equivalent for each export, based on the average unit value of that particular export in the year preceding the devaluation of the rupee. The results of our calculation are outlined in column (4) of the Table. It is clear

[5] This assumption is based on the stated government policy, and the fact that exporters continued to get their actual import content at the official exchange rate even after the devaluation. In practice, however, import entitlements often tended to be more than twice the actual import content. Unfortunately, the absence of precise data and information on departures from stated policy prevents an alternative assumption. One can only say that the figures in Table 11.1 probably underestimate the subsidy equivalent of the import entitlement schemes.

[6] For details, see Chapter 10, pp. 222–5.

[7] Cf. ibid.

[8] Cf. RBI Bombay, *Report on Currency and Finance*, *1966/67*, Statement 87.

[9] Calculated from Table 2.6.

[10] The export duty on mica, leather and coir manufactures was fixed in ad valorem terms; cf. *Report on Currency and Finance*, *1966/67*, Statement 87.

TABLE 11.2 *The incidence of export duties imposed after devaluation*

Commodity	(1) Export duty in rupees per unit weight	(2) Average dollar unit value of exports in 1965/66	(3) Average unit value in post-devaluation rupees (2) × 7.50	(4) Implicit ad valorem duty (1) ÷ (3) × 100 in percentages
Jute manufactures				24.5*
a. carpet backing	900/ton	640.30/ton	4802.25/ton	18.7
b. hessian	900/ton	449.00/ton	3367.50/ton	26.7
c. sacking	600/ton	335.70/ton	2517.75/ton	23.8
d. other jute goods	600/ton	268.40/ton	2013.00/ton	29.8
Iron ore	10/ton	7.20/ton	54.00/ton	18.5
Manganese ore	20/ton	17.15/ton	128.63/ton	15.5
Oilcakes	125/ton	87.89/ton	659.18/ton	19.0
Raw cotton	750/ton	567.00/ton	4252.50/ton	17.6
Tea	2/kg	1.22/kg	9.15/kg	21.9
Coffee	0.50/kg	1.03/kg	7.73/kg	6.5
Black pepper	1.25/kg	0.89/kg	6.68/kg	18.7

Source:

For column (1): RBI Bombay, *Report on Currency and Finance, 1966/67*, Statement 87.

For column (2): Statistics published by DGCIS, Calcutta, on the quantity and value of exports.

* The average export duty for the commodity group 'jute manufactures' has been calculated as a weighted average of its four sub-divisions. The weights used are the actual quantities of carpet backing, hessian, sacking and other jute products exported in 1965/66; cf. Table 3.7, p. 47.

from the data that the incidence of these export duties was quite significant.

Having quantified the impact of the pre-devaluation export incentives and the post-devaluation export duties, it is now possible to estimate the net devaluation in the selected exports. Table 11.3 lists the rate of tax credits available, the cash subsidy equivalent of the import entitlement schemes, and the rates of export duties imposed with effect from June 1966. We have calculated the net rupee returns per dollar of exports *before* devaluation for each of the selected commodities, simply by adding to Rs4.76 the cash values of the tax credit and the import entitlement. These net returns are entered in column (6) of Table 11.3. Similarly, we have calculated the net rupee returns per dollar of exports *after* devaluation, this time deducting the cash value of the export duty payable on each of the selected exports, from Rs7.50. The post-devaluation net realisations of exporters are entered in column (7). The effective *net* devaluation is therefore equal to the percentage difference between the net rupee returns (per dollar of exports) of exporters before and after devaluation, and has been computed as such in Table 11.3.

A mere glance at the estimates of net devaluation reveals that it varied substantially from commodity to commodity, and in almost all cases, was far less than the gross parity change of 57.5 per cent. It is striking that the net devaluation was only about 15 per cent in cotton textiles, chemicals and engineering goods. To the extent that our method underestimated the subsidy implicit in the import entitlements available in these industries, the actual net devaluation was probably close to negligible. The *de facto* devaluation was substantial only in cashew kernels, coffee and coir manufactures, while it was slightly less than half the *de jure* figure of 57.5 per cent in the case of tobacco, oilcakes, black pepper, leather and raw cotton. For the remainder of the selected exports, i.e. jute manufactures, tea, iron ore and manganese ore it worked out in the range 15 to 20 per cent, whereas it was negative in the case of mica. In order to obtain an index of the overall change, we computed a weighted average of our net devaluation estimates and found that it was only 21.3 per cent for the selected commodities,[11] which together constituted three-fourths of India's exports at the time of devaluation. Therefore, it is only reasonable to infer that a significant proportion of the devaluation in June 1966 was neutralised by the elimination of prevalent export incentives and the imposition of export duties.

[11] The weights used are the percentage share of each of these commodities in India's total exports during the year 1965/66; cf. Table 2.6.

	Pre-devaluation incentives			Post-devaluation duties				
Commodity	(1) Tax credit as a percentage of the f.o.b. value of exports	(2) Cash value of tax concession in rupees per dollar of exports	(3) Cash subsidy equivalent of import entitlements in rupees per dollar of exports	(4) Ad valorem rate of export duty in percentages	(5) Export duty actually payable in rupees per dollar of exports	(6) Net rupee returns per dollar of exports *before* devaluation Rs4.76 + (2) + (3)	(7) Net rupee returns per dollar of exports *after* devaluation Rs7.50 − (5)	(8) Estimated *net* devaluation [(7) − (6)/(6) + 100] in percentages
Jute manufactures	2	0.10	–	24.5	1.84	4.86	5.66	16.5
Tea	2	0.10	–	21.9	1.64	4.86	5.86	20.6
Cotton textiles	2	0.10	1.71	–	–	6.57	7.50	14.2
Cashew kernels	2	0.10	–	20.0	1.50	4.86	7.50	54.3
Tobacco	–	–	–	20.0	1.50	4.76	6.00	26.1
Iron ore	10	0.48	–	18.5	1.39	5.24	6.11	16.6
Engineering goods	2	0.10	1.65	–	–	6.51	7.50	15.2
Leather	2	0.10	0.45	10.0	0.75	5.31	6.75	27.1
Manganese ore	15	0.71	–	15.5	1.16	5.47	6.34	15.9
Mica	–	–	–	40.0	3.00	4.76	4.50	−5.5
Oilcakes	–	–	–	19.0	1.43	4.76	6.07	27.5
Coffee	–	–	–	6.5	0.49	4.76	7.01	47.3
Chemicals and allied products	2	0.10	1.67	–	–	6.53	7.50	14.9
Black pepper	–	–	–	18.7	1.40	4.76	6.10	28.2
Coir manufactures	–	–	–	10.0	0.75	4.76	6.75	41.8
Raw cotton	–	–	–	17.6	1.32	4.76	6.18	29.8

Source:

For column (1): Bhagwati and Desai, *India: Planning for Industrialisation*, Tables 19.7 and 19.8, pp. 432–3; For column (3): Table 11.1.

For column (4): Table 11.2, and in the case of mica, leather and coir manufactures, RBI Bombay, *Report on Currency and Finance, 1966/67*, Statement 87. The duty on mica was revised with effect from 15 June 1966 and we have taken that rate.

Note:

Column (2) has been calculated as the percentage rate of tax credit times Rs4.76 which was the equivalent of one dollar at the pre-devaluation exchange rate; and column (5) has been calculated as the rate of export duty in column (4) times Rs7.50, which was the equivalent of one dollar at the post-devaluation exchange rate.

At this stage, it must be pointed out that some of the policy changes outlined above were shortlived. In fact, the post-devaluation period witnessed several modifications in the Government's export policies. For example, the export duties on the main traditional exports, i.e. jute manufactures and tea were gradually reduced.[12] But a far more important development was the revival and steady increase of subsidisation measures to promote the growth of non-traditional exports of manufactures. As we have shown in an earlier chapter, scarcely two months after the devaluation, the Government introduced cash subsidies for a wide range of exports of manufactures, and brought back the import entitlements in the guise of import replenishment schemes. Clearly, all these export promotion policies must have raised the net rupee returns per unit of foreign exchange for Indian exporters. It may have been possible to quantify the net effect of the new policy measures if the changes brought about by them had been uniform or once-and-for-all. As it happened, the cash subsidy and import replenishment rates not only varied from product to product, but were also revised every once in a while. Therefore, we have not made any attempt to adjust our calculations of net devaluation for subsequent policy changes. However, in our analysis, we shall allow for the fact that the effective exchange rate for exporters of non-traditional products improved continuously even after the devaluation of the rupee.

The picture would not be complete without considering the net effect of the devaluation on the import sector of the economy. Along with the devaluation, a number of import tariffs were scaled downwards. At the same time, import policy for raw materials and intermediate inputs was liberalised, which meant that the scarcity premium on import licences was substantially reduced. Clearly, the net devaluation on imports was also less than the apparent depreciation in the exchange value of the rupee, so that import prices did not rise by the amount of the devaluation. Detailed calculations might have involved too much of a digression and may have been beyond the scope of our work; fortunately however, we can rely on available evidence. It has been estimated that the *de facto* 'overall devaluation on the import side was 40 to 45 per cent'.[13] On the surface, this suggests that the devaluation of June 1966 raised the profitability of the import-

---

[12] See Tables 3.13, and 5.13. However, there were virtually no changes in the export duties on other traditional exports until 1970/71; see *Report on Currency and Finance, 1970/71*, pp. S182–4.

[13] Philip S. Thomas, *The 1966 Devaluation and Import Liberalization in India*, mimeo (December 1966), p. 3.

competing sector more than that of the export sector. However, the above figure relates only to actual imports, and it has been pointed out that 'for importables, the average effective devaluation was probably appreciably less than 40–45 per cent'.[14] What is more, in the case of non-traditional exports, the relative profitability was improved further, after the devaluation, by the introduction of cash subsidies and import replenishment schemes. On balance, therefore, the 1966 exchange rate policy changes probably did not worsen the relative profitability of non-traditional exports vis-à-vis the import-competing goods. However, it is likely that traditional exports were discriminated against even after the formal elimination of the overvalued exchange rate.

The influence of exogenous factors

So far we have been concerned only with the changes in trade policy that coincided with the devaluation, and therefore influenced its net effect. However, in view of the fact that the devaluation of the rupee in June 1966 was preceded and followed by some very important changes that affected the entire economy, it would not be appropriate to leave them out of account. These factors were: (a) the serious agricultural drought in the mid-1960s, (b) the resulting inflation, (c) the recession in the industrial sector from 1965/66 to 1967/68, and (d) the closure of the Suez Canal in 1967. Let us examine the impact of each of these exogenous factors on India's export performance in the post-devaluation period.

Consider first, the droughts of 1965/66 and 1966/67. The poor harvests in these two years affected the export performance adversely in two ways: (a) directly, by reducing the supply of agricultural products that were exported; and (b) indirectly, by reducing the supply of agricultural raw materials that were the basis of some manufactured exports like jute goods and cotton textiles. Table 11.4 outlines the trends in the output of such directly and indirectly exportable agricultural products during the period 1964/65 to 1967/68.

We find that the output of tea, coffee and black pepper was totally unaffected, except for minor cyclical fluctuations, while the tobacco

---

[14] See Ian Little, T. Scitovsky and Maurice Scott, *Industry and Trade in Some Developing Countries* (Oxford, 1970), p. 467, where it is argued that there was an implicit 'tariff reduction' in the case of consumer good importables (because imports were banned both before and after devaluation while the prices of domestic substitutes did not certainly rise by the amount of the devaluation), which is not taken into account by Thomas.

TABLE 11.4   *Index numbers of production for selected agricultural commodities in India*

1950 = 100	1964/65	1965/66	1966/67	1967/68
Raw jute	182.4	135.7	162.4	191.6
Raw cotton	215.7	176.8	191.9	210.5
Oilseeds	164.9	126.5	125.8	161.7
Tobacco	123.2	111.1	134.0	139.8
Tea	140.1	137.9	141.5	144.8
Coffee	250.3	282.1	346.6	252.7
Black pepper	150.2	141.6	150.2	145.9
All agricultural commodities	158.4	131.7	131.6	161.1

Source: RBI Bombay, *Report on Currency and Finance, 1966/67*, p. S11 and *1970/71*, p. S16. All figures, except for black pepper, relate to agricultural years beginning 1 July and ending 30 June. The data for black pepper have been computed from production figures in FAO, *Factors Affecting the World Pepper Economy*, document no. CCP. 71/9/1 (Rome, 11 July 1971), p. 13, which relate to calendar years and use the average output in 1950–1952 as base year production. Estimated production of black pepper in India was 23.3 million kg in 1950–1952 and 35, 33, 35 and 34 million kg in the years 1965–1968.

output fell in 1965/66[15] but more than recovered by 1966/67. Other than that, it was only the production of raw jute, raw cotton, and oilseeds that was seriously affected by the drought. Clearly, the fall in the production of oilseeds during the years preceding and following the devaluation must have reduced the exportable supplies of oilcakes and vegetable oils. In the case of jute and cotton, 1965/66 was a particularly bad agricultural year. In 1966/67, the output of raw jute and raw cotton recovered somewhat, but not completely. Thus it is most likely that the exports of jute manufactures and cotton textiles were seriously affected by the poor harvests, not only through the shortage of raw materials but also because of subsequent increases in the prices of raw jute and raw cotton.

This raises the question of the effect of the agricultural droughts on the general price level in the economy. While a few agriculture-based principal exports suffered directly, there was also a serious shortfall in total agricultural production during 1965/66 and 1966/67.[16] Thus, not only was the devaluation immediately preceded by a poor harvest, it was also followed by an equally poor one. The substantially lower level of agricultural output had a marked effect on

[15] The fall in the output of flue-cured Virginia tobacco, which accounted for the bulk of Indian tobacco exports, was even greater; cf. Table 6.14.

[16] Total agricultural production in 1965/66 and 1966/67 was nearly 17 per cent lower than in 1964/65; calculated from Table 11.4.

TABLE 11.5   *Movements in the price indices of selected commodity groups: 1963–1967*

1961/62=100	1963/64	1964/65	1965/66	1966/67	1967/68
Foodgrains	115.2	145.5	154.3	182.9	228.4
Industrial raw materials	100.2	115.9	132.8	158.4	156.4
All agricultural commodities	108.4	130.9	141.7	166.6	188.2
All commodities	110.2	122.3	131.6	149.9	167.3

Source: RBI Bombay, *Report on Currency and Finance*, 1969/70, pp. S30–31.
Note: With the exception of minerals, the group entitled industrial raw materials is constituted primarily by agricultural products.

the price level. Although the Indian economy had experienced a steady inflation since the early 1960s, there was a sharp upward movement in the trend after the 1965/66 harvest. This is brought out clearly in Table 11.5 which reveals a marked increase in the price of foodgrains and raw materials following the poor harvest. It is quite likely that the rise in prices of agricultural commodities, resulting from the two successive droughts, contributed to the general inflation in the economy. But there is no doubt that at least a part of this inflation was attributable to the devaluation itself, for the increased rupee prices of imports of foodgrains, machinery, capital equipment and manufactured intermediate goods must have had some effect on the price level.[17] The data in the above table show that the average price level in 1966/67 was 13.9 per cent higher than in 1965/66, and rose by another 11.6 per cent in 1967/68. It becomes obvious that a significant proportion of the net devaluation, such as it was, must have been neutralised by the inflation in the two following years.

Not surprisingly, inflation in the agricultural sector was accompanied by a recession in the industrial sector,[18] which brings us to the

[17] However, it must be said that the bulk of the increase in prices of foodgrains and agricultural raw materials was probably due to the scarcities created by the drought (as imports of these were not a large proportion of the total consumption) and would have occurred even in the absence of a devaluation. Only to that extent was the inflation that followed a factor independent of the exchange rate depreciation.

[18] For a detailed analysis of this apparently contradictory situation, see A.M. Khusro, 'Recession, Inflation and Economic Policy', *Economic and Political Weekly* (14 October 1967).

TABLE 11.6 *Some indicators of monetary and fiscal restraints after devaluation*

In Rs million	1965/66	1966/67	1967/68	1968/69
1 Increase in currency with the public	2652	1625	1793	3059
2 Increase in net bank credit to the Government	4667	1986	2459	4435
3 Developmental capital outlays of the central Government	5790	5131	4653	4989
4 Developmental capital outlays of the State Governments	4039	4032	4262	5156

Source: RBI Bombay, *Report on Currency and Finance, 1969/70.* For rows 1 and 2: Statement 26; for row 3: Statement 61; for row 4: Statement 64, except figures for 1965/66 and 1966/67 in this last row which have been taken from ibid. *Report on Currency and Finance, 1966/67*, Statement 57.

impact of the third exogenous factor. We have explained earlier that it all began with the bad harvest in 1965/66, which reduced the supply of some agricultural raw materials.[19] However, only the beginnings of the recession are to be found in supply factors. Lower farm incomes after the drought meant a fall in the demand for industrial consumer goods. At the same time, the Government sought to check the inflation in food and other consumer necessities. For this purpose, it adopted restrictive monetary and fiscal policies to curb private investment expenditure, and simultaneously reduced public outlays. These deflationary policies, which are evident from the data in Table 11.6, were probably partially prompted by the devaluation itself, in the belief that a devaluation can improve the balance of payments only if it is accompanied by an overall disabsorption in the economy.[20] As would be expected, such cutbacks in investment reduced the demand for intermediate and capital goods. And this is how almost the entire industrial sector came to be affected by a recession. In theory, the reduction in domestic absorption of manufactured goods (which was inevitable in the recession) should have helped exports immediately after the devaluation. In fact, in the case of engineering goods, we found fairly definite evidence that the recession was one of the factors

[19] pp. 195–7.
[20] To the extent that the deflationary policies were prompted by the devaluation, the recession that followed cannot be treated as a completely exogenous factor.

underlying the acceleration in export growth after 1965/66. However, the engineering industries provided an isolated example of a favourable impact of the recession on exports. Output in the traditional manufacturing industries, e.g. jute goods and cotton textiles was constrained by a shortage of raw materials.

The fourth exogenous factor which might have affected India's export performance soon after the devaluation was the closure of the Suez Canal in mid 1967. Owing to the resulting increase in transport costs, it improved India's competitiveness in the markets east of Suez, but worsened it in markets west of Suez. It might be useful to consider its possible impact on India's principal exports.

In the case of jute manufactures, tea and cotton textiles, this factor probably made little difference because India's main competitors viz. Pakistan in jute goods, Ceylon and East Africa in tea, and Pakistan, Hong Kong, Taiwan, South Korea and Japan in cotton textiles, all lay east of Suez and were confronted with a similar increase in transport costs. India's exports of iron ore were hardly affected because her principal market was Japan. As for cashew kernels and mica, transport costs had little significance owing to India's monopolistic position in the world market. Coffee exports were determined essentially by the quota under the International Agreement. Together, the above commodites accounted for 56.4 per cent of India's total exports in 1966/67.[21] Thus we see that a very large proportion of India's traditional exports was not adversely affected by the Suez closure. It is possible that the competitiveness of Indian tobacco, oilcakes and manganese ore suffered because her main competitors – USA, Nigeria and Gabon respectively – enjoyed a transport cost advantage in the European markets. However, these commodites constituted a relatively small proportion of India's traditional exports.

As for the non-traditional exports of manufactures, the closure of the Suez Canal improved India's competitiveness in the West Asian, East African and South East Asian countries vis-à-vis her European and American competitors, although it put them at a disadvantage in the West European and North American markets. But in view of the fact that most of India's exports of 'new manufactures' were sold in the developing countries of Asia and Africa, this exogenous factor probably had a favourable effect on non-traditional exports. Our inference is borne out by the rapid growth in India's engineering exports as a result of the Suez closure.[22]

Clearly, it is difficult to measure precisely the quantitative significance of these exogenous factors, and say anything conclusive. How-

[21] Calculated from Table 2.6.   [22] See pp. 209–11.

ever, our brief discussion did reveal the consequences of the two harvest failures. In the first place, the agricultural drought which coincided with the devaluation had a direct adverse effect on exports such as jute manufactures, cotton textiles, and oilcakes. Second, to the extent that the shortfalls in agricultural output contributed to the overall increase in the price level, the drought partially neutralised the possible favourable effects of the devaluation on exports, through inflation. On the other hand, the industrial recession and the closure of the Suez canal probably had a favourable net effect on the non-traditional exports of manufactures.

Export performance since 1966

Among several Indian economists, there has been a marked tendency to reject devaluation as a meaningful policy variable because it did not lead to any improvement in the balance of payments in the following year, and in fact, led to a fall in the dollar value of exports.[23] On the other hand, some others like Bhagwati and Desai have disputed such judgements for not being based on any rational economic evaluation. They argue that the net devaluation was relatively small, and that in any case there was little likelihood of an increase in exports in the short run.[24] This latter argument certainly has a substantial element of truth in it, specially in view of the fact that devaluations are generally followed by a short term fall in the foreign exchange value of exports owing to the initial terms of trade loss. In the case of India, it was also preceded and followed by a number of exogenous factors which had a marked influence on the export sector of the economy. Therefore, before making any assessment of the effect of the devaluation on export performance, it is necessary to place it in perspective.

We have shown that the imposition of export duties reduced the *de facto* devaluation for most traditional exports to a range of 15–25 per cent, as against the *de jure* figure of 57.5 per cent. The agricultural drought, which coincided with the devaluation, directly affected the supplies of some principal traditional exports, i.e. jute manufactures, cotton textiles and oilcakes. This was not all. The inflation which followed (to the extent that it was a result of the drought) further

[23] See, for example, the Introduction and Part II of the symposium in L. M. Singhvi (ed.), *Devaluation of the Rupee: its Implications and Consequences* (New Delhi, 1968).

[24] For details of the argument, see Bhagwati and Desai, *India: Planning for Industrialisation*, pp. 488–90. As a matter of fact, it is suggested that an immediate fall in the value of exports was likely because removal of the export incentives eliminated not only the need to overinvoice exports, but also the inefficient exports.

eroded the export incentives created by the devaluation. A long-term shift of resources into the production of traditional export commodities was perhaps also pre-empted by the fact that the effective devaluation was greater for the import sector of the economy. In view of these factors, the exchange rate depreciation of June 1966 could not have brought about any marked growth in traditional exports.

In the case of non-traditional exports of manufactures, such as engineering goods and chemical products, we have seen that the net devaluation was close to negligible. However, for industries which were not so heavily subsidised before 1966, the devaluation may have created a positive export incentive.[25] In terms of other factors, the picture was completely different from that in traditional exports. In the first place, most of these manufactures were not based on agricultural raw materials and were therefore not directly affected by the drought. Second, the devaluation was accompanied by a liberalised import policy which should have eased the supply bottlenecks for these industries. Third, exogenous factors in the form of an industrial recession and the Suez closure probably had a favourable net effect on these exports. And finally, subsidisation of non-traditional exports of manufactures continued, even after the devaluation, in the form of cash subsidies and import replenishment schemes. Clearly, the post-1966 trend in non-traditional exports must be considered in the context of all the aforesaid factors.

The aggregative view outlined so far highlights the interaction of the devaluation and the other economic forces which had a bearing on the export performance of the economy, at that time. A brief commodity-wise analysis of export trends since .1966 would provide us with a greater insight into the problem. For that purpose, we shall consider the traditional and non-traditional exports in turn.

In considering the effects of the devaluation on export growth it is obviously not sufficient to compare the actual trend in exports before and after the devaluation. As we have shown above, other factors must also be taken into account. However, some economists go further; they argue that it is necessary to consider what would have happened in the absence of a devaluation, i.e. if some alternative policy had been adopted by the Government.[26] From this it is inferred

---

[25] This would be particularly true for new exports which had escaped the attention of export promotion policies, and probably did not really exist in any significant magnitude.

[26] Prominent among this group of economists are the ardent advocates of devaluation. See, for example, Bhagwati and Desai, *India: Planning for Industrialisation*, pp. 486–90, and Little, Scitovsky and Scott, *Industry and Trade in Some Developing Countries*, pp. 382–84.

that, in the Indian case, the situation on the export front might have been worse without the devaluation.[27] In empirical terms, it is difficult to establish or to refute this proposition, but on the basis of available evidence we shall attempt to examine its validity.

Traditional exports

The phrase 'traditional exports' generally refers to raw materials and primary or semi-processed agricultural products. Such commodities constitute the bulk of the exports in most developing countries. Strictly speaking, this is not true for India because manufactured goods accounted for about half her exports in the 1960s. For the purpose of our analysis, however, we include jute manufactures and cotton textiles in the grouping of traditional exports from India, because these products have been exported for a very long time, and are essentially agriculture-based manufactures.

Elasticity pessimism about traditional exports was widely prevalent in the early 1950s, and it was one of the factors which resulted in India, and many other developing countries, pushing import substitution to the limit, on the assumption that it was not possible to increase exports. Such policies have recently come in for a great deal of criticism[28] inasmuch as import-substitution-based development strategies neglected not only export promotion but also the domestic supply factors affecting exports, by focusing attention on the stagnant world demand for the typical LDC exports. Moreover, in the long run, even if the total foreign demand for a commodity is price inelastic, the price is important for an individual exporting country to the extent that some degree of substitution is always possible as between different sources of supply. Available evidence suggests that this was indeed the case for India's main traditional exports.[29] Therefore it may have been possible for India to increase her traditional exports by increasing her share of the given world market. However, this would not have been possible for commodities in which India had a near-monopoly in world trade, and would have been rather difficult for commodities in which

---

[27] Cf. ibid.

[28] See, for example, Little, Scitovsky and Scott, pp. 231–4.

[29] Benjamin Cohen found that in the UK market, the elasticity of substitution between Indian tea, cotton cloth, manganese ore and leather and these very commodities from other sources was quite high; cf. 'The Stagnation in Indian Exports: 1951–61', *Quarterly Journal of Economics* (November 1964). See also, G.C. DaCosta, 'Elasticities of Demand for Indian Exports', *Indian Economic Journal* (July–September 1965), pp. 50–4, who came to much the same conclusion.

India was an important seller in an oligopolistic world market environment.[30]

Let us now turn our attention to the post-1966 trends in the principal traditional exports and an analysis of the possible effects of devaluation on each of them.

(a) *Jute manufactures*:   In 1965, India accounted for a little over 70 per cent of the world exports of jute manufactures. In view of the fact that Pakistan held the remainder of the world market, it might appear that any attempt by either of the two countries to increase its relative share would have been resisted by the other. As it happened, however, in the post-devaluation period, India rapidly lost her share of the world market to Pakistan and there was a marked decline in her exports of jute goods. Matters were made worse by the increasing pressure of domestic demand; while domestic production registered a marked decline, because of the drought and other factors, the home consumption of jute goods increased.[31] The devaluation, such as it was, did not reverse these trends.

Apart from domestic demand and supply conditions, the fall in India's exports of jute manufactures after 1965/66 was almost entirely attributable to the poor competitive position of the Indian jute industry. The Pakistan jute industry benefited not only from cheaper availability of raw jute, but also from heavy subsidisation by the Government. Under these circumstances, the devaluation may have been a good defensive measure against Pakistan's aggressive export policy based on the bonus voucher scheme, for it could have helped India to maintain her relative share in the world market for jute manufactures. In fact, however, a large part of the potential benefit of devaluation was neutralised by the levy of export duties. The net devaluation of 16.5 per cent was also wiped out by the increase in raw jute prices in that very year.[32] Although there may have been some valid reasons for imposing export duties,[33] there is little doubt that a

---

[30] In the latter case, rival oligopolists would have resisted attempts by India to increase her relative share of the world market, but this was certainly not out of the realm of possibility as, in some traditional export commodities, other oligopolists did manage to increase their relative shares.

[31] See Table 3.11.

[32] The wholesale price index of raw jute rose from 131.6 in 1965/66 to 156.4 in 1966/67; cf. p. 50.

[33] Export duties may have been justified in order to: (*a*) avert a possible terms of trade loss; and (*b*) reduce the incentive for farmers to switch from rice to jute, for that might have cut the availability of food for domestic consumption and thus led to inflation.

larger net devaluation would have helped India's exports of jute manufactures. But since the devaluation was almost completely neutralised, one might think that the trend in exports in the absence of the devaluation would not have been very different from the actual one, because the reduction in output and the increase in raw jute prices resulting from the drought would have been the same. However, there was a small *net* devaluation and an inflation which would have occurred anyway. Thus, to the extent that the effective devaluation helped absorb the rise in prices, the competitive position of the Indian jute industry might have been that much worse in the absence of the devaluation. It is extremely difficult to estimate how this would have affected the export earnings from jute goods; one can only say that they might have been slightly lower in 1966/67. After that it could not have made a difference, one way or the other, because the incentive effect of the devaluation had ceased to exist.

(*b*) *Tea*: The foreign exchange earnings derived from exports of tea were virtually stagnant until 1964/65, but declined to a lower level thereafter. We found that the main reason for India's relatively poor export performance was the increasing pressure of domestic demand. In the post-devaluation period, while home consumption continued to rise rapidly because of the high income elasticity of demand for tea and the growth in population, the domestic production of tea increased at a much slower rate.[34] The possible effects of the devaluation must be considered in this context.

Despite the export duties, the net devaluation was significant at 20.6 per cent. It is generally accepted that the production of tea cannot respond quickly to such relative price changes because there is a long lag between the time a tea bush is planted and the time it yields an output. Therefore, the supply available for export could have been increased only by reducing domestic absorption. In fact, internal consumption continued to increase steadily. There were two reasons why the devaluation was unable to counteract the domestic demand pull: (1) the price elasticity of demand for tea in India is very low,[35] and (2) the tax policy adopted by the Government discriminated against exports and in favour of home sales. It is, of course, possible that in the absence of the devaluation, domestic consumption may have grown faster than it did, but, in view of the above reasons, that appears unlikely – at least in any significant measure. In any case, as

[34] Cf. Tables 5.10 and 5.11.
[35] See G. K. Sarkar, *The World Tea Economy* (Calcutta, 1972), pp. 77–81.

we have shown earlier, the export incentive created by the devaluation did not last beyond eighteen months.[36] Thus it is clear that the downward trend in India's tea exports during the late 1960s had nothing to do with the devaluation, and the actual situation would not have been far different if there had been no devaluation. In fact, on balance, the low elasticity of supply was probably a good thing, because in the face of inelastic foreign demand, it prevented terms of trade from worsening.[37]

(c) *Cotton textiles*: The stagnation in India's cotton textile exports during the 1960s was primarily due to: (1) poor price competitiveness of the Indian textile industry which was the result of increases in the cost of raw cotton, rising labour costs and relatively old capital equipment; and (2) the pressure of domestic demand coupled with the relative attractiveness of the home market.[38] The devaluation of the rupee did little to improve competitiveness or make exports more attractive because, given the previous export incentives, its net effect was negligible.[39] During the two years following the devaluation, the dollar value of exports fell because of the drought, and then recovered to its previous level. The trend would have been the same even if the previous incentives had not been replaced by the devaluation.

(d) *Cashew kernels*: The net devaluation in the cashew industry was quite substantial at 54.3 per cent. In the two years following the devaluation, the dollar value of exports was virtually stagnant, but rose significantly towards the end of the 1960s. *Prima facie* it would appear that the devaluation had a favourable impact on export growth. However, a look at the trend in export volume reveals a somewhat different picture. The quantity exported fell slightly from an annual average of 53.4 million kg in 1964/65–1965/66 to 50.5 million kg in 1966/67–1967/68 and rose to 58.2 million kg during

---

[36] It was neutralised almost completely by: (a) the higher excise duties imposed in early 1967; and (b) the British and Ceylonese devaluations of November 1967; see p. 106.

[37] In Chapter 5, we adduced sufficient evidence to show that the price elasticity of world demand for tea is close to negligible. India could not also have increased her exports by raising her relative share of the world tea market which is dominated by a few suppliers, including India. Any such attempt would have certainly been resisted by the main rivals – Ceylon and East Africa. As it is, there was a steady decline in world prices of tea; an attempt by India to increase the volume of its exports would only have worsened the terms of trade.

[38] For a detailed examination of all these factors, see Chapter 4.

[39] Even if the devaluation had been positive, the quality factor would have continued to act as a constraint on export performance.

1968/69–1970/71.[40] The reduction in export volume immediately after the devaluation was probably because of the drought, and was not related to the exchange rate adjustment in any way. The maintenance of export earnings in that period, and the much faster growth thereafter was mainly attributable to the continuous increase in unit value,[41] which also had nothing to do with the devaluation of the rupee. Given the fact that world prices of cashew nuts rose steadily throughout the 1960s, export earnings would have risen even in the absence of a devaluation. On the other hand, it might be argued that the foreign exchange earned could have been lower, to the extent that there may have been a smaller or no increase in quantity exported beyond the pre-devaluation level. Available evidence, however, does not lend support to the latter view.[42]

(e) *Tobacco:* Although the levy of export duties reduced the net devaluation to 26.1 per cent, it was still significant enough to have helped exports. However, the devaluation in June 1966 was preceded by an extremely poor harvest of Virginia tobacco, as a result of which the supplies available for export were already at a very low level. Clearly, it was impossible to increase exports in the short run, and given the background of the drought, it is not surprising that exports of tobacco fell to an all time low in the year of the devaluation. The tobacco crop did recover in 1967 but by that time, as we have shown earlier, the competitive advantage bestowed by the devaluation

[40] At the same time, the average annual export earnings were stagnant at $59.3 million in the first two periods, and rose to $75.7 million in the third period; calculated from Table 6.1.

[41] Ibid.

[42] If we make the simple assumption that without the devaluation, the export volume during 1968/69–1970/71 would have been no higher than in 1964/65–1965/66, then, at prevalent world prices, export earnings at the end of the decade would have been $6.4 million lower than they actually were, i.e. $69.3 million instead of $75.7 million. However, this extreme assumption is not justified for the following reason. Our analysis of the trends in India's cashew exports revealed that the main constraint on increasing exports was the availability of raw nuts, about 70 per cent of which were imported. The substantial net devaluation should have raised significantly the incentive to grow more cashew nuts, not only because the net rupee returns from exports increased, but also because the import of raw nuts became more expensive. In fact, however, the production of raw cashew nuts in India did not increase even after the devaluation and the cashew industry relied more than before on imports (cf. Table 6.6). This inelasticity of supply, which may be attributable (among other things) to the time lags involved in production, confirms that the trend in the export earnings derived from cashew would not have been different in the absence of a devaluation.

was almost entirely neutralised.[43] Thus, while production returned to its earlier level, domestic consumption increased rapidly so that, in the post-devaluation period, exports were somewhat lower than their peak level in the early 1960s.[44] Obviously, the downward trend was independent of the devaluation. Given the facts that (1) the exchange rate depreciation coincided with the drought, and (2) it was all but neutralised within eighteen months (when the production of tobacco returned to normal), the trend would not have been markedly different if the devaluation had not taken place.

(*f*) *Iron ore*: India's exports of iron ore increased very rapidly throughout the 1960s both in terms of value and volume. In our earlier analysis we found that this growth was almost entirely attributable to the considerable expansion in world demand, and as such, had little to do with the devaluation of the rupee in 1966. In the period under study, Japan was the principal market for Indian iron ore. Given the boom in Japanese import demand for iron ore,[45] and the fact that most of the exports to Japan were under long term contracts, it is clear that foreign demand and price competitiveness never constituted a problem during the period 1960 to 1970. Therefore, it is almost certain that the net devaluation of 16.6 per cent made little difference either way, and the export growth would have taken place even without it.[46]

(*g*) *Manganese ore*: The foreign exchange value of India's manganese exports fell steadily throughout the decade. This poor export performance was primarily due to: (1) a general fall in the world prices of manganese ore, (2) a deterioration in the quality of Indian ore, and (3) the restricted nature of the world market, although supply constraints may also have been partially responsible.[47] In the post-devaluation period, the downward trend in export earnings continued, but it was not as marked as the fall in average unit value because there was an increase in the volume of exports.[48] It is possible that the net devaluation of 15.9 per cent stimulated the supply of exports by improving the profitability of mining through higher domestic currency returns, in which case one could infer that export earnings may

[43] See p. 132; the Suez closure increased freight costs and the UK devaluation worsened competitiveness in the principal market.

[44] Cf. Tables 6.14 and 6.9.

[45] See Table 7.6.

[46] It is possible that the devaluation increased the relative profitability of exports vis-à-vis home sales, but domestic demand pressure was no constraint in the case of iron ore. The basic constraints on the supply of exports were the infrastructural bottlenecks such as inadequate transport and port facilities.

[47] These factors emerged from our analysis in Chapter 7.

[48] Cf. Table 7.8.

have fallen even more in the absence of the devaluation. But it must be pointed out that a significant proportion of the competitive advantage created by the devaluation was eliminated by the Suez closure in 1967 which escalated the transport costs of shipments to Europe and North America.[49]

(*h*) *Mica*:   The commodities we have discussed so far experienced *some* devaluation in June 1966. However, in the case of mica, the net devaluation was negative at −5.5 per cent, and the dollar value of exports was stagnant throughout the 1960s. Given the predominance of the American market, and the US Government decision to run down its mica stockpile,[50] any attempt to stimulate demand by lowering the price through a devaluation would only have worsened the terms of trade substantially. Therefore, it was just as well that the devaluation was completely neutralised by a large export duty. Clearly, the trend in mica exports would have been no different (from what it was) without the devaluation, because it did not affect the mica industry at all.

(*i*) *Other exports*:   Let us now consider the remaining traditional exports viz. coffee, oilcakes, black pepper, raw cotton and coir manufactures, for each of which the net devaluation was greater than 25 per cent. In the post-1966 period, there was a marked decline in the exports of oilcakes, raw cotton and coir manufactures, while exports of coffee and black pepper remained virtually unchanged.

As we have shown earlier in the chapter, exports of oilcakes and raw cotton were seriously affected by the two poor harvests that coincided with the devaluation. What is more, the competitive advantage bestowed by the exchange rate depreciation was wiped out completely by the increase in prices of oilseeds and raw cotton in that very year.[51] Since the net effect of the devaluation did not even last until the economy had recovered from the drought, it could not have brought about any increase in exports. For lack of sufficient evidence, it is difficult to say what the trend in these exports would have been in the absence of a devaluation. However, in view of the fact that there was no significant increase in the production of raw cotton and oil-seeds even after 1966/67 it seems unlikely that the situation could have been any worse.

In the case of coffee, exports from all countries were restricted by

---

[49] See p. 155.   [50] For details see Chapter 7, pp. 158–60.

[51] The wholesale price index of oilseeds rose from 154.4 in 1965/66 to 194.7 in 1966/67, while that of raw cotton rose from 131.6 to 156.4. It is worth noting that prices did fall in the following year: cf. *Report on Currency and Finance, 1970/71*, pp. S30–1.

quotas under the International Coffee Agreement of 1962. Since a large proportion of the world coffee market was regulated by this agreement, the foreign elasticity of demand for Indian coffee was effectively zero once the quota was filled.[52] The only possible additional outlet was socialist countries of Eastern Europe, all of whose trade was conducted through bilateral agreements. Given these factors, it is quite apparent that a devaluation could not have increased exports and the trend would have been the same, even in its absence. As for coir manufactures, the net devaluation of 41.8 per cent was very shortlived. The rate of export duty was raised from 10 to 25 per cent in July 1966,[53] thereby neutralising most of the devaluation. Thus, even without the devaluation, the trend in exports would not have been very different.

Exports of black pepper did not change very much, during the post-devaluation period, either in terms of value or volume, even though the net devaluation was 28.2 per cent. In response to the possibly higher domestic currency returns from exports, there was no increase in the total production of pepper,[54] perhaps because of the long time lag before a new pepper vine yields an output. However, to the extent that it made possible a lower foreign currency price, it may have improved the price competitiveness of exports.[55] But it should be pointed out that the world pepper market is dominated by India, Malaysia and Indonesia,[56] so that any attempt by India to increase her relative share through lower prices would have been resisted by the other two. Given the sharp fluctuation in world pepper output and prices, and the lack of any information on stocks held in the principal trading countries,[57] it is not possible to say what India's pepper exports would have been in the absence of the devaluation. However, in view of the factors stated above, it seems that a devaluation could have done little to foster exports of black pepper.

Non-traditional exports

Essentially, non-traditional exports from India are constituted by manufactured products other than jute goods and cotton textiles. The characteristic common to all these products is that India is only a

---

[52] Of course, as long as the quota is not filled the demand is infinitely elastic.

[53] Cf. *Report on Currency and Finance, 1966/67*, p. S150.

[54] See FAO, *Factors Affecting the World Pepper Economy*, p. 13.

[55] It is possible that price competitiveness was a problem for Indian exports of black pepper; for details see pp. 319–20.

[56] Cf. FAO, *Factors Affecting the World Pepper Economy*, p. 14.

[57] Stocks held in the main producing and importing countries have a crucial impact on the world pepper market; for a detailed discussion, see ibid.

marginal supplier in the world market. Therefore, in theory, she faces a perfectly elastic foreign demand curve and should be able to increase her exports substantially, as long as she can sell at the given world prices. Actually, however, this may not be possible because of the importance of non-price factors such as quality and marketing efficiency. Price competitiveness is clearly necessary for export, but it may not be sufficient if the quality is not competitive. Moreover, in the case of non-traditional exports of manufactures, product differentiation results in a much greater importance for brand names, designs and packaging. In these circumstances, export growth requires not only a competitive price but also an elaborate and efficient marketing network.

How could the devaluation of the rupee in June 1966 have helped export performance? To the extent that it led to an increase in domestic currency returns on exports, it may have enabled exporters to incur higher selling costs in marketing. To the extent that it lowered the foreign exchange price of exports, it may have improved competitiveness. Not only that, in manufactured goods lower prices are often, though not always, acceptable as a substitute for better quality, and the devaluation may have compensated for the lack of competitive quality. However, it is necessary to point out that there may have been other important factors such as salesmanship, marketing ability, designing, brand names and delivery dates which could not have been taken care of by the exchange rate depreciation *per se*. In other words, devaluation may in some sense be a necessary condition, but it is certainly not sufficient to bring about an increase in exports.

Having commented upon the usual assumption of perfectly elastic foreign demand and considered the possible favourable effects of the devaluation, let us now turn our attention to the post-1966 trends in non-traditional exports from India. A look back at Table 2.3 reveals that there was a phenomenal increase in the exports of engineering goods, chemical products and manufactured leather during the period 1966/67 to 1970/71. It would be interesting to consider how this performance was related to the depreciation in the exchange value of the rupee, and what the trend would have been in the absence of the devaluation.

In the case of engineering goods and chemicals, the net devaluation worked out at approximately 15 per cent. However, the method of calculation underestimated the subsidy implicit in the import entitlement schemes so that the actual effective devaluation was probably close to negligible. To the extent that there was any real devaluation, it must have helped export performance in the ways outlined above.

But, for these non-traditional exports, the exchange rate depreciation was basically a replacement for the previous export incentives. As such, it could not have led to any dramatic increase in exports, and *prima facie*, if the old incentives had continued, the trend may not have been very different in the absence of the 1966 devaluation. However, the exchange rate adjustment did eliminate the delays and uncertainties inherent in the cumbersome system of export incentives which existed before. This rationalisation, although shortlived, probably created a more efficient basis for exporting, without which exports may not have increased as much, but at the same time it eliminated the socially uneconomic exports which were made possible by heavy subsidisation. This was certainly a change for the better. In purely quantitative terms, however, it suggests that export earnings would not have been markedly lower without the devaluation.

In fact, both these industries experienced rapid export growth. Our empirical analysis revealed that the impressive export performance of the engineering industries in the late 1960s was due to the recession in the home market from 1965/66 to 1967/68, the closure of the Suez Canal in 1967 and heavy subsidisation by the Government even after devaluation.[58] On the other hand, the rapid expansion in exports of chemicals after 1967/68 was the result of the liberalisation of imports that accompanied devaluation, the continuation of export subsidies and other incentives, and the compulsory export obligation scheme operated by the Government.[59] Thus it appears that export subsidisation, which followed the 1966 policy package, was a major factor underlying the growth in engineering and chemical exports. In principle, a larger net devaluation would have had the same favourable effect, provided other things did not change as a consequence. However, it must be pointed out that domestic supply and demand conditions were *equally important* factors underlying the trend, and, by itself, an exchange rate adjustment would not have been enough. The importance of demand and supply conditions in the home market is obvious enough. We found that exports of engineering goods were boosted in a period of slack domestic demand. As for chemicals, export supplies, which were constrained by increasing domestic demand pressure and inadequate production, were mobilised through compulsory export obligation schemes.

Exports of manufactured leather, which were virtually stagnant until 1965/66, grew very rapidly thereafter. It seems quite plausible that the net devaluation of 27.1 per cent was one of the factors underlying this trend. We found that the rapid growth in leather

[58] See Chapter 9, pp. 215–6.　　[59] p. 179.

exports was attributable to the development of the chrome tanning industry in India and a shift away from the relatively stagnant UK market to other rapidly expanding markets.[60] It is possible that higher domestic currency returns stimulated production for export in the chrome tanning industry, and lower foreign exchange prices following the devaluation helped the Indian leather industry to capture new markets. Hence, *prima facie*, it might appear that without the devaluation, exports of manufactured leather would not have increased as much as they did, but it should be noted that the potential favourable effect of the devaluation must have been significantly neutralised by the inelastic supply of hides and skins. After all, the reason other leather-exporting countries fared better than India, was not poor price competitiveness of Indian leather but increasing domestic demand pressure and difficult supply conditions. The legislation against cattle slaughter not only made for an inelastic supply of hides but also affected the quality of the leather. Clearly, the devaluation could have done little to relax such supply constraints on the exportable surplus of leather.

There is no doubt that the engineering and chemical industries provided a significant proportion of the non-traditional exports of manufactures. However, there were other industries which were not subsidised so heavily in the period before 1966, or did not exist as export industries at all. In these cases, the net devaluation must have been substantial and close to the *de jure* figure of 57.5 per cent. Clearly, this must have provided a very positive export incentive, and available evidence suggests that there was a marked growth in such exports.[61] It is, of course, necessary to point out that some of these products received substantial export assistance, in the form of cash subsidies and import replenishments, *after* the devaluation.[62] What

---

[60] For details, see Chapter 8.

[61] Consider, for example, the post-devaluation trend in the exports of the following non-traditional items:

In Rs million	1966/67	1967/68	1968/69	1969/70	1970/71
Fish and fish products	172.5	179.5	221.7	308.3	305.4
Rubber manufactures	35.2	30.4	46.5	47.2	68.9
Glass and glassware	4.4	5.9	9.0	13.0	15.0
Mineral manufactures	17.2	12.2	23.0	27.0	20.0
Lime and cement materials	3.0	6.6	26.0	24.0	24.0
Sports goods	3.2	8.5	8.6	14.8	21.5

Source: Statistics published by DGCIS, Calcutta.

[62] Therefore, subsidisation measures introduced after 1966 may have been partially responsible for the export growth.

is more, the increase in foreign exchange earnings attributable to these new exports, while impressive in absolute terms, is not that significant when expressed as a proportion of total exports. For these reasons, one must be careful not to overstate the success of the devaluation in this context.

Implications and evaluation

An examination of trade statistics reveals that there was no significant increase in India's exports during the second half of the 1960s.[63] However, it is apparent from our discussion in this chapter that the impact of the devaluation of the rupee on export performance needs to be considered in the context of changes in government policies and the influence of certain exogenous factors, which coincided with the depreciation in the exchange value of the rupee. Therefore, a brief assessment of the complex interaction of factors and policies might provide the basis for some conclusions.

The imposition of export duties on a wide scale meant that the *de facto* devaluation for most traditional exports was far less than the *de jure* change in parity. The two poor harvests which preceded and followed the exchange rate depreciation had a direct adverse effect on the exportable supplies of jute manufactures, cotton textiles, tobacco and oilcakes. Under these circumstances, there was obviously no possibility of domestic disabsorption in the short run, because the total output available fell drastically. The following inflation, which was partially a result of the drought, precluded the possibility of increased production of these exportables in the long run, for it eroded most of the incentives created by the devaluation. As for the remaining traditional exports, in some, the net devaluation was not very significant. Clearly, the devaluation could not have brought about an increase in such traditional exports. However, even in cases where the net devaluation was positive and significant, the export performance did not improve. In general, this was because the exchange rate depreciation did not lead to any reduction in domestic absorption or any increase in the production of these exportables.[64]

---

[63] As a matter of fact, in the post-devaluation period the only exports that registered a marked increase were cashew kernels, iron ore, leather, engineering goods and chemical products. Foreign exchange earnings from the remaining principal exports declined, or were stagnant; cf. Table 2.3.

[64] The stagnation in the output of exportable commodites is, of course, attributable to a number of complex factors. It would involve too much of a digression to go into them here.

As it happened, there was in fact a noticeable decline in the foreign exchange earned from several traditional items. But our commodity-wise analysis revealed that this was the result of independent factors which had nothing to do with the devaluation. Therefore, it would be perfectly correct to say that the fall in the dollar value of some traditional exports was not because of the devaluation. It would have occurred in any case. At the same time, it must be stressed that the export performance would not have been much worse without the devaluation. Although the exchange rate depreciation may have been of some help to exports of jute manufactures and manganese ore for a short period, we have seen that, on the whole, it did not make any significant difference.

In the case of non-traditional exports of manufactures, such as engineering goods and chemical products, the devaluation sought only to replace the complicated system of export incentives that existed before, and its net effect was almost negligible. Thus, the trend in these exports would have been much the same even without the devaluation unless we attribute some export growth to the rationalisation of the structure of incentives. However, export subsidisation continued in one form or another even after June 1966 (so that the complexity of the earlier system was not entirely removed) and was one of the main factors underlying the rapid export growth. But it is necessary to point out that the continuing subsidisation was not the only factor responsible for the increase in these exports, and factors such as the industrial recession, the Suez closure and the import liberalisation were also of considerable importance.

In contrast with the engineering and chemical industries, the devaluation provided a positive export incentive to industries which were either not subsidised as heavily before 1966, or had escaped the network of export promotion policies altogether. The growth in exports of certain non-traditional items during the post-devaluation years substantiates this point, although it would not have been possible to the same extent without the extensive subsidisation that followed the change in parity of the rupee.

It is evident from the above that summary conclusions about the success or failure of the devaluation are not possible. A meaningful analysis can only attempt to place it in its correct context and perspective, while trying to separate its impact on export performance from that of other factors and policies. Can any lessons for policy be drawn from this experience? An unequivocal answer is rather difficult but some broad guidelines do emerge. The timing of a devaluation decision is obviously quite crucial. Apart from that, one must learn to be sceptical about simple neo-classical policy prescriptions which suggest that an exchange rate adjustment is all that is necessary to resolve balance of payments problems on the export front. While a devaluation is one method of improving the price competitiveness and the relative profitability of exports, it may not be successful in bringing about higher exports, unless it is accompanied by policies designed to raise the supplies available for export.[65] In the case of non-traditional exports of manufactures there may be additional obstacles in the form of non-price factors which need to be overcome before exports can be increased.

[65] This may be achieved either by reducing domestic absorption or by increasing production of exportables.

12

Bilateral rupee trade and export growth

Having analysed India's export policies in the 1960s and the impact of the devaluation on exports, we shall now attempt to evaluate India's trade with the socialist countries of Eastern Europe. The purpose of this chapter is to consider the extent to which Indian exports benefited from increased trade with these countries.

TABLE 12.1   *India's exports to Eastern Europe*

Year	Value in $ million	Value index 1970/71 = 100	Percentage share in total exports
1960/61	104.4	22	7.7
1961/62	135.6	28	9.8
1962/63	195.1	40	13.6
1963/64	229.2	48	13.8
1964/65	302.9	63	17.7
1965/66	329.0	68	19.5
1966/67	301.0	62	19.4
1967/68	301.2	62	18.9
1968/69	355.2	74	19.6
1969/70	410.1	85	21.8
1970/71	482.3	100	23.6

Source: Table 2.10.
Note:
(*a*) The figures include the USSR in East Europe.
(*b*) The value index has been computed.

Table 12.1 shows that, over the decade, India's exports to the socialist bloc increased at a compound rate of 16.5 per cent per annum, rising from $104.4 million in 1960/61 to $482.3 million in 1970/71. As a result, the combined share of Bulgaria, Czechoslovakia, East Germany, Hungary, Poland, Rumania, USSR and Yugoslavia in India's total export earnings more than trebled, increasing from 7.7 to 23.6 per cent. From the table, it is also quite apparent that, except for the decline in 1966/67 and 1967/68,[1] the growth in exports was continuous. However, the most striking fact to emerge from these trends is that increased exports to the socialist countries accounted for 54.2 per cent of the total increment in India's exports during the period 1960 to 1970.[2]

This remarkable export growth occurred in a framework of bilateral trade agreements with the East European countries,[3] the principal feature of which was that payments for all transactions were made in rupees. Therefore, in order to analyse the rapid expansion in exports to the socialist countries, a necessary first step is to examine the working of trade and payments arrangements. The next step in the analysis is a consideration of the possible costs and benefits of such bilateral rupee trade at a theoretical level, which is followed up by a review of the trends in the commodity composition and market distribution of these exports. Finally, the chapter attempts an evaluation of India's rupee trade in the 1960s by considering the factors underlying the increase in exports and the terms of trade obtained.

The working of trade and payments agreements

Bilateral trade is an integral part of the overall system of economic relations between the socialist countries and India. All trade is channelled through agreements which have three distinct features:

---

[1] This break in the trend can be explained in terms of two main factors. First, 1965/66 was a very poor agricultural year which affected exports to *all* markets adversely. Second, the devaluation of the rupee in June 1966 had a dislocating effect, particularly on trade with the socialist countries, because the agreements had to be adjusted for the exchange rate alteration and this took some time. For an enumeration of the short run administrative problems encountered in rupee trade following the devaluation, see *Economic and Political Weekly* (22 October 1966), pp. 396–7.

[2] India's total export earnings rose from $1349.4 million in 1960/61 to $2046.9 million in 1970/71 – an increase of $697.5 million; cf. Table 2.1.

[3] Such trade agreements were not unique to the Socialist Bloc. In the 1960s, India negotiated trade agreements with several other countries. However, most of them, e.g. those with France, Greece, Indonesia, Iran, Iraq, etc., were no more than a gesture of political goodwill and economic co-operation between the signatories. Although a list of tradable commodities was generally incorporated in the agreements, nothing was specified, and the pattern/volume of trade was determined by the usual considerations of international commerce. A few agreements like those with Afghanistan, Sudan and the UAR were more meaningful in as much as specific commodities and the amounts to be traded were written into the agreements; although here again, trade was on a commercial basis and payments were made in convertible currencies. Therefore, our analysis in this chapter is concerned *only* with bilateral trade agreements between India and the socialist countries of Eastern Europe including the USSR.

(*a*) the mode of payment; (*b*) a long term contractual approach coupled with specific annual arrangements; and (*c*) an automatic conversion of aid as well as debt repayments into trade flows. We shall discuss each of these characteristics in turn,[4] and, in the process, highlight the mechanism and working of the trade and payments arrangements.

Consider first, the mode of payment. To begin with, in the early 1950s, all payments were made in convertible currencies. Gradually, the emphasis of trade agreements shifted to bilateralism, and by 1956, East European countries had adopted the rupee as the unit of account in their trade with India. In practice, however, trade did not balance each year and the surpluses or deficits which arose had to be settled in sterling. In 1959/60, there was a radical change in the payments mechanism. It was decided that payments for *all* transactions were to be made in inconvertible rupees. Balances outstanding each year were to be settled through exports or imports of mutually agreed products. This complete transition to rupee payments brought about a genuine shift to bilateralism in India's trade with the socialist countries. Throughout the 1960s, India's exports to these countries were effected through the mechanism of bilateral rupee trade. However, in the agreements, the exchange value of the rupee was pegged to its gold equivalent, so that the East European countries were protected from the devaluation of the rupee in June 1966.[5]

The second distinct feature of the bilateral arrangements is their long term contractual approach. Generally, the duration of trade

---

[4] This discussion is based on three main sources: (*a*) A study by the Indian Institute of Foreign Trade, *India's Trade with Eastern Europe* (New Delhi, 1966), pp. 46–8; (*b*) Dharm Narain, *Aid Through Trade*, UNCTAD document no. TD/B/C.3/57 (Geneva, 16 December 1968), pp. 20–4; and (*c*) Asha Datar, *India's Economic Relations with the USSR and Eastern Europe* (Cambridge, 1972), pp. 87–90. In our analysis, we shall draw on some of the findings of these studies. However, it is necessary to point out that whereas the above works were concerned with the overall impact of India's economic ties with Eastern Europe, our main objective is to analyse the impact of bilateral rupee trade on India's exports. Furthermore, the three studies, referred to above, relate to the period 1950 to 1965, while this chapter considers the period 1960 to 1970.

[5] India has to fulfil the unimplemented portions of its long term export contracts in terms of the earlier value of the rupee. It follows that the sudden increase in the rupee value of India's exports to the socialist countries after June 1966, does not reflect a genuine increase in trade. Therefore, in order to make post-devaluation trade figures comparable with the earlier ones, it is necessary to deflate them. We have tried to solve the problem by converting all statistics into US dollars at the official exchange rate. This might appear paradoxical as all trade was actually transacted in rupees, but the dollar should be looked upon only as a *numeraire*.

and payments agreements was three to five years, although they were sometimes extended for longer periods.[6] Originally, the main purpose of such agreements was to outline the long term objectives of economic co-operation between the partner countries. But after 1960, more specific clauses were introduced. For example, in some cases, quantitative targets for the expansion of trade, the value of goods to be exchanged, or the intention of increasing the proportion of manufactures in India's exports[7] were written into the agreement as special provisions. All the same, even such clauses were quite general and aggregative in their very nature. In actual fact, trade flows were determined by the annual trade plan. At the beginning of each year, the contracting parties decided upon the aggregate total value of trade between them for that year. A list of possible importables and exportables was appended to this plan, but the commodity pattern of trade remained flexible. Therefore, it is clear that although the long term agreement provides the framework 'the annual trade plan continues to be the specific operational document'.[8]

The ex-ante determination of the annual value of trade is most interesting. The trade target is calculated in such a way that after taking the credit inflows from the socialist countries to India and the debt servicing outflows from India to the socialist countries into account, the trade is bilaterally balanced each year. Hence, it is apparent how aid from the socialist countries and debt repayments by India are automatically converted into trade flows through the bilateral agreements. However, this does not preclude the possibility of short term imbalances that might arise during, and at the end of, each plan. Surpluses and deficits outstanding at the end of a year are usually adjusted for in the next annual trade plan. In the very short run, imbalances are met through an extension of temporary swing credit facilities by the partner in surplus.

So much for the principles underlying rupee trade. It is also quite crucial to understand how the trade transactions actually take place in this framework. The procedure is indeed quite complex. Each East European country maintains four accounts with banks in India:

---

[6] For a detailed description of India's trade and payments agreements with the socialist countries, see a case study prepared by the UNCTAD Secretariat on *Trade and Economic Relations between India and the Socialist Countries of Eastern Europe*, TD/B/129 (Geneva, 21 July 1967), pp. 20–30.

[7] To take an illustration, the 1966 agreement with the USSR stipulated that the proportion of manufactures in India's exports to the Soviet Union would increase from less than one-third in 1964 to 40 per cent in 1970; cf. p. 24, ibid.

[8] Narain, *Aid Through Trade*, p. 21.

(*a*) a central clearing account with the Reserve Bank of India; (*b*) another special account with the Reserve Bank in which it deposits any credits extended to India as aid; (*c*) a similar corresponding account, again with the Reserve Bank, in which debt repayments by India are deposited; and finally (*d*) a current account with one or more commercial banks. In this system, India pays for its imports from the socialist countries by depositing inconvertible rupees into the first central account or by withdrawals from the second account. On the other hand, socialist countries finance their imports from India by incurring expenditure through their current account with commercial banks. If they want to spend their credit in the third account, it must be transferred to their account with a commercial bank through the central clearing account. Despite the complexity in accounting, the equilibrating mechanism is fairly simple. If a particular socialist country exhausts its rupee balances, India extends temporary swing credit facilities, and the repayment is made as soon as possible. In the opposite situation, when a socialist country accumulates a large rupee surplus, India uses import licensing to restore the balance. Whatever happens, in the long run, the accounts are bilaterally balanced.

The central accounts of the socialist countries are protected against any alterations in the exchange value of the rupee, and these countries are free to transfer the rupee balances from any of their other accounts into it. For this reason, accounts in the commercial banks hold just what is necessary for current transactions.

In this section, we have been concerned with the operational aspects of bilateral trade and payments arrangements. It is now necessary to examine the possible costs and benefits of such agreements. There is no doubt that any evaluation of a particular economic policy must be based on carefully defined theoretical concepts. Hence the need for an analytical framework is obvious. To this, we now turn.

Bilateralism: a theoretical approach

Little attention has been paid to bilateral agreements in the theory of international trade. Bilateralism is generally subsumed in the set of non-optimal trade policies that diverge from free trade. However, in situations where import restrictions are widely practised, under certain conditions, even orthodox economic theory does allow for bilateral trade and payments arrangements. The hypothesis is that a country which applies import restrictions on a non-discriminatory basis, could improve its welfare through bilateral trade adjustments.[9] Although in such analysis, multilateral free trade is the optimum policy, if, for some reason, the import restrictions cannot be dispensed with, bilateralism does provide a second-best solution. It has been shown that a bilateral trade adjustment would bring about an improvement in welfare if the prices of commodities so traded are higher in the importing country as compared with the exporting country,[10] i.e. import restrictions are used in both countries. It is widely known that, during the 1950s, the Eastern Bloc countries followed fairly autarkic policies and India fostered import substitution through protection. Therefore, it is only reasonable to infer that before the expansion of bilateral trade between India and Eastern Europe, prices of traded commodities in the importing country were in most cases higher than in the exporting country.

From India's viewpoint, the benefits of bilateral rupee trade are even more obvious. First, trade with the socialist countries could not have grown as rapidly as it did in the 1960s, except through the media of bilateral agreements. Second, given the extreme shortage of foreign exchange, the introduction of rupee trade (*a*) added to India's import capacity, at the same time underwriting an expansion in exports;[11] and (*b*) reduced the burden of debt servicing, in so far as repayments could be made in exports or domestic currency, instead of scarce convertible foreign currencies.

Although the benefits appear to be quite straightforward, any measurement or quantification poses a problem. It is clear that the expansion of bilateral trade *per se* is no index of the gain to India. After all, it is quite possible that a part of the increase in exports to the bilateral agreement markets is illusory in as much as it represents a diversion of exportable commodities away from the other traditional markets. Therefore, the real benefit of rupee trade is determined by two factors: (*a*) the extent to which it constitutes a net increase in exports; and (*b*) the terms of trade obtained.

Let us try and illustrate the above argument with a simple partial equilibrium diagram. In Figure 1, the volume of exports is represented on the horizontal axis and the price of exports on the vertical axis. Suppose that *SS* is the domestic supply curve of exports and *DD*

[9] For a detailed analysis, see J. M. Fleming, 'On Making the Best of Balance of Payments Restrictions on Imports' in *Essays in International Economics* (London, 1971), pp. 23–45.

[10] Ibid, pp. 25–27.

[11] This is particularly significant in view of the stagnation in India's exports during the period 1950 to 1960.

Figure 1

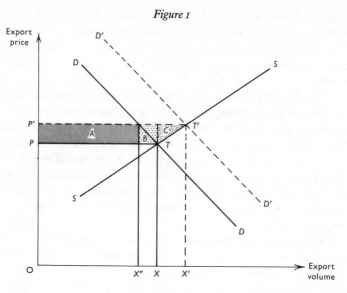

the foreign demand curve for them. In this situation, India exports
an amount *OX* at the price *OP*. At this stage, if the socialist countries enter the world market for Indian products, the demand curve
will shift outwards – let us say to *D'D'*. Thus, the introduction of
rupee trade increases India's exports to *OX'*, and pushes up the
export price to *OP'*. Although bilateral trade exports to the socialist
countries increase from zero to *X''X'*, this does not constitute a net
increase in India's exports, because we find that her exports to the rest
of the world fall by *X''X*. Therefore, the net increase in exports made
possible by rupee trade is *XX'*. The amount *X''X* is just diverted from
the other traditional markets to the new bilateral partners. In this
diagrammatic analysis it is also possible to pinpoint the real benefit
India obtains by trading with the socialist countries. On the assumption that import prices remain unchanged (i.e. India can purchase its
import requirements from the socialist countries at world prices),
India's gain from bilateral trade is *PP'T'T*. This gain can be divided
into three components. The area *A* represents a terms of trade gain
obtained from the rest of the world, as a result of socialist countries
entering the world market. Area *B* is the terms of trade gain obtained
on the diverted exports to the socialist countries. Thus we see that a
mere diversion of exports does not mean a loss for India – in this
particular case it results in a gain because of the terms of trade improvement. It is only if terms of trade actually worsen that diverted

exports will entail a loss. However, if the terms of trade remain unchanged, diverted exports, which represent a part of the increase in exports to socialist countries are not a net benefit to India. Finally, area C represents the gain accruing to India from the net increase in exports.

No sanctity should be attached to the above exposition as it suffers from all the numerous limitations of static partial equilibrium analysis. Moreover, the shift in the demand curve for Indian exportables from DD to $D'D'$ is nothing unique to bilateral rupee trade. It could also come about as a result of increased multilateral world demand for Indian products. As it happened, however, the rapid expansion in trade with the socialist countries after 1959 probably did result in such a shift of the demand curve. Hence, it does serve to illustrate our argument that any evaluation of India's bilateral trade with the socialist countries must be based on the extent to which it led to a net increase in exports and the terms of trade obtained. Therefore, it is necessary to examine the factors which determine net export growth and the terms of trade.

The apparent growth in exports to the socialist countries may be greater than the net increase for two reasons. First, if the supply of Indian exportables is inelastic, additional export commitments made in bilateral agreements might have to be met by diverting exports away from other traditional markets to the new trading partners. Second, it is possible that socialist countries re-export Indian products to the rest of the world. This kind of practice is easily distinguishable if shipments from India are directly reconsigned to other ports without being actually unloaded in any socialist country, or if distinctly Indian products are re-exported after import. However, when we consider commodities which were produced and exported by the socialist countries even before they began trading with India, several complications arise. It is no longer possible to identify the Indian origin of such exports. But to the extent that imports of these commodities from India enhance the exportable surplus in socialist countries, there is an implicit re-export. As far as India is concerned, all such re-exports are the equivalent of exports diverted away from her traditional markets to her bilateral trading partners, and do not constitute a net increase in exports. On their part, the socialist countries might re-export Indian goods for the following reason. Most of them suffer from acute foreign exchange shortages, and the resales of products imported from India (under rupee agreements) might be one way of obtaining convertible currencies. Alternatively, it is possible that under the bilateral arrangement they have to import some Indian products for which there is little demand; these products might then be dumped on the world market, again for the purpose of obtaining foreign exchange. Apart from diversion, such dumping would probably reduce world prices thereby worsening India's terms of trade with the rest of the world. In general, however, an increase in bilateral trade is likely to improve India's terms of trade with the rest of the world − as illustrated in Figure 1; and it is far more important to examine the factors which determine India's terms of trade with the socialist countries.

Under bilateral agreements, terms of trade are directly dependent on prices received for exports and prices paid for imports. Therefore, in order to compare the terms of trade obtained from the socialist countries with those obtained from the rest of the world it is necessary to compare: (a) prices fetched by exports under rupee trade and in the world market; and (b) prices paid for imports under rupee trade and in the world market. Let us illustrate this statement with an example. Suppose that India can procure her import requirements in the socialist countries at world market prices; then, if the socialist countries pay higher prices for Indian exports than the rest of the world, the terms of trade under bilateral agreements are favourable to India. On the other hand, if the Eastern Bloc countries pay lower prices, the terms of trade are relatively unfavourable. Similarly, we can allow for differences in import prices and include their impact on the terms of trade.

From the above discussion it is clear that if the terms of trade obtained from the bilateral partner countries are no worse than those obtained from other countries, any net increase in exports as a result of rupee trade constitutes a real benefit to India. It also follows that although diverted exports are no gain, they do not necessarily constitute a loss. But it might be argued that a premium attaches to convertible foreign exchange earned, so that even at equivalent terms of trade, any diversion of exports constitutes a 'cost' imposed by bilateral trade. On the other hand, it might be said that the uncertainty and risk of convertible currency markets are largely eliminated in bilateral trade markets owing to the contractual nature of long term agreements, thereby yielding a 'benefit'. Although these types of arguments have some element of truth, such costs and benefits are extremely difficult to quantify.

Having set out a clarification of the theoretical issues involved, it is now possible to attempt an evaluation of India's bilateral rupee trade through an empirical analysis of net export growth and the terms of trade obtained. However, before doing that, it will be most useful to review the export trends and to examine the changes in the market distribution and the commodity composition of India's exports to the rupee payment countries.

Export trends in the 1960s

We have shown that bilateral rupee trade led to a rapid growth in the aggregate value of India's exports to the socialist countries of Eastern Europe.[12] Clearly, it is necessary to go beyond such aggregative data and analyse the export trends in some detail. Two important questions arise in this context. First, how were the exports distributed as between different Eastern Bloc countries? And second, what were the changes, if any, in the commodity composition of these exports?

Table 12.2 outlines the market distribution of India's rupee trade exports and brings out the changes in relative shares of different countries. The main trends emerging from these figures can be summed up as follows.

(a) Among the socialist countries, the USSR was by far the most important buyer of Indian products. Its share in India's total exports to the Eastern Bloc countries increased from an average of 50 per cent in the three-year period 1960/61–1962/63 to 57 per cent during 1968/69–1970/71. In absolute terms also its imports from India grew very rapidly rising from $60.5 million in 1960/61 to $279.8 million in 1970/71. This growth was continuous except for the decline in 1966/67, which we have explained earlier.

(b) Although exports to Bulgaria, Hungary, and Rumania increased substantially in the 1960s, they remained relatively unimportant buyers of Indian goods, accounting for less than 10 per cent of India's rupee trade exports throughout the decade.

(c) Apart from the Soviet Union, India's main trading partners in Eastern Europe were Czechoslovakia, East Germany, Poland and Yugoslavia. However, with the exception of Czechoslovakia, exports to which registered a slow but steady growth during the period under

---

[12] Table 2.1. It is worth nothing that this rapid expansion was not unique to India. In fact, during the 1960s, the socialist countries of Eastern Europe (excluding Yugoslavia) increased their trade with developing countries at an extremely rapid rate, and India's share in this trade fell slightly from 9.3 per cent in 1960 to 8.8 per cent in 1970. See *Review and Analysis of Trends and Policies in Trade between Countries having Different Social and Economic Systems*, UNCTAD document no. TD/112 (Geneva, 20 January 1972), p. 21.

TABLE 12.2   Market distribution of India's rupee trade exports
(in $ million)

	1960/61	1961/62	1962/63	1963/64	1964/65	1965/66	1966/67	1967/68	1968/69	1969/70	1970/71
Bulgaria	0.1	1.9	3.6	5.9	6.4	4.6	6.3	5.3	9.7	8.9	12.8
Czechoslovakia	15.3	18.3	24.3	33.9	33.4	33.3	38.1	38.9	42.3	40.1	39.3
East Germany	6.9	9.6	17.8	21.2	27.1	28.8	25.9	27.1	26.4	26.7	32.7
Hungary	2.9	10.0	13.5	12.7	17.3	14.5	15.1	17.1	13.4	12.5	17.6
Poland	8.1	9.5	24.3	20.3	23.5	19.2	18.0	29.3	33.2	28.4	29.5
Rumania	2.9	5.5	7.1	5.8	6.6	9.5	7.8	5.6	7.3	13.1	18.3
USSR	60.5	67.8	80.5	109.6	164.0	195.4	164.5	162.4	197.7	235.1	279.8
Yugoslavia	7.0	13.0	23.7	19.5	24.2	23.7	25.3	15.5	25.2	45.3	52.2
Total	104.4	135.6	195.1	229.2	302.9	329.0	301.0	301.2	355.2	410.1	482.3

Relative shares (in percentages)

	1960/61	1961/62	1962/63	1963/64	1964/65	1965/66	1966/67	1967/68	1968/69	1969/70	1970/71
Bulgaria	0.4	1.4	1.8	2.6	2.1	1.4	2.1	1.8	2.7	2.2	2.7
Czechoslovakia	14.7	13.5	12.5	14.8	11.0	10.1	12.7	12.9	11.9	9.8	8.1
East Germany	6.6	7.1	9.1	9.2	8.9	8.8	8.6	9.0	7.4	6.5	6.8
Hungary	2.8	7.4	6.9	5.5	5.7	4.4	5.0	5.7	3.8	3.0	3.6
Poland	7.8	7.0	12.5	8.9	7.8	5.8	6.0	9.7	9.3	6.9	6.1
Rumania	2.8	4.1	3.6	2.5	2.2	2.9	2.6	1.9	2.1	3.2	3.8
USSR	58.2	50.0	41.3	47.8	54.1	59.4	54.7	53.9	55.7	57.3	58.0
Yugoslavia	6.7	9.6	12.1	8.5	8.0	7.2	8.4	5.1	7.1	11.0	10.8
Total	100.0	100.0	100.0	100.0	100.0	100.0	100.0	100.0	100.0	100.0	100.0

Source: Statistics published by DGCIS, Calcutta.
Note: All figures relate to Indian fiscal years, and have been converted into dollars. The columns may not add up to the total owing to the rounding off in calculations.

study, the growth in India's exports to these countries was quite discontinuous. Exports to Poland and East Germany increased rapidly in the early 1960s, but were virtually stagnant thereafter. The trend in exports to Yugoslavia is even more interesting; between 1960/61 and 1962/63 exports more than trebled. This rapid growth was followed by a period of stagnation until 1968/69. In the last two years of the decade, however, imports by Yugoslavia from India recorded a sudden jump, and more than doubled.

From market distribution, let us now turn to the question of changes in the commodity composition. Table 12.3 outlines the trends in India's principal exports to the rupee payment countries during the period 1960 to 1970. These twenty commodity groups accounted for most of India's rupee trade exports,[13] which is hardly surprising, as they also constituted her major exports to the rest of the world. A careful study of the data reveals the following trends.

(1) Exports of some products like cashew kernels, coffee, oilcakes, mica and leather increased very rapidly throughout the decade.

(2) There were other products such as jute manufactures, tea and unmanufactured tobacco, exports of which also registered a substantial increase between 1960/61 and 1970/71, but the bulk of this growth occurred before 1965/66. In fact, in the latter half of the 1960s, jute and tobacco exports fell markedly,[14] whereas tea exports were quite stagnant.

(3) Exports of hides and skins, vegetable oils, raw wool, manganese ore and lac fluctuated widely, but the general picture is one of decline or stagnation. The value of iron ore, pepper and footwear exports also fluctuated, but on balance, showed a slight increase over the decade.

(4) In the late 1960s, some new products acquired importance in the export basket; these were, engineering goods, clothing, chemicals and related products and cotton piecegoods. Export earnings from these commodities increased rapidly but remained only a small proportion of the total.[15]

Although the above trends identify the commodities which were responsible for the rapid export growth, they provide no index of the changes in commodity composition. In order to see if there was any diversification in India's exports to the socialist countries, it is neces-

---

[13] They constituted 96.6 per cent of India's total exports to the socialist countries in 1960/61, 91.8 per cent in 1965/66, and 81.1 per cent in 1970/71.

[14] Jute exports recovered significantly in 1970/71, but were still lower than their peak level in 1965/66.

[15] For example, in 1970/71, together they constituted only 13.5 per cent of the exports to rupee payment countries.

TABLE 12.3 India's principal exports to rupee trade countries (in $ million)

	1960/61	1961/62	1962/63	1963/64	1964/65	1965/66	1966/67	1967/68	1968/69	1969/70	1970/71
Jute manufactures	9.6	21.7	22.6	32.5	53.2	71.5	66.8	56.1	48.9	41.0	63.2
Tea	17.0	19.5	24.3	26.6	36.3	36.7	28.4	30.8	30.7	35.7	39.7
Cashew kernels	5.3	7.5	9.3	10.9	18.1	16.4	22.1	14.9	28.2	36.1	24.5
Oilcakes	4.9	8.2	25.1	33.3	49.8	41.2	35.9	44.9	46.6	34.0	48.2
Coffee	4.5	6.1	12.6	8.0	16.1	17.3	11.7	14.0	17.7	19.5	26.4
Iron ore	13.8	14.6	20.0	18.2	18.3	18.2	14.2	17.0	18.4	18.3	17.8
Pepper	9.1	5.1	4.5	6.7	7.8	11.6	8.7	12.5	9.3	15.6	10.7
Engineering goods	–	0.1	0.2	0.5	1.2	3.0	4.0	8.8	12.0	14.2	16.4
Chemicals and related products	0.3	1.0	2.0	1.2	5.2	7.4	4.5	5.8	7.8	12.9	16.1
Mica	4.2	4.4	5.4	6.1	5.8	8.6	6.2	8.9	8.8	10.3	11.9
Tobacco	1.5	3.0	12.6	17.3	21.0	13.9	4.4	7.1	6.3	10.0	8.4
Hides and skins	12.6	9.5	15.0	12.5	12.5	12.4	16.3	7.4	3.8	7.3	4.4
Footwear	3.4	1.9	2.0	3.6	3.7	5.7	5.6	5.6	4.2	4.1	6.2
Vegetable oils	3.1	4.9	5.3	7.0	4.9	3.6	–	2.5	8.1	4.4	7.7
Cotton piecegoods	–	–	0.5	0.3	2.3	8.6	5.1	0.5	7.8	8.7	13.7
Raw wool	3.4	8.6	6.9	3.6	7.7	8.5	4.1	4.6	3.9	3.2	4.4
Manganese ore	2.7	2.2	3.2	3.5	3.5	5.3	2.3	1.8	2.6	1.7	1.1
Lac	1.2	1.4	1.5	2.0	1.4	2.2	1.1	1.0	1.2	1.5	0.9
Leather	0.3	0.9	3.4	5.1	5.0	3.9	24.1	17.9	28.1	49.6	46.6
Clothing	0.2	0.1	0.3	0.9	3.3	5.9	6.1	7.8	12.0	12.2	23.2
Total, including others	104.4	135.6	195.1	229.2	302.9	329.0	301.0	301.2	355.2	410.1	482.3

Source: Statistics published by DGCIS, Calcutta, except for: (a) engineering goods, for which data published by the Engineering Export Promotion Council are used; and (b) chemicals and related products for which figures have been taken from RBI Bulletin (Bombay, July 1971), p. 991 and include manufactures of wood, cork, paper, paperboard and glass.

Note: All data relate to Indian fiscal years beginning 1 April and have been converted into US dollars.

TABLE 12.4   *Commodity composition of India's exports to the socialist countries*

	1960/61–1962/63 Annual average		1965/66		1968/69–1970/71 Annual average	
	$ million	%	$ million	%	$ million	%
1 Food, beverages and tobacco	64.5	44.5	140.7	42.8	155.9	37.5
2 Raw and crude materials	43.5	30.0	55.2	16.8	40.5	9.7
3 Manufactured goods	21.7	15.0	106.0	32.2	148.2	35.6
Total of above	129.7	89.5	301.9	91.8	344.6	82.8
Total rupee trade exports	145.0		329.0		415.9	

Source: Table 12.3

Note:

(a) Group 1 includes tea, cashew kernels, oilcakes, coffee, pepper, tobacco and vegetable oils; Group 2 includes iron ore, mica, hides and skins, raw wool, manganese ore and lac; Group 3 includes jute manufactures, engineering goods, chemicals and related products, footwear, cotton piecegoods, leather and clothing.

(b) The three groups together do not add up to the total exports because our data is not exhaustive, i.e. there are items other than the twenty principal exports on which this table is based.

sary to group products according to the degree of processing involved in the output finally exported. Table 12.4 does just that by classifying India's rupee trade exports into food, raw materials, and manufactured goods. It shows that, over the decade as a whole, exports of manufactured goods grew very rapidly; exports of food, beverages and tobacco (a group constituted mostly by primary and semi-processed agricultural products) also increased substantially, but raw material exports were quite stagnant. However, it is the changes in relative shares that are more important. We find that, in the early 1960s, the bulk of India's exports to the socialist countries consisted of primary and semi-processed agricultural products and raw materials. In the period 1960/61–1962/63, food, beverages, tobacco and unprocessed materials accounted for nearly three-fourths of the total rupee trade exports. Since then, the situation has changed considerably. Manufactured goods which were only 15 per cent of the total in 1960/61–1962/63 increased their share to 35.6 per cent during 1968/69–1970/71. At the same time, the share of raw materials fell sharply from 30 per cent to a little less than 10 per cent. This diversification was largely the result of specific clauses about increased exports of manufactures from India in the trade and payments agreements. Despite this change, however, the socialist countries absorbed a relatively lower proportion of manufactures as compared to the rest of the world, which is obvious from the fact that, during 1968/69–1970/71, 53.3 per cent of India's total exports to the world consisted of manufactured goods.[16]

Net export growth: some estimates

Our theoretical analysis has shown that any attempt at a quantification of net export growth must determine two things: first, the extent to which India diverted export supplies from convertible currency areas to the socialist countries; and second, the proportion of Indian products re-exported by the latter. Once such diversion has been estimated, it is fairly simple to discern the net impact of bilateral rupee trade on export growth.

Export supplies diverted by India

As long as there is no constraint on increasing the domestic production of an exportable product, the question of diversion does not arise. However, supply conditions might be such that domestic production cannot be stepped up adequately to meet all increases in demand. If the supply of Indian exportables was less than infinitely elastic during the period under study, it is quite possible that India diverted export supplies away from her traditional markets to meet her export commitments under the bilateral agreements. An exact measure of this diversion would be the difference between the actual exports to convertible currency areas, and what these exports would have been in the absence of rupee trade with the socialist countries. Such a hypothetical question raises immense problems of measurement, and could only be answered by extrapolating past trends. But there are two glaring limitations in this extrapolation methodology. First, the factors underlying the trends might well change over time. And second, there may be no past trends in the case of non-traditional exports. In view of these serious conceptual problems and the statistical difficulties involved, there does not seem much point in estimat-

[16] Cf. Table 2.7.

ing what India's exports to the rest of the world would have been in the absence of trade with the Eastern Bloc countries.[17]

A less exact, but more pragmatic approach would be to measure the actual reduction in India's exports to the rest of the world as a result of increased exports to the socialist countries,[18] i.e. the amount $X''X$ as illustrated in Figure 1. For this purpose, it is necessary to distinguish between India's exports to the rupee payment countries from her exports to convertible currency areas, and then compare the trends over the period under study.

For each commodity, statistically, there are four possible combinations: an increase in India's exports both to the socialist countries and to the rest of the world; an increase in exports to the rest of the world accompanied by a fall in exports to the socialist countries; an increase in exports to the socialist countries accompanied by a reduction in exports to the rest; and finally, a falling trend in exports to both groups of countries. Let us consider the possibility of diversion in each case.

(1) An increase in exports to both sets of countries means that, as a result of bilateral trade, there is no visible reduction in exports to convertible currency areas, but it does not eliminate the possibility of implicit diversion. It might be argued that were it not for trade with the socialist countries, exports to the rest of the world may have

[17] Nevertheless, Asha Datar employs a variant of this method in her study of India's trade with the East European countries. For each commodity, diversion is estimated as the difference between the increase in world (other than socialist countries) import demand and the projected increase in India's exports to her traditional markets, i.e. the convertible currency areas. The latter figure does not relate to actual exports but is based on an extrapolation of past trends, e.g. the assumption that in the period 1960–1965 exports would have declined no faster than they did during 1954–1959. Some adjustments are made for changes in factors like competitiveness that underlie the long term export trends. For details, see *India's Economic Relations with the USSR and Eastern Europe*, pp. 132–9.

In my opinion, this methodology is unsatisfactory for two reasons. First, it ultimately reduces to conjecturing about changes in the factors underlying long term trends and the extent to which they would have affected Indian exports. Some of the assumptions used in her analysis substantiate our point. For example, in the case of jute manufactures Miss Datar assumes that India would have lost her share in the world market at the same rate as it did in 1959/60 when the bonus voucher scheme was introduced in Pakistan (pp. 143–4). This is indeed a dubious assumption because it implies that there were no changes in the factors underlying competitiveness after 1959/60. We know that there were changes, and in fact, the rate of subsidy implicit in the bonus voucher scheme also increased substantially in the 1960s. Second, this approach cannot be applied to non-traditional exports which emerged in the 1960s.

[18] A similar approach is adopted by Narain, *Aid Through Trade*, p. 6.

increased even more. However, such a proposition rests on the assumption that there would have been sufficient import demand in the convertible currency areas. This might be difficult to establish one way or another because one does not know what the world demand would really have been in the absence of socialist countries. All the same, on the basis of evidence available about trends in world demand, we shall try to assess the possibility of implicit diversion. It would be worth remembering that such an exercise may yield somewhat uncertain results.

(2) If an increase in exports to the convertible currency areas is accompanied by a reduction in exports to the socialist countries, it would be perfectly reasonable to assume that there is no diversion.

(3) A reduction in exports to the rest of the world accompanied by an increase in exports to the socialist countries suggests a strong possibility of diversion, but may not always mean that India diverted export supplies from the former to the latter. First, it is possible that there was a falling trend in exports (of a particular commodity) even before the socialist countries emerged as important markets, in which case, the decline may be independent of increased exports to rupee payment areas. Second, there may be exogenous changes in factors such as world demand and India's relative competitiveness. These may be quite independent of the expansion in rupee trade and might yet lead to a fall in India's exports to the rest of the world. But if there are no such factors, and the decline in exports to convertible currency areas began only after the socialist countries became important markets, it is most likely that India diverted export supplies.

(4) By itself, a falling trend in exports to both groups of countries does not establish or refute the possibility of diversion. However, if exports to the socialist countries fall faster, or even at the same rate as exports to the rest of the world it would be reasonable to assume that there is little likelihood of diversion. On the other hand, if exports to convertible currency areas fall relatively more than those to rupee payment countries, it is likely that India diverted export supplies from the former to the latter.

So much for a general methodology. Let us now consider the trends of each of India's principal exports to the Eastern Bloc countries in order to determine the extent to which limited exportable supplies were diverted away from convertible currency areas. The method outlined above provides us with a broad framework which is supplemented with other available and relevant evidence for particular exports.

(*a*) *Jute manufactures*: Table 12.3 shows that India's exports of jute goods to the socialist countries increased most rapidly between 1960/61 and 1965/66; they rose from an average annual value of $18 million during 1960/61–1962/63 to $52.4 million in 1963/64–1965/66. At the same time, exports to the rest of the world increased from $287 million to $303.8 million.[19] This was roughly in the same proportion as the increase in import demand in the two sets of countries.[20] Moreover, throughout the first half of the 1960s India maintained her share of the world market at a little over 70 per cent.[21] Clearly, in this period, increased exports to the socialist countries did not reduce India's exports to the rest of the world.

In the second half of the decade, the trends were completely different. After 1965, India rapidly lost her share of the world market to Pakistan and there was a marked decline in her exports of jute manufactures. We have shown earlier that this was largely because of the poor competitive position of the Indian jute industry.[22] Exports to convertible currency areas fell sharply from the peak level of $312.6 million in 1965/66 to an average annual value of $238.3 million during the period 1966/67–1970/71: a decline of.23.8 per cent. But over the same period of time, exports to the socialist countries also fell by 22.8 per cent, declining from a peak level of $71.5 million to $55.2 million. Thus it seems extremely unlikely that India diverted any export supplies even after 1965/66.

It is worth noting that the bulk of India's jute exports to the Eastern

[19] These figures have been calculated from the data in Tables 2.3 and 12.3. Unless specified otherwise, the same sources have been used to calculate exports to convertible currency areas in the following analysis.

[20] Cf. Table 3.3.

[21] Cf. Table 3.2.

[22] One of the factors responsible for this poor competitiveness was the increasing pressure of domestic demand. In the second half of the 1960s, rising domestic consumption was accompanied by a fall in the output of jute goods (cf. Table 3.11). Therefore, it could be argued that a reduction in the supplies available for export may have led India to divert supplies away from convertible currency areas. In reality, however, this could not have happened to any significant extent, because most of the domestic demand was for jute bags which were exported to the rupee payment countries, and *not* for carpet backing, which was exported to the Western countries. If anything, increasing domestic demand is likely to have reduced the potential exports under rupee trade.

Bloc countries was constituted by sacking and jute bags,[23] which were increasingly difficult for India to sell in the rest of the world because of: (1) intense competition from Pakistan, the bulk of whose exports were sacking and jute bags, and (2) the development of substitute materials and handling techniques in North America and Western Europe.[24] To the extent that this was true, India found additional markets for her jute goods through the bilateral agreements.

(*b*) *Tea*: India's exports of tea to the socialist countries grew rapidly in the early 1960s and stagnated thereafter, but over the decade as a whole they registered an increase. The average annual value of tea exports to the rupee payment countries rose from $26.7 million in the period 1960/61–1965/66 to $33 million during 1966/67–1970/71, but at the same time, exports to the rest of the world fell from $225.6 million to $169.9 million.[25] Given the fact that the increasing pressure of domestic demand reduced the exportable surplus,[26] it is likely that India might have diverted some export supplies away from convertible currency areas. However, it is interesting that although exports to the socialist countries increased by only $6.3 million, exports to the rest of the world fell by $56.7 million. Clearly, most of the fall in India's tea exports to the convertible currency areas *cannot* be explained in terms of supplies diverted to the rupee payment countries. In fact, we have shown that the main reasons for India's poor export performance were increased competition from East African teas in the UK market, and the relative attractiveness of the domestic market. Both these developments were quite independent of bilateral rupee trade.

In view of the above factors, it is difficult to say how much of the increase in exports of tea under rupee trade was diversionary. To the extent that the traditional markets were saturated and the world demand for the tea was quite stagnant, the East European countries did provide a new demand for Indian tea. It is possible that India may have been able to create such additional demand elsewhere, e.g. North America and Western Europe, but that would have meant

---

[23] In the period 1968/69–1970/1, jute bags alone accounted for 57.3 per cent of the value of the jute manufactures exported by India to the rupee payment countries. A large proportion of the remainder was constituted by sacking and hessian cloth (calculated from statistics published by DGCIS, Calcutta). For evidence on the overwhelming importance of sacking in the early 1960s, see Datar, *India's Economic Relations with the USSR and Eastern Europe*, p. 146.

[24] For a detailed discussion, see Chapter 3.

[25] There was a similar trend in export volume. The average annual quantity of tea exported to the Eastern Bloc countries increased from 18.1 million kg in the period 1960–1965 to 26.4 million kg during 1966–1970, whereas exports to other countries fell from 189.3 to 158.6 million kg (calculated from Table 5.5).

[26] Cf. pp. 100–3.

incurring substantial advertising costs – an expense not necessary in the framework of bilaterial agreements.

(c) *Cashew kernels*:   Exports of cashew kernels from India increased substantially in the 1960s. The annual average value of cashew exports to the socialist countries increased from $10.2 million in the quinquennium 1960/61–1964/65 to $23.7 million during 1965/66–1970/71. At the same time, exports to the rest of the world also increased from $34.8 million to $43.4 million. Clearly, the expansion in rupee trade did not reduce exports elsewhere. In fact, we have shown that the additional demand created by the socialist countries pushed up the world cashew prices thereby improving India's terms of trade.[27] However, it might be argued that given the rising trend in world demand, cashew kernels sold under bilateral agreements could easily have been sold in convertible currency markets. One might go further and say that this led to the creation of alternative sources of supply, as a result of which, India began to lose her monopolistic share of the world market. But, in fact, the erosion in India's share during the period 1964–1969 cannot be ascribed to increased trade with the socialist countries for the following reasons. Between 1964/65 and 1967/68, India's cashew exports to the rupee payment countries were quite stagnant while her share of the world market fell from 92.3 to 80.7 per cent.[28] We have shown that this was because of increasing competition from Tanzania, Mozambique and Brazil. Historically, the basis of the Indian monopoly had been the labour skills necessary for processing. The development of a mechanical processing plant in Italy eliminated the monopoly element,[29] and induced the African countries to process their own nuts rather than export them to India for that purpose. Obviously, this factor had nothing to do with the expansion in rupee trade.

(d) *Unmanufactured tobacco*:   India's exports of tobacco to the socialist countries increased at a fast pace in the early 1960s, rising from an annual average value of $2.3 million in 1960/61–1961/62 to $17 million during 1962/63–1964/65. Over the same period, exports to the rest of the world were virtually unchanged, falling very slightly from $27.8 million to $27.4 million. However, between 1960/61 and 1964/65, India's total tobacco exports increased faster than world exports, as a result of which her share in the world market also increased.[30] Therefore, it would seem that bilateral trade provided

[27] See Chapter 6, p. 115.
[28] Table 6.3.
[29] See pp. 112–13.
[30] Cf. Table 6.10.

India with additional markets for her tobacco at the cost of a very minimal diversion of export supplies.

After 1964/65, however, the trends were completely reversed. Exports to the socialist countries dropped sharply, falling from the peak level of $21 million in 1964/65 to an average of $8.3 million during 1965/66–1970/71, whereas exports to the rest of the world increased from $30.2 million to $32.7 million. The contrast in export volume trends is even more pronounced. Exports to the rupee payment countries fell from 42.2 million kg in 1964/65 to an annual average of 10.4 million kg during 1965/66–1970/71, while exports to convertible currency areas increased from 35.2 to 38.8 million kg.[31] It appears that tobacco exports were actually diverted away from socialist countries to convertible currency markets.[32]

(e) *Iron ore*: Although India's total exports of iron ore grew at a phenomenal pace in the 1960s, her exports to the socialist countries were quite stagnant. The average annual value of iron ore exported to the rupee payment countries hardly changed from $17.2 million during 1960/61–1965/66 to $17.1 million in 1966/67–1970/71, whereas exports to the rest of the world more than doubled rising from $41.5 million to $101.5 million. In view of these trends it is most unlikely that export supplies were diverted away from convertible currency areas.

(f) *Manganese ore*: There was a distinct falling trend in India's exports of manganese ore during the 1960s. Her exports to the convertible currency areas fell from an annual average value of $19.3 million in the period 1960/61–1965/66 to $15.2 million during 1966/67–1970/71; a decline of about 20 per cent. But at the same time, exports to the rupee payment countries fell by more than 40 per cent from $3.4 million to $1.9 million. Obviously, there was no diversion of export supplies. In fact, given the deteriorating quality of its ore, and the restricted nature of the world market,[33] India was having

[31] Calculated from statistics published by the DGCIS, Calcutta.

[32] This sudden reversal in the trend does need some explanation. Our analysis in Chapter 6 showed that one of the main reasons for India's poor export performance after 1964 was the increasing pressure of domestic demand. Domestic consumption of Virginia tobacco which had fluctuated around 24 million kg in the early 1960s, increased rapidly thereafter, and reached a level of 40 million kg in 1969/70 (cf. Table 6.14). As it happened, the demand from the socialist countries was for low and medium grades of Virginia tobacco (see NCAER, *Export Prospects of Tobacco* (New Delhi, 1966), pp. 111 and 116) which coincided with the domestic consumption needs. Exports to the convertible currency areas were not affected by this trend in internal demand, because they were constituted by relatively high quality flue-cured Virginia tobacco.

[33] For details, see the section on manganese ore in Chapter 7.

problems in selling its manganese. Sales through bilateral agreements were therefore a welcome addition.

(*g*) *Mica*: Over the decade, India's total mica exports were virtually stagnant. However, exports to the socialist countries increased from an annual average of $5.8 million in 1960/61–1965/66 to $9.2 million during 1966/67–1970/71, while exports to the rest of the world fell from $15.4 million to $10.5 million. Thus, *prima facie*, it would appear that exportable supplies were diverted away from convertible currency areas in order to meet commitments under bilateral agreements. But our analysis in Chapter 7 showed that owing to the importance of the US market, the changes in American demand for mica were an extremely important factor underlying the export trends. The following facts provide further confirmation. Between 1960/61 and 1964/65, when the American demand for mica registered a slight increase, India's exports to the Eastern Bloc countries were quite stagnant. In the second half of the decade, American import demand fell sharply,[34] because of the decision to run down the stockpile and the new technological developments in the electronics industry. Both these factors were completely independent of rupee trade, and would have led to a much greater fall in India's mica exports, had it not been for the additional demand created by the socialist countries.

(*h*) *Oilcakes*: These emerged as an important commodity in India's export basket during the 1960s. Between 1960/61 and 1964/65, total oilcake[35] exports nearly trebled rising from $30 million to $83.5 million. In this period, exports to the socialist countries jumped from $4.9 million to $49.8 million, and exports to the rest of the world increased only moderately. In view of the fact that world import demand for oilcakes, particularly in Western Europe, rose sharply in these years,[36] it is quite plausible that a significant proportion of the oilcakes exported by India under bilateral trade agreements could have been sold in convertible currency areas. There were reasons for this 'implicit' diversion of exportable supplies and we shall go into them presently.

However, the growth in exports of oilcakes came to an abrupt end after 1964/65, and there was a marked change in the trends. Exports to the Eastern Bloc countries fell from their peak level of $49.8 million in 1964/65 to an average annual value of $41.8 million during the period 1965/66–1970/71, but in proportional terms,

[34] Cf. Table 7.18.
[35] Oilcakes are an important constituent of compound animal feed.
[36] See FAO, *Trade Yearbook, 1965*, p. 212.

exports to the rest of the world registered a greater decline from $33.7 million to $24.2 million. The difference is even more pronounced if we compare the trends in export volume. The quantity of oilcakes exported to the convertible currency countries dropped sharply from 609 million kg in 1964/65 to an annual average of 318 million kg during 1965/66–1970/71, whereas the quantity exported to the rupee payment countries declined only from 654 million kg to 484 million kgs.[37]

What must have happened is quite apparent. In the latter half of the 1960s, there was a shortfall in India's exportable surplus of oilcakes which was met by a cut in exports. Perhaps because of the commitment under bilateral agreements, the reduction in exports to the socialist countries was far less than in exports to the rest of the world. Available evidence suggests that, owing to the growth of livestock and dairy farming, the rapid expansion in West European demand for oilcakes continued during this period.[38] Therefore, it is likely that India implicitly diverted scarce supplies of oilcakes to rupee trade countries, when they could have been sold in convertible currency areas. There were two main reasons for this diversion. First, some West European countries restricted imports of groundnut oilcakes (which constituted the bulk of India's oilcakes exports) because groundnuts harvested under humid conditions sometimes led to a fungal poison content in the crushed cake.[39] Second, the landed c.i.f. prices of Indian oilcakes in Western Europe were not competitive.[40] This was largely because of high shipping costs which amounted to 18.3 per cent of the f.o.b. value of oilcake exports.[41] The central trade agencies of the socialist countries got around the problem of high transport costs by making bulk purchases on an f.o.b. basis and arranging to transport them by chartered vessels which were much cheaper. In fact, the normal conference freight rates were nearly 20 per cent higher than the charter rates. A part of this freight cost

---

[37] Calculated from statistics published by DGCIS.

[38] For an analysis of the growth in demand, see a study by the UNCTAD-GATT International Trade Centre, *The Major Import Markets for Oilcake* (Geneva, 1972).

[39] Ibid. pp. 10–11.

[40] Asha Datar (*India's Economic Relations with the USSR and Eastern Europe* p. 153) points out that Nigerian oilcakes had a transport cost advantage in Western Europe, and were therefore cheaper, but fails to analyse why the transport cost problem did not arise in the case of the socialist countries.

[41] Cf. T. K. Sarangan, *Linear Shipping in India's Overseas Trade*, United Nations (New York, 1967), p. 72.

advantage was passed on to the Indian exporters in the form of high f.o.b. prices, which provided an incentive for diverting supplies.[42] (*i*) *Coffee*: India's exports of coffee to the socialist countries increased rapidly in the 1960s rising from an average annual value of $10.8 million in 1960/61–1965/66 to $17.9 million during 1966/67–1970/71. There is little point in comparing the trend in exports with the rest of the world because all of India's coffee trade with the convertible currency areas was regulated by an International Coffee Agreement with effect from 1962. Except for two years, India filled her export quota throughout this period.[43] In 1965/66 and 1969/70 her exports fell short by 6.1 and 8.8 million kg respectively.[44] Valued at prices prevailing in the world market at that time, these two short-falls amount to a foreign exchange loss of $11 million. We know that none of the Eastern Bloc countries was a signatory to the Agreement.[45] Therefore, it is clear that all of India's coffee exports to the rupee trade countries, except for the diversion worth $11 million in 1965/66 and 1969/70, were a net addition to her exports.

(*j*) *Pepper*: It is difficult to extract a general trend from statistics on pepper exports owing to the sharp fluctuations, which in turn are attributable to erratic supplies and consequent variations in world pepper prices.[46] To some extent, the fluctuations can be eliminated by averaging the data. Table 12.3 shows that average annual value of pepper exports to the socialist countries increased from $7.5 million in the period 1960/61–1965/66 to $11.3 million during 1966/67–1970/71. However, exports to the rest of the world declined from $8.9 million to $6.4 million.[47] On the surface it appears that $2.5 million worth of pepper exports were diverted from convertible currency areas to bilateral trade markets each year. But in fact, it is quite possible that India's poor export performance in the convertible currency markets was because of the competitiveness factor.

---

[42] For a detailed discussion on this point, see ibid. pp. 70–3.

[43] See document no. EB 1189/72 of the International Coffee Organisation (London, 14 November 1972).

[44] Ibid.

[45] Cf. *International Coffee Agreement, 1962*, p. 230, and *1968*, p. 39, published by HMSO (London).

[46] Pepper crops in the main producing countries India, Indonesia and Malaysia are constantly vulnerable to diseases that can destroy the entire crop. Therefore, a good crop gluts the market and a poor crop sends prices shooting up. For a detailed discussion, see FAO, *Factors Affecting the World Pepper Economy*, document no. CCP 71/9/1 (Rome, 11 July 1971).

[47] Calculated from statistics published by the DGCIS, Calcutta.

Throughout the 1960s, Indian pepper prices were consistently higher than the prices of her main competitors, Indonesia and Malaysia.[48] It has been suggested that the average unit value of Indian exports may have been pushed up because of higher prices paid by the USSR.[49] However, even in the USA, the average import price of Indian black pepper was 19 per cent higher than that of Indonesian black pepper during the period 1966 to 1970.[50] Perhaps this was the reason why Indonesia sold the bulk of its pepper in the USA.[51] The above discussion suggests that in years when Indonesia had a normal crop, it would have been difficult for India to sell more of its pepper in convertible currency markets, owing to the price disadvantage. Thus, in such years, it is unlikely that there was any diversion of export supplies by India. On the other hand, in years when Indonesian exports dropped sharply as they did in 1962, 1965 and 1970,[52] because of poor crops, India could have sold more pepper than she did to the convertible currency countries. On balance, therefore, it is difficult to say how much of the decrease in India's exports of pepper to the rest of the world was because of increased exports to the socialist countries.

(k) *Leather*: We have shown earlier that India's exports of leather and leather manufactures were virtually stagnant in the first half of the 1960s, but grew rapidly thereafter. A considerable proportion of this growth was attributable to bilateral rupee trade. The average annual value of India's leather exports to the socialist countries rose from \$3.1 million in the period 1960/61–1965/66 to \$33.3 million during 1966/67–1970/71. At the same time, exports to the conver-

---

[48] The following data on average prices of pepper exports illustrates our point:

Unit values of exports of pepper from selected countries in US cents/kg

	1960–1965 (annual average)	1966	1967	1968	1969	1970
India	82.8	84.1	72.2	68.9	79.3	113.9
Indonesia	68.9	76.8	50.3	56.1	66.2	114.4
Sarawak, Malaysia	79.4	81.3	58.5	48.9	59.8	75.2

Source: FAO, *The Marketing of pepper*, document no CCP 71/9/2 (Rome, 21 July 1971), p. 14. (The annual average for 1960–1965 has been computed.)

[49] See NCAER, *Export Prospects of Pepper* (New Delhi, 1965), p. 48.

[50] The annual average of f.o.b. unit value of black pepper imported into the USA from India was 85.9 cents per kg, whereas it was only 72.2 cents per kg for Indonesian black pepper; calculated from statistics published in ibid. p. 15.

[51] Cf. A. Hone and V. K. Saxena, 'India's Spice Trade', *South Asian Review* (January 1971), p. 151.

[52] The shortfall was particularly acute in 1970; see FAO, *Factors Affecting the World Pepper Economy*, p. 14.

tible currency areas increased relatively slowly from $50.8 million to $57.9 million. To the extent that India's principal market for leather, viz. UK, was relatively stagnant, the shift in markets probably helped exports. What is more, increased exports to the East European countries did not reduce exports elsewhere.

In the 1960s, however, there was a substantial expansion in the import demand for leather in some West European countries such as Italy, France, Spain and West Germany.[53] Thus, it is possible that India could have sold more leather in these convertible currency markets. In fact, Pakistan, which exported roughly the same type of leather did achieve a remarkable growth in exports,[54] and most of its markets were in the West.[55] Our discussion in Chapter 8 revealed that there were several supply constraints on the export performance of the Indian leather industry. Hence, it seems likely that there was an 'implicit' diversion of exportable supplies under the bilateral trade agreements, in the absence of which India's exports of leather to convertible currency areas might have increased faster than they actually did.

(*l*) *Other exports*: So far we have considered the important traditional exports to the socialist countries. Apart from jute manufactures and leather, these consisted entirely of raw materials and primary or semi-processed agricultural products. However, in the second half of the 1960s, there was a change in the commodity composition of exports and some non-traditional products were also sold to the rupee payment countries. In this category, the most important groups were clothing, engineering goods and chemicals and related products. Between 1965/66 and 1970/71, exports of engineering goods to the Eastern Bloc countries increased from $3 million to $16.4 million, and of chemicals and related products from $7.4 million to $16.1 million. Over the same period, exports to the rest of the world increased from $36.7 million to $139.1 million in the case of engineering goods and from $15.9 million to $32.4 million in the case of chemicals. The story was much the same in clothing, exports of which to the socialist countries increased from $7.8 million in 1967/68 to $23.2 million in

---

[53] See FAO, *The World Hides, Skins, Leather and Footwear Economy*, Commodity Bulletin series no. 48 (Rome, 1970), pp. 79–80; and UNCTAD-GATT International Trade Centre, *Hides, Skins and Leather – Major Markets in Western Europe* (Geneva, 1968), statistical annex.

[54] Table 8.3.

[55] In the period 1967/68–1969/70, only 14 per cent of Pakistan's leather exports went to the Eastern Bloc countries, and the rest were sold in convertible currency markets; cf. M. Kidron, *Pakistan's Trade with Eastern Bloc countries* (New York, 1972), p. 78.

1970/71, while exports to the rest of the world rose from $4.2 million to $16.8 million.[56] It is patently clear that the growth of these non-traditional exports under bilateral rupee trade did not displace exports to the convertible currency areas. In fact, the socialist countries provided additional markets for these products without the marketing efforts and advertising expenses, which were unavoidable in the convertible currency markets.[57]

The commodites discussed above account for the bulk of India's exports to the socialist countries in the 1960s. Our analysis has shown that except in the case of oilcakes and to some extent in tea, pepper, coffee and leather, India did not divert scarce export supplies away from convertible currency areas to meet her commitments under the rupee trade agreements.

Re-exports by the socialist countries

There are two methods by which the East European countries could have resold the products obtained from India under bilateral agreements, in convertible currency markets. In the first place, shipments from India could have been directly reconsigned to ports in the Western countries without ever actually arriving in a socialist country. Alternatively, Indian products could have been re-exported after import. Let us explore each of these possibilities in turn.

Reconsignment in transit: Cargoes loaded in transit may be diverted from their stated destinations in Eastern Europe, either by reconsignment at an intermediate port or by unloading in transit at a West European port. In both cases, such shipments do not constitute a net addition to India's exports and amount to 'switch trading' on the part of her bilateral partners. Clearly, it is almost impossible to measure the extent of this diversion separately for every commodity. Even if all the necessary data on shipping were available, which is inconceivable, it would be a stupendous task to estimate the extent of switch trading in each of India's exports to the socialist countries during the period under study.

It would be far more practical to resort to an aggregative test. If there is switch trading, and some of the purchases made in India do

---

[56] In this period, India's total exports of clothing increased from $12 million to $40 million; cf. Table 4.12.

[57] Bilateral trade agreements do away with the risk and uncertainty of convertible currency Western markets. This indirect benefit is particularly crucial in the case of non-traditional exports wherein product differentiation, brand names, and selling costs are all an important part of any successful export effort.

TABLE 12.5   *A comparison of Indian and East European trade statistics: 1960–1969* (in $ million)

	(1) Imports from India as recorded by the socialist countries	(2) Exports from India as recorded by Indian trade statistics	(3) Percentage difference (2) − (1) ÷ (2) × 100
USSR	1422.2	1437.5	1.06
Bulgaria	55.9	53.0	−5.47
Czechoslovakia	324.9	317.9	−2.20
East Germany	229.9	217.5	−5.70
Hungary	189.2	129.0	−46.66
Poland	205.9	213.8	3.69
Rumania	67.6	71.2	5.06
Yugoslavia	216.1	222.4	2.83

Source:
For column (1)' UN *Yearbook of International Trade Statistics, 1964* and *1969*.
For column (2): Table 12.2.
Note: All figures have been converted into dollars at the official rates of exchange. The exact conversion factors used for *one* US dollar are: 1.17 Bugarian leva, 7.2 Czech korunas, 4.2 East German marks, 11.737 Hungarian forints, 4 Polish zlotys, 6 Rumanian lei, 0.90 USSR roubles and 12.50 Yugoslav dinars. However, for the period 1960–1964, the exchange rate in Yugoslavia was 300 dinars = $1, and this has been used for those years.

not actually reach the socialist countries, it is only reasonable to infer that these products do not enter their import statistics. Therefore, a comparison of: (*a*) India's total exports to the socialist countries as reported in Indian trade statistics *with* (*b*) total imports from India by the socialist countries as reported in their statistics, should provide us with some idea of the extent of switch trading. Such comparisons of trade figures, however, are not free of limitations. First, it is possible that the basis of recording import and export statistics varies from country to country. As it turns out, this is not a serious problem because all Indian exports are recorded f.o.b., and fortunately, most Eastern Bloc countries also record their imports on an f.o.b. basis. But import data in the case of Hungary and Yugoslavia is on a c.i.f. basis, for which some adjustment might be necessary. Second, the time lag inevitable in shipping, i.e. the ocean journey for the cargo, might lead to discrepancies in annual trade statistics between countries. We have tried to overcome this problem by aggregating the data over the ten years for the entire period 1960–1969.

The results of the exercise are outlined in Table 12.5, which shows a very close correspondence between the statistics of partner countries involved in bilateral rupee trade. In fact, the percentage difference between the total value of Indian exports to the rupee payment countries in the 1960s as reported in India's trade statistics and as recorded by the socialist countries works out at 5 per cent or less for each East European country,[58] with the exception of Hungary. There seems to be no feasible explanation for the 46.7 per cent difference between the Hungarian and Indian trade figures.[59] The fact that Hungary records its imports on a c.i.f. basis can account only for a part of this gap, but certainly not all of it. For our purpose, however, it is sufficient to know that the Hungarian figure substantially exceeds the Indian one; the extent is immaterial because the possibility of Indian shipments being diverted away from their original destination is eliminated.

Thus, in as much as any sanctity can be attached to trade statistics, it seems that there was no significant or apparent switch trading of Indian products by the socialist countries. It is necessary to point out that the validity of this conclusion depends on one crucial assumption, which is, that socialist countries recorded imports only after the goods entered the country. However, if the Eastern Bloc countries recorded a product as imported as soon as the rupee payment was made to the exporter in India, without actually waiting for it to arrive, our result above becomes relatively uncertain and one can only take guesses about the amount of switch trading. Needless to add that such a statistical practice is most unusual and unlikely.

Re-export after import: Let us now consider the possibility of actual re-exports of Indian products by the socialist countries of Eastern Europe. It is most unlikely that they could have resold any of India's non-traditional exports like clothing, engineering goods, footwear, chemicals and other related products, in convertible currency areas. The reason is quite straightforward. In such goods, product differentiation and brand names are rather important and exporting involves marketing expenses like advertising, etc. Moreover, as discussed earlier, even India found it difficult to increase her exports of such

[58] Even these small differences can be explained in terms of the time lag for exports effected at the end of the period; particularly as Indian data relates to fiscal years so that exports during January–March 1970 are also included in the 1969 figure, whereas statistics from the East European countries relate to calendar years. In any case, the Bulgarian, Czechoslovak and East German figures are higher than the Indian ones, thereby ruling out a direct reconsignment of shipments from India.

[59] Perhaps the Hungarian trade statistics are based on an exchange rate different from the official one.

products to the developed countries of Western Europe and North America owing to non-price factors such as quality and marketing. In view of these factors, one can safely rule out the possibility of the above non-traditional Indian products having been re-exported by the Eastern Bloc countries.

Among the traditional exports of manufactures, exports of cotton textiles to the bilateral trade markets were quite insignificant throughout the 1960s, in as much as they constituted a very small proportion of India's total cotton textile exports, and an even smaller proportion of India's total exports to the socialist countries. On the other hand, exports of jute manufactures under the bilateral agreements were indeed substantial. The bulk of these exports were constituted by jute bags and sacking. As such, it is quite unlikely that these could have been re-exported to the convertible currency areas because the development of bulk handling techniques and consumer packaging retail methods had reduced the demand for jute bags and sacks in the Western countries to a minimum level.[60] Although there was a substantial import demand for leather in Western Europe, it is highly unlikely that Indian manufactured leather was re-exported because exports of leather from the socialist countries of Eastern Europe were negligible throughout the period under study.[61]

We are now left only with raw materials and primary or semi-processed agricultural products that could have been re-exported by India's bilateral rupee trade partners. These commodities can be classified into two groups: those which were *not* produced domestically in the socialist countries, and those which were produced domestically.

In the first group, the three main Indian exports were pepper, coffee and cashew kernels. In the absence of domestic production, any exports of these products by the socialist countries would certainly suggest re-export. Let us consider each of the three commodities in turn. An examination of official international trade statistics shows that none of the Eastern Bloc countries exported black pepper throughout the period 1960 to 1970.[62] Exactly the same is true for

---

[60] Cf. Chapter 3, pp. 40–1. Of course, re-exports in small quantities were always possible but these could not have been significant. For the period 1961–1965, Dharm Narain has shown that even if all the jute goods exported by the socialist countries were Indian in origin (and if this figure was larger than actual Indian exports, he took the latter as the maximum possible re-export), such re-exports could not have been more than 8.6 per cent of India's exports of jute goods to the East European countries (Appendix B, pp. 18–19).

[61] Cf. FAO, *World Hides, Skins, Leather and Footwear Economy*, pp. 76–7.

[62] See FAO, *Trade Yearbook, 1965*, p. 201 and *1971*, p. 262, except for Rumania which exported 0.03 million kg in 1966.

coffee.[63] In fact, with the inception of the International Coffee Agreement in 1962, the socialist countries, which were non-quota countries, could not have legally exported coffee to convertible currency areas which were quota countries under the Agreement.[64] Unfortunately, it is not possible to say anything definite about cashew kernels because they are generally included in the broader category of 'edible nuts' in most trade statistics. As such, it is virtually impossible to identify the extent of cashew exports, if any, from the socialist countries. However, there have been reports of Indian cashew nuts being resold by the socialist countries in convertible currency markets. It has been shown how cashew nuts purchased under bilateral rupee trade are marketed at a price discount in New York by some Eastern Bloc countries.[65] But owing to the lack of necessary data, no quantification is possible. One can only infer that such exports by the socialist countries could not have been significant, otherwise they would have appeared separately in the trade statistics. On basis of the evidence outlined above, one can say that the East European countries did not re-export any pepper or coffee imported from India, although some amount of cashew kernels may have been re-exported.

An analysis of re-exports in the second group of commodities is far more difficult. Since most of these products were produced and exported by the socialist countries even before they began trading with India, it is quite impossible to identify the Indian origin of such exports. Although it may be possible to say something about it, the lack of necessary data poses another major problem. Therefore, we shall restrict our analysis to three commodities viz. tea, tobacco and oilcakes, the choice of which was determined entirely by the statistical information available.

(a) *Tea*:   The bulk of India's tea exports under bilateral rupee trade were absorbed by the USSR, which was also the only socialist country that exported tea in the 1960s.[66] As such, it would be quite reasonable to confine our analysis of re-exports to the USSR. It is necessary to

---

[63] Ibid., *1965*, pp. 185–6, and *1971*, pp. 243–4, except for the USSR which exported small amounts of coffee in 1960 and 1961.

[64] There were, however, some illicit inflows of 'tourist' coffee from the non-quota countries into Western Europe; see Paul Streeten and Diane Elson, *Diversification and Development: The Case of Coffee* (New York, 1971), p. 20. But no quantitative estimates are available, and it is extremely difficult to pinpoint how much of this coffee was Indian.

[65] See M. Goldman, *Soviet Foreign Aid* (New York, 1967), pp. 110–11.

[66] None of the other East European countries exported any tea except for minute quantities in one or two stray years; cf. FAO, *Trade Yearbook, 1965*, pp. 192–3, and *1971*, pp. 252–3.

point out that the Soviet Union has been a producer and exporter of tea for quite sometime, and well before it started trading with India. In the 1960s, however, there was a marked increase in its exports which rose from an annual average of 8.1 million kg in the period 1961–1965 to 11.7 million kg during 1966–1970.[67] At the same time, the annual average imports of tea from India increased from 17.5 million kg to 22.5 million kg.[68] On the surface this seems to suggest that Indian tea must have been re-exported, but we find that the annual average domestic production of tea in the USSR also increased from 45.5 million kg to 58.5 million kg.[69] Therefore, it is extremely difficult to say what proportion of the growth in the Soviet Union's tea exports in the 1960s was due to re-exports of Indian tea, and what proportion was due to increased domestic production. To the extent that imports from India added to the total stock of tea in the USSR and hence to the exportable surplus, some element of re-export is implicit. But this may not have been any loss to India in the convertible currency markets, because available evidence suggests that almost all Soviet tea exports went to other Eastern Bloc countries and Mongolia.[70]

(b) *Tobacco*: After a careful and detailed examination of statistics relating to exports of unmanufactured tobacco by the Eastern Bloc countries and their imports from India, Dharm Narain has shown that in the period 1961/62–1965/66 there were no significant re-exports of Indian tobacco by the socialist countries.[71] The possibility of such re-exports after 1965/66 is even more remote because of the very rapid decline in exports of tobacco from India under rupee trade.

(c) *Oilcakes*: Among the socialist countries, Poland was by far the most important buyer of oilcakes from India,[72] and official international trade statistics show that Poland did not export any oilcakes in the period 1960 to 1970.[73] Except for very small quantities in the early 1960s, there were no exports of oilcakes from Bulgaria, East Germany, Hungary and Rumania.[74] This leaves us with the USSR,

[67] Calculated from FAO, *Trade Yearbooks*, ibid.
[68] Cf. Table 5.5.
[69] See FAO, *Production Yearbook, 1971*, p. 270.
[70] Dharm Narain, *Aid Through Trade*, Table A-7.
[71] Ibid. Appendix B, pp. 20–1.
[72] In terms of volume, exports to Poland accounted for 25 per cent of India's oilcakes exports to the socialist countries during the period 1960/1–1965/6 (calculated from ibid. Table A-10). This proportion was 33 per cent in 1970/71 (calculated from statistics published by DGCIS).
[73] Cf. FAO, *Trade Yearbook, 1965*, pp. 210–11, and *1971*, pp. 274–5.
[74] Ibid.

Czechoslovakia and Yugoslavia who might possibly have re-exported Indian oilcakes. However, the Soviet Union was always a large exporter of oilcakes and exported substantial quantities of oilcakes even before it started importing them from India.[75] Therefore, it is impossible to say how much of its imports from India were re-exported. In the case of Czechoslovakia and Yugoslavia, the evidence is more definite in as much as exports of oilcakes from these countries showed a marked increase after 1960.[76] This suggests that Indian oilcakes might have been re-exported, but once again it is extremely difficult to quantify the extent of it, owing to the lack of data on domestic production and consumption of oilcakes in these countries.

The above discussion on the re-export of Indian goods by the socialist countries is certainly not exhaustive, but it does cover most of India's exports to these countries under bilateral agreements.[77] On the basis of limited statistical evidence, our analysis has shown that: (*a*) there was no switch trading on a significant scale; (*b*) it seems extremely unlikely that manufactured goods imported from India could have been re-exported by the socialist countries; and (*c*) as for primary or semi-processed agricultural products, some of them were definitely not re-exported (at least legally), whereas others were, although the extent of such re-exports was probably small. However, these findings should not be taken to mean that the socialist countries did not indulge in any switch trade or re-export of Indian products. In fact, during the 1960s, there were several instances of such practices, and a parliamentary committee specifically pointed to the resale of Indian cashew nuts, oilcakes, hides and skins, coffee, tea and spices, by the socialist countries in convertible currency markets.[78] The Indian Government was quite aware of some of these instances,[79]

[75] Ibid. For example, in 1960, the USSR exported 496.4 million kg of oilcakes.

[76] Ibid.

[77] It is not possible to comment on the remaining exports owing to the lack of necessary data.

[78] 'Eleventh Report of the Fourth Lok Sabha's Estimates Committee', entitled *Utilisation of External Assistance*, quoted in Asha Datar, *India's Economic Relations with the USSR and Eastern Europe*, pp. 161–2.

[79] Personal discussions with the people concerned at UNCTAD in Geneva, and with the officers of the Foreign Trade and Shipping Ministries in New Delhi, confirmed this awareness. It was felt that there were very few complaints about reconsignment and re-export against the USSR, but evidently, all the other East European countries had indulged in these practices. In his study on *Pakistan's Trade with the Eastern Bloc Countries*, Michael Kidron also found that the USSR absorbed all its imports, whereas the others indulged in switch trade; see p. 26.

but in the absence of definite proof, it was unable to do anything about it.[80]

All the same, in so far as any reliance can be placed on available statistical evidence, it seems that only a very small proportion of Indian exports under bilateral rupee trade were resold by the socialist countries through reconsignment or re-export. Given the limitation of the data examined, any attempt at a quantification of such resale must necessarily be based on guesswork. Dharm Narain estimated it at 3.5 per cent of India's total exports to the socialist countries,[81] and 'official circles' evidently put it at around 5 to 10 per cent.[82]

The terms of trade

Thus far, we have been concerned with an analysis of the extent to which bilateral rupee trade led to a net increase in India's exports during the 1960s. However, in order to evaluate the benefits of this export growth, it is necessary to examine the terms of trade obtained from the socialist countries under bilateral agreements.

We have shown that the terms of trade are directly dependent on the prices paid for imports and the prices received for exports. A detailed investigation of the prices paid by India for the commodities imported from the Eastern Bloc countries would be quite complex, and is beyond the scope of our work. Hence, we shall rely on available evidence on this point. Information on import prices is scarce, but all the studies so far have shown that the prices of goods imported from the socialist countries have generally been lower and very rarely higher than the prices of similar goods imported from the rest of the world.[83] According to Dave, 'a study of about 100 unit values of imports of chemicals, fertilisers, newsprint and iron and steel products from these countries for three years 1957−59 suggests that no higher prices were charged (and) ... the findings indicate that except for some dyes, chemicals and high grade steel, prices charged by these countries were less than the multilateral prices'.[84] For the period 1961/62−1965/66, Dharm Narain also computed

---

[80] This was the testimony of the Ministry of Foreign Trade Representative to the Lok Sabha Committee, quoted in Asha Datar, p. 162.

[81] p. 13.

[82] Reported in Asha Datar, p. 161.

[83] See Dharm Narain, pp. 16−19; Asha Datar, pp. 175−6; and *India's Trade with Eastern Europe*, pp. 26−8 and 69−76.

[84] S. Dave, 'India's Trade with East European Countries − Rejoinder', *Indian Economic Journal* (April 1962), p. 482.

average unit values of selected imports viz. base metals, paper, petroleum and petroleum products, organic and inorganic chemicals and iron and steel products, and compared the prices charged by the socialist countries with those charged by the rest of the world. He found that except in one year, the prices charged by the rupee payment countries were significantly lower than the prices India paid to convertible currency countries.[85] However, these selected imports constituted only 35 per cent of India's total imports from the East European countries in the first half of the 1960s.

In a more recent study, relating to the period 1958/59–1969/70, Sebastian compared the average unit value of twenty-four items, which accounted for 60 per cent of India's imports from the USSR, with the unit value of the same imports from Western countries.[86] He concludes that, except in a few cases, the prices charged by the Soviet Union were definitely lower than those charged by other countries.[87] Nevertheless, a sizeable proportion of total imports is constituted by machinery and transport equipment, for which it is quite impossible to obtain comprehensive price data, and unit value comparisons are meaningless because of the wide quality variations.[88] Asha Datar suggests that 'a significant proportion of the imports of machinery and equipment from the East European countries has been financed by tied credits'.[89] Therefore, it would not be appropriate

---

[85] The unit value comparisons were made for narrowly defined 'homogeneous' products within each of the broad commodity groups. A weighted average of the unit import prices yielded the following interesting result:

Ratios of unit values of imports of selected industrial materials and intermediate products from socialist countries and rest of the world.

1961/62	1962/63	1963/64	1964/65	1965/56
92.4	92.1	88.7	93.2	101.1

Source: Dharm Narain p. 18. The prices paid to socialist countries are expressed as a percentage of those paid to the rest of the world.

[86] See M. Sebastian, 'Does India Buy Dear from and Sell Cheap to the Soviet Union?'. *Economic and Political Weekly* (1 December 1973), pp. 2141–50. Some of the selected imports were: fertilisers, newsprint, iron and steel refractory bricks, tractor ploughs, drilling machines, bulldozers, etc.

[87] Ibid. p. 2146.

[88] Dharm Narain compared the unit values of ten specific items of machinery (Table A-28) and found that import prices under bilateral trade were lower than world prices for seven of these items. In the remaining three items the prices charged by the socialist countries were slightly higher. However, this sample is much too small for any general conclusions to be drawn from it.

[89] Asha Datar, p. 176.

to compare these prices with the prices from the cheapest source.[90]

Although the evidence adduced above is not exhaustive, and it is not possible to say anything definite about import prices of machinery, it does indicate that imports under bilateral agreements were sometimes cheaper and usually not any dearer than in the world market. As such, it would be reasonable to assume that the purchasing power of Indian exports under rupee trade varied directly with the prices received for them.

Data on export prices is extremely hard to come by. Thus we have to resort to a comparison of the average unit value of exports to the socialist countries and the average unit value of the same exports to the rest of the world. The major drawback of this method is that it does not take any account of quality differences. However, it is the only way by which one can get some idea of the terms of trade.

For a comparison of unit values we have selected ten commodity groups which constituted about two-thirds of India's exports to the Eastern Bloc countries during the period under study. These are: jute manufactures, tea, cashew kernels, oilcakes, iron ore, coffee, pepper, manganese ore, lac and unmanufactured tobacco. Apart from jute goods, all the selected commodities are raw materials and primary or semi-processed agricultural products. Admittedly, there are quality differences within each of our selected commodity-groups, but they are much less than would be in the case of non-traditional exports of manufactures.

Table 12.6 outlines the trend in the average unit value of selected exports and brings out the differences between the prices received from the socialist countries and the prices received from the rest of the world. Table 12.7 summarises the results of Table 12.6 and shows that except for jute manufactures, cashew kernels and tobacco, the Eastern Bloc countries paid consistently higher prices than the convertible currency countries. In the case of tobacco and jute manu-

---

[90] There have been reports that credit financed imports from Eastern Europe were priced higher than world prices. But, in this, the socialist countries were not unique. It has been shown that aid-tied imports from the Western countries were also overpriced significantly; cf. Michael Kidron, *Foreign Investments in India* (London, 1965), pp. 122–3. According to Asha Datar (p. 257) 'there is no evidence that the prices charged by East European credits are higher than in the case of tied credits from other sources'. There may have been some other disadvantages in tied credits from the socialist countries, such as limited choice for Indian importers, but in this chapter we are concerned with an evaluation of trade and *not* aid. Therefore, it is the prices of goods purchased in exchange that are important.

TABLE 12.6 Average unit value of selected Indian exports to the socialist countries and others

Exports	Destination	In rupees per	1960/61	1961/62	1962/63	1963/64	1964/65	1965/66	1967/68	1968/69	1969/70	1970/71
Jute manufactures	SCs	kg	1.95	1.98	1.73	1.68	1.70	2.00	2.89	2.73	3.03	3.30
	Others		1.57	1.80	1.75	1.67	1.78	2.05	3.16	3.50	3.75	3.62
Tea	SCs	kg	5.70	7.23	7.36	6.45	6.31	6.70	9.79	9.39	7.99	8.15
	Others		6.60	5.86	5.73	5.82	5.82	5.69	8.74	7.58	6.95	7.29
Cashew kernels	SCs	kg	5.23	4.42	3.90	4.13	5.10	5.21	7.96	9.21	9.23	9.79
	Others		3.27	4.33	3.99	4.23	5.27	5.40	8.62	10.17	9.71	10.69
Oilcakes	SCs	kg	0.37	0.33	0.38	0.38	0.36	0.44	0.63	0.57	0.73	0.66
	Others		0.34	0.35	0.37	0.38	0.26	0.39	0.56	0.66	0.45	0.59
Iron ore	SCs	ton	66.53	49.50	48.87	43.83	44.27	41.73	60.86	60.69	62.73	61.03
	Others		47.42	17.38	20.91	35.15	33.11	30.12	53.31	55.37	56.34	54.69
Coffee	SCs	kg	4.76	3.02	3.86	3.68	4.41	5.21	5.66	6.97	6.59	8.00
	Others		3.28	3.05	3.24	3.47	4.25	4.29	5.00	5.00	4.72	6.58
Pepper	SCs	kg	5.09	3.89	3.21	3.21	3.95	4.27	5.22	5.15	7.57	8.57
	Others		4.33	3.68	2.97	3.02	3.85	4.17	5.79	5.11	6.78	8.40
Manganese ore	SCs	ton	138.71	136.36	122.22	116.78	108.39	133.68	150.56	173.21	167.95	156.36
	Others		119.23	105.45	101.89	81.53	81.31	73.15	101.88	95.68	90.10	82.99
Lac	SCs	kg	2.61	2.44	2.43	2.38	2.75	2.92	3.45	2.84	3.03	3.63
	Others		2.34	2.20	2.27	2.21	2.33	3.07	2.18	1.93	1.82	3.78
Tobacco	SCs	kg	1.59	1.41	2.00	2.50	2.37	2.57	5.14	5.68	6.17	7.26
	Others		2.54	3.68	3.97	4.15	4.02	4.19	6.55	6.37	5.98	6.46

Source: Statistics published by DGCIS, Calcutta.

Note:
(a) The figures have been computed from statistics on the quantity and value of exports.
(b) All figures are in rupees and no adjustment has been made for the devalua-

tion in June 1966, because it affects the unit value to both groups of countries equally.
(c) The year 1966/67 has been left out of account, data for which is difficult to aggregate owing to the devaluation part of the way through.
(d) SCs = socialist countries.

TABLE 12.7 *A comparison of average unit values for selected exports*

Export	In Rs per	Annual average 1960/61–1962/63		Annual average 1963/64–1965/66		Annual average 1967/68–1970/71	
		Socialist countries	Others	Socialist countries	Others	Socialist countries	Others
Jute manufactures	kg	1.89	1.71	1.79	1.83	2.99	3.50
Tea	kg	6.76	6.06	6.49	5.78	8.83	7.64
Cashew kernels	kg	4.52	3.86	4.81	4.97	9.05	9.80
Oilcakes	kg	0.36	0.35	0.39	0.34	0.65	0.57
Iron ore	ton	55.00	28.57	43.28	32.79	61.33	54.93
Coffee	kg	3.88	3.19	4.43	4.00	6.81	5.33
Pepper	kg	4.06	3.66	3.81	3.68	6.60	6.52
Manganese ore	ton	133.43	108.86	119.62	78.66	162.02	92.66
Lac	kg	2.49	2.27	2.68	2.54	3.24	2.43
Tobacco	kg	1.67	3.40	2.48	4.12	6.11	6.34

Source: Table 12.6.

TABLE 12.8   *A comparison of unit values in some
specific export items*
(in Rs per kg for the year 1970/71)

Product	Socialist countries	Rest of the world
Black leaf tea	8.22	7.37
Coffee: Arabica Plantation 'A'	8.28	7.84
Jute hessian bags	3.55	3.39
Jute sacking bags	2.72	2.51
Varnishes	6.45	2.66
Synthetic enamels	5.72	3.52
Potassium permanganate	4.65	4.03

Source: DGCIS, *Monthly Statistics of the Foreign Trade of India* (March 1971).
Note: Calculated from data on the quantity and value of exports.

factures the price difference is almost certainly attributable to the quality composition. It is generally accepted that as compared with the rest of the world, the Eastern Bloc countries bought relatively low quality Virginia tobacco from India;[91] this fact was bound to be reflected in the average unit value. As for jute manufactures, the bulk of the socialist countries' imports consisted of jute bags and sacking, whereas a large proportion of India's exports to the Western countries consisted of carpet backing. We know that gunny bags fetch a much lower price per unit of weight as compared to carpet backing.[92] Thus it is not surprising that the average unit value works out slightly lower for the socialist countries, even though they paid higher prices than the rest of the world for jute bags.[93] In the case of cashew kernels, however, the rupee payment countries did pay lower prices than the convertible currency countries.

In view of the fact that differences in the quality composition of exports can significantly affect the average unit values, it might be useful to compare the unit prices of more specifically defined qualities in some of these products. Table 12.8 does just that, and also compares the unit values obtained in selected exports of chemicals during the year 1970/71. In all the selected qualities and products the socialist countries were important buyers. Although these figures relate to only a few products in one particular year, they do suggest

[91] See pp. 315–6.
[92] Carpet backing fetched more than Rs4 per kg in 1970/71, whereas jute hessian bags and jute sacking bags fetched only Rs3.39 and 2.51 respectively.
[93] See Table 12.8.

TABLE 12.9   *An aggregate index of prices paid by socialist countries expressed as a percentage of prices paid by other countries for selected Indian exports*

Year	Relative price index	Selected exports as a percentage of total Indian exports to Eastern Europe
1960/61	118.5	67
1961/62	136.6	66
1962/63	123.0	70
1963/64	101.9	69
1964/65	108.4	74
1965/66	108.3	71
1967/68	103.2	66
1968/69	99.3	59
1969/70	114.6	52
1970/71	105.3	50

Source: Tables 12.3 and 12.6.
Note: The year 1966/67 has been left out owing to the devaluation which affected the unit values sharply after June 1966.

that the socialist countries paid better prices than the rest of the world even in some comparable quality products.

All the data discussed so far have been fairly detailed. One might ask if it is at all possible to make an overall comparison of export prices received through bilateral rupee trade and the export prices obtained in the world market. A weighted average of the price differentials provides one obvious solution. Starting from the data in Table 12.6, we computed an index of the unit value obtained from socialist countries expressed as a percentage of the unit value obtained from the rest of the world, for each commodity in each year. These indices were then weighted by the corresponding share of each commodity in the total exports to socialist countries in that particular year, and finally averaged for each year. This weighting method eliminates the importance of large price differentials in individual commodities which might have constituted only a small proportion of total rupee trade exports. It also provides us with one overall relative price index for each year. The end results of the statistical exercise are outlined in Table 12.9, which reveals that except for 1968/69, when the prices received from socialist countries were marginally lower than those obtained from other countries, India obtained higher prices for her exports under bilateral rupee trade than she did in the world market, throughout the 1960s. It is interesting that the rupee payment countries offered much higher prices in the early 1960s. Once trade flows through the bilateral agreements became regular, the price differential registered a marked decline.

Although price data is not available for about one-third of India's exports to the East European countries, the evidence that we have examined does show that, in general, they paid higher prices than the rest of the world. A comparison of import prices is even more difficult, because machinery and equipment accounted for more than half of India's imports under rupee trade. However, available evidence does suggest that the prices paid for imports to the socialist countries were no higher than those paid to the rest of the world. Hence, it is quite reasonable to infer that India probably obtained somewhat better, and at any rate no worse, terms of trade from the socialist countries.

A summary assessment

The main conclusions emerging from the above analysis can be summed up as follows:

India's exports to the socialist countries increased most rapidly in the period 1960 to 1970. This rapid growth occurred in a framework of bilateral trade agreements, the distinct feature of which was that payments for all transactions were made in rupees. The USSR was by far the largest market, although Czechoslovakia, East Germany, Poland and Yugoslavia were also important buyers of Indian products. To begin with, the bulk of India's exports to the Eastern Bloc countries consisted of raw materials and primary or semi-processed agricultural products. Gradually, however, the commodity composition shifted towards manufactured goods. All the same, at the end of the 1960s, the East European countries imported a relatively smaller proportion of manufactures than the rest of the world.

A theoretical analysis of bilateralism showed that any evaluation of rupee trade depended upon the extent to which it led to a net increase in exports and the terms of trade obtained. Our empirical analysis revealed that most of the increase in India's exports to the socialist countries was a real one.

The estimation of net export growth raised several conceptual and statistical difficulties. However, a detailed examination of available evidence showed that except in the case of oilcakes and to some extent tea, pepper and leather, India did not divert any scarce exportable supplies away from convertible currency areas in order to meet her export commitments under the bilateral agreements. In fact, in the case of traditional exports like manganese ore and mica and non-traditional exports like clothing, engineering goods and chemicals, the socialist countries provided welcome new markets. As for the resale of Indian products by the Eastern Bloc countries in convertible currency markets, the problems of measurement were even more acute. Although there were some instances of switch trading and re-exports by the socialist countries, it was not on any significant scale. A comparison of Indian and East European trade statistics revealed almost no evidence of switch trading. We also found that there was little possibility of the socialist countries having re-exported Indian manufactured goods. The lack of necessary data prevented a complete commodity-wise analysis of the remaining raw material and primary product exports. However, we did examine some commodities on the basis of available statistical information and found that the Eastern Bloc countries did not re-export any pepper, coffee, tobacco or tea to the convertible currency markets. There may have been stray instances of re-export, but these were obviously not large enough to show up in the trade statistics. On the other hand, it is quite possible that the East European countries re-exported some of the cashew nuts and oilcakes imported from India to the Western countries, but no quantification was possible.

On the whole it is clear that the diversion of export supplies by India and the re-export of Indian products by the socialist countries, constituted a relatively small proportion of India's exports under bilateral rupee trade. Thus it is reasonable to conclude that most of the increase in India's exports to the socialist countries of Eastern Europe was a net addition to her exports.

The terms of trade obtained under bilateral agreements were also, on balance, probably favourable to India. Existing work on the subject suggests that the prices of a significant proportion of goods imported from the socialist countries were not higher than prices of similar goods imported from the rest of the world. On the other hand, the evidence that we examined clearly showed that the socialist countries paid higher prices for Indian exports (except cashew kernels) as compared to the rest of the world.

Bilateral rupee trade was responsible for more than half the growth in India's total exports in the 1960s. In view of the fact that a large proportion of it constituted a net increase in exports and was probably at better terms of trade, the benefit to India is unquestionable. It might be argued that the availability of an easier outlet through these trade agreements may have reduced the pressure on Indian exporters to sell in convertible currency markets. This may well be true, but given the trends in world demand and increasing competition in most of India's major exports, it is most unlikely that, in the absence of bilateral trade agreements with the socialist countries of Eastern Europe, India could have increased her total exports as much as she did in the 1960s.

13
Concluding observations

Our analysis of India's export performance and policies in the 1960s revealed that the process of export growth was influenced by a variety of domestic and external factors. Given the diverse commodity composition and the complicated structure of policies, generalisations are no doubt difficult. Nevertheless, it is possible to identify the salient features of the Indian export experience during the period under study.

Export performance

The relative importance of the different factors underlying the trends in India's principal exports varied considerably as between commodities. External factors played a significant role in the export performance of some industries, while domestic factors and policies were crucial in others. It need hardly be stressed that aggregative explanations are not representative of the actual experience. However, they are necessary in order to arrive at any policy conclusions. Thus it is worthwhile to group the major factors affecting India's export performance in accordance with the approach outlined at the beginning, and to comment on their significance.

The impact of world demand

The rapid growth in world import demand for cashew kernels, iron ore, chemicals and engineering goods was certainly one of the factors which stimulated the exports of these commodities from India. On the other hand, many of India's major exports such as jute manufactures, cotton textiles, tea, tobacco, manganese ore and mica were faced by a very slowly growing world market. In view of the fact that these traditional exports accounted for almost half of India's total export earnings until the mid-1960s, it might be argued that the sluggishness of world demand operated as a constraint on export growth. This sounds particularly plausible in the case of jute manufactures, tea and manganese ore, in all of which, world trade was dominated by India and a few other countries. For if there was no significant in-

339

crease in the size of the market, India could have increased her exports only at the expense of her competitors. In an oligopolistic market environment, the other exporting countries may have been willing to let India maintain her share of the world market, but they would have certainly resisted any attempt by a large supplier such as India to increase her relative share. As it turned out, however, in these commodities, India did not even maintain the absolute level of export earnings, let alone her share of the world market. The case of mica, in which India had a virtual monopoly, was different, and stagnant world demand did put a limit on further export expansion.

This leaves exports of cotton textiles and tobacco, in both of which India accounted for less than 10 per cent of world exports. Although the Indian cotton textile industry managed to retain its share of the world market, it failed to capture the markets lost by the UK, the USA and Japan. Similarly, in tobacco, India was not able to increase her share of world trade despite the fact that one of the principal competitors – Rhodesia – was largely eliminated by the imposition of trade sanctions. Therefore, it appears that India failed to exploit even the limited opportunities which were available, and although world demand for a large proportion of her exports increased very slowly, it did not, except in mica, constitute an effective constraint on export growth. It was domestic factors and policies that were basically responsible for the relatively poor export performance.

Changes in commodity composition

There is little doubt that at the start of the decade under review, the commodity composition of India's exports was an unfortunate one. In 1960, more than half the export earnings were derived from the traditional commodities discussed above, which faced stagnant or slowly growing world demand. Given this commodity composition and the rapid expansion of world trade in non-agro-based manufactures, her share in world exports was bound to fall. But, during the 1960s, there was a marked change in the composition of Indian exports. The contribution of jute manufactures, cotton textiles and tea, which accounted for 48.3 per cent of the average annual export earnings in 1960/61–1962/63, fell to 30.5 per cent during 1968/69–1970/71.[1] At the same time, the share of non-traditional exports of manufactures rose from 10.6 per cent to 30.2 per cent.[2] Although

[1] Calculated from Table 2.6.
[2] Cf. Table 2.9.

the growth is exports of products such as engineering goods, iron and steel, and chemicals was quite phenomenal, it did not make up for the stagnation and decline in the foreign exchange earned by the principal traditional exports. It is unlikely that it could have because, in absolute terms, the new manufactured exports were still fairly small. On the other hand, had India been able to maintain her exports of jute manufactures and tea, the impact of this diversification on export growth would have been much larger.

Shifts in market distribution

The changes in export markets were almost as pronounced as the changes in commodity compostion. The UK lost her traditional position as the largest market of Indian exports, an increasing proportion of which went to Japan, Eastern Europe and the USSR. In general, these shifts in the market distribution had a favourable effect on export growth. For instance, the shift away from UK provided the necessary impetus to exports of manufactured leather, while the booming Japanese market was the basis of the striking growth in India's exports of iron ore. However, by far the most significant development was the rapid expansion of exports to the socialist countries of Eastern Europe including the USSR. We found that a very large proportion of it was a net addition to India's exports and was constituted by traditional items that India was finding difficult to sell in convertible currency markets.

Competitiveness: the role of domestic factors

The factors which affected the supply and competitiveness of Indian exports were the basic determinants of export performance. In the first chapter, we outlined the manner in which domestic factors such as the costs of production, the pressure of domestic demand and the bottlenecks in supply could affect the performance of export industries. This section takes a brief look at the actual experience, and is followed by an evaluation of the policies towards exports.

Costs of production: The remarkable price stability of the 1950s gave way to a sharp rise in costs and prices during the decade under study. While the inflation in India was quite moderate by world standards, it did create problems for some exports. The competitiveness of the jute manufactures and the cotton textile industries was particularly afflicted by rising production costs. We found that this was largely the result of shortages of raw jute and raw cotton which led to sharp increases in their prices. The nature of the problem was somewhat different in the case of non-traditional manufactured exports, where the relatively high prices of intermediates and inputs were, to a large extent, a direct consequence of import substitution policies. The cost competitiveness of some of these export industries was ensured through subsidisation policies.

Pressure of domestic demand: The ever increasing absorption of exportables in the home market was one of the most important factors that affected India's export performance during the 1960s. Our analysis of the trends in India's principal exports established that rising domestic demand, coupled with the higher relative profitability of the home market, pre-empted a growing proportion of the total output of jute manufactures, cotton textiles, tea, tobacco, manufactured leather and chemical products. The demand for intermediate products such as jute manufactures was bound to increase with the expansion in agricultural and industrial production. In the case of consumer good exportables such as cotton textiles, tea, tobacco, leather footwear, sugar, spices and vegetable oils, there were two basic factors underlying the pressure of domestic demand. In the first place, the rapid increase in population naturally led to rising domestic consumption. Second, the income elasticity of demand for most of these goods was quite high in the domestic market. In any case, given the relatively slow growth in the output of exportables, the gigantic size of the home market meant that even small increases in per capita consumption had serious repercussions on the supplies available for export. It is somewhat difficult to disentangle the population effect from the income effect, but taken together, both these factors were responsible for the rising domestic consumption of exportables. As for the chemicals and engineering industries, they were established with the sole objective of import substitution, so that an overwhelming proportion of their total output was taken up by the domestic market. The fact that in a period of industrial recession, exports of engineering industries registered a marked increase, bears testimony to the impact of the level of home demand on export performance.[3] But for this exception of the recession, there seems little doubt that, in relation to production, the domestic absorption of ex-

---

[3] The favourable effect of the recession was confined to the engineering industries because it was only in this sector that the underutilisation of capacity arose from a lack of effective demand. In the traditional manufacturing industries such as jute manufactures and cotton textiles, the excess capacity was attributable to a shortage of raw materials.

portables was rather high, and this imposed a fundamental constraint on the possibilities of export expansion.

The mounting pressure of domestic demand, which is easily explicable in terms of the above factors, also reinforced the inflationary pressures in the economy. We have see that, between 1961/62 and 1970/71, wholesale prices in India rose by 81 per cent.[4] Insofar as this was not counteracted either by an increase in the world price of Indian exports, or by a change in relative prices in favour of exports through subsidisation and the devaluation, it must have made the sale of exportables at home relatively more profitable as compared to exports.

Supply bottlenecks: In some commodities, physical contraints on supply restricted the output available for export. For instance, we found that exports of iron ore could have increased even more than they did had it not been for infra-structural bottlenecks like inadequate port and shipping facilities. Stagnant production of raw cashew nuts limited the exports of cashew kernels.[5] The inelastic supply of hides, which was a direct consequence of the legislation against cattle slaughter, reduced the potential exports of manufactured leather. The export performance of the engineering and chemical industries was constrained by shortages of intermediates and inputs.[6] It is worth noting that, despite such limitations, all these exports accounted for a significant proportion of the increase in India's foreign exchange earnings during the period under study. Were it not for the difficult production conditions encountered by these industries, their contribution to export growth would have been even greater.

---

[4] Cf. Table 10.4.

[5] Further imports of raw nuts would have been rather difficult and, as such, could not have provided a permanent solution to the problem. This is because imports of raw cashew nuts were already quite high and the main producing countries were much more interested in setting up their own processing capacity rather than exporting raw nuts to India.

[6] For a short time, in the period of the industrial recession and the import liberalisation that followed the devaluation, these industries did not suffer from such a shortage of intermediate inputs, as a result of which export growth was accelerated. Clearly, further import liberalisation would have eased the problem, but it would also have had one undesirable effect. Given the choice, exporters would not have used domestically produced inputs at all because the latter were not really competitive in terms of either price or quality. In this situation, if domestic intermediate goods industries required a reasonably large market to exploit economies of scale, export promotion requiring a liberal import policy would have precluded the possibility.

Export policies

In sharp contrast with the 1950s, when exports were largely neglected, the period under review witnessed a deliberate and conscious attempt to promote exports. As a result, the past stagnation in export earnings gave way to a rising trend in exports. Yet the increase in the total value of exports, brought about by the elaborate network of export promotion policies, was relatively limited. What is more, a significant proportion of export growth was attributable to a small range of commodities. The factors underlying this outcome emerged clearly from our analysis of export policies adopted by the Government.

Export promotion efforts were almost exclusively concentrated on non-traditional exports of manufactures, while most traditional exports were neglected. Very little was done to prevent or slow down the decline in India's relative share of the world market for its major traditional exports. In fact, the combination of trade policies actually employed added up to a positive discrimination against them. The overvalued rupee, supported by import restrictions and accompanied by incentives for non-traditional exports, constituted an effective tax on traditional exports. It is quite possible that this policy was intended, as the elasticity of foreign demand for many of these commodities was less than infinite, and there may have been a terms of trade argument for taxes on exports. However, it did not justify the extent of the discrimination implicit in the overvalued exchange rate. As we have argued earlier, this policy was not in India's long term export interests, for traditional commodities which suffered on its account contributed a little more than two-thirds of the country's foreign exchange earnings even in the late 1960s.

The devaluation of the rupee did not turn out to be a panacea for problems faced by the export sector of the economy. In fact, as far as traditional exports were concerned, it did little to remedy the situation. This is because a large part of it was neutralised by the imposition of export duties, so much so that the *de facto* devaluation for most traditional exports worked out in the range 15–25 per cent, whereas the *de jure* figure was 57.5 per cent. Not only that, the devaluation also coincided with a severe agricultural drought which had the direct effect of reducing the exportable supplies of some important traditional items. The following inflation, which was a result partially of the drought and partially of the devaluation itself, further eroded the incentives created by the exchange rate depreciation. However, even in cases where the *net* incentive provided by the devaluation was significant and the influence of the drought was not predominant, there was no marked improvement in the export performance because it did not lead to a reduction in domestic absorption or an increase in the production of such exportables. Under these circumstances, the June 1966 devaluation could not have fostered the growth of traditional exports.

Thus it appears that while policy makers were concerned with promoting exports of non-traditional products, India's traditional exports fared rather badly in the world market. In absolute terms, of course, this loss was made up for by the extremely rapid growth in non-traditional exports of manufactures, which, in turn, was almost certainly attributable to the incentive schemes operated by the Government, even though defective methods of subsidisation probably reduced the potential favourable effects of these policies. In general, export promotion efforts were concentrated on a few selected groups of non-traditional manufactured exports, which were engineering goods, iron and steel and chemical products. Consequently, it was these products that were the basis of the rapid expansion in exports. Given the overvalued exchange rate and the higher relative profitability of import substitution, export promotion was clearly necessary as a compensatory measure. However, available evidence suggests that, in the early 1960s, some exports were granted excessive and indiscriminate subsidisation. In these cases, it seems that the objective of export growth was paramount, and little attention was paid to the domestic resource costs of bringing about such an increase in exports. The problem was removed only temporarily, at the time of the devaluation when the prevalent export incentives were abolished. In fact, the net devaluation for the engineering and chemicals industries was close to negligible; its alleged contribution lay in the rationalisation of the structure of export incentives. However, this policy change was rather shortlived, and subsidisation measures to promote the growth of non-traditional manufactured exports were revived a few months later.

The neglect of traditional exports and the excessive subsidisation of a few, select, non-traditional exports were not the only serious drawbacks of export policies adopted in India. The failure to develop other new manufactured exports, which would have been domestic-resource-based and employment-creating, was an equally serious shortcoming. This was largely because the Government took the existing industrial base in the economy as a starting point and sub-sidised heavily, without attempting to see what other sorts of in-dustrial exports could have been developed. It is only in recent years that products such as clothing, sports goods, processed foods, plastic goods, canned fish and marine products have emerged as export items. Before 1966, most of these escaped the extensive export promotion network, partially because some of them did not even exist as ex-port industries. To some extent, it was the devaluation of the rupee which provided the first substantial incentive for these new 'dynamic' exports to be developed, although it was accompanied by a number of other subsidisation measures.

To recapitulate, during the 1950s, the overvalued exchange rate and import licensing policies had raised the relative profitability of import substitution and discriminated against the export sector of the economy. In the following decade, export incentives were employed to compensate for this bias implicit in the policy of protection. How-ever, the structure of relative incentives created by the subsidisation policies was far from appropriate because it concentrated attention on a narrow range of non-traditional manufactured exports, to the relative neglect of traditional exports (which accounted for a sizeable proportion of total foreign exchange earnings) and of other promising new exports that were relatively insignificant, but could have been developed.

An overview

The foregoing paragraphs sought to identify the significance of the different variables that could have influenced the trend in Indian exports during the 1960s. It should now be possible to abstract from these concluding observations, and outline the most important factors underlying India's relatively poor export performance. Clearly, such an overview cannot be exhaustive, but it might enable us to pinpoint the basic reasons.

An examination of foreign demand conditions revealed that there was scope for further expansion in most of India's exports, and al-though world import demand for many of them increased rather slowly, it did not constitute an effective constraint on export growth. In fact, the fundamental explanation for the actual trends in exports is to be found in internal rather than external factors.

Apart from factors such as the severe agricultural droughts, which were beyond the reach of policy, it appears that there were two basic reasons why Indian exports did not fare better. In the first place, throughout the decade under review, rising domestic absorption outpaced the growth in production of exportables. Second, promotion policies which attempted to compensate the export sector of the economy for the bias implicit in prevalent trade policies, did not do so in an appropriate manner. These two issues are clearly not separable, as export policies are bound to affect the production and consumption of exportables. Therefore, we shall take them up together with a view to providing some assessment of the extent to which the relatively poor export performance was attributable to policies in the foreign trade and payments field, and the extent to which it was attributable to domestic policies in other spheres. It is obvious that a higher level of exports could have been attained either by reducing domestic absorption or by increasing production of exportables faster than the growth in absorption. Let us briefly consider these possibilities.

The pressure of domestic demand in the case of consumer-good exportables was attributable to the rapid growth in population and the relatively high income elasticity of demand, whereas, in the case of intermediate and capital-good exportables, it was a direct consequence of the growth in output. In principle, it should have been possible to reduce absorption, or at least curb the growth in it. However, as far as consumer-good exportables are concerned, such a consumption squeeze may not have been politically feasible, particularly because a large number of these constituted items of mass consumption. Exporting them forcibly through physical procurement would only have created scarcities at home and might have generated an import demand, while mobilising supplies for export through drastic changes in relative prices would have created obvious political problems. What is more, at the existing low levels of per capita consumption, any attempt at diverting wage-goods out of the home market, for exports, was certainly not desirable because it would have squeezed the consumption of the poor. In this context, it should be noted that the use of the price mechanism or of policies designed to operate on relative prices would have been regressive, because it would have penalised the poor by pricing them out of the market while the relatively well-off could have maintained their consumption levels. But this does not mean that there was no room for manoeuvre. Indeed, fiscal policy could have been used more effectively than it was to check rising consumption of some exportable commodities bought by the rich; higher taxation of superior quality textile fabrics, or Virginia tobacco, are obvious examples. Similarly, where needed, export policies could have been employed to improve the relative profitability of export, as compared to home sales. Unfortunately, the effective taxation of most traditional exports implicit in trade policy meant that their relative profitability was no higher than it had been in the 1950s, while for some it may even have been worse, owing to rising costs and prices at home. Controlling the rising domestic absorption of inter- mediate- and capital-good exportables through trade policy would have been less problematic as compared to consumer goods, but the effect of the necessary disinflation on the level of industrial produc- tion would have had to be taken into account.

In the ultimate analysis, therefore, a higher level of exports could only have been sustained by a growth in the output of exportables which was relatively greater than the increase in domestic absorption. In considering why the production of exportables did not increase any faster, it would be useful to distinguish between agriculture- based and non-agricultural exports, as the nature of production problems was quite different in the two sectors.

Exports such as jute manufactures, cotton textiles, tea, cashew kernels, tobacco, coffee, oilcakes, vegetable oils, sugar, spices and raw cotton, which were based on production in the agricultural sector, accounted for a sizeable proportion of India's export earnings during the 1960s. Our detailed analysis of the export trends in many of these commodities revealed that export performance was seriously con- strained by the inadequacy of supplies available for export. In some cases, this may have been attributable to temporary shortfalls in out- put, but there is no doubt that stagnant yields and the consequent failure of agricultural production to rise fast enough imposed a fun- damental constraint on increasing agriculture-based exports.[7] To a large extent, this was the result of inappropriate policies towards agriculture. We will not here enter into any controversies about whether it was the land tenure system, the lack of credit and other material inputs, the failure to spread the new technology to cash crops, or faulty government policies in the agricultural sector. Suffice it to say that domestic policies, which led to stagnant yields, were responsible for the extremely slow growth in output. Under these con- ditions, trade policies more favourable to agriculture-based traditional

---

[7] Available evidence suggests that, during the decade under study, there was no significant improvement in the average yield per acre for any of the directly or indirectly exportable cash crops, i.e. raw jute, raw cotton, tea, cashew nuts, tobacco, spices, coffee and oilseeds; cf. *Estimates of Area and Production of Prin- cipal Crops in India, 1971/72*, Ministry of Agriculture, Government of India (New Delhi, 1972), pp. 182–3.

exports may have provided some incentive for bringing about an increase in productivity, thereby raising the total output of exportable crops.[8]

The situation was substantially different in the case of industrial exports. Admittedly, production may have been constrained by domestic policies like investment licensing or by inadequate infra-structural facilities, but even in export industries such as engineering and chemicals, which were heavily subsidised, the shortage of inter-mediate goods and material inputs was the principal bottleneck in supply. If exporters had been allowed to import all the necessary inputs, a considerable proportion of these bottlenecks would have been removed, although, as pointed out earlier, this would have created problems of survival for the domestic industries producing the inputs used by export industries. Of course, a large number of non-traditional manufactured exports such as processed foods, marine products, sports goods, toys, electronic equipment and precision instruments were not produced in any significant measure because of the bias implicit in exchange rate policies. And it was only in the late 1960s that these items emerged as exports.

Another, quite different, reason why manufactured exports from India did not fare as well as they could have was that exporters tended to neglect non-price factors such as designing, effective advertising techniques, after-sales service and the keeping of delivery dates. This lack of an export consciousness stemmed from the domestic market orientation of industrial production in India, which was an inevitable consequence of the import-substitution based industrialisation strategy. Manufacturers who had been used to the sellers' market at home did not acquire the attributes necessary for a successful export effort. In effect, this failure was attributable to trade policies pursued in the past. Thus it seems that policies in the foreign trade and pay-ments field were a very important factor underlying India's relatively poor performance in industrial exports.

On balance, it is rather difficult to say how much of India's re-latively poor export performance was due to faulty trade policies, and how much to domestic policies in other spheres. Many factors outside

[8] It must be stressed that if an increase in the output of exportables had been ob-tained by extending the acreage under them, at the expense of foodgrains, it would probably have reduced the output of the latter. Export growth of this kind would have been accompanied by food shortages, inflation and eventually food imports, thereby neutralising any foreign exchange gain that might have accrued to the economy. Therefore, efforts would have had to be directed at raising productivity.

the domain of trade policy adversely affected exports, but it is clear that inappropriate trade policies were equally, if not more, responsible. Therefore, any future export policy which ignores, or does not sufficiently recognise, the lessons of this experience is unlikely to fare better than its predecessors.

14
Postscript – the early 1970s

This book has sought to analyse India's export performance and export policies during the 1960s. At the time it was written, 1970/71 was also the latest year for which comprehensive information was available. The years since then have witnessed certain new developments such as the recent boom in prices of primary commodities, the sharp rise in prices of crude oil, a marked acceleration in the rate of inflation and a serious economic crisis in India. Clearly, all these occurrences have an important bearing on India's export performance in the past few years, and need to be investigated in detail. But it is almost impossible for any book to incorporate the latest developments in a constantly changing economic scene. Nevertheless, in the following pages, I have attempted to bring the analysis of export trends up to date and to discuss the broader implications of these recent developments for India's export sector. It should, however, be stressed that the objective is only a limited one. A brief account, such as the one below, cannot provide a complete analysis of export performance in the 1970s.

As a first step, it would be useful to examine the overall trend in exports since 1970. In doing so, we shall outline the changes in commodity composition as well as the changes in market distribution of exports. This is followed by a section which discusses the performance of each of the principal export industries and seeks to analyse the factors underlying the growth in export earnings. The final section of the postscript attempts to place the export performance of the early 1970s in perspective, and considers the impact of the commodities boom, the oil crisis and the rapid inflation on the external sector of the Indian economy.

Export trends since 1970: an overview

The trend in Indian exports since 1970 is outlined in Table 14.1. It shows that export earnings increased rapidly in the early 1970s. In fact, between 1970/71 and 1974/75, the rupee value of exports, in current prices, increased at an average rate of 21.5 per cent per

TABLE 14.1   *India's exports in the 1970s*

Year	Export earnings in Rs million	Export volume index 1958 = 100	Unit value index 1958 = 100
1970/71	15351.8	153	173
1971/72	16031.5	151	180
1972/73	19643.9	168	202
1973/74	25183.4	174	247
1974/75	32986.2	179	319

Source: Statistics published by the Director General of Commercial Intelligence and Statistics (DGCIS), Calcutta.

annum. *Prima facie*, these figures tend to suggest an unprecedented success on the export front. However, the rapid growth in terms of current rupee value is rather deceptive because a very significant proportion of it is a consequence of the global inflation. For confirmation, one has only to consider the movement in the volume index. The volume of exports increased at a much slower rate of 4.1 per cent per annum and it appears that the basic factor underlying the growth in export proceeds was a sharp increase in the average unit value of commodities exported by India.

Even after allowing for the inflation, it would be misleading to identify an expansion in rupee value with a real and sustainable growth in exports. This is so for three reasons: the steady depreciation in the exchange value of the rupee since 1971; the emergence of Bangladesh as a new trading partner in late 1971; and the boom in the prices of primary commodities, the impact of which was felt in 1973 and, to some extent, in 1974. It is necessary to examine how each of these factors affected the growth in Indian exports after 1970.

(*a*) Consider first, the depreciation of the rupee. The crisis in the international monetary system during 1971 led to the Smithsonian Agreement at the end of the year and a realignment of exchange rates between the major world currencies. A salient feature of the new arrangement was the devaluation of the US dollar in December 1971. At the same time, the rupee was marginally devalued. Six months later, in June 1972, the rupee was pegged to the pound and floated.[1] This has meant a steady depreciation of the rupee *vis-à-vis*

[1] In September 1975, the rupee was officially delinked from the pound and tied to a basket of currencies: the US dollar, the Deutsche mark, the Japanese yen and the pound sterling.

TABLE 14.2   *The foreign exchange value of Indian exports*
(in US $ million)

Year	(1) Dollar value of exports at current exchange rates	(2) Dollar value of exports at exchange rates prevalent before December 1971
1970/71	2046.9	2046.9
1971/72	2151.9	2166.4
1972/73	2541.3	2340.7
1973/74	3204.0	2656.1
1974/75	4133.6	3426.7

Sources and method: (1) The series on the rupee value of exports in Table 14.1 has been converted into US dollars. The exact conversion factors used for $1 are: Rs7.50 in 1970/71, Rs7.45 in 1971/72, Rs7.73 in 1972/73, Rs7.86 in 1973/74 and Rs7.98 in 1974/75. These rates have been worked out from the quarterly average exchange rates published by the IMF (see *International Financial Statistics* (September 1975), pp. 184–5), and relate to Indian fiscal years. (2) The dollar value of exports at exchange rates prevalent in 1970/71 is derived from the figures in column (1), which have been deflated by an average depreciation factor for each year. In December 1971, the US dollar was devalued and the price of gold was raised from $35 per ounce to $38 per ounce; in February 1973 it was devalued further, and the price of gold was raised to $42.22 per ounce (see *International Financial Statistics* (July 1975), p. 2). To obtain the figures in column (2), the dollar values at current exchange rates have been divided by 1.0857 (i.e. $38 ÷ $35) for 1972/73 and by 1.2063 (i.e. $42.22 ÷ $35) for 1973/74–1974/75. The figure for 1971/72 has been divided by 0.9933 (i.e. Rs7.45 ÷ Rs7.50).

Note: All figures are in terms of current prices and relate to Indian fiscal years beginning 1 April.

most currencies of the world. Therefore, data on export earnings expressed in terms of rupees tend to overstate the foreign exchange value of exports. In the earlier chapters we resolved the problem by using the US dollar as a numeraire. However, in a regime of floating rates, where the exchange rate adjustments have been frequent as well as significant, it is impossible to find a numeraire currency, the parity of which remained unchanged throughout the period under consideration. For this reason, all data in the postscript are presented in terms of current rupee values.

Nevertheless, it is extremely important to provide some idea of the extent to which rupee export proceeds overstate the foreign exchange value of exports. What is more, it should be possible to make a comparison with export performance in the 1960s. Towards these ends, Table 14.2 sets out the dollar value of Indian exports, both at current exchange rates and at exchange rates prevalent before December 1971. While this method of conversion is not a perfectly accurate measure of the foreign exchange earnings derived from exports, it does provide a suitable approximation.[2] Between 1970/71 and 1974/75, the rupee value of exports increased by 115 per cent. Over the same period, however, the dollar value of exports at 1970/71 exchange rates rose by only 67 per cent, which works at an average rate of 14.1 per cent per annum. It should be stressed that even the dollar figures are in terms of current prices. Thus it is apparent that the real export growth was far less than the expansion in the nominal value of exports.

(*b*) During the early 1970s, a second factor which had a distinct impact on the country's export earnings was the emergence of Bangladesh as a trading partner in late 1971. India's exports to Bangladesh in 1971/72 amounted to Rs423.4 million and were responsible for 62.3 per cent of the total increase in the value of exports over the preceding year; in 1972/73 these exports attained a much higher level, at Rs1671.2 million, but accounted for 46.3 per cent of the total increment in the rupee value of exports.[3] This contribution to export growth is clearly not sustainable, for two reasons. In the first place, it constituted a once-and-for-all increase in exports, because trade with Bangladesh was virtually non-existent until then.[4] Second, a very large proportion of these exports was aid-financed. During 1971/72–1972/73, Indian aid utilised by Bangladesh amounted to Rs1589.5 million[5], which financed a little over 75 per cent of the total exports in these two years. It is very likely that these exports would not have materialised in the absence of aid flows. Our argument is borne out by the fact that, as aid flows diminished in 1973/74 and 1974/75, exports to Bangladesh fell markedly.[6]

(*c*) The third factor which must be taken into consideration while analysing the overall export trends since 1970, is the recent boom in

[2] An exact measure would require an *average* figure for the depreciation of the rupee each year, *vis-à-vis* the currencies of the country's principal trading partners, weighted by the shares of each such partner in India's exports. In principle, this calculation would certainly be worth while but, for our limited purpose here, it involves too much of a digression.

[3] The data on exports to Bangladesh are taken from the statistics published by DGCIS, Calcutta.

[4] In 1970/71, such exports amounted to a paltry sum of Rs3.3 million.

[5] See RBI, Bombay, *Report on Currency and Finance*, 1974/75, vol. II p. 183. The composition of this aid was as follows: (*a*) grants – Rs1229.8 million, (*b*) loans – Rs189.7 million, and (*c*) relief goods – Rs170 million. It is therefore worth noting that 88 per cent of this aid was non-repayable and took the form of grants or relief goods.

[6] In these two years, the amount of aid utilised was much smaller at Rs227.6 million. Correspondingly, the level of exports was also lower: Rs587.8 million in 1973/74 and Rs421.8 million in 1974/75.

the prices of primary commodities. That there was a marked rise in the prices fetched by Indian exports, starting in 1973, is confirmed by the movement in the average unit value index for exports. In fact, during 1973/74, only 12.7 per cent of the increase in export earnings, over the preceding year, was accounted for by the growth in export volume, while the remaining 87.3 per cent was attributable to higher unit values realised; for 1974/75, these proportions work out at 9.3 per cent and 90.7 per cent respectively.[7] Available evidence suggests that a large proportion of the increase in export earnings during 1973/74–1974/75 was attributable to substantial price gains in a limited number of commodities. However, the prices of many of these commodities have come down from the peak levels attained in 1973. Therefore, the commodities boom cannot be looked upon as a sustainable basis of export growth. We shall examine the evidence on this particular aspect of the problem a little later. Before turning to that, it might be useful to discuss the changes in the commodity composition of exports and the changes in export markets.

The discussion so far has confined itself to an aggregate view. Let us now consider how these overall trends relate to the performance in the major export commodities. Table 14.3 outlines changes in the rupee value of India's principal exports during the early 1970s. It reveals that the trends were rather complex and export performance varied substantially from commodity to commodity. Between 1970/71 and 1974/75, there was a rapid and continuous growth in the exports of cashew kernels, tobacco, coffee, engineering goods, handicrafts and clothing. In addition, the earnings from exports of oilcakes, manufactured leather and marine products registered a remarkable expansion until 1973/74, but declined to lower levels in 1974/75. A third group of exportable commodities, constituted by cotton textiles, chemicals, iron ore, spices and sugar revealed little or no growth until 1972/73, but recorded substantial increases in the rupee value of exports during 1973/74–1974/75. The performance in sugar, of course, was a freak occurrence insofar as it was a consequence of the phenomenal increase in world prices. None of the remaining principal exports showed any significant increase in the period under consideration. Exports of manganese ore, mica, footwear and raw cotton were stagnant throughout, while the major traditional exports – jute manufactures and tea – also fared poorly with little change in the rupee

---

[7] The proportion of export growth attributable to a rising volume of exports has been calculated as follows. As a first step, assume that export earnings increase in the same proportion as export volume. This notional increase is then expressed as a percentage of the actual increase in the value of exports.

TABLE 14.3   *Trends in the value of India's principal exports: 1970/71–1974/7*
(in Rs million at current prices)

	1970/71	1971/72	1972/73	1973/74	1974/75
Jute manufactures	1904.3	2632.9	2472.0	2255.3	2929.2
Tea	1482.5	1563.1	1472.9	1448.5	2239.9
Cotton textiles	975.0	1000.5	1267.1	2352.9	2147.9
Cashew kernels	520.5	613.3	688.2	744.3	1181.4
Tobacco	314.3	422.5	610.7	684.1	803.6
Iron ore	1173.0	1047.0	1097.9	1328.3	1603.9
Engineering goods	1166.3	1252.7	1410.8	2012.9	3528.0
Leather and leather manufactures	721.5	907.7	1745.1	1713.5	1449.1
Manganese ore	139.5	106.0	86.7	90.0	95.5
Mica	156.0	153.8	166.1	126.8	181.8
Oilcakes	554.3	401.5	747.7	1706.0	957.0
Coffee	251.1	220.7	329.3	460.1	513.6
Sugar	276.0	302.0	132.7	422.2	3397.1
Spices	388.1	361.8	291.3	549.0	613.3
Chemicals	363.8	320.7	403.6	570.0	1036.7
Footwear	114.8	117.6	128.6	133.9	204.7
Raw cotton	164.3	166.4	215.8	324.0	170.5
Handicrafts	803.0	905.2	1306.2	1807.8	1904.4
Marine products	305.4	413.9	537.9	881.0	649.8
Clothing	302.0	376.7	560.2	995.9	1360.4
Total including others	15 351.8	16 031.5	19 643.9	25 183.4	32 986.2

Source: Statistics published by DGCIS, Calcutta.

value of earnings derived from them, except for a sudden increase in 1974/75.

It is worth noting that the growth in the nominal value of exports, on a relatively stable basis, was attributable to a fairly wide range of commodities: clothing, handicrafts, engineering goods, manufactured leather, marine products, oilcakes, cashew kernels, tobacco and coffee. Of all these commodities, only cashew kernels and engineering goods had registered a continuous growth throughout the previous decade. Coffee and leather exports did begin a steady expansion around 1965, and this was perhaps a continuation of the earlier trend, but the foreign exchange earnings derived from tobacco and oilcakes had been virtually stagnant since 1964/65. Exports of clothing, handicrafts and marine products did exhibit a dynamic potential even earlier but, in absolute terms, they were not very significant until the late 1960s. In general, the traditional exports, which had been the principal foreign exchange earners in the 1950s, continued to experience stagnation and an almost certain decline in their relative importance. For example, the contribution of jute manufactures, cotton textiles and tea, which accounted for nearly half the average annual export earnings in 1960/61–1962/63 fell to less than 25 per cent during 1972/73–1974/75.

Surprisingly enough, there was little change in the overall commodity composition of exports after 1970. The average annual share of food, beverages and tobacco in total export earnings rose from 28.4 per cent in 1968/69–1970/71 to 30.9 per cent in 1972/73–1974/75, while that of raw materials and unprocessed products fell from 17.6 per cent to 13.5 per cent.[8] Over the same period, the average share of manufactured goods in total exports remained almost unchanged at 53 per cent. Within the category of manufactured goods, however, non-traditional exports of manufactures continued to acquire an increasing significance.

The shifts in the market distribution of exports were somewhat more pronounced. This is confirmed by Table 14.4, which outlines the directional changes in exports and brings out the changes in the relative shares of different export markets during the early 1970s. A study of the table reveals that the rupee value of exports to the USA, the USSR, the ECAFE countries (excluding Japan) and Western Europe increased most rapidly. On the other hand, exports to the UK, Japan, Eastern Europe, Africa and West Asia were relatively stagnant in the first three years, but registered substantial increases in 1973/74 and 1974/75.

To some extent, these trends in the absolute value of exports are reflected in the changing relative shares of different markets. The share of the US in India's exports fluctuated but, on the whole, maintained itself around the 1970 level. Much the same was true for the USSR market. As it turned out, the pace of expansion in exports to the ECAFE countries (excluding Japan) and Western Europe was much faster, so that the share of both these regions increased steadily. However, the proportion of Indian exports sold in Eastern Europe and Africa diminished gradually. A similar downward trend is discernible in the case of the UK and the Japanese markets. Whereas the declining importance of the UK as India's partner in trade is nothing new, the reduced share of Japan and Eastern Europe does stand out in sharp contrast with the experience of the 1960s when these markets were, perhaps, the most dynamic.

It is worth noting three striking features of the changes in relative

[8] Calculated from statistics published by DGCIS, Calcutta.

TABLE 14.4 *India's export markets by countries and regions: 1970/71–1974/7*
(in Rs million at current prices)

	1970/71	1971/72	1972/73	1973/74	1974/75
USA	2073.8	2627.9	2753.7	3763.3	4189.9
USSR	2098.5	2086.8	3047.6	2858.9	4181.2
UK	1704.0	1680.8	1718.7	2627.4	3063.4
Japan	2034.8	1817.1	2167.5	3585.2	2949.1
ECAFE countries					
excluding Japan	2067.8	2410.5	3386.9	3785.5	6100.6
Eastern Europe	1518.8	1348.0	1647.4	2015.0	2622.2
Western Europe	1288.0	1568.1	2740.5	3971.3	4415.3
Africa	1392.8	1319.1	1010.4	1017.0	2349.2
West Asia	606.6	515.7	611.8	1195.6	2562.8
Total including others	15 351.8	16 031.5	19 643.9	25 183.4	32 986.2

Relative shares: in percentages

	1970/71	1971/72	1972/73	1973/74	1974/75
USA	13.5	16.4	14.0	14.9	12.7
USSR	13.7	13.0	15.5	11.4	12.7
UK	11.1	10.5	8.7	10.4	9.3
Japan	13.3	11.3	11.0	14.2	8.9
ECAFE countries					
excluding Japan	13.5	15.0	17.2	15.0	18.5
Eastern Europe	9.9	8.4	8.4	8.0	7.9
Western Europe	8.4	9.8	14.0	15.8	13.4
Africa	9.1	8.2	5.1	4.0	7.1
West Asia	4.0	3.2	3.1	4.7	7.8
Total including others	100.0	100.0	100.0	100.0	100.0

Source: Statistics published by DGCIS, Calcutta
Note:
(a) West Asia includes Abu Dhabi, Bahrein, Dubai, Iraq, Jordan, Kuwait, Lebanon, South Yemen, Saud Arabia, Syria and the Yemen Arab Republic. Owing to this wider coverage, the figure for 1970/71 does no tally with that in Table 2.10.
(b) Western Europe includes the EEC (apart from the UK), EFTA and the rest of Europe other than th socialist countries.

market shares, which also need some explanation. (*a*) The first was the remarkable growth in exports to the ECAFE countries which rose from Rs2067.8 million in 1970/71 to Rs6100.6 million in 1974/75. This is attributable to the emergence of Bangladesh as a new export market in 1971, and the dramatic increase in exports to Iran, starting in 1973/74.[9] (*b*) A second significant feature was the sudden increase

[9] The average annual exports to Iran during the period 1970/71–1972/73 were Rs236.8 million; this figure stood at Rs427.8 million in 1973/74 and jumped to Rs2144.6 million in 1974/75.

in exports to the Middle Eastern OPEC countries.[10] During 1970/71–1972/73, these exports averaged Rs703 million per annum; they increased to Rs1447.9 million in 1973/74 and Rs4137.4 million in 1974/75.[11] To a large extent, this may have been a direct consequence of the recent affluence acquired by the OPEC countries, but it does also reflect India's efforts at exploiting new opportunities. (*c*) The third feature worth noting is the emergence of Western Europe as an increasingly important market in the 1970s. Exports to this region – characterised by the overwhelming importance of the EEC – more than trebled, rising from Rs1288 million in 1970/71 to Rs4415 million in 1974/75. This growth in rupee value was due to a considerable depreciation in the exchange value of the rupee *vis-à-vis* major West European currencies, rising commodity prices and a booming import demand in Western Europe.

At this juncture, a comment on India's bilateral trade with the socialist countries might be in order. While exports to Eastern Europe did not increase as rapidly as in the past, exports to the USSR continued to grow at a steady pace. In fact, taken together, the average annual share of the socialist countries in India's export earnings remained almost unchanged from 21.6 per cent during 1968/69–1970/71 to 21.3 per cent in 1972/73–1974/75. There is little doubt that India continued to derive substantial benefits from her trade with the socialist world. A very large proportion of this trade constituted a net addition to India's exports and the terms of trade obtained under the bilateral agreements were, on balance, favourable to India even in the early 1970s.[12] In terms of export growth, however, the contribution was not as significant as before. The socialist countries accounted for only 18.1 per cent of the total increment in the rupee value of exports between 1970/71 and 1974/75, in contrast with the 1960s when this proportion was 54.2 per cent.

Analysis of export performance

It is clearly not sufficient to outline the overall trends in exports. One must also examine the causal factors underlying these trends. For that purpose, it is necessary to consider the basic determinants of performance in each of the principal export industries. However, given the diverse commodity composition of exports, an exhaustive analysis

[10] Abu Dhabi, Bahrein, Dubai, Iran, Iraq, Kuwait and Saudi Arabia.
[11] Calculated from statistics published by DGCIS, Calcutta.
[12] For evidence on this point, see Deepak Nayyar, 'India's Trade with the Socialist Countries', *World Development* (May 1975).

such as the one in the second part of this book is obviously beyond the scope of a postscript. In what follows, an attempt is made to analyse, very briefly, the trends in the major exportable commodities and commodity groups. From that, it might be possible to extract a few generalisations.

Jute manufactures

During the early 1970s, the export performance of the jute industry was rather poor. This was nothing new. It was a mere continuation of the trend which began in 1965. There was little change in the volume of jute manufactures exported from India, which fluctuated around a level somewhat below 600 thousand tons per annum; 1971/72 provided the solitary exception when the volume of exports attained a higher level.[13] In that year, India's exports of jute goods gained on account of buoyant demand conditions abroad. This was largely attributable to the civil war in what was then East Pakistan, which disrupted supplies from the main competing source. In the sellers' market which developed, Indian jute goods also fetched higher prices thereby pushing up the value of exports. After that, however, as supplies from Bangladesh reappeared on the world market, both the volume and value of Indian exports slipped back to the earlier levels. Internal factors, such as shortages of raw jute and the increasing pressure of domestic demand continued to operate as constraints on export performance. What is more, external factors in the form of foreign demand conditions were also not favourable. The principal market for jute manufactures – carpet backing – suffered due to two factors. As rising food and fuel costs squeezed consumer incomes in the rich countries, the demand for carpets fell sharply. At the same time, synthetic materials continued to erode the market for jute carpet backing at an extremely rapid rate. All the same, in 1974/75, the rupee value of jute exports recorded a substantial increase. This was almost entirely because of higher world prices; in fact, the average unit value of Indian exports increased by 25 per cent over the preceding year. Given the state of the world market for jute manufactures, and the increasing competition from synthetic substitutes, it is unlikely that these high prices can be maintained in the near future.

Cotton textiles

The stagnation in India's cotton textile exports continued until 1971/72. The first sign of change was the significant increase in

---

[13] See Table 14.5. In the following pages, references to the volume and the average unit value of India's principal exports are based on this table.

TABLE 14.5 *Trends in the volume and average unit value of selected Indian exports*
(volume: in million units)

Commodity	Unit	1970/71	1971/72	1972/73	1973/74	1974/75
Jute manufactures	kg	561.0	671.0	581.0	563.0	586.0
Tea	kg	199.0	207.4	193.2	190.3	224.8
Cashew kernels	kg	50.0	60.4	66.3	52.3	65.0
Tobacco	kg	50.0	57.3	94.5	78.2	78.0
Iron ore	ton	21.0	19.9	20.6	23.7	22.3
Oilcakes	kg	879.0	741.7	1001.3	1224.5	832.3
Coffee	kg	32.0	35.7	50.9	52.7	49.5
Sugar	kg	348.0	316.7	101.8	248.9	694.6
Cotton fabrics: mill-made	sq m	415.0	382.0	449.0	646.0	370.0
Handloom cotton fabrics	m	28.0	29.0	47.0	68.0	49.0
Semi-finished tanned leather	kg	34.1	41.8	72.9	35.8	25.5
Marine products	kg	33.0	33.0	35.0	48.3	38.9
Average unit values: in rupees per unit						
Jute manufactures	kg	3.39	3.92	4.25	4.00	5.00
Tea	kg	7.45	7.54	7.62	7.61	9.96
Cashew kernels	kg	10.41	10.51	10.38	14.23	18.18
Tobacco	kg	6.29	7.37	6.46	8.75	10.30
Iron ore	ton	55.86	52.61	53.30	56.05	71.92
Oilcakes	kg	0.63	0.54	0.75	1.39	1.15
Coffee	kg	7.85	6.18	6.47	8.73	10.38
Sugar	kg	0.79	0.95	1.30	1.70	4.89
Cotton fabrics: mill-made	sq m	1.63	1.74	1.88	2.48	3.50
Handloom cotton fabrics	m	2.79	3.45	3.51	4.72	5.89
Semi-finished tanned leather	kg	20.99	21.56	23.38	46.32	39.88
Marine products	kg	9.25	12.54	15.37	18.24	16.70

Source: Statistics published by DGCIS, Calcutta.
Note: The average unit values have been calculated from data on the volume and value of exports.

export earnings during 1972/73, although this was largely attributable to the new trade with Bangladesh.[14] In 1973/74, however, there
was a very marked expansion and the rupee value of exports almost
doubled to attain a peak level of Rs2352.9 million. The sudden growth
can be explained in terms of three factors: (*a*) a vastly improved supply
position of raw cotton at home (owing to higher output and yields),
as a result of which the volume of textile exports rose sharply; (*b*)
extremely favourable demand conditions abroad because the prices of
synthetic materials and blended textiles increased considerably; and
(*c*) a boom in world prices which is reflected quite clearly in the
average unit values realised by India.[15] It is clear that this growth was
not sustained. Export earnings expressed in terms of current rupee
value declined by almost 10 per cent in 1974/75, but the volume of
exports fell drastically by a little more than 40 per cent. Thus, had it
not been for the continued increase in the world price of cotton
fabrics, export earnings would have suffered far more.

Tea

There was no improvement in the export performance of Indian
tea even after 1970. The volume as well as value of exports remained
virtually unchanged until 1973/74. The percentage contribution
of tea to total export earnings fell steadily. This was no different
from the experience of the previous decade. An almost stagnant
world demand coupled with fierce competition from Kenya obviously
limited the room for manoeuvre. What is more, tea was one of the
few which did not benefit from higher prices during the commodities
boom. In 1974, however, a poor crop in Kenya led to a sharp increase
in London auction prices. As a result, the unit value of Indian tea
rose from an average of Rs7.55 per kg during 1970/71–1973/74 to
Rs9.96 per kg in 1974/75. At the same time, diminished supplies from
Kenya increased the demand for Indian tea abroad, particularly in the
UK. The net outcome was an increment of more than 50 per cent
in the rupee value of exports. Clearly, such factors do not constitute
a sustainable basis for export growth.

Cashew kernels

On the surface, the steadily rising trend in the rupee value of cashew
exports is quite impressive. As before, it can be explained largely in
terms of the favourable impact of a rapidly growing world demand and
a marked improvement in prices obtained. But this is a rather decep-

[14] Cf. *Economic Survey, 1973/74*, Government of India (New Delhi, 1974), p. 43.
[15] See Table 14.5.

tive picture. India has continued to lose its predominant share of the world market even after 1970. The average annual volume of exports increased very little from 58.2 million kg in 1968/69–1970/71 to 61.2 million kg in 1972/73–1974/75, whereas world trade registered a substantial increase. The supply position of raw cashew nuts in India did not improve either. During the early 1970s, domestic production fluctuated in the range of 70–80 million kg which was no higher than in the 1960s. Therefore, exports of cashew kernels from India continued to be overwhelmingly dependent on the import of raw nuts from Mozambique, Tanzania and Kenya. However, as the East African countries increase their processing facilities, it is perfectly possible that India would be deprived of her principal sources of raw nuts in the near future. Surprisingly enough, India has been content to sit back and receive high prices for the superior quality whole kernels sold in the US, while the standard or broken grades have been marketed very easily in the socialist countries. Almost no effort has been made to step up the domestic production of raw cashew nuts. This is all the more puzzling as cashew trees can be grown with relatively little effort on poor and arid soils.

Tobacco

Between 1970/71 and 1974/75, there was a continuous growth in the exports of tobacco from India, the rupee value of which rose from Rs314.3 million to Rs803.6 million. The increase in 1971/72 was primarily due to higher unit values realised. On the other hand, in 1972/73, it was largely attributable to the increased volume of exports which, in turn, stemmed from a substantial offtake by Bangladesh.[16] In contrast with many other commodities, the growth in tobacco exports was sustained and, in 1973/74–1974/75, exports returned to the peak levels attained in the early 1960s. This was, of course, accompanied by much higher average unit values on account of the boom in primary commodity prices so that the export earnings derived from tobacco increased rapidly.

Minerals

India's mineral exports did not fare too well in the early 1970s. The rupee earnings from exports of manganese ore and mica revealed no trend other than stagnation or decline. What is more, the commodities boom did not lead to any increase in the price of either manganese or mica. Exports of iron ore, also, did not exhibit the dynamism of the

---

[16] Cf. *Economic Survey, 1973/74*, Government of India (New Delhi, 1974), p. 43.

1960s. From 1970/71 to 1972/73, there was virtually no change in the value or volume of iron ore exports. The supply bottlenecks – relatively inefficient mining methods, inadequate transport networks, poor port facilities – discussed at length earlier in the book, operated as the fundamental constraint on export performance. The serious recession in the Japanese steel industry posed further problems. However, 1973/74–1974/75 witnessed a moderate growth in the value of exports, but there was still no significant increase in export volume.[17] The rupee earnings were pushed up by higher unit value realisations. In this context, it is worth pointing out that India did not take full advantage of the increase in world prices of iron ore because of the long-term contractual arrangements the MMTC had entered into earlier. While iron ore did not benefit as much from the commodities boom as some other minerals, prices in the world market rose from around $9 per ton during the late 1960s to $12 per ton in 1973/74 and to even higher levels in 1975. It needs to be said that Indian iron ore was sold at an average price of $7 per ton in 1973/74 and $9 per ton in 1974/75.[18] The MMTC did not negotiate successfully, and was able to secure only two small increases in the price of iron ore in order to offset the devaluations of the US dollar.[19]

Manufactured leather

The rapid expansion in the export earnings derived from leather, which began in 1965/66, continued in the early 1970s. The rupee value of leather exports jumped from Rs721.5 million in 1970/71 to Rs1745.1 million in 1972/73. As a result, the share of manufactured leather in India's total exports increased from 4.7 per cent to 8.9 per cent. It is important to note that the mainstay of leather exports continued to be semi-finished tanned leather, as indeed it was in the 1960s. The one significant difference was that whereas, until 1970, only chrome tanned leather contributed to the increase in foreign exchange receipts, vegetable tanned leather also contributed to export growth thereafter. But this period of phenomenal growth turned out to be shortlived. The rising trend tapered off into a slight decline during 1973/74–1974/75. Clearly, the factors underlying these trends need some explanation. The rapid growth in world demand was

---

[17] The outer harbours at Madras and Vishakapattnam have, at long last, been commissioned. These improved port facilities will help to alleviate one of the principal bottlenecks that constrain export growth. As such, exports in 1975/76 are likely to be significantly higher.

[18] The average unit values, set out in terms of rupees in Table 14.5 have been converted into US dollars at current exchange rates.

[19] Cf. *The Times of India*, New Delhi, 27 August 1974, p. 4.

obviously an important determinant throughout. The peak level attained in 1972/73 was also due to a much higher quantity of leather exported and a moderate increase in prices.[20] In 1973/74, however, the volume of exports fell by more than 50 per cent, but the rupee value of exports was almost maintained as the prices of leather doubled thanks to the commodities boom. Had India been able to maintain the quantity of exports, the earnings would have been much higher. The supply bottlenecks discussed earlier in the book continued to restrict the exportable surplus. The following year, 1974/75, witnessed a further decline in export volume as well as a significant fall in prices, both of which were attributable to a downturn in the world markets.

Chemicals

During the early 1970s, there was almost no increase in the exports of chemicals from India. In 1973/74, the rupee value of these exports increased moderately and then almost doubled in 1974/75. This sudden growth was due entirely to higher unit values realised[21], which followed the hike in prices of crude oil and petrochemicals. The long term export prospects of the Indian chemicals industry are obviously not favourable because it is essentially uncompetitive. It suffers from high costs of production and a perennial shortage of inputs. What is more, its main feed-stocks have to be imported at rather high prices.

Engineering goods

In marked contrast with the 1960s, engineering exports increased rather slowly in the early 1970s. In fact, at exchange rates prevalent before December 1971, there was hardly any growth in the dollar value of exports during the period 1970/71–1972/73. Even in 1972/73, the increase in the rupee earnings was due primarily to the trade with Bangladesh.[22] The principal reasons underlying this stagnation were: a shortage of steel as well as other intermediates, uncompetitive export prices and the higher relative profitability of the domestic market. The outlook changed thereafter. The rupee value of engineering exports increased from an annual average of Rs1277

---

[20] See Table 14.5; the volume of leather exports was 75 per cent higher than that in the previous year.

[21] The index of export volume for chemicals, compiled by the DGCIS, actually fell from 311 in 1973/74 to 268 in 1974/75 whereas the index of average unit value rose from 415 to 874.

[22] See *Economic Survey, 1973/74*, Government of India (New Delhi, 1974), p. 43.

million during 1970/71–1972/73 to Rs2013 million in 1973/74 and Rs3528 million in 1974/75. For the reasons set out at the beginning of this postscript, it needs to be stressed that the nominal value of these exports is not indicative of the real growth, which was probably much less than what the data suggest. Nevertheless, there was a marked expansion in the exports of engineering goods. It seems that there were three basic factors responsible for this growth. The first was the demand boom in West Asia, particularly the OPEC countries. India's engineering exports to West Asia increased from Rs253.5 million in 1970/71 to Rs1100.7 million in 1974/75. Despite this increase, however, India's share in the overall imports of these countries is still rather small and much of the potential remains untapped. The second factor was the industrial recession at home[23], which led to slack domestic demand and increased the supplies of engineering goods available for export. In other respects too, the favourable impact was probably similar to that of the recession in the mid 1960s. The third factor was the marked depreciation of the rupee *vis-à-vis* the currencies of the major importing countries coupled with the continued sub-sidisation programme, both of which improved competitiveness and raised the relative profitability of exports as compared to domestic sales.

Oilcakes

The stagnation in exports of oilcakes continued until 1971/72. An examination of Table 14.3 reveals that these exports picked up in 1972/73, attained a peak level in 1973/74 (accounting for nearly 7 per cent of the country's total export earnings in the year), and declined sharply once again in 1974/75. The trend in volume was much the same, though somewhat less pronounced. In the good years, these exports benefited from tight supply conditions in the world market and markedly higher prices. Between 1972/73 and 1973/74, world prices almost doubled and the average unit value of oilcakes exported by India rose from Rs0.75 per kg to Rs1.39 per kg. The sharp increase in prices was due to three unrelated factors which reduced the supplies of cattle feed in the world market: the US imposed restrictions on exports of soyabean meal, fish meal from Peru was not readily available, and there was an extremely poor groundnut crop in West Africa. Consequently, in 1973, there was an immense increase in the demand for oilcakes from the EEC and Japan, but this opportunity

---

[23] The general index of industrial production increased by only 0.7 per cent in 1973 and 1.2 per cent in 1974, as compared to the 7.1 per cent increase in 1972; see *Report on Currency and Finance*, 1974/75, vol. I, pp. 29–31.

could not be fully exploited owing to the constraints on domestic production.[24] While oilcakes were one of the few exportable commodities in India to benefit from the commodities boom, exports were not sustained at the peak level. In 1974/75 the quantity of exports fell sharply leading to a drastic reduction in the rupee value of exports. This occurrence is not very surprising, given that Indian oilcake exports are based on uncertain production and that there has been a complete stagnation in the average yields and total output of oilseeds during the 1970s.[25] Matters were made worse by a fall in world prices as production conditions in competing cattle feed products improved during 1974.

Sugar
Exports of sugar revealed almost no trend in the early 1970s. The earnings derived from the sale of sugar fluctuated considerably, as they had in the past, but did not register any significant change. In 1974/75, however, the rupee value of sugar exports leaped to Rs 3397 million as compared to Rs 422 million in 1973/74, accounting for 38 per cent of the total increment in export earnings over the preceding year. As a result, sugar became the largest single foreign exchange earner for India and contributed a little more than 10 per cent of the country's export earnings in 1974/75. This freak occurrence needs some explanation. In 1974, the major sugar exporting countries – Cuba and Brazil – experienced a very poor sugar-cane crop. At the same time, the beet crop in Europe also failed leading to a dramatic increase in world sugar prices. The price of sugar in the London market, for instance, shot up from less than £100 per ton to £600 per ton. India sought to exploit this opportunity by exporting large quantities of sugar, and the volume of Indian sugar exports rose from 248.9 million kg in 1973/74 to 694.6 million kg in 1974/75. This was achieved by diverting supplies of sugar out of the home market and squeezing domestic consumption through higher prices. It is worth noting that much of the Indian sugar was sold in the range £250–300 per ton – the average unit value of Indian exports during 1974/75 works out at £260 per ton – as against the market peak of £600 per ton. The latest available evidence suggests that India will export 1100 million kg of sugar in 1975/76, but the prices in the world market have slumped[26], following expectations of improved sugar availability.

[24] See *Economic Survey, 1974/75*, Government of India (New Delhi, 1975), p. 45.
[25] See *Report on Currency and Finance, 1974/75*, vol. II, pp. 22–3.
[26] In June 1975, prices in the London market were about £130 per ton although, later in the year, prices rose to about £170 per ton.

Obviously, it will not be possible to sustain the earnings from sugar exports at the high level attained in 1974/75, not only because prices are bound to come down but also because domestic consumption cannot be squeezed in the long run.

Marine products

Shrimps and prawns form 90 per cent of the marine products exported from India. Lobsters and fish meal are the other major components of the commodity group. In 1965/66, exports of these products were not very significant and amounted to only Rs72 million. Since then, there has been a steady growth in the export earnings derived from them; the rupee value of fish exports rose to Rs305 million in 1970/71 and Rs881 million in 1973/74. The rising trend, which is reflected both in value and volume, can be traced to the rapid growth in world import demand, particularly in Japan and the US which constitute the principal markets for Indian marine products.[27] In 1974/75 however, the volume, prices and value of fish exports registered a noticeable decline. This was because of a poor catch at home and unfavourable demand conditions in the US and Japan. Available evidence suggests that it was only a temporary occurrence, and prices as well as demand are bound to pick up. If the catch and production can be stepped up, marine products have an extremely good export potential.

Clothing

The current rupee value of clothing exports increased at a phenomenal pace during the early 1970s. It shot up from Rs302 million in 1970/71 to Rs1360 million in 1974/75. Over the same period, the contribution of clothing to the country's export earnings increased from 2 per cent to 4 per cent. This was clearly an improvement on the past performance[28], but it should be pointed out that India's exports of clothing are still relatively small as compared to those of its principal competitors: Hong Kong, Taiwan and South Korea. Thus, while India did not altogether miss out on the opportunities available, it could certainly have done better in the favourable demand conditions that prevailed abroad. The basic factors underlying the recent export success of Indian garments were the rising wage costs in competing Asian countries and the strong fashion for Indian handloom fabrics in the Western world. However, the clothing industry in India, which is predominantly export-oriented, may run into difficulties because (a)

[27] During the period 1970/71–1974/75, 50 per cent of the Indian marine products were sold in Japan and another 33 per cent in the US.
[28] Cf. Chapter 4.

the high prices and poor quality of mill-made cotton fabrics in India still detract from competitiveness, (*b*) the excessive dependence on handloom cloth makes it vulnerable to changes in fashion, and (*c*) its exports are likely to face stringent import quotas, in Western Europe and North America, under the new Multi-Fibre Agreement.

Handicrafts

The data in Table 14.3 show that handicrafts were one of the fastest growing Indian exports in the period after 1970. Like marine products and clothing, this item also appears to have developed in the late 1960s. Exports of handicrafts fetched just Rs276 million in 1965/66, but this figure rose to Rs803 million in 1970/71 and Rs1904 million in 1974/75. As a commodity group, handicrafts are a composite of three major categories: (*a*) gems and jewellery, (*b*) carpets, and (*c*) art metalware and woodware. During the period 1970/71–1974/75, the average annual shares of these categories in total handicrafts exports were 56.6 per cent, 15.7 per cent and 10.6 per cent respectively. The other principal handicrafts exported from India were: hand-printed textiles and scarves, imitation jewellery, *zari* and embroidered goods. Nearly 75 per cent of these handicrafts were sold in North America and Western Europe. The phenomenal expansion in the rupee value of exports is obviously not a good index of the real export growth owing to the global inflation and the steady depreciation in the exchange value of the rupee. Quite apart from that, however, the export figures for handicrafts are rather deceptive because such a large proportion originates in gems and jewellery where the net foreign exchange earnings range from 25–30 per cent of the gross value of exports. This is because the trade in gems relies on imported raw materials and is entirely export-oriented; rough diamonds, emeralds and precious stones are imported into India to be cut and polished for re-export. Hence, a more accurate picture might emerge if we exclude gems and jewellery from the data on handicraft exports. For the years from 1970/71 to 1974/75, these adjusted figures work out at Rs375 million, Rs382 million, Rs518 million, Rs726 million and Rs920 million respectively. The data still reveal an impressive growth in the export of handicrafts but, in absolute terms, it is much smaller.

It might be useful to recapitulate. The striking fact to emerge from the above discussion is the extremely favourable impact of foreign demand and high world prices on India's export performance in the early 1970s. The rapid growth in world import demand for cashew kernels, tobacco, oilcakes, manufactured leather, engineering goods, cotton textiles, clothing, handicrafts and marine products was certainly an important factor which stimulated the exports of these commodities from India. Much more significant, however, was the marked increase in prices of cashew kernels, tobacco, oilcakes, manufactured leather, cotton fabrics and marine products. This price gain was an outcome of the commodities boom which started in 1973. It is clear that the rupee value of exports would not have increased as rapidly as it did in the absence of these price increases, simply because the problems of producing for export in India remained as serious as before. Supply constraints restricted the exportable surplus in the case of cashew kernels, tobacco, oilcakes, cotton fabrics, leather and marine products. Had it not been for these bottlenecks, the earnings derived from most such exports would, of course, have increased even more. But it is important to remember that the price gains of the early 1970s were a temporary phenomenon which will be difficult to sustain in the long run. The prices of oilcakes and leather have already fallen, and available evidence suggests that the prices of many other commodities are likely to come down from the peak levels attained in 1973–1974. Freak occurrences such as the recent boom in sugar exports cannot be relied upon as an even remotely stable factor. Given that a very large proportion of the expansion in the nominal value of exports was price induced, the experience of the early 1970s obviously cannot provide a sustainable basis for export growth. It should also be stressed that much of the discussion in this section has been based on the trends in export earnings expressed in terms of current rupee values. For an accurate understanding, one must also keep in mind the global inflation and the steady depreciation in the exchange value of the rupee both of which are implicit in the data.

There is little doubt that favourable demand conditions abroad and high world prices provided a boost to Indian exports. Apart from these external developments, however, there was probably another factor underlying the rapid growth in export earnings during the early 1970s. This was the export promotion policies followed by the Government. Such subsidisation of exports was, of course, nothing new and represented a continuation of past policies. In the period under consideration, the total export promotion expenditure undertaken by the Government increased steadily, rising from Rs407 million in 1970/71 to Rs764 million in 1974/75.[29] A very large proportion of this expenditure was constituted by cash subsidies to exporters. If we take account of the subsidies implicit in customs and excise duty refunds, fiscal incentives, import replenishment schemes and railway freight concessions, the degree of subsidisation undertaken by the Government was probably far greater than is apparent from the data on export promotion expenditure.

The wider context

The analysis so far has attempted to focus attention on export performance alone. But, it would be unrealistic to consider the export sector in isolation from the rest of the economy. This is particularly true because the years since 1970 have witnessed certain important developments such as the oil crisis, an unprecedented inflation and a serious economic crisis in India. All these occurrences are bound to have significantly influenced the external sector of the economy. Therefore, it is imperative that we consider India's export performance during the early 1970s in its wider context.

The preceding section sought to examine the impact of the commodities boom on the prices of Indian exports and, hence, on total export earnings. It is, however, equally important to consider the other side of the coin. For, as a buyer on the world market, India also had to import commodities at much higher prices. The world prices of non-ferrous metals, steel, newsprint and foodgrains, all of which are important components in India's import basket, registered a marked increase in 1973–1974. It might be worth citing the example of wheat which accounted for more than 80 per cent of India's foodgrain imports during the period 1970/71–1974/75. The world price of wheat which had fluctuated in the range $60–70 per ton throughout the 1960s, rose to approximately $150 per ton in 1973 and a little over $200 per ton in 1974. But that was not all. In October 1973, and once

[29] The composition of this export promotion expenditure is brought out clearly by the following figures: (in Rs million)

	1970/71	1971/72	1972/73	1973/74	1974/75
Cash subsides to exporters	349.9	465.8	522.7	532.4	599.3
Export credit development scheme	37.0	40.0	50.0	45.0	72.5
Grants for export promotion	19.8	31.5	49.7	45.9	92.5
Total	406.7	537.3	622.4	623.3	764.3

Source: Ministry of Commerce, Government of India.

Note: The data on cash subsidies include product promotion assistance for non-traditional exports, commodity development assistance for traditional exports, and assistance offered to exporters of cotton textiles through the Indian Cotton Mills Federation.

TABLE 14.6   *India's import bill in the 1970s* (in Rs million)

Commodity group	1970/71	1971/72	1972/73	1973/74	1974/75
(a) Foodgrains	2 130.1	1 312.1	807.9	4 731.5	7 637.6
(b) Petroleum	1 359.0	1 941.4	2 040.0	5 602.8	11 569.5
(c) Fertilisers	612.0	812.0	962.6	1 628.4	4 251.8
Total of above	4 101.1	4 065.5	3 810.9	11 962.7	23 458.9
Total imports	16 342.0	18 245.4	18 674.4	29 553.7	44 613.5
(a + b + c) as a percentage of imports	25.1	22.3	20.4	40.5	52.6
(a + b + c) as a percentage of export earnings	26.7	25.4	19.4	47.5	71.1

Source: Statistics published by DGCIS, Calcutta.
Note:
  (i) All figures are in terms of current rupee values, and relate to Indian fiscal years beginning 1 April.
  (ii) The data on petroleum include imports of unrefined petroleum as well as petroleum products.
  (iii) The percentages have been computed.

again in January 1974, the petroleum exporting countries announced dramatic increases in the price of crude oil. The posted price of Saudi Arabian crude oil, for instance, was raised from \$2.69 per barrel in the middle of 1973 to \$11.65 per barrel in early 1974. There is no doubt that, among the poor oil-consuming countries, India was one of the most seriously affected by this sudden rise in oil prices. Its direct impact was a massive escalation in the foreign exchange expenditure on oil imports which, in turn, imposed a severe pressure on the balance of payments. However, the inflated cost of oil was only one of the consequences. The import bill on account of fertilisers and other oil-based chemicals also rose by substantial amounts. The data set out in Table 14.6 highlight the magnitude of the problem faced by India because of the phenomenal increase in the prices of its major imports: foodgrains, pertroleum and fertilisers.

Successive shortfalls in agricultural production during the early 1970s — a fundamental factor underlying the current economic crisis in India — meant that large quantities of foodgrains, constituted mostly by wheat, had to be imported. The volume of India's foodgrain imports increased from 0.8 million tons in 1972/73 to 4.4 million tons in 1973/74 and 5.6 million tons in 1974/75. The problems were compounded by the high prices that prevailed in the world market. The consequent increase in the import costs of food is brought out clearly in Table 14.6. As a result, the average annual share of foodgrains in the country's total imports doubled, rising from 8.2 per cent during 1970/71–1972/73 to 16.6 per cent in 1973/74–1974/75.

At roughly the same time, the oil price increase announced by the OPEC countries also came into effect. In 1974/75, the first fiscal year in which the full impact of higher crude oil prices was felt, imports of petroleum shot up to Rs11 570 million accounting for 26 per cent of India's import bill and 35 per cent of the country's export earnings. This constituted a drastic change from previous years. In the three-year period 1970/71–1972/73, the average annual value of petroleum imports was only Rs1780 million and made up just 10 per cent of the import bill as well as export earnings. Following the price hike, the prices of petrochemical based fertilisers were also raised and that pushed up the cost of imports further. In 1974/75, fertilisers constituted nearly 10 per cent of the total value of imports as compared to a figure of about 5 per cent in earlier years.

Taken together, the imports of foodgrains, petroleum and fertilisers have cost India a staggering sum in recent years. At current exchange rates, the foreign exchange value of these major imports rose from an average annual sum of $529 million during 1970/71–1972/73 to $1522 million in 1973/74 and $2940 million in 1974/75. Consequently, their share in the total import bill increased from less than one fourth in the early 1970s to more than half in 1974/75. In relation to export earnings, the figures are even starker. Until the recent increase in import prices, approximately 25 per cent of the foreign exchange earnings derived from exports was sufficient to finance the three categories of imports; this proportion rose to 47.5 per cent in 1973/74 and 71.1 per cent in 1974/75.

Although the nominal value of India's exports increased rapidly after 1970, it appears that the country's capacity to import fell sharply. So did the purchasing power of its exports. These facts are brought out very clearly in Table 14.7. Between 1970/71 and 1974/75, the average unit value of exports rose by 84 per cent but the average unit value of imports increased by 131 per cent, so that there was a marked deterioration in India's terms of trade. Similarly, the proportion of imports financed by export earnings, which had been rather high in the period 1969/70–1972/73, declined markedly in subsequent years. In absolute terms, this meant that the small trade surplus, which existed in 1972/73, was transformed into a huge deficit. The import bill exceeded export earnings by Rs4370 million in 1973/74 and by Rs11 627

TABLE 14.7   *The purchasing power of Indian exports*

Year	Unit value index of imports (1958 = 100)	Unit value index of exports (1958 = 100)	Terms of trade index (1958 = 100)	Export – import ratio
1970/71	147	173	118	0.94
1971/72	149	180	121	0.88
1972/73	155	202	130	1.05
1973/74	226	247	109	0.85
1974/75	339	319	94	0.74

Source: Statistics published by DGCIS, Calcutta.

million in 1974/75.[30] Therefore, if the purpose of exports is to increase the import capacity of the economy and to provide the external resources required to finance economic development, India's export performance in the early 1970s was far less impressive than it appears on surface. While the commodities boom enabled India to increase the rupee value of her exports, it increased her import bill even more, thereby worsening the terms of trade.

Apart from the escalation in import prices, the other occurrence which needs examination is the inflation experienced by the Indian economy in recent years. Table 14.8 outlines the movement in the general price level in the years since 1970, as reflected in the wholesale price index and the consumer price index. It shows that, between 1970/71 and 1974/75, wholesale prices rose by 73 per cent at a compound rate of 14.8 per cent per annum and retail prices registered an increase of 70 per cent at a compound rate of 14.2 per cent per annum. This inflation was quite unprecedented by Indian standards, and stands out in sharp contrast with the 1960s when prices increased at less than 7 per cent per annum. It is worth noting that there was a marked acceleration in the rate of price increase after 1971/72. Starting in 1972/73, prices rose at more than 20 per cent per annum.

Other things being equal, this inflation may have had two adverse

[30] It is estimated that the balance of trade deficit in 1975/76 will be around Rs 15 000 million. These extraordinarily large trade deficits are probably an important factor underlying the price stability attained by the Indian economy during 1975/76. *Ceteris paribus*, in a regime of foreign exchange controls, a deficit on account of trade must have enabled the Government to mop up a significant proportion of the growth in domestic money supply.

TABLE 14.8   *Indices of wholesale and retail prices in India
during the 1970s*

Average of months in	Wholesale price index all commodities: 1961/62 = 100	Consumer price index for industrial workers 1960 = 100
1970/71	181.1	186
1971/72	188.4	192
1972/73	207.1	207
1973/74	254.3	250
1974/75	313.7	317

Source: RBI, Bombay, *Report on Currency and Finance, 1974/75* vol. II, pp. 12–13.

effects on export performance. In the first place, if world prices of Indian exports did not rise as much, the inflation might have reduced the relative profitability of exports *vis-à-vis* sales in the domestic market. However, it is unlikely that this happened because export prices rose at the same rate as the general price level. Second, it is possible that the sharp increase in prices worsened the cost competitiveness of exports. In view of the fact that inflation has been a global phenomenon during the early 1970s, one might expect that India's inflation was not excessive when compared with inflation in the rest of the world. But available evidence suggests the inflation rate in India was higher than that in the industrial countries and in the world economy as a whole, though it was no greater than inflation in the other underdeveloped countries.[31] Under normal circumstances, this would have reduced the competitiveness of exports. However, since June 1972, the rupee has been pegged to the pound sterling which has meant a steady depreciation *vis-à-vis* most currencies of the world. It seems likely that this depreciation in the exchange value of the rupee

[31] The annual percentage charge in consumer prices, during the 1970s, was as follows:

	1971	1972	1973	1974
World	5.9	5.8	9.5	15.1
Industrial countries	5.1	4.5	7.5	12.6
LDCs	9.5	12.4	20.2	29.3
Asia	5.3	7.9	16.4	29.7
India	3.1	6.4	17.0	28.5

Source: IMF, *International Financial Statistics*, (September 1975), pp. 34 and 36.

more than compensated for the adverse effect of inflation on competitiveness.[32]

The relative profitability of exports as compared to sales at home may not have diminished after 1970. Nevertheless, the increasing pressure of domestic demand and the size of the home market remain important determinants of export performance. In fact, there is little doubt that the domestic consumption of exportables continued to increase at a rapid pace, as it did in the 1960s. This is evident from the fact that the volume of total exports increased rather slowly in the early 1970s, and there was no sustained growth in the volume of any of the principal exports. Indeed the average share of exports in GNP barely changed from 4.46 per cent in 1960/61–1963/64 to 4.45 per cent in 1970/71–1973/74.[33] Therefore, it needs to emphasised that a higher level of exports could have been sustained only by a growth in the output of exportables which was relatively greater than the increase in domestic absorption. In the long run, export growth based on a squeeze of domestic consumption, such as that in sugar, is neither feasible nor desirable, for the reasons set out in the preceding chapter. In sum, the basic hypothesis of the book remains unchanged. The problem of Indian exports is a problem of production. In the ultimate analysis, exports can be increased on a sustainable basis only if there is a growth in real national income.

The conclusions set out above appear to contradict a rather popular axiom of neo-classical economics, which looks upon exports as a leading sector in the development process. Among economists of this school, there is a widely held view that export-led industrialisation is a viable strategy of development in all poor countries. The small Asian economies – Hong Kong, Taiwan and South Korea – are cited as the success stories, whereas India is the frequently quoted example of failure. But this is not a policy prescription that is feasible across the board in the underdeveloped world, and even if it were it is probably not desirable. The argument needs a little elaboration. In the first place, the traditional view of trade as an engine of economic growth is considerably discredited, particularly in the context of poor capitalist countries. In fact, radical economists have convincingly argued the opposite suggesting that trade between unequal partners might be responsible for the international transmission of inequality and for the perpetuation of underdevelopment. What is more, it is not possible to

[32] The rupee was delinked from the pound sterling in September 1975, and pegged to a basket of currencies. However, latest available evidence suggests that inflation has also slowed down very substantially in 1975/76.

[33] Calculated from *Economic Survey, 1974/75*, Government of India, (New Delhi, 1975), p. 59.

transplant the Hong Kong, Taiwan or South Korea model of export growth elsewhere in the Third World, because such a recipe suffers from the fallacy of aggregation. While it is perfectly possible for one, two or a few small countries to pursue export-oriented policies without worrying about the impact it might have on world trade, an adoption of this strategy on a global basis – especially by large countries like India – would certainly bring about a wave of protectionism in the importing countries, largely as a reaction. Finally, if such export growth is based on substantial inflows of foreign capital, and the participation of multinational corporations, the net benefits derived by poor countries may not be very significant. It would involve too much of a digression to embark on a discussion of these issues here. Suffice it to say, for reasons developed earlier in the book, that export-led growth is a curiously naive prescription for the problems faced by the Indian economy. This does not mean that the export sector is irrelevant. On the contrary, it is crucial. But its role is akin to that of a link in a bicycle chain which is needed to keep the economy running. Put more simply, exports provide the much needed import capacity and external resources necessary in the process of development. In the Indian context, however, export performance is likely to be determined by economic growth rather than the other way round. This is hardly surprising in an economy where exports account for less than 5 per cent of the national output.

To conclude, it might be worth summing up the salient features of India's export performance during the early 1970s. The remarkable expansion in the rupee value of Indian exports since 1970 is rather deceptive. There is no doubt that, in real terms, the export growth was considerably less, because of the global inflation and the steady depreciation in the exchange value of the rupee implicit in the trade statistics. What is more, two of the important factors underlying the export expansion – the new trade with Bangladesh and the commodities boom – cannot be looked upon as a sustainable basis for export growth. The export performance looks even less impressive when considered in the wider context. The oil crisis and the sharp increase in the prices of India's major imports led to a marked deterioration in the terms of trade and a dramatic reduction in the purchasing power of exports. In fact, India's ability to mobilise the external resources necessary to finance development, through export earnings, diminished significantly after 1973. The problem of Indian exports remains very much a problem of production, and it would be unrealistic to expect that exports will grow any faster than real national income.

Select bibliography

This is not a complete bibliography. Full references to the works cited can be found in the footnotes throughout the book. There would not be much point in reproducing these references here, as many of them are specific to the individual commodity chapters. The following is a list of principal sources that were most useful in the process of research. For the convenience of readers, these are grouped into three categories: publications of international organisations, official Indian publications, and other documents.

PUBLICATIONS OF INTERNATIONAL ORGANISATIONS

1. Commonwealth Secretariat, London
Industrial Fibres: A review, several annual issues.
Non-Metallic Minerals, no. 2, 1967.
Plantation Crops, no. 13, 1970
Tobacco Intelligence, several monthly issues.

2. Food and Agriculture Organisation, Rome
Commodity Reviews, annual.
Monthly Bulletins of Agricultural Economics and Statistics.
Production Yearbooks, annual.
State of Food and Agriculture, annual.
Trade Yearbooks, annual.
Factors Affecting the World Pepper Economy, CCP 71/9/1, 11 July 1971.
Impact of Synthetics on Jute and Allied Fibres, Commodity Bulletin Series no. 46, 1969.
Marketing of Pepper, CCP 71/9/2, 21 July 1971.
Report of the First Session of the Consultative Comittee on Tea, CCP 70/3, 8 December 1969.
Tea – Trends and Prospects, Commodity Bulletin Series no. 30, 1960.
World Hides, Skins, Leather and Footwear Economy, Commodity Bulletin Series no. 48, 1970.

3. General Agreement on Tariffs and Trade, Geneva
Arrangement Regarding International Trade in Cotton Textiles, 1971.
A Study in Cotton Textiles, 1966.
International Trade, annual issues.

Select bibliography

4. United Nations
Monthly Bulletins of Statistics.
Statistical Yearbooks.
Yearbooks of International Trade Statistics.
Survey of World Iron Ore Resources, New York, 1970.
World Market for Iron Ore, New York, 1968.

5. United Nations Conference on Trade and Development
Commodity Surveys 1966 and *1968,* New York.
Incentives for Industrial Exports, TD/B/C.2/89/Rev.I, New York, 1970.
Leather and Leather Products: A Summary Report, TD/B/C./2/101, Geneva, 19 January 1970.
Problems of the World Market for Manganese Ore, TD/B/C.1/105, Geneva, 4 May 1971.
Problems of the World Market for Iron Ore, TD/B/C.1/104, Geneva, 30 April 1971.
Review and Analysis of Trends and Policies in Trade between Countries having different Social and Economic Systems, TD/112, Geneva, 20 January 1972.
Restrictions on Exports in Foreign Collaboration Agreements in India, TD/B/389, New York, 1971.
Trade and Economic Relations between India and the Socialist Countries of Eastern Europe, TD/B/129, Geneva, 21 July 1967.
World Trade in Mica: Problems and Possible Remedial Policies, TD/B/C.1/SYN/14, Geneva, 9 October 1968.

6. UNCTAD–GATT International Trade Centre, Geneva
Cashew Marketing, 1968.
Hides, Skins and Leather – Major Markets in Western Europe, 1968.
The Major Import Markets for Oilcake, 1972.
The Major Markets for Unmanufactured Tobacco, 1968.

7. Others
Annual Bulletin of Statistics, International Tea Committee, London.
Cotton – World Statistics, quarterly publication of the International Cotton Advisory Committee, Washington.
Yearbook of Labour Statistics, International Labour Office, Geneva.
International Coffee Agreement, HMSO, London.
Modern Cotton Industry, A Capital-Intensive Industry, OECD (Paris, 1965).

OFFICIAL INDIAN PUBLICATIONS

1. DGCIS, Calcutta
Monthly Statistics of the Foreign Trade of India, March issue for every year.

2. Indian Institute of Foreign Trade, New Delhi
India's Trade with Eastern Europe, 1966.

Tobacco Exports, 1967.

Verghese, S.K. *Export Credit and Credit Insurance Policies in India and Abroad*, 1970.

3. Ministry of Commerce/Foreign Trade, New Delhi

Annual Reports.

Brochure of Statistics of Imports and Exports, 1966.

Home Bulletins, Engineering Export Promotion Council, Calcutta.

Import Trade Control Policy, 1968/69 and *1970/71*, vol. I and II.

Indian Cashew Journal. Periodically published by the Indian Cashew Export Promotion Council, Ernakulum.

Report of Import and Export Policy Committee, 1962.

Report on Leather and Allied Industries of India, 1966.

4. National Council of Applied Economic Research, New Delhi

Export Prospects of Pepper, 1965.

Export Prospects of Tobacco, 1966.

Export Strategy for India, 1969.

India's Export Potential in Selected Countries, vol. I and II, 1970.

Underutilization of Industrial Capacity, 1966.

5. Planning Commission, New Delhi

First Five Year Plan, 1951.

Second Five Year Plan, 1956.

Third Five Year Plan, 1961.

6. Reserve Bank of India, Bombay

Reports on Currency and Finance, annual.

Reserve Bank of India Bulletins, monthly.

Foreign Collaboration in Indian Industry, 1968.

7. Others

Economic Surveys, annual, Ministry of Finance, New Delhi.

'Fourteenth Report of the Fifth Lok Sabha's Estimates Committee', *Ministry of Foreign Trade: Export Promotion Measures*, Lok Sabha Secretariat, New Delhi, April 1972.

Indian Labour Statistics, Labour Bureau, Simla.

Indian Textile Bulletins, Textile Commissioner, Bombay.

Jute Development: Retrospect and Prospects, Ministry of Food and Agriculture, New Delhi, April 1967.

Monthly Abstract of Statistics, Central Statistical Organisation, New Delhi.

Report of the Plantation Enquiry Commission, New Delhi, 1956.

Report of the Textile Enquiry Committee, New Delhi, 1958.

Survey of India's Export Potential in Leather and Leather Products, vol. I, Gokhale Institute of Politics and Economics, Poona, and the Central Leather Research Institute, Madras, October 1969.

Tea Statistics, several annual issues, Indian Tea Board, Calcutta.

Select bibliography

OTHER DOCUMENTS

Annual Departmental Report of the Commissioner of Labour, 1968/69, Hong Kong.

Annual Statistical Handbooks, British Steel Corporation.

Annuaro Estatistico do Brasil, Brazil.

Census of Manufacturing Industries, Central Statistical Organisation, Karachi.

Cotton and Allied Textiles. A Report by the Textile Council, Manchester, 1969.

Government Annual Reports, Hong Kong.

Jute Chronicle, a bi-monthly publication of the Indian Jute Mills Association, several issues, Calcutta.

Mineral Yearbooks, US Bureau of Mines, Department of the Interior, Washington.

Monthly Statistical Bulletins of Pakistan, Central Statistical Organisation, Karachi.

Pakistan Jute Enquiry Commission Report, Karachi, 1961.

Pakistan Statistical Yearbooks, Central Statistical Organisation, Karachi.

Quarterly Statistical Reviews, Textile Council, Manchester.

Report of the Tea Commission, Government of Ceylon, 1968.

INDEX